THE SOCIAL ROLE OF THE GĪTĀ
HOW AND WHY

THE SOCIAL ROLE OF
THE GĪTĀ
HOW AND WHY

SATYA P. AGARWAL
Ph. D. (UC, Berkeley)
CENTER FOR SOUTH ASIAN STUDIES
UNIVERSITY OF CALIFORNIA,
BERKELEY, CALIFORNIA
U.S.A.

MOTILAL BANARSIDASS PUBLISHERS
PRIVATE LIMITED • DELHI

First Edition: New Delhi, 1993
Reprint: Delhi, 1997

ISBN: 81-208-1524-6

Also available at:

MOTILAL BANARSIDASS
41 U.A. Bungalow Road, Jawahar Nagar, Delhi 110 007
8 Mahalaxmi Chamber, Warden Road, Mumbai 400 026
120 Royapettah High Road, Mylapore, Chennai 600 004
Sanas Plaza, Subhash Nagar, Pune 411 002
16 St. Mark's Road, Bangalore 560 001
8 Camac Street, Calcutta 700 017
Ashok Rajpath, Patna 800 004
Chowk, Varanasi 221 001

PRINTED IN INDIA

BY JAINENDRA PRAKASH JAIN AT SHRI JAINENDRA PRESS,
A-45 NARAINA INDUSTRIAL AREA, PHASE I, NEW DELHI 110 028
AND PUBLISHED BY NARENDRA PRAKASH JAIN FOR
MOTILAL BANARSIDASS PUBLISHERS PRIVATE LIMITED,
BUNGALOW ROAD, DELHI 110 007

To

My mother
the late Shrimati Sitadevi
and
My mother-in-law
Shrimati Saraswati Mital

Contents

Preface to the Second Reprint

I feel much pleasure in introducing to the readers the second reprint of my book "The Social Role of the Gītā: How and Why". The fact that this reprint is being brought out in the year 1997 has, according to me, a special significance because four important events connected with the social applications of Karmayoga, that occurred fifty or hundred or one hundred and twenty-five years ago, will be celebrated during the course of this year. These celebrations will afford an opportunity to understand afresh how the social message of the Gītā played such an important role in bringing about far-reaching changes in the society through non-violent means.

Some readers might wonder as to why I am referring to four important events (rather than one), because their limited view might be confined to the celebrations connected with the achievement of India's independence in 1947. Undoubtedly, in popular mind, the year 1997 is characterized as the golden jubilee year of India's independence. However, scholars and thinkers also want to recall, with equal enthusiasm, the events that significantly contributed to the achievement of not only political independence, but also the spirit of awakening and social regeneration. Two such events that occurred in 1897, and which, according to me, deserve special recognition in the current year, are the following:

(i) Establishment of the Ramakrishna Mission by Swami Vivekananda in May 1897 with the motto "atmano mokṣartham jagaddhitaya ca", that is, attaining simultaneously "one's highest freedom and the good of the world".

(ii) Lokamanya B.G. Tilak's speech of June 1897 which advocated Gītā-based resistance to foreign rule and which marked the beginning of the process of political imprisonment in modern India.

It should be added that the fourth important event which will be celebrated in 1997 is Sri Aurobindo's birth that occurred 125 years ago, that is, on 15th August 1872.

Why are the above-mentioned events so important to the readers of this book? The basic message of this book is that social applications of the Karmayoga approach of the Gītā can effectively lead to all-round development and progress in the social, economic, political and cultural fields. But this calls for the rise of Karmayogins who are guided, not by considerations of selfish or family gains, but by "the desire for the good of all"—or "cikirsurlokasaṁgraham" as the Gītā calls them in verse III.25. A careful understanding of how the social applications of Karmayoga have been made during the last two hundred years can help in the process of the rise of future Karmayogins.

Part One of the book contains five case studies on the social applications of Karmayoga—beginning from Raja Rammohun Roy in 1815 and ending with Mahatma Gandhi till the middle of this century. Each of the five leaders had something unique to contribute. For example, Rammohun Roy warned that people ignorant about the real meaning of Niskāma Karma are often exploited and misled by orthodox priests who give false allurements about going to heaven. Although Roy's warning was given during his debate with the supporters of the inhuman custom of suttee (or widow-burning) in 1818, his assessment of the social damage caused by orthodox priests—irrespective of the faith that they might profess—is equally valid today. Terrorists are pushed along the path of violence by means of false allurements that these acts will take them to heaven. Social damage caused by terrorists can be averted, at least partly, if modern Karmayogins take up this cause in the spirit of Rammohun Roy. Although Roy's activities might not be specifically recalled during the various celebrations of 1997, his role as the initiator of the social reform movement in India—with particular relevance to the cause of women—always deserves careful attention on the part of social activists.

The wonderful work that the Ramakrishna Mission has done during the last hundred years will undoubtedly be recalled in connection with the centenary celebrations that will reach their climax in May 1997. Swami Vivekananda—who is the subject of the second case study in this book—emphasized the "social ser vice" component of the Mission's programme of work, and his final message to the disciples (quoted below) was in response to the difficulty of establishing social unity and harmony in India:

"Your duty is to serve the poor and the distressed, without distinction of caste and creed. What business have you to consider the fruits of your actions? ....Let the reading of the Vedānta and the practising of meditation and the like be left to be done in the next life! Let this body go in the service of others—and then I shall know you have not come to me in vain!"

According to Madeleine Biardeau, "the influence of Vivekananda... and of his Ramakrishna Mission as well, lent great credence to the idea of selfless service. It is nevertheless more than likely that all of this took place within pre-existing ideological frames of references, and that the Bhagavad-Gītā was its greatest source of inspiration".

The third case study relates to Lokamanya B.G. Tilak. Although he did not establish any new institution, his speech of June 1897 and his subsequent trial and imprisonment gave a new direction to the Indian National Congress and thus marked a turning point in the history of India's fight for independence. In fact, the popular title "Lokamanya" now began to be used for Tilak, who advocated Gītā-based resistance to foreign rule. Tilak's famous book "Gītā-Rahasya" was published later—in 1915—but his basic idea about Karmayoga and Lokasaṁgraha was presented in a nutshell in 1897. The golden jubilee celebrations of India's independence are bound to recall how a major step in that direction was taken by Tilak in 1897.

The fourth case study describes the contribution of Sri Aurobindo, not only when he was a Karmayogin (during the years 1905-10) but also during his ascent to the status of a Purnayogin (during the years 1910-50). It is significant that the date and month of Sri Aurobindo's birth (15th August 1872) also became (after 75 years) the date and month of India's independence (15th August 1947). Sri Aurobindo himself saw an inner meaning in this coincidence:

"August 15th 1947 is the birthday of free India....

August 15th is my own birthday and it is naturally gratifying to me that it should have assumed this vast significance. I take this coincidence, not as a fortuitous accident, but as the sanction and seal of the Divine force that guides my steps on the work with which I began life, the beginning of its full fruition."

Nearly six months prior to his departure for Pondicherry, that is, on 31st July 1909, Sri Aurobindo wrote, almost prophetically, in his journal "The Karmayogin":

"The (Congress Nationalist) party is there, not less pervading and powerful than before but in want of a policy and a leader. The first it may find, the second, only God can give. The men who have led hitherto, have been strong men of high gifts and commanding genius, great enough to be protagonists of any other movement; but even they were not sufficient to satisfy one which is the chief current of a worldwide revolution. Therefore, the Nationalist Party, custodians of the future, must wait for the man who is to come, calm in the midst of calamity, hopeful under defeat, sure of eventual emergence of triumph and always mindful of the responsibility which they owe not only to India, but to the world."

The closing words of Sri Aurobindo describe "the man who is to come" in a way practically similar to how the Gītā has depicted a Sthitaprajñā, that is, a Karmayogin engaged in Lokasaṁgraha. This was the ideal aimed at by Mahatma Gandhi who is the subject of the fifth—and the last—case study in this book. By deriving the technique of non-violence from the Gītā, Mahatma Gandhi not only achieved India's independence but also showed the way to Sarvodaya, the uplift of all. The golden jubilee celebrations of India's independence will, of course, recall the crucial role played by Lokamanya Tilak, Sri Aurobindo, and Mahatma Gandhi in the freedom struggle.

The various celebrations of 1997 will undoubtedly be accompanied with a keen desire to find out how the Karmayoga spirit of selfless service—which was prominent during the freedom struggle but is no longer visible now—can be regenerated. It is hoped that the spreading of the social message of the Gītā through the above-mentioned case studies will make some contribution in this respect—howsoever small.

While the case studies of Part One describe 'how' selected leaders of social movements applied the Karmayoga technique, the theoretical question as to 'why' such applications could possibly be made is discussed in Part Two. To summarize in brief, the main objective of Part Two is to show that in addition to the individual goals of 'Preyas' and 'Śreyas'—i.e. the 'Pleasant' and the 'Good'—the Gītā also contains the broad social goal of 'Lokasaṁgraha'—the 'Good of the Society'.

Readers may be interested in knowing that the study and research which enabled me to bring out the first edition of this book in 1993 continued to influence my subsequent writings. For example, my second book entitled "The Social Message of the Gītā"—which was published in 1995—differed from the first, not so much in the realm of ideas as in regard to the language of expression, namely the use of two hundred self-composed Sanskrit verses, the language of the commentary being English (which meant partial similarity with the first book). After these two Gītā-based publications, the latest writing of mine conveys the social message of the Rāmāyaṇa of Tulsidas—the popular Hindi version of the Rāmāyaṇa composed in 1573. This publication of mine is in Hindi, and it has just been brought out under the title "Tulsi Rāmāyaṇa—Jagmaṅgal-Parāyaṇa" which means Tulsi Rāmāyaṇa's devotion to the cause of the good of the world. Irrespective of the language used in my books—English, Sanskrit, Hindi—the essence of my writings is that the Gītā as well as the Tulsi Rāmāyaṇa conveys the message of the good of all, and that this message can play an important role in tackling problems of disharmony, conflict, social backwardness, etc.

Before concluding this preface, I want to thank Prof. Robert P. Goldman, Chairman, and Dr. Steven M. Poulos, Vice-Chairman, Center for South Asia Studies, Berkeley, for having extended my Honorary Research Associateship for all these years. It is gratifying to see the warm welcome that has been showered on me from all the quarters. To mention only a few, Mr. William Donald Schaefer, Governor of the State of Maryland, conferred upon me, in November 1994, the Governor's Citation "as an expression of our admiration, gratitude and great respect for your talent, dedication and service to your fellowmen". The President of India, Dr. Shankar Dayal Sharma, received the first copy of my book "The Social Message of the Gītā" in July 1995, and honoured it as a valuable contribution to social causes. My Hindi book on Tulsi Rāmāyaṇa received the International Kunti Goyal Award for 1996, based on a competition organized by Satish-Kunti Goyal Foundation which has offices at Jodhpur, India and Northboro, Massachusetts, USA. On 31st January 1997, the President of India, Dr. Shankar Dayal Sharma received the first copy of this book too at Rashtrapati Bhavan, New Delhi and spoke words of praise. I am grateful to him as also to the Governor of Maryland for the honour bestowed on me by them.

I do hope the second reprint of "The Social Role of the Gītā" will receive similar appreciation and welcome as has been extended not only to the first edition of this book but also to my other writings published during recent years.

Center for South Asia Studies
University of California
Berkeley, California, USA
February 5, 1997

SATYA P. AGARWAL

Preface

It gives me great pleasure to have the opportunity to write a few words to accompany the publication of this most meritorious work from one of Berkeley's distinguished alumni. Although the author's training has been in a field other than religious studies, he has put his wide knowledge of the social history of India to use to produce this study of the Bhagavad-gītā. In this introduction I propose to give a summary of the book and of the impression it has made on me. In brief, Dr. Satya Agarwal in this study examines the role that the Bhagavad-gītā, the inspired poem of ancient India, has played in guiding modern man in the performance of his day-to-day duties. To that end he takes the reader through a long and fascinating tour of recent and modern Indian history, showing us how important the Gītā has been in the lives and thoughts of a few selected Indian statesmen and religious leaders. He then points out that this sacred poem continues even at present to stir the imagination of social and cultural theoreticians and that from its well-spring flow forth an inexhaustible flood of new insights. Hopefully, through these new perspectives mankind may re-interpret the nature of the problems it faces from one day to the next and perhaps partake of the same insight that was granted of old by Lord Kṛṣṇa to Arjuna.

Although the Bhagavad-gītā has traditionally been regarded as a poem of primarily religious significance, Dr. Agarwal shows that with the proper interpretation its message may be transformed into a set of practical ethical guidelines. This practical aspect of the Gītā's teaching, its insistence that involvement with the world is an ethically correct function of human behaviour, is the focus of this book. That involvement with the world is expressed by the term "Lokasaṁgraha". The term covers a multitude of social and political forms of behaviour and attitudes of mind and is perhaps more central to the meaning the Gītā should have for modern man than its traditional otherworldly interpretation.

The book opens with a survey of the intellectual, political and religious history of Hindu India in the past two centuries. In the minds of most people superficially acquainted with modern Indian history, the last fifty years have been dominated by the towering figures of Mohandas Gandhi and Pandit Nehru, perhaps because their voices still reverberate in living memory. However, Dr. Agarwal points out that these great liberators of India are the last torchbearers of a movement that began more than two hundred years ago with the Bengali scholar, statesman and author, Ram Mohun Roy. Living at a time when colonial powers were gradually encroaching upon land ruled by the Mughal Emperors and slowly converting from trade into territorial interests, he clearly foresaw that if India was to survive, it would have to come to terms with the ideologies developed by Western thinkers. For better or worse, the ancient civilization of India was destined to confront the powerful new ideas of the Enlightenment, the notions that all men were created equal, the libertarian ideas of John Stuart Mill, and sometime later still, the seductive theories of economic equality for all people. At Roy's time the Mughal empire was crumbling, Marathan warriors fought disorganized battles, India was seriously divided by opposing ideologies, none of them by themselves able to define to everybody's satisfaction the position India should take to maintain its integrity. Even the idea of a nation in the abstract as opposed to a community of independent states had never been worked out systematically. The colonial powers, on the other hand, had clearly defined goals, goals that were fed by economic policies calculated to enrich the mother nations. With the support of the Church whose avowed mission was the conversion of nonbelievers to the Christian faith, the foreign merchants gradually made major advances in their conquest of India and became a serious threat to the economic, social and religious integrity of the Indian subcontinent.

Dr. Agarwal has examined the various ways in which India has reacted to the impact of many powerful foreign influences over the past two centuries. He has done so by studying the lives and the activities of select Hindu thinkers who through their writings and their ways of life showed their awareness of a need to preserve an Indian identity. All of them undertook to define these differences and thus established their views on what might be acceptable alternatives for India and the Indian genius vis-á-vis those principles and customs that run counter to the Indian tradition. But they were not unanimous in either their conclusions or the strategies they devised for attaining their common goal. The author has concentrated on the role the Bhagavad-gītā has played in the lives and works of these thinkers and points out how its inspiration guided their thoughts and led them to their views on what is the essential nature of the Hindu identity. There is a good reason to focus on the role that the Bhagavad-gītā played in that period. Apart from the fact that it is one of the most influential and beautiful philosophical works that ancient India has created, its translation into Western languages in the last century had begun to stir an interest in Indian religion. Many Westerners had become aware of the Gītā and its teachings. The book was generally well received and even highly praised by a few prominent Western religious thinkers and literati. Therefore, it might possibly serve as a vehicle for intellectuals of both cultures, East and West, to bridge the unexplored realm of conflicting ideologies that separated them. Thus they might hope to reach a common ground to begin a dialogue aimed at reaching a degree of consensus about the intrinsic value of the Indian tradition from the more global perspective of world history.

There was a great need for a critical review of the forms of worship and the social customs that have become known as Hinduism. Apart from its glorious concept of a structured society where every member contributes to a common goal, the perpetuation of the community through universally understood religious and ethical principles, Hinduism had inherited from its past a number of acute social problems that cried out for a solution. Some of these problems have been summarized by Dr. P. N. Chopra in *The Cultural Heritage of India,* vol. II, pp. 627-39 in a chapter entitled "Some experiments in social reform in Mediaeval India". For him they concern the observance of proper marriage customs, as well as the glaring injustices of child marriage, sati, and the prohibition of a remarriage for a widow. Serious as these may be, the excesses associated with the rigorous application of measures to preserve the caste hierarchy and the inhumane treatment of untouchables proved to be equally disturbing to those Indians who began to examine India's society more objectively. More recently, many of these points have been reiterated and examined very thoughtfully by the Western author V.S. Naipaul in a number of books.

The Gītā with its message of transfiguring earthly experience into an experience of the divine may seem to have little relevance for solving the manifold social problems confronting Indian society in the 1850s and even less relevance for helping solve India's immense task of emerging from beneath the firmly established stranglehold of colonial rule. However, the essential Indianness of the Gītā qualifies it as a serious, authoritative pronouncement about the values that are dear to the Hindu. As such it could develop into an instrument not only of religious rejuvenation, but also for solving social and political problems, both domestic and foreign.

It is Dr. Agarwal's central thesis that the Gītā contains a very clear and important message relevant to finding a solution for the social and political impasse confronting modern India. That message can be summarized as "Lokasaṁgraha", literally "involvement with the world", and more broadly, the willingness of people to undertake action, especially selfless action (*niṣkāmakarma-*) on behalf of the community in which they find themselves. He traces the discovery and elaboration of this aspect of the Gītā's teaching to the work of a series of Indian political thinkers beginning with Ram Mohun Roy. The Gītā's message of Lokasaṁgraha was again eloquently formulated by the brilliant thinker Vivekananda who urged the monks of the Ramakrishna Mission to transform their strategies for achieving spiritual liberation. A sannyasin, in his view, must not be content with the practice of austerities (tapas) in the privacy of his monastery or forest abode, but instead he must go out into the world and make the benefit of the entire world (sarvalokahita) the aim of his selfless actions. In a similar vein, the great Maharashtran reformer Tilak propounded in his *Gītārahasya* that not only devotion and compassion lie at the root of the Gītā's teachings, but also an admonishment to perform unselfish action. The Gītā, in Tilak's opinion, is a revolutionary work, a dynamic doctrine which instructs people to act for the benefit of the world. It differs from the Western doctrines of social activism in that it adds a dimension of self-realization to the process of serving mankind. Applied to the political situation of India in the early 1900s it also meant identifying the "good" and the "wicked" parties in India's struggle and the Gītā clearly sanctions the use of force to overthrow the enemy.

Dr. Agarwal continues describing the roles of Aurobindo and Gandhi in the formulation of a programme for liberation from British rule. The latter especially found in the teachings of the Gītā not so much a call to arms, but a call to every human being to live his or her life in harmony with the principle of truth. With Aurobindo he advocated resistance, but passive resistance, resistance based on a personal conviction that one's actions are prompted by satya, truth. Only in this way should resistance against the colonial powers be carried out. Dr. Agarwal shows how Gandhi's reliance on the Gītā, as well as other works, inspired him to develop this form of Lokasaṁgraha.

In Part II of this Work Dr. Agarwal tries to answer the question why the Gītā can and should be used to find a solution to the social problems facing independent India.

The principal social problems facing India before the arrival of the British were: widow burning, the treatment of untouchables, the role of the Muslim in a Hindu society, the role of the women and of the Ādivāsīs. Several of these problems have remained since independence. I leave it to the reader to follow Dr. Agarwal's account as he carefully develops his thesis and shows how a modern karmayogin would evolve a personal way of life that would relate his individual goal to mankind's ultimate goals in life and how these goals can be realized by engaging in Lokasaṁgraha. Some of the most original and challenging ideas of the book are found in Chapter 11 where he explores the various practical ways in which the concept of Lokasaṁgraha may be applied to the modern world. Quoting from many thinkers, both Indian and Western, he finds applications of the Gītā not only to the development of mankind's mental discipline, but also to the formulation and ways of attaining goals that a modern society has to envisage, such as proper economic practices, the wise management of environmental resources, the maintenance of a desired level of mental health, a just legal system, to mention only a few. Always carefully quoting his sources, Dr. Agarwal shows how the concept of Lokasaṁgraha has been applied, to develop economic theories on the village level and to give a rationale for protecting endangered environment against pollution and natural hazards. The concept is especially powerful when it is invoked to join together people with a sense of common purpose and forge them into one community, be it local, regional, national, or global.

The work is written in a scholarly style with numerous footnotes and references. It is a commendable and daring attempt to establish a new sense of Indian unity based on age-old Indian principles.

Associate Professor of Sanskrit BAREND A. VAN NOOTEN
University of California
Berkeley

Acknowledgements

The ideas presented in this book have been formulated, slowly but steadily, as a result of over fifty years of close association with Gītā-scholars and activists, and to all of them I want to express my indebtedness and gratitude.

To begin with, it was my father, the late Shri Ram Swarup, who tried to explain to me in simple Hindi, as early as in 1942, some of the new ideas contained in Tilak's *Gītārahasya*.

Although my study of the various interpretations of the Gītā went on, during my stay at Berkeley from 1948 onward, practical examples of Karmayoga on a modest scale, under Indian conditions, were provided by my father-in-law, the late Shri Dwarka Prasad Mital, and my uncle-in-law, the late Shri Dilip Singh Mital.

After my retirement from the United Nations, the Indian community in Cairo, Egypt, led by Dr. R.S.S. Sarma and Dr. M. Sivamurthy, who organized so many socio-religious activities, enabled me, during 1988-89, to share my views on the Gītā, on a weekly basis, with members of an active Study Group.

During July-August 1990, I and my wife Urmila had an excellent opportunity to hold discussions on *Lokasaṁgraha* with Gītā-scholars in Canada, of whom special mention should be made of Prof. J.G. Arapura, Prof. V. Subramaniam, Prof. Arvind Sharma, Dr. K. Mishra (then visiting from Banaras Hindu University), and the late Prof. K. Sivaraman. Those who made these discussions possible included Ashwini and Neeta Gupta, Mahendrajit and Sarla Goyal, Rohit and Usha Goel, Vijay and Manju Chandra, Jainarain and Shashi Goel, and Alok and Gauri Goel.

In June 1991, Urmila and I had the privilege of talking about *Lokasaṁgraha* with Swami Chinmayananda and his associate, Swami Tejomayananda. Subsequently, in January 1992, we can never forget how Swami Ranganathananda, under medical advice to take rest, asked Urmila and me to come and see him, to consult about *Lokasaṁgraha*. During the same month, Dr. V.

Madhusudan Reddy and Dr. Karan Singh provided an insight into Sri Aurobindo's interpretation of *Lokasaṁgraha*. Shri Shivanand of Meerut reviewed for us what he has himself written on this subject in Hindi, while Prof. Gopal Reddy and Dr. K. Kamala of Osmania University gave useful references.

From February 1992, the renewal of my old ties with the University of California, Berkeley, enabled me to start giving a concrete shape to my ideas on *Lokasaṁgraha*. Prof. Robert P. Goldman, Chairman, and Dr. Steven M. Poulos, Vice-chairman, Center for South Asia Studies, kindly obtained for me a new University-linked identity, namely, as an honorary Research Associate. At the technical level, Dr. Barend A. van Nooten and Dr. Linda Hess of the Berkeley campus, and Swami Aparnananda of the Berkeley-based Ramakrishna Mission, provided several sessions of useful discussion on *Lokasaṁgraha*. Furthermore, Prof. van Nooten's generosity and spirit of encouragement are vividly reflected in the Preface to this book which he has written, in spite of heavy pressure of work. For this I am particularly indebted to Prof. van Nooten.

Within my own family or svajanam, in the language of the Gītā, my wife Urmila's role as an active research partner has already been referred to in the above paragraphs. Over and above that, she provided not only constant companionship and encouragement but also very valuable feedback, based on a thorough reading of all the drafts. My son Nishkam obtained books and articles from so many different sources, and helped bring into prominence the linkage between *Lokasaṁgraha* and environmental protection. Nishkam also provided, to a large extent, the technical skills, time and energy needed to convert a hand-written draft into a computer-processed manuscript, containing so many references and footnotes—and whatever else was needed to complete this job was provided by other svajanam, particularly Kokila and Seema. Valuable feedback and technical help also came from Shri Harish Kashyap, Shri T.P. Gupta, Shri I.C. Gupta, Renu Mital, Rai Ajay Kumar, Rashmi Gupta, M.M. Agarwal and Dr. David Harding. Even grandchildren, particularly Isha and Kiran, helped keep alive the spirit of devotion to the cause of book-writing, by asking what I was writing and by listening attentively to stories connected with the Gītā. The grandchildren's support was made possible because of excellent help received from Barbara Smith at the right time. Still referring to the important role of svajanam, special mention must be made of the entire families of Shri Arya Bhushan and Mr. Abhaya Bhushan, of Palo Alto, California, for strong moral and intellectual support provided by them.

The topic of *Lokasaṁgraha* is undoubtedly vast and complex, and it is only through the generosity and blessings of Gītā-scholars and others—some of whom have been specified above—that I have arrived at the present stage of research and writing. While reiterating my deep sense of gratitude to all of them, I express the hope that similar support will be forthcoming when I continue study and research on *Lokasaṁgraha*, accompanied with modest practical applications thereof.

Center for South Asia Studies SATYA P. AGARWAL
University of California
Berkeley, California, U.S.A.
August 15, 1993

Part One

Case Studies on Social Applications of Karmayoga

Chapter One

Leaders of Social Movements in India: Selective Identification for Case Study

1.1. Robert N. Bellah, after making a comparative study of religious responses to the challenges of the modern age in the various Asian countries, has identified four types of such responses, namely:

(i) conversion to Christianity;
(ii) traditionalism;
(iii) reformism; and
(iv) neo-traditionalism.

According to Bellah, India provides a good example of "reformism" which has been defined by him as "a movement that re-interprets a particular religious tradition to show not only that it is compatible with modernization but also that, when truly understood, the tradition vigorously demands at least important aspects of modernity."[1]

RAMMOHUN ROY

1.2. It is generally agreed that Rammohun Roy (1772-1833) initiated the process of reformism in India, symbolized by his successful leadership of the suttee-abolition movement[2] and also by his founding of the Brahmo Samaj.[3] But what were the sources of inspiration and strength which enabled Rammohun Roy to face the challenges of reformism, which involved, in Embree's words, "fighting on two fronts":

> At the same time that he was urging reform on his fellow Hindus, Rammohun felt it necessary to defend Hinduism

against the attacks that were made on it by a number of Europeans, especially the missionaries who had begun to come to Bengal in increasing numbers. Believing that their denunciations of Hinduism were unfair in that they identified it completely with its worst features, he countered by charging that Christianity in its current forms was as much marred by superstition as was Hinduism. He was fighting, then, on two fronts: against the orthodox Hindus who accused him of injecting Christian ideas into the Upaniṣads, and against orthodox Christians who thought his interpretation of the Bible had been colored by Hinduism.[4]

1.3. A detailed study of Rammohun Roy's life and works reveals how he utilized the Upaniṣads and the Bhagavad-Gītā to derive support for his reformist ideas. However, not everything that Roy initiated was equally able to stand the test of time. For example, within two generations, the Brahmo Samaj (founded in 1828) was split into rival factions, and serious limitations adversely affecting its appeal to the vast majority of the population became obvious. On the other hand, the success associated with the abolition of the evil custom of suttee (in 1829) proved to be more enduring. It also became clear that the arguments with which Roy was able to score victory over the suttee-advocates were based mainly on the teachings of the Bhagavad-Gītā . Eric Sharpe views this as the "first entry" of the Gītā "into the field of modern Indian politics"—the word 'politics' probably standing for 'social affairs' in general.[5]

1.4. The social reform movement in India, initiated by Rammohun Roy, was carried further by several leaders including Mahadev Govind Ranade (1842-1901). He and other members of the Prarthana Samaj tried to change public opinion against the evil practice of "child marriage", and were instrumental in getting "The Age of Consent" Bill passed in 1891.[6] They also attempted to change public opinion in favour of widow remarriage. However, none of these reform-advocates invoked the ancient scriptures to the same extent as was done by Rammohun Roy in connection with suttee-abolition.

1.5. Although social reformers like Roy wanted the society itself to voluntarily discontinue evil customs, they did not protest when the British Government enacted legislation to impose a ban on such customs. (Roy's protest was before, but not after, the ban was imposed.) The attitude of complete or partial collaboration which the reformers displayed vis-a-vis a foreign government, arose out of a feeling of indebtedness to European values and ideas that had helped generate abhorrence among the reformers themselves towards the Indian evil customs. However, this phase of the reformist approach, adopted by the so-called "Moderates", began yielding ground (from 1875 onward) to new approaches rooted in revivalism and self-sufficiency, associated with the so-called "Revolutionary Thinkers" or "Leaders of Hindu Renaissance". Embree has summarized how the process of reformism developed into revivalism and how this brought in new assertions as to the sources of inspiration for social and religious changes:

> In the last half of the nineteenth century the intellectual movement associated with Rammohun Roy and his successors, which was characterized by a general tendency to adapt the Hindu tradition to Western values, met strong opposition. The criticism of Hindu institutions and beliefs which had been engendered by the first contacts with modern Western thought was replaced by a mood of resurgent self-confidence. Instead of an attempt to show that pure Hinduism was basically similar to the highest reaches of Western thought, there was a proud assertion that the Hindu tradition needed no support from the finding of identities, real or fancied, with Christianity. . . . To this new movement the title "Hindu Renaissance" is sometimes given. . . .[7]

DAYANANDA

1.6. When serious searches were taken in hand to identify indigenous sources of inspiration for bringing about socio-religious transformation, a variety of movements came into existence because of the richness of the Indian tradition. In this context, the first major event was the founding of the Arya Samaj in 1875 by Dayananda Saraswati (1824-1883). Dayananda reinterpreted the Vedas and asserted that by following the

Vedas alone (to the exclusion of the Epics and the Puranas), the Hindus could rise again from the depths of degradation into which they had fallen. For Dayananda, the Vedas were not only true, but they contained all truth, including the ideas of modern science. Above all, they taught a rigorous monotheism, giving no sanction to either the polytheism or idol-worship of later Hinduism. From these two basic principles—the infallibility of the Vedas and monotheism—he mounted a wide-ranging criticism of all aspects of contemporary Hinduism. Along with this went a fierce polemic against other religious groups, particularly Islam and Christianity, as false alien religions that sought to destroy the Hindu faith.

1.7. The fact that the Arya Samaj drew its inspiration solely from indigenous sources, and not from the West, partly accounted for its wider appeal among the Indian people, as compared to the Brahmo Samaj. Another factor contributing to the relatively greater popularity of the Arya Samaj was its efforts to raise the social status of the neglected sections of the society, including women, low-caste Hindus, untouchables, etc. Educational institutions called 'Dayananda Anglo-Vedic Schools and Colleges' attracted large numbers of students, boys as well as girls, especially in the Punjab and United Provinces (later called Uttar Pradesh). The Arya Samaj also became known for its philanthropic activities, such as orphanages, workshops for boys and girls, homes for widows, and exemplary works of social service at the time of public calamities, epidemics, famines, etc.

1.8. The above-mentioned characteristics of the Arya Samaj enabled it to make a significant contribution to the so-called Hindu Renaissance, but wide gaps and deficiencies obviously remained to be filled. For one thing, Dayananda's strong opposition to the doctrine of Divine Incarnations (including Rāma and Kṛṣṇa whom so many Hindus worshipped) created confusion among the large numbers of Hindus who had been deeply inspired by the Rāmāyaṇa and the Gītā. Similarly, Dayananda's fierce attacks on some of the beliefs and practices of Islam and Christianity were viewed by many as an obstacle in the path of creating feelings of religious tolerance and social harmony—so important in a country like India.

RAMAKRISHNA AND VIVEKANANDA

1.9. While acknowledging that "Dayananda transfused into the languid body of India his own formidable energy, his certainty, his lion's blood", Romain Rolland finds Dayananda to be "in default of outpourings of the heart and the calm sun of the spirit", or, in other words, "in default of the warm poetry radiating from the entire being of a Ramakrishna or the grandiose poetic style of a Vivekananda".[8] In fact, in 1873, that is, a couple of years prior to establishing the Arya Samaj, Dayananda himself had gone to Bengal and met Sri Ramakrishna, whom Embree describes as "the most famous of nineteenth-century Indian saints", possessing "a totally different temperament from that of Dayananda".[9] It was the same Sri Ramakrishna (1836-1886) whose teachings enabled his disciple Vivekananda to start, in 1897, what can be called the "next" major socio-religious institution, namely the Ramakrishna Mission—the word "next" obviously referring to chronology or time sequence. However, before coming to that, it may be of interest to see what came out of the meeting between Dayananda and Ramakrishna in 1873.

1.10. Romain Rolland says that prior to meeting Dayananda, Sri Ramakrishna had seen the Brahmo Samaj leader, Devendranath Tagore, who left on Ramakrishna an impression of "a very profound man—but an aristocrat remaining aloof—secure in his paradise of idealism".[10] Romain Rolland indicates, next, how Dayananda's approach also failed to come up to standards of universalism, aimed at by Ramakrishna:

> When Ramakrishna examined Dayananda, he found in him 'a little power', by which he meant, 'real contact with the Divine'. But the tortured and torturing character, the bellicose athleticism of the champion of the Vedas, his feverish insistence that he alone was right, and therefore had the right to impose his will, were all blots on his mission in Ramakrishna's eyes. He saw him day and night disputing concerning the scriptures, twisting their meaning, and striving at all costs to found a new sect. But such preoccupation with personal and worldly success sullied the true love of God, and so he turned away from Dayananda.[11]

1.11. Whereas the Arya Samaj had singled out the Vedas as the sole source of inspiration, the Ramakrishna Mission based itself on a very wide foundation because Sri Ramakrishna had personally experienced communion with the Divine, as he put it, through all the deities, including Kālī, Christ, Allah. Embree describes Sri Ramakrishna as "one who accepted the Hindu tradition in all its richness and contradictions" and also the one "who showed to his generation that sainthood, as understood within the Hindu tradition, had a unique value for India's life in the modern world".[12] In this context, one of the main reachings that he, by his own example, gave to his favourite disciple, Vivekananda, was "to worship Jīva as Śiva".[13] And this enabled Vivekananda to coin the famous word "Daridra-Nārāyaṇa"to convey the message that "service to the poor is service to God".[14]

1.12. Vivekananda (1863-1902) formulated a socio-spiritual approach to India's problems based on a harmonious synthesis of Karma-Yoga and Vedānta, which he designated as "Practical Vedānta". The main source of the doctrine of Karma-Yoga was obviously the Bhagavad-Gītā, but Vivekananda often cited the example of the Buddha as an "Ideal Karma-Yogin". Thus, although the immediate source of inspiration for the founding of the Ramakrishna Mission was the life and teachings of Sri Ramakrishna, the ultimate sources, belonging to the long Indian tradition, also included the Upaniṣads, the Gītā, the Buddha, and wandering monks and *bhaktas* for whom rendering selfless service to the needy was a spontaneous act.

1.13. The social service activities of the Ramakrishna Mission were broadly similar to those of Arya Samaj—including, as they did, educational institutions, and exemplary dedication to the cause of helping the needy in times of famines and epidemics. However, an important difference between the two, from the viewpoint of the present study, is in regard to the underlying source of inspiration. In this context, two points need to be highlighted. First, that an extremely selective approach of the Arya Samaj (basing everything on the Vedas alone) was replaced by a practically all-inclusive view of the Ramakrishna Mission. Secondly, that the Gītā (which had no role in the Arya

Samaj) was one of the main sources of inspiration for the Ramakrishna Mission.

TILAK

1.14. The year 1897 is highly significant for the present study, not only because the Ramakrishna Mission was founded in May that year, but also because the political application of the Gītā was publicly initiated by Bal Gangadhar Tilak (1856-1920) in June the same year. Among the institutions referred to above, both the Arya Samaj and the Ramakrishna Mission were, by their charters, "non-political", although some of the members of the Arya Samaj (including Lala Lajpat Rai) later participated in political activities. Tilak too did not start any Gītā-based political institution as such. He was a member of the Indian National Congress which, although founded in 1885, confined itself, in pre-Tilak days, to holding a short, annual session in December and "requesting" the British Government to grant favours like giving more positions of responsibility to qualified Indians. What Tilak wanted was to change the character of political activities and to obtain mass participation therein.

1.15. To achieve his political objectives, Tilak had to adopt a rather indirect approach in the sense that he started organizing "Gaṇapati Festival" and "Śivājī Festival" as public functions. While the Gaṇapati Festival was essentially a Hindu religious function, Tilak utilized it for giving politically oriented speeches also. To the Śivājī Festival, Tilak gave a distinctly political flavour by highlighting Śivājī's seventeenth century battles as "heroic struggles to protect the Motherland, and drawing inspiration from the Gītā". Commenting on Tilak's approach, William Holland has tried to analyse why religion started playing an important role in India's freedom struggle: "Like all empires, the British suppressed political meetings but they generally observed a hands-off policy with regard to religion. This provided a loophole which nationalists like Tilak exploited to the full for political purposes".[15]

1.16. The political application of the Gītā, initiated by Tilak in 1897, was conceived by him as one of the elements of "Lokasaṁgraha"—a Gītā-concept made more explicit in Tilak's subsequent writings and speeches, culminating in the *Gītā-Rahasya* (published in 1915). This was a significant expansion of the social role of the Gītā—an addition, so to say, of a new dimension. Tilak's assertion was that the Karma-Yoga doctrine of the Gītā, centred on the ideal of "Lokasaṁgraha" (the good of the society), was kept suppressed by most of the traditional commentators. His interpretation was thus, as he put it, only an attempt to understand the real message of the Gītā—almost like a rediscovery—but by no means a superimposition of his own ideas. Panikkar broadly agrees with Tilak, and highlights the great importance of widening the scope of applications of the Gītā—namely, from the religious to the socio-political sphere: "Hindu Reformation. . .was indeed a significant fact, but it would have remained basically a religious movement but for the re-discovery of the Bhagavad-Gītā as the political and social gospel of Hindu India".[16]

POST-TILAK LEADERS

1.17. Once Tilak had identified the Gītā as the most appropriate sourcebook of concepts and ideas needed for pursuing socially beneficial causes—be they religious, social or political—subsequent studies and researches by scholars and activists provided general support to Tilak's finding—albeit with some modifications. The twentieth century literature on the Gītā—and particularly on the Karma-Yoga—is immense, both in English and in modern Indian languages. Ursula King observes that the Gītā's attainment of supremacy "in popular thought and practice" has gone hand-in-hand with the vast increase in Gītā commentaries:

> There can be no doubt that the influence of this text (i.e. the Gītā) in modern Hinduism, with numerous editions and countless commentaries, goes far beyond anything in previous periods in Indian history. The Bhagavad-Gītā has so displaced the orthodox Vedic scriptures, at least in popular thought and practice, that some speak of a new Hindu orthodoxy based on the modern interpretations of what is now considered to be the central message of the Bhagavad-Gītā.[17]

1.18. Since the emphasis in the present study is intended to be on "leaders of social movements drawing inspiration from the Gītā," mention needs to be made of at least the following persons in the post-Tilak period:

(i) Aurobindo Ghose
(ii) Mohandas Karamchand Gandhi
(iii) Annie Besant
(iv) C. Rajagopalachari
(v) K.M. Munshi
(vi) Sri Prakasha
(vii) Vinoba Bhave

AUROBINDO

1.19. Aurobindo (1872-1950) was, till 1910, a close political associate of Tilak—and of course, a great political leader in his own right. Furthermore, Aurobindo, like Tilak, was also a very famous journalist. The weekly paper, the *Karmayogin,* which Aurobindo edited during 1909-10, depicted on the title page the "Kurukshetra Battlefield—with Krishna teaching Karma-Yoga to Arjuna". According to Ursula King: "Religious and political nationalism are closely intertwined in this review (i.e. paper) which preaches a new Karma-Yoga through the very effective vehicle of the ideal Karmayogin symbol."[18]

1.20. Although Aurobindo withdrew from active politics in 1910, to practise his Sādhanā at Pondicherry, the Gītā continued to engage his attention. In his *Essays on the Gītā,* written at Pondicherry, he gave a new interpretation, but the emphasis on Lokasaṁgraha was maintained throughout.

GANDHI

1.21. Gandhi (1869-1948) occupies a special place among Gītā-practitioners, because of his long and successful leadership of the Indian freedom movement based on Satyāgraha. By equating an ideal Satyāgrahī with the Sthitaprajña of the Gītā—i.e. a Karmayogin working for Lokasaṁgraha but having no desires for selfish gains—a very close link was established between the freedom fighters and the Gītā-ideals, with particular emphasis on *Ahiṁsā* (non-violence). From this consideration, Gandhi made a significant modification to Tilak's interpretation of Niṣkāma-karma and Lokasaṁgraha. Panikkar believes that Tilak's ideas "set right" by Gandhi's *Ahiṁsā,* produced a new ideal of great practical importance:

> To Gandhiji it was not sufficient that the ideal should be Lokasaṁgraha or the welfare of all. . . .
>
> There was a suggestion in Tilak's Gītā-Rahasya that the Karma-Yogin's action, as it was dedicated to God, was above moral laws so long as the object was clearly understood to be the common weal. It is this unexpressed doctrine of Tilak that Gandhiji sought to set right by his commentary on the Gītā and the practical interpretation he gave to it through his own life.[19]

OTHERS

1.22. Annie Besant, C. Rajagopalachari, K.M. Munshi and Sri Prakasha—all of them were not only prominent political leaders, who participated in India's freedom struggle, but they were also known as Gītā scholars. Vinoba Bhave's association with Gandhi was primarily in the Ashram-activities, viz. constructive programme and scholarly support to Gandhi's Gītā-commentary. However, it was in the post-independence period, that Vinoba made a new application of the Gītā to the country's land distribution problem, through the movement called "Bhūdāna-yajña".

SELECTION FOR CASE STUDY

1.23. In order to delimit the scope of the present study, only five leaders of social movements, who drew inspiration from the Gitā, are included therein, viz. the following:

(i) Rammohun Roy
(ii) Vivekananda
(iii) Tilak
(iv) Aurobindo

(v) Gandhi

It is hoped that case studies on some of the other activists, who drew inspiration from the Gītā for their social movements, will be presented in a subsequent publication.

CHAPTER TWO

Rammohun Roy: Using the Gītā for Social Reform

A BRIEF LIFE-SKETCH

2.1. Rammohun Roy was born in 1772 when the British administration in Bengal was being consolidated. The surname "Roy" was a title given to his great grandfather, Krishna Chandra Banerji. Rammohun's grandfather, Braja Binod, served under Siraj-ud-dowla. Rammohun's father, Ramakant was a small Zamindar, and, being also an orthodox Brahmin, commanded respect from the village community. Rammohun's mother, Tarini Devi, was a woman of great piety, descending from a family of priests.

2.2. Rammohun's parents wanted to give him good education, but the only place of learning in the village was either a Hindu Pandit's *Pāthasālā* or a Persian Moulvi's *Muktab.* After learning Bengali and Persian in the village, Rammohun was sent to Patna for studying Arabic and to Banaras for studying Sanskrit. As a result of new ideas that arose from all these studies, seeds of discord with his orthodox father were sown because Rammohun had become a strong opponent of idol-worship.

2.3. Leaving his parental home, Rammohun travelled from place to place within India, and also went to Tibet to obtain first-hand knowledge of Buddhism. According to the writings of Brahmo Samaj biographers, Rammohun's dispute with the Tibetan idol-worshippers and the protection that he received from women, in the face of a risk of attack by the fanatics, left a long-lasting impression on his mind:

> Rammohun's assertion of monotheistic doctrines gave offence

to the Lama worshippers, so much so that in their fanatic fury, they even resolved to lay violent hands on him, and they would certainly have executed their resolve but for the help which the poor Hindu (Rammohun) received from a quarter whence it was least expected. Some kind-hearted Tibetan women readily came to his rescue and by their timely help, saved him from imminent danger. This circumstance made a very deep impression on Rammohun's mind, and ever after he became a warm friend and staunch advocate of the tender sex. No wonder that he laboured hard for the emancipation of women.[1]

2.4. After Rammohun's return from Tibet, a reconciliation between him and his father took place. Rammohun's willingness to get married in the usual orthodox style further restored peace and harmony in the family. This enabled Rammohun to widen the scope of his language studies, by including, at this stage, a study of English, Latin, Greek, and Hebrew.

2.5. Rammohun soon got a lesson in the functioning of the Hindu orthodox society of his days. When he openly expressed his views against idol-worship, the Hindu religious leaders wanted him to be expelled from his parental home. Forced to choose between the society and the son, Rammohun's father yielded to social pressure and asked Rammohun and his wife to look for another house and to find their own means of sustenance.

2.6. Rammohun's knowledge of English and Persian and his willingness to work hard under the supervision of British officers enabled him to secure a job in the Revenue Department of the East India Company. The birth of his first son added to his happiness, and according to Brahmo Samaj biographers, "Rammohun named his first son Radha Prasad, after Lord Krishna's favourite wife Radha".[2]

2.7. Rammohun worked for the British administration till 1815, the last six years of his job being at Rangpore. The significance of the Rangpore residence as a preparatory phase for Rammohun's further activities in the religious field has been highlighted by Sarma:

The period of six years (1809-15) of Rammohun's residence at Rangpore may be said to be the period of preparation for his future work. He then made a careful study not only of Vedānta texts but also of Tāntric works and Jain scriptures. He started informal discussions on religious subjects with various men who assembled at his house for the purpose. And he began to disseminate his views by his talks and his publications.[3]

2.8. Rammohun's interest in "religious studies and in the investigation of truth" was so keen that, as soon as he had obtained adequate financial resources, he wanted to give up his job and to devote all his time and energy to philosophic pursuits. This he was able to do from 1815 onward, because, in addition to his own savings, he also got a large portion of the ancestral property. This phase of his life was spent mainly in Calcutta. But his "retired" life proved to be full of challenges, as his biographer observes:

> With all his love of retired life, Rammohun never neglected the call of duty which the then miserable condition of his country imperatively made on him, and being right earnest in his love of mankind, he readily responded to the call. Rammohun was, so to say, a born reformer, and even before he left Government service, he had formed the resolution to reform the social and religious life of his country. Now that he had got the sinews of war, he gave full and free vent to the workings of his mind, and proceeded to give his thoughts and feelings a permanent, tangible shape and form.[4]

2.9. Among the many activities which Rammohun pursued from 1815 onward, only one—the abolition of suttee—is covered in detail in this case study. Suttee was a Hindu custom whereby a widow burned herself to death along with the body of her dead husband. Besides giving details of Rammohun Roy's work for the abolition of suttee, a brief mention is also made in this study of two more activities, namely:

(i) religious reform through Brahmo Samaj and
(ii) pleas for starting modern education, for boys as well as girls.

2.10. By 1829, two of Rammohun's biggest "missions" had yielded tangible results—Suttee was abolished, and Brahmo Samaj was established. He then wanted to pay a visit to Europe. Since the suttee-advocates appealed to the Privy Council to overrule the ban imposed by the Governor-General, Rammohun too wanted to personally pursue the cause of abolition, and so felt it necessary to go to England. His journey to England in 1830 was facilitated because the Moghul Emperor of Delhi—now reduced to a mere shadow of a sovereign—nominated Rammohun Roy as his ambassador to His Majesty the King of England. The Moghul Emperor also conferred upon Rammohun Roy the title of "Raja", with a view to adding dignity and importance to the person nominated as his ambassador. The Moghul Emperor hoped that Raja Rammohun Roy would be able to obtain from the King of England additional financial grant as well as expanded territorial jurisdiction (for the Moghuls) in the vicinity of Delhi.

2.11. While in England, Rammohun Roy had the satisfaction that the abolition of suttee was finally confirmed in 1832. However, his plea on behalf of the Emperor of Delhi was only partly successful, in the sense that only some extra money—but no territory—was sanctioned for the Moghuls.

2.12. Rammohun Roy was unable to return to India because of his illness to which he succumbed, while still in England, in 1833. Dwarka Nath Tagore got a tomb erected over his grave near Bristol, with the following inscription.

> Beneath this stone rest the remains of Raja Rammohun Roy. A conscientious and steadfast believer in the unity of the Godhead, he consecrated his life with entire devotion to the worship of the Divine Spirit alone. To great natural talents he united a thorough mastery of many languages and early distinguished himself as one of the greatest scholars of the day. His unwearied labours to promote the social, moral and physical condition of the people of India, his earnest endeavours to suppress idolatry and suttee rite, and his constant zealous advocacy of whatever tended to advance the glory of God and welfare of man live in the grateful remembrance of his

countrymen. This tablet records the sorrow and pride with which his memory is cherished by his descendants.[5]

SUTTEE: A SYMBOL OF RELIGIOUS AND SOCIAL ORTHODOXY, EXPLOITED BY PROPERTY-GRABBING RELATIVES OF THE WIDOW

2.13. Although some instances of suttee occurred in different parts of India during the ancient and the middle ages, it was mainly during the seventeenth century that it became relatively more frequent, particularly in Bengal. Obviously, this was associated with religious and social orthodoxy. Historical evidence from various sources shows that this evil custom almost took the shape of conspiracy between the priests and the newly emerging richer sections of the Hindu society. Because of the prevalence of the Dāyabhāga law of inheritance in Bengal (which gave the widow practically the same rights over joint family property as her deceased husband), the property-grabbing instincts of the widow's relatives appear to have assumed a major role in this conspiracy.

2.14. Hindu priests strengthened their hold on the society by laying stress on rituals and regulations of all sorts which only they could specify. Separatist tendencies between the different castes that were encouraged by restricting inter-group dining and marriages generated a feeling of competition to gain higher social status with the help of priests. Evil customs like child-marriage, polygamy, and suttee received priestly support. At the same time, threats of expulsion from the caste-groups on grounds of sea-voyage, widow-marriage, etc. became more and more common.

2.15. The active role that the priestly class played in motivating, and even forcing, the widows to burn themselves has been documented by Tavernier and Bernier who travelled through India in the seventeenth century. For example, Tavernier says:

> The Brahmins that accompany the widow exhort her to give public testimonies to her constancy and courage, and to take away the fears of death, which naturally terrify humanity, the

priests do give her a certain beverage to stupefy and disorder the senses, which takes from her all apprehension of her preparations for death. This for the Brahmins' interest that the poor miserable creatures should continue in their resolutions; for all their bracelets, as well about their legs as their arms, the pendants in their ears, their rings, sometimes of gold and sometimes of silver, all these belong to the Brahmins who rake for them among the ashes, when the party is burned.[6]

2.16. Bernier's account (referring to the years 1656-1668), confirms that of Tavernier. William Johns remarks:

> The amicable Bernier, indignant at this horrible spectacle, indignantly exclaims against a religion which could permit such a sacrifice, but still more so against 'les demons de brahmens' who not only encouraged these deluded females, but were the most active persons throughout the infernal tragedy.[7]

2.17. Priests imposing superstitious customs on the society joined hands with those who, on the basis of quick money earned by trading with the English merchants wanted religious sanction for securing higher status in the society. B.B. Roy gives details of how this process worked:

> During 1680-83, English merchants imported into Bengal silver worth £200,000 to pay for their purchases. This huge influx of silver effected a sudden change in Bengal's economy. The upper classes of our society grew richer, and came to possess more articles of luxury than before; and the Government officials and revenue collecting middlemen made more money on large scale than they did in Akbar's days. The people of Bengal were able to buy products of other provinces or countries to an extent inconceivable in the earlier times when barter was the chief method of our trade. Money also affected the social life of Bengal, because persons accumulating wealth wanted to enjoy higher status in the society. So they had to follow the injunctions of the Brahmins. At that time, building a temple and maintaining within it a set of priests was believed to be the best action which human virtue could be capable of.

2.18. A sudden increase of wealth in several of the joint Hindu families in Bengal created problems of distribution amongst the various claimants, particularly when one of the brothers died. In other parts of India (not covered by the Dāyabhāga law of inheritance) a widow living in a joint Hindu family was only entitled to maintenance, and, by herself having no other right over the family property, did not appear as an obstacle in the property claims of other relatives. In Bengal, on the other hand, the Dāyabhāga law permitted even a childless widow to become an heir to her husband, so long as she was alive. In such a situation, the option of burning the widow with her husband could appear to other property claimants as a convenient way of getting rid of an obstacle. B.B. Roy considers this as "circumstantial evidence" linking property disputes with suttee:

> From the overall picture of participation (in the suttee custom) it may be concluded that in Bengal, most of the participating families of upper castes were opulent. From circumstantial evidence it may not be ruled out that property relation was the dominant factor in leading the participants to homicide. For an explanation the law of inheritance of Bengal should be discussed.[9]

2.19. This is more explicitly stated by P.V. Kane:

> It appears from all accounts of travellers and others that widow burning prevailed more in Bengal during the century immediately preceding its abolition than anywhere else in India. If that was so, there were certain good reasons for that state of things. In the whole of India, except Bengal, the widows as members in a joint Hindu family are only entitled to maintenance and have no other rights over the property of the family. In Bengal, wherever the Dāyabhāga prevails, the widow of a sonless member even in a joint Hindu family is entitled to practically the same rights over joint family property which her deceased husband would have had. This must have frequently induced the surviving members to get rid of the widow by appealing at the most distressing hours to her devotion to and love for her husband.[10]

2.20. A similar reasoning, supported by a magistrate's report, is contained in William Crooke's paper included in the British Parliamentary Papers. In Crooke's opinion, widow marriage was disallowed with a view to preventing her "second husband" from putting forth a claim to her "first husband's" property.[11] Then the widow was taught to recognize the spiritual benefit which would arise from the annual performance of the death rites. In some instances it was also seen that to obtain the property, relatives often induced the wife of the deceased member to commit suicide. In fact, the Magistrate of Rangpore reported in 1824.

> In the instance which occurred in this district, the Magistrate thought there was a strong suspicion that the brothers of a deceased husband might obtain some property to the value of 3000 or 4000 rupees left by him, to which she would, had she lived, succeed.[12]

2.21. B.B. Roy concludes that the custom of homicide was started by upper classes to serve only their personal interests. Of course, the priests' connivance gave it a religious flavour. Why, then, did the custom spread to poorer sections of the society? B.B. Roy raises this question and also provides an answer.

> Then comes the question why a portion of the poor people took resort to suttee practice. In this case also, poverty of those people compelled them to encourage the widow burning in order to relieve themselves from the additional burden of maintaining the widow member. Moreover, they were eager to uplift their social status by following the custom which was preponderant among the members of high society. The widow-burning on the whole became a status-giving socio-religious activity.[13]

SUTTEE IN THE LIGHT OF HINDU SCRIPTURES: A DEBATE BETWEEN RAMMOHUN ROY AND SUTTEE-ADVOCATES

2.22. After several years of preparatory work, Rammohun Roy assumed, in 1818, the leadership of the movement to create public opinion against the suttee custom. A key question arose whether this custom had the sanction of the Hindu scriptures or not. Some of the Hindu scholars (organized by Radhakanta Deb and Kashinath Turkabagish) argued that, although the *Manusmṛti* makes no mention of suttee, later *smṛti*-writers like Angiras and Harita speak in favour of the custom in the following words:

> That woman who, on the death of her husband, ascends the burning pile with him, is exalted to heaven. (Angiras)[14]
>
> That woman who follows her husband in death purifies three families, viz. of her mother, of her father and of her husband. (Harita)[15]

2.23. Realizing that the authoritativeness of the later *smṛtis* was less in comparison to that of the *Manusmṛti*, the advocates of suttee also tried to gain support from a distorted version of *Ṛgveda* X.18. 7-8, which was translated by them as follows:

> O fire ![16] let these women, with bodies anointed with clarified butter, eyes coloured with collyrium, and void of tears, enter thee, the parent of water, that they may not be separated from their husbands, but may be, in unison with excellent husbands, themselves sinless and jewels amongst women.[17]

2.24. In order to refute the arguments of suttee-advocates, Rammohun Roy adopted a step-by-step approach. First, he reminded the advocates that neither any scripture nor the prevailing custom viewed the burning of a widow as obligatory. Rather, it was, at the most, an option on which a decision is taken by the widow herself. Secondly, he quoted Manu who directs that a widow should pass her whole life as an ascetic:

> Let the widow emaciate her body, by living voluntarily on pure flowers, roots and fruits, but let her not, when her lord is deceased, even pronounce the name of another man. Let her continue till death forgiving all injuries, performing harsh duties, avoiding every sensual pleasure, and cheerfully practising the incomparable rules of virtue which have been

followed by such women as were devoted to only one husband.[18]

2.25. The suttee-advocates sensed in Rammohun Roy's approach a possibility of reconciling the views of Angiras and Harita with those of Manu, and they accepted that even the later *smṛti*-writers consider suttee as optional, the basis of their advocacy being that a suttee receives a reward in the form of heaven:

> When Angiras says that there is no other way for a widow except concremation (suttee), and when Harita says that the omission of it is a fault, we reconcile their words with those of Manu, by considering them as used merely for the purpose of exalting the merit of concremation, but not as prescribing this as an indispensable duty. All these expressions, moreover, convey a promise of reward for concremation, and hence it appears that concremation is only optional.[19]

2.26. As soon as a stage was reached, involving a comparison between a life of asceticism (without hankering after any reward) and a reward-promising concremation, Rammohun Roy was able to argue convincingly against suttee by drawing strong support from the Upaniṣads and even more so from the Bhagavad-Gītā. The significant role of the Bhagavad-Gītā in particular can be inferred from the fact that, in Rammohun Roy's statements, as many as fourteen verses of the Gītā were quoted, in comparison to only six from the Upaniṣads. Furthermore, at a crucial stage in the course of arguments and counter-arguments, the wider issue of discrimination between men and women was raised, and Rammohun Roy quoted from the Gītā in ruling out any trace of discrimination in spiritual matters, on grounds of sex.

WHO IS SPIRITUALLY SUPERIOR—THE WIDOW OR THE SUTTEE?

2.27. Rammohun Roy quoted three verses from the Upaniṣads and six verses from the Gītā to highlight the superiority of a life of asceticism (without hankering after any reward) to a reward-oriented act like suttee:

Faith in God which leads to absorption is one thing, and rites which have future fruition for their object, another. Each of these, producing different consequences, holds out to man inducements to follow it. The man who, of these two, chooses faith is blessed, and he, who, for the sake of reward practises rites, is dashed away from the enjoyment of eternal beatitude.[20] (*Kathopaniṣad*)

Knowledge and rites together offer themselves to every man. The wise man considers which of these two is better and which the worse. By reflecting, he becomes convinced of the superiority of the former, despises rites, and takes refuge in knowledge. And the unlearned, for the sake of bodily gratifications, has recourse to the performance of rites.[21] (*Kathopaniṣad*)

Rites, of which there are eighteen members, are all perishable; he who considers them as the source of blessing shall undergo repeated transmigrations; and all those fools who, immersed in the foolish practices of rites, consider themselves to be wise and learned, are repeatedly subjected to birth, disease, death and other pains. When one blind man is guided by another, both subject themselves on their way to all kinds of distress.[22] (*Mundakopaniṣad*)

2.28. Before starting to quote from the Gītā, Rammohun Roy characterized it as "the essence of all śāstras" and mentioned that its main theme is "the praise of works performed without desire for fruits".[23] The six verses quoted from the Gītā in support of this viewpoint are from five different chapters, namely, third, fifth, second, eighteenth, and twelfth (the last of these chapters accounting for two verses). In each case, Rammohun Roy's own translation of the Gītā-verses is given below:

Works performed, except for the sake of God, only entangle the soul. Therefore, O Arjuna, forsaking desire, perform works with the view to please God. III 9.

The person who performs works without desire of fruition, directing his mind to God, obtains eternal rest. And the person who is devoted to fruition and performs works with desire, he is indeed inextricably involved. V. 12

O Arjuna, rites performed for the sake of fruition are

degraded far below works done without desire, which lead to the acquisition of the knowledge of God. Therefore perform thy works without desire of fruition, with the view of acquiring divine knowledge. Those who perform works for the sake of fruition are most debased. II.49

It is my firm opinion that works are to be performed forsaking their consequences, and the prospect of their fruits. XVIII. 6

If you are unable to acquire by degrees divine knowledge, be deligent in performing works with a view to please Me, that by such works you may acquire a better state. If you are unable even to perform rites solely for My sake, then, controlling your senses, endeavour to perform rites without the desire of fruition. XII. 10-11[24]

2.29. It is important to appreciate how heterodox and non-traditional was Rammohun Roy's statement according a higher spiritual status to a widow living as an ascetic (without hankering after any reward), in comparison to a suttee (who burnt herself with the desire for reward in heaven). The traditional Hindu view during the middle ages, mentioned by later *smṛti*-writers and supported by superstitious beliefs and socially oppressive customs, had glorified the suttee and put the widow in a pathetic situation. Alaka Hejib and Katherine Young have compared the traditional Hindu images of the widow and the suttee:

> The appearance of a traditional widow suggested destitution. Her tonsured head or her flowing hair unadorned with flowers indicated her miserable status. . . . Not only was she denied enjoyments, but every other opportunity for pleasure, such as participation in social gatherings, festivals, the partaking of rich food, indeed, entertainment or pleasure of any sort. . . . Even when the family and society grieved ostensibly for her plight, they had more regret for her karmic crime of "causing her husband's death." Thus widowhood of a woman entailed spiritual misfortune and implied the temporary absence of dharma in relation to the family. Not only she but also the family, the lineage and the community too had to share the blame for this adharma.

Whereas most Hindus looked down on the widow, they had a diametrically opposite attitude towards the suttee. . . . The suttee was viewed as a perfect wife, the very embodiment of the goddess, for she expedited immediately her bad karma that caused her husband's death. . . . The suttee never had the title of widow. Because of the immediacy of her self-imposed death, she circumvented any rite of passage to another stage of life. Rather, she donned her wedding garments, and thereby reaffirmed symbolically her marital status and auspiciousness. It was as though suttee were an event of spiritual and cosmic significance.[25]

2.30. Rammohun Roy knew that a lessening of the popular support for suttee could be brought about only by making the people realize that the sentiments traditionally associated with this custom were unjustified. To this end, he put forward not only the philosophic argument based on the Upaniṣads and the Bhagavad-Gītā, but also practical considerations of morality and civilized behaviour in society. It seems appropriate to draw attention to some of these related issues before specifying further references to the Upaniṣads and the Bhagavad-Gītā in Rammohun's arguments with the suttee-advocates.

Rammohun Roy's Charges of Cruelty and Murder

2.31. Apart from drawing scriptural support for his statement favouring the ascetic life of a widow, Rammohun Roy pointed out to the suttee-advocates, how their glorified image of a suttee was largely hypocritical because of the extreme cruelty involved in the burning of living human beings. Rammohun had personal knowledge of the physical force applied to a widow to prevent her from changing her mind and escaping from the flames at the last minute:

At the death of his elder brother Jagamohun in 1811 the widow became a suttee. It is said that Rammohun had endeavoured to persuade her beforehand against this terrible step, but in vain. When, however, she felt the flames, she tried to get up and escape from the pile, but her orthodox relations and the priest forced her down with bamboo poles, and kept her there to die, while drums and brazen instruments were loudly sounded to drown her shrieks. Rammohun, unable to save her and filled with unspeakable indignation and pity, vowed within himself then and there that he would never rest until the atrocious custom was rooted out.[26]

2.32. Theoretically, a woman, on the death of her husband, had the option whether to perform suttee or to undergo the rite of passage to widowhood. Every precaution was to be taken that the suttee knew what she was doing and had the strength to endure the consequences of her resolve. While recognizing the apparent availability of the option to the widow, Alaka Hejib and Katherine Young argue that "the proleptic model instilled in her from childhood was the society's or family's choice, not truly hers."[27] Apart from the pressure of traditional values and customs, if there was overt pressure by family or priests prior to her resolve, a suttee could be called homicide, according to the tradition. In fact any action that influenced directly a woman's decision so that it was not her own resolve was considered adhārmic.

2.33. In the course of his arguments with the suttee-advocates Rammohun told them that suttee performed by force is a "woman murder":

> Those who, in direct defiance of the authority of the śāstras, act the part of woman-murderers, in tying down the widow to the pile and subsequently applying the flame, burn her to death, can never expurgate themselves from the sin of woman-murder.[28]

2.34. Stung by the charge of cruelty, the suttee-advocates lodged a protest to Rammohun Roy:

> You have repeatedly asserted that from want of feeling we promote female destruction. This is incorrect, for it is declared in our Veda and codes of law that mercy is the root of virtue and from our practice of hospitality etc. our compassionate dispositions are well known.[29]

2.35. In reply, Rammohun explained how a long and repeated exposure to cruel customs, surcharged with religious sentiments, makes one insensitive to the cries of innocent victims:

> That in other cases you show charitable dispositions is acknowledged. But by witnessing from your youth the voluntary burning of women amongst your elder relatives, your neighbours and the inhabitants of the surrounding villages, and by observing the indifference at the time when the women are writhing under the torture of the flames, habits of insensibility are produced.[30]

2.36. The suttee-advocates realized that Rammohun Roy's charges of cruelty, force and insensibility are too strong to be set aside lightly, and so they expressed willingness to look into them, by saying "what you have said we shall carefully consider".[31]

Spiritual Versus the Ritual

2.37. To the suttee-advocates it appeared essential that Hindus should carry on the ritualistic practices in the traditional manner. They even asserted that the performance of rites with a desire for fruits was approved of by the Vedas themselves, and they quoted, in support, the following Vedic verse: "He who desires heavenly fruition shall perform the sacrifice of horse."[32]

2.38. In reply, Rammohun Roy explained the limitations associated with Vedic ritualistic practices. For example, he stated that "the (Vedic) passages directing works for the sake of fruition are meant only for the most ignorant. Learned men should endeavour to withdraw all those ignorant persons from works performed with desire, but should never, for the sake of profit, attempt to drown them in the abyss of passion".[33] What Roy meant was that, within the Hindu tradition, the school of Uttara-Mīmāṁsā ultimately superceded that of Pūrva-Mīmāṁsā, that the spiritual content of the tradition was finally regarded as transcending the ritual content thereof. He continued:

> There are indeed *śāstras* directing the performance of rites for the sake of fruition, but these are acknowledged to be of less authority than those which prohibit such rites, as is proved by the following text from the Mundaka Upaniṣad:

> Śāstras are of two sorts, superior and inferior; of these, the superior are those by which the Eternal God is approached.[34]

2.39. Rammohun Roy quoted the Bhagavad-Gītā also to establish the superiority of the spiritual over the ritual: "Krishna says: Amongst śāstras I am those which treat of God". (X.32)

Rammohun further quoted three Gītā verses which criticize Vedic ritualism as an obstacle in the spiritual path, and he reminded the suttee-advocates that all Hindus consider the Gītā as authoritative and most sacred:

> The Bhagavad-Gītā whose authority is considered the most sacred by Hindus of all persuasions, repeatedly condemns rites performed for fruition. I here quote a few passages of that book:
>
> All those ignorant persons who attach themselves to the words of the *śāstras* that convey promises of fruition, consider those extravagant and alluring passages as leading to real happiness, and say, besides them there is no other reality. Agitated in their minds by these desires, they believe the abodes of the celestial gods to be the chief object, and they devote themselves to those texts which treat of ceremonies and their fruits and entice by promises of enjoyment. Such people can have no real confidence in the Supreme Being. (Gītā II. 42-44)[35]

2.40. Faced with overwhelming evidence from authoritative scriptures like the Gītā and the Upaniṣads, the suttee-advocates had to admit that "pious works performed without desire are preferable to works performed for the sake of fruition".[36] However, they tried to equate the "desire for heaven" and the "desire for God", and thus to deny the ascetic widow spiritual superiority over the suttee, which Rammohun Roy was attempting to establish all the time. To this end they interpreted Manu's advice to the widow in such a way as to bring it within the range of "having a desire for reward". The suttee-advocates adopted a two-stage argument:

> Manu directs that a widow should continue till death as an ascetic, aiming to practise the incomparable rules of virtue

that have been followed by such women as were devoted to only one husband. From the word "aiming", it follows that the duties of an ascetic, to be practised by widows, are of the nature of those performed with desire. Secondly, from the subsequent words of Manu it appears that those widows who lead austere lives ascend to heaven; thefore, from the words "ascending to heaven" it is obvious that the austerities that may be performed by them are for reward.[37]

2.41. Rammohun Roy questioned the validity of the interpretation applied by the suttee-advocates to Manu's words. He clarified that practising virtue for acquiring the knowledge of God and "with the object of final beatitude" is entirely different from what the Gītā has called "desire-prompted acts", and further that "no *śāstras* nor any of the learned has ever classed this (aiming for final beatitude) amongst works performed with desire of fruition. For no man possessed of understanding performs any movement of mind or body without an object. It is those works only, therefore, that are performed for the sake of corporal enjoyment, either in the present or in a future state of existence, that are said to be with desire, and that are, as such, prohibited, as Manu defines: "Whatever act is performed for the sake of gratifications in this world or the next is called Prabarttak; and those that are performed according to the knowledge of God, are called Nibarttak". (*Manusmṛti*)[38]

2.42. This took care of the first argument of the suttee-advocates related to the meaning of the word "aiming". Their second argument was that "ascending to heaven" being common between the widow and the suttee, there was no justification for viewing the widow as spiritually superior to the suttee.

2.43. Rammohun Roy utilized the Bhagavad-Gītā in pointing out a fallacy in the above argument. He explained that "ascending to heaven" was only the first stage of the journey which happened to be common between the widow and the suttee, and that it was necessary to take into account the second stage of the journey also for appreciating the difference between the two women. According to the Gītā, those whose actions are motivated by desire are entitled to only a limited spell of heavenly enjoyment, after which they fall again in *saṅsāra* and have to face the problems of the world of the mortals. In contrast to this, says the Gītā again, that those who perform righteous actions without desire are assured of a continuous, upward spiritual mobility, for in their case, a heavenly stay is followed by a birth in the home of the pure, to enable them to complete their yoga till they attain final beatitude.

2.44. Rammohun's explanation clarified the subtle distinction between *karma-kāṇḍa* (ritualistic, desireful karma) and Karma-yoga (desire-free, righteous karma). The Gītā-verse quoted by him for describing the limited heavenly stay obtainable through *karma-kāṇḍa* was:

> Observers of rites, after the completion of their rewards, return to earth. Therefore they, for the sake of rewards, repeatedly ascend to heaven and return to the world, and cannot obtain bliss. (*Gītā*, IX. 21)[39]

And the Gītā-verse quoted by Rammohun for describing the unimpeded, upward spiritual mobility of the karmayogin was:

> A man whose devotions have been broken off by death, having enjoyed for an immensity of years the rewards of his virtues in the regions above, at length is born again in some holy and respectable family. (*Gītā,* VI.41)[40]

Discriminatory Attitude Towards Women in Spiritual Matters

2.45. At this stage, the suttee-advocates realized that, on philosophical grounds, they could not deny the spiritual superiority of the ascetic widow in comparison to the suttee. Therefore, they adopted a new line of argument, questioning the capability of widows to follow an ascetic mode of life in accordance with the karma-yoga teachings of the Gītā. In a way, this raised the basic issue of a discriminatory attitude towards women in spiritual matters, reflecting the traditional gender-bias of orthodox Hindus. Furthermore, since Rammohun Roy was making extensive use of the Gītā in his arguments, the suttee-advocates themselves picked up a Gītā-verse out of context and quoted it in support of their own argument. This is how the suttee-advocates gave expression to their distrust in the inherent spiritual capability of women:

> The real reason for the anxiety to persuade widows to follow their husbands, and for our endeavours to burn them pressed down with ropes is, that women are, by nature, of inferior understanding, without resolution, unworthy of trust, subject to passions, and void of virtuous knowledge. They, according to the precepts of the *śāstras*, are not allowed to marry again after the demise of their husbands, and consequently despair at once of all worldly pleasure. Hence it is evident that death to these unfortunate widows is preferable to existence; for the great difficulty which a widow may experience by living a purely ascetic life, as prescribed by the *śāstras*, is obvious. Therefore, if she does not perform concremation, it is probable that she may be guilty of such acts as may bring disgrace upon her paternal and maternal relations, and those that may be connected with her husband. Under these circumstances, we instruct them from their early life in the idea of concremation, holding out to them heavenly enjoyments in company with their husbands, as well as the beatitude of their relations, both by birth and marriage, and their reputation in this world. From this, many of them, on the death of their husbands, become desirous of accompanying them; but to remove every chance of their trying to escape from the blazing fire, in burning them we first tie them down to the pile.
>
> Furthermore, since women are naturally devoted to works productive of fruits, to persuade them to forsake concremation in order to attempt the acquisition of knowledge is to destroy their hopes in both ways. Even the Gītā advises that "ignorant persons who are devoted to works ought not to be dissuaded from performing them. (*Gītā,* III. 26)[41]

2.46. On both the issues, viz., women's inherent capability and entitlement in the spiritual field, and doubts about their continued adherence to asceticism while living as widows, Rammohun Roy put forth a strong and detailed refutation and also quoted two Gītā-verses. He then clarified why the Gītā-quotation employed by the suttee-advocates was invalid, being out of context and inapplicable in the present case.

2.47. Rammohun Roy's defence of the fine qualities of women and their virtuous conduct in the face of gross injustice by men covered five aspects of their mutual relationship and behaviour:

> Firstly, the male part of the community, taking advantage of the women's corporal weakness, have denied to them, those excellent merits that they are entitled to by nature, and afterwards they are apt to say that women are naturally incapable of acquiring those merits. Is men's accusation against women consistent with justice? When did you ever afford them a fair opportunity of exhibiting their natural capacity?. How then can you accuse them of want of understanding. As you keep women generally deprived of education and acquirements, you cannot in justice pronounce on their inferiority. Līlāwatī, Bhānumatī and other women in the past were celebrated in their thorough knowledge of all the *śāstras*, and Yājñavalkya imparted divine knowledge of the most difficult nature to his wife Maitreyī who was able to follow and completely attain it.
>
> Secondly, you charge them with want of resolution, at which I feel exceedingly surprised; for we constantly perceive, in a country where the name of death makes the male shudder, that the female, from her firmness of mind, offers to burn with the corpse of her deceased husband.
>
> Thirdly, with regard to their trustworthiness, if we enumerate such women in each village or town as have been deceived by men, and such men as have been deceived by women, I presume, that the number of the deceived women would be found ten times greater than that of the betrayed men.
>
> Fourthly, with respect to their subjection to the passions, this may be judged of by the custom of marriage as to the respective sexes; for one man may marry two or three or sometimes even ten wives, while a woman who marries but one husband, desires at his death to follow him, forsaking all worldly enjoyments, or to remain leading the austere life of an ascetic.
>
> Fifthly, the accusation of the want of virtuous conduct is an injustice. At marriage the wife is recognized as half of her husband, but in after-conduct they are treated worse than inferior animals. Respect to virtue and their reputation makes women forgive even such ill-treatment. What I lament is that

> seeing the women thus dependent and exposed to every misery, you feel for them no compassion that might exempt them from being tied down and burnt to death.[42]

2.48. Rammohun Roy then explained the directive of the *śāstras* in general, and of the Gītā in particular, according to which men as well as women are equally entitled to make spiritual progress:

> By leading an ascetic life in the performance of duties without desire, widows may purify their minds and acquire divine knowledge, which may procure for them final beatitude. Consequently, there is no reason why they should lose both objects of future hope by forsaking concremation. We have Shri Krishna's assurance in the Gītā that "by placing their reliance on me, women, and those of the lower classes of Vaiśya and Śūdra may obtain the highest exaltation. (*Gītā,* IX. 32)[43]

2.49. Referring to the fears expressed by the suttee-advocates that great harm was likely if the widow failed to maintain an ascetic life, Rammohun Roy explained that such fears arose from the warnings given in the *śāstras*, but that they referred only to reward-oriented ceremonies, and so were not applicable to desire-free acts:

> Should even the least part of any ceremony performed for reward be omitted or mistaken, the fruits are destroyed, and evil is produced. But there is no bad consequence from a failure in works performed without desire, for the completion of these, even in part, is advantageous. In proof I quote the Bhagavad-Gītā:
>
> Works without desire, if only commenced, are never without advantage, and if any member be defective, evil consequences do not ensue, as in works performed with desire. And the performance of even a small portion of a work without desire brings safety. (*Gītā,* II. 40)[44]

2.50. Finally, Rammohun Roy clarified why the Gītā-quotation resorted to by the suttee-advocates was invalid:

As to your quotation from the Gītā, to show that persons devoted to works ought not to be dissuaded from the performance of them, it may be observed that this text applies only to rites offered without desire of rewards, though applied by you to works performed for the sake of future enjoyment, in direct inconsistency with the authority of the Gītā. The object of this, as well as of all the texts of the Gītā, is to dissuade men from works performed with desire.[45]

SUTTEE DECLARED ILLEGAL BY GOVERNOR-GENERAL IN 1829

2.51. The idea behind Rammohun Roy's debates with the suttee-advocates was that the Hindu society itself should become aware of the need to put an end to this evil custom, and take action accordingly. He was not in favour of the Government (led by adherents of a different religion) interfering directly in Hindu religious matters. He knew how during a part of the Moghul rule, government interference had taken the form of forcible conversion of Hindus to Islam, and he did not want any such thing to happen again. Even non-governmental interference, for example, by Christian Missionaries, was viewed with suspicion, as being part of their design to convert the Hindus to Christianity. The sermons preached by Rev. Claudius Buchanan of the Church of England (who came to Bengal in 1790) strengthened such fears among the Hindus, because he divided human history, since the beginning of Christianity, into three eras: (1) the first era was that of the promulgation of the Gospel by Christ Himself; (2) the second was the era of reformation; and (3) the third era of light is the present period when Christianity has assumed its true character as "Light of the world". The holy scriptures, said Buchanan, are multiplying without number and preachers are going forth into almost every region to make the ways of God known upon the earth. So as a historical process, as viewed by Buchanan, Christianity was bound to come to a heathen land like India. In Buchanan's view, a religion like Hinduism which included a horrible custom like suttee could not be worth sticking to. In any case, as a first step, Buchanan advocated abolition of the custom of suttee by law.

2.52. The Christian missionaries tried to mould public opinion, in India as well as Britain, against the Indian custom of suttee. Buchanan's writings were widely read in Britain, and they contained statistics of widows burnt, which were brought to the attention of British Parliament by William Wilberforce in 1813. Subsequently, Fowell Buxton moved in the Parliament for publication of copies or extracts of all communications from India dealing with the subject of widow-burning. As to whether the custom should be abolished by law, he said that he was aware that a feeling of delicacy, upon the superstition of the natives, alone restricted the British authorities from interfering to prevent these dreadful spectacles. Still the question was not, in fact, one of religious toleration, but whether murder and suicide ought tacitly to be permitted under British jurisdiction.

2.53. The British administration in Bengal, coming under pressure from various directions, felt the need to depart from the policy of non-interference in religious matters. Three aspects of the question had to be taken into account. Firstly, what did the Hindu religious scriptures say about the suttee? Secondly, what was the opinion of the judges and officers of the Government? Thirdly, how to ascertain native Indian opinion?

2.54. The arrival of Lord William Bentinck as Governor-General of India in 1828 marked a quickening of the pace of action. He already had before him a statement by Mṛtyuñjaya Vidyālaṅkār, who was the Chief Pundit of Sanskrit and Bengali in the College of Fort William and who was held in high esteem by other pundits as well. At the request of the Chief Judge, Mṛtyuñjaya submitted a report in Sanskrit after consulting about thirty religious works. He stated clearly that, after the death of her husband, the widow may either embrace a life of abstinence and chastity, or mount the burning pile; but according to his opinion, the life of abstinence and chastity was the most sensible. A widow by burning herself with her husband may obtain conjugal bliss in heaven, while by a life of abstinence and chastity she would attain sacred wisdom and final beatitude. Hence to destroy herself for the sake of a little evanescent bliss should not be her duty.

2.55. The judges and officers of the Government in India also expressed their views in favour of putting an end to the suttee. Finally, to ascertain native Indian opinion, Lord Bentinck sought a meeting with Rammohun Roy. However, when the Governor-General's aide-de-camp first conveyed this message to Rammohun, the latter replied: "I have now given up all worldly avocations, and am engaged in religious culture and in the investigation of truth. Kindly express my humble respects to the Governor-General and inform him that I have no inclination to appear before his august presence and therefore I hope that he will kindly pardon me."[46]

2.56. The above words the aide-de-camp conveyed to the Governor-General who enquired, "What did you say to Rammohun Roy?" The aide-de-camp replied, "I told him that Lord William Bentinck, the Governor-General, would be pleased to see him." The Governor-General answered, "Go back and tell him again that Mr. William Bentinck will be highly obliged to him if he will kindly see him once."[47] This the aide-de-camp did and Rammohun Roy could no longer refuse the urgent and polite request of the Governor-General.

2.57. The meeting between the Governor-General and Rammohun Roy took place in July 1829. The Governor-General expressed his anxious desire to put an end to a custom constituting so foul a blot. While Rammohun Roy expressed his strongest disapproval of the custom, he did not approve of the principle of imposing a legal ban by the Government. In Lord Bentinck's words:

> It was Rammohun Roy's opinion that the practice might be suppressed quietly and unobservedly by increasing the difficulties and by the indirect agency of the police. He apprehended that any public enactment would give rise to general apprehension, that the reasoning would be, while the English were contending for power they deemed it polite to allow universal toleration and to respect our religion, but having obtained the supremacy their first act is a violation of their profession, and the next will probably be, like the Mohammedan conquerors, to force upon us their own religion.[48]

2.58. While appreciating Rammohun Roy's viewpoint, Lord Bentinck realised that, in the absence of a legal ban, the burning of widows by orthodox Hindus would continue, leading to widespread condemnation of the policy of the Government. He therefore decided to act, and on 4 December 1829, the suttee-custom was declared illegal by Regulation XVII of the Bengal Code. Once the Governor-General's decision was announced, Rammohun Roy came out in open support for it.

CONFIRMATION OF GOVERNOR-GENERAL'S DECISION BY PRIVY COUNCIL IN 1832

2.59. Even after the declaration of the ban on suttee, orthodox Hindus tried to convince the Governor-General that this custom was in accordance with their tradition based on scriptures. However, after going through the memorandum submitted by suttee-supporters, Lord Bentinck replied that, widows, in the religious writings of the Hindus, were not commanded to destroy themselves. He said he had no intention to attack the Hindu religion, but for the security of human life and the preservation of social order, he could not prohibit the regulation enacted by him. If the petitioners were of opinion that the regulation was not in conformity with the enactments of the British Parliament, then they could send an appeal to the King-in-Council.

2.60. Orthodox Hindus decided to pursue the matter and asked an Englishman, Francis Bathie to go to England and file an appeal on their behalf, that is, for the removal of the ban on widow-burning.

2.61. Liberal Hindus opposed to suttee realised, that, to win the final battle, their own interpretation of the scriptures must be presented to the British public and the appellate authorities. They collected money and decided to send Rammohun Roy to England to present their point of view. Rammohun gladly agreed to go but he said he would not take any money from the society because he was determined to fight for the just cause of the widows in the spirit of Karma-yoga. Rammohun also wanted to demonstrate his opposition to the ban on sea-voyage which orthodox priests had imposed on the Hindus. He was aware of the risk to which he was thus exposing himself, because some of the orthodox Hindus even thought of assassinating him, as B.B. Roy (referring to the *Asiatic Journal* of August 1830) says:

> When the anti-abolitionists heard that Rammohun would go to England to counter their petition before the House of Lords, they decided to assassinate him. As a consequence, Francis Keith Martin came forward for his help and accompanied him, armed with a brass pistol and sword stick, when he came to town during those perilous days. Rammohun himself also kept a naval dagger in his pocket and a sword stick in his hand. His attendants were also well armed.[49]

2.62. Realizing that the debate as to which scriptures deserve priority was again open, Rammohun Roy summarized the long arguments that he had earlier put forward, and published in 1830 an "Abstract of the arguments, regarding the burning of widows considered as religious rite". Being a summary of what he had written in the preceding years, this Abstract included references to the Bhagavad-Gītā "whose authority is considered the most sacred by Hindus of all persuasions".[50]

2.63. During his stay in England, Rammohun Roy was requested by the Attorney and Solicitor General, who was to argue on behalf of the Governor-General, to clarify to him the views of the Hindu authorities on suttee. Rammohun accordingly sent him a paper entitled "Some remarks in vindication of the resolution passed by the Government of Bengal in 1829 abolishing the practice of female sacrifices in India." This paper contained, among other things, a reference to the statement of Mṛtyuñjaya Vidyālaṅkār, the Chief Punḍit in the College of Fort William. What Rammohun tried to prove was that the suttee-supporters wanted to serve their property interests "under the cloak of religion", and that therefore the banning of suttee did not constitute any interference in such of the religious matters as are guided by sacred principles. B.B. Roy has summarized this part of Rammohun's paper in the following words:

(i) The real cause of suttee was the worldly interest, but not the religious interest. The worldly interest is served under the cloak of religion. The law of inheritance prevailing in Bengal was Dāyabhāga, whereas, in the Upper Provinces Mitākṣhara was respected as the law of inheritance. According to the law of inheritance in Bengal (i.e. Dāyabhāga) a widow was entitled to inherit the property of her deceased husband without regard to his condition in life, and therefore completely barred the claims of the father, mother, brothers, sisters and daughters of the deceased, who had all consequently a direct interest in the destruction of his widow. Whereas according to Mitākṣhara the rights of surviving wives were more circumscribed, so the relatives of the husband were not much interested in her death. Actually the number of suttees in the Upper Provinces was comparatively very low.

(ii) The ban on suttee did not constitute any interference with what can be called "religious matters". The duty of the government was to support only those religious observances which were considered incumbent on the people according to authorized principles of their faith and which were not a nuisance and outrageous to human feeling. So the government prohibition on suttee was just.

(iii) After the abolition of suttee nearly two years had elapsed, still no accounts of burning widows in opposition to the regulatión of the government were received nor even any attempt made to spread commotion. In fact, the suttee-supporters themselves were conscious of the unworthiness of the cause that they advocated to achieve worldly interest.[51]

2.64. Rammohun Roy also took such a keen interest as to be present on the occasion of the hearing of the appeal before the Privy Council. He was there on 11 July 1832 when the judgement of the Privy Council, confirming the Governor-General's decision, was announced.

SIMULTANEOUS MOVES FOR RELIGIOUS REFORM THROUGH BRAHMO SAMAJ

2.65. Whereas Rammohun Roy's work for the abolition of suttee belonged mainly to the domain of social reform and appealed to religious scriptures only for authoritative support, he worked simultaneously for religious reform as well. Two aspects connected with the practice of the Hindu faith in those days seemed to him to be in urgent need for reform, namely, idolatry and polytheism. His contention was that the original Hinduism, as taught in the Vedas and the Upaniṣads, did not worship idols, nor did it acknowledge the large number of gods and goddesses; rather the true Hindu faith believed in one supreme God without form. Rammohun Roy, therefore, began translating the Vedas and the Upaniṣads into Bengali and English to propagate his views, and in 1828 he founded the Brahmo Samaj.

2.66. Rammohun Roy's concept was that of a universal religion which recognized no distinction of colour, creed or caste. He invited all to the "worship and adoration of the Eternal, Unsearchable, Immutable Being who is the Author and Preserver of the Universe". In the Brahmo Samaj house of prayer, the Supreme Being alone was to be worshipped under "no name, designation or title, peculiarly used by any man or set of men for any particular Being". The trust deed specifically mentioned that:

> No religion should be reviled or slightingly or contemptuously spoken of or alluded to, and that worship should be conducted in such a way as would tend to promote the contemplation of the Supreme Being as well as to promote charity, morality, piety, benevolence, virtue and for strengthening of the bond of union between men of all religious persuasions and creeds.[52]

2.67. Like many other reformers in the history of Hinduism, Rammohun Roy claimed that he was not starting a new sect, but only purifying the old religion. He represented, in a way, the initial response of Hinduism to the challenges of the modern age symbolized by British rule and the proselytizing activities of the Christian missionaries. Bellah has identified four types of religious response, in non-Christian societies of Asia, to new ideas brought in through European colonialism, namely;

(i) conversion to Christianity;

(ii) traditionalism;
(iii) reformism; and
(iv) neo-traditionalism

Rammohun Roy is generally acknowledged as the initiator of Hindu reformism, which Bellah defines as "a movement that re-interprets a particular religious tradition to show not only that it is compatible with modernization but also that, when truly understood, the tradition vigorously demands at least important aspects of the modernity".[53]

2.68. Just as Rammohun Roy tried to "separate the essentials and non-essentials" of Hinduism, based on his own studies of the Vedas and the Upaniṣads, he attempted something similar for Christianity in his book entitled *The Precepts of Jesus—The Guide to Peace and Happiness.* However, neither the Hindu religious leaders nor the Christian missionaries appreciated the usefulness of Rammohun Roy's attempts for bringing about religious reforms. Embree describes this as "Rammohun Roy's fight on two fronts":

> At the same time that he was urging reform on his fellow Hindus, Rammohun felt it necessary to defend Hinduism against the attacks that were made on it by a number of Europeans, especially the missionaries who had begun to come to Bengal in increasing numbers. Believing that their denunciations of Hinduism were unfair in that they identified it completely with its worst features, he countered by charging that Christianity in its current forms was as much moved by superstition as was Hinduism. He was fighting, then, on two fronts: against the orthodox Hindus who accused him of injecting Christian ideas into the Upaniṣads, and against orthodox Christians who thought his interpretation of the Bible had been coloured by Hinduism.[54]

2.69. Although the Brahmo Samaj attracted only a small percentage of the Hindus, it did help strengthen attitudes of rationality in religious matters. After the lapse of nearly half a century since it was founded, association with Brahmo Samaj for a limited period of time influenced Vivekananda also, prior to his becoming a disciple of Sri Ramakrishna. A point of interest, in a comparative sense, for the present study is that, whereas for the suttee-abolition movement Rammohun Roy utilized the Upaniṣads as well as the Bhagavad-Gītā, the Brahmo Samaj referred exclusively to the Vedas and the Upaniṣads and not to the Bhagavad-Gītā.

PLEAS FOR STARTING MODERN EDUCATION FOR BOYS AS WELL AS GIRLS

2.70. Rammohun Roy knew that his efforts for bringing about social and religious reform would not produce long-lasting results unless Hindu boys and girls had the opportunity to receive modern education. Although a well-known Sanskrit scholar himself, he felt that merely learning Sanskrit language and grammar in the traditional style would close the door to the study of English, social sciences, physical sciences and mathematics. He therefore made strong pleas to the British authorities to start an institution which would be mainly devoted to modern education, providing some funds at the same time to enable the continuation and promotion of traditional Sanskrit teaching. Decision-making was, however, a slow process in those days, partly because of conflicting views among prominent members of the Hindu society, and partly also because the British Government was still debating about the kind of education that they wanted to promote in India.

2.71. Rammohun Roy's efforts were put into as many as five educational "issues and/or projects", of which only three took shape during his life time, and two remained undecided till some years after his death. These are:

(i) an English school for boys;
(ii) Hindu college;
(iii) choice between Sanskrit college and a college for modern education;
(iv) choice between Oriental and English education; and
(v) an English school for girls.

2.72 Rammohun Roy started the Anglo-Hindu school in Calcutta in 1822, where Hindu boys got free instruction through English medium. The entire expenses of this school were borne by him. Among the prominent men who had their early education there, special mention may be made of Debendranath Tagore who took over the leadership of the Brahmo Samaj after the death of Rammohun Roy.

2.73. Rammohun Roy, in consultation with his friend, David Hare, suggested to the Chief Justice of the Supreme Court, Sir Hyde East, the desirability of establishing a college for the education of Hindu boys on modern lines as in Europe. The suggestion was communicated to the Governor-General who approved of the idea, subject to the moral and financial support of selected leaders from the Hindu community. The scheme went through, but some of the orthodox Hindus insisted that Rammohun Roy must resign from the college committee. Since Rammohun Roy was more interested in the college than in remaining on the committee, he acceded to the demand of the orthodox Hindus who were opposed to him because of his zeal for social and religious reforms. The Hindu College of Calcutta was founded in 1817, and in due course became the Presidency College.

2.74. In 1823, the British authorities had before them a proposal to establish a Sanskrit College under Hindu Punḍits, for the teaching of Sanskrit language, grammar and *Darśanas* on traditional lines. Rammohun Roy strongly felt that the funds available for education should mainly be spent for the study of English, social sciences, physical sciences and mathematics, and only partly for the study of Sanskrit. He wanted the college to be run by those who had their education in Europe, rather than by Sanskrit pundits. Rammohun's views were contained in a letter addressed to the Governor-General, Lord Amherst. Rammohun also organized a public agitation by his supporters. His plea for modern education was eventually accepted, and it enabled the Hindu College to acquire a new building, well-equipped with books, scientific apparatus and other educational aids.

2.75. The 1820s also saw the beginning of the great controversy between the "Orientalists"—who wanted a continuation of traditional education—and the "Anglicists" who favoured modern education through the medium of English. Princep and Macaulay, respectively, were the leaders of the two groups. Rammohun Roy supported the Anglicists, but he did not live long enough to see the Anglicists, led by Macaulay, emerge as victorious in the great controversy.

2.76. Rammohun Roy's advocacy of modern education for Hindu girls was as strong as that for boys, but on this issue, the progress was extremely slow because of fierce opposition by the orthodox Hindus. It was nearly ten years after Rammohun Roy's death that an English medium school for girls was set up in Calcutta by Bethune.

ROLE OF THE BHAGAVAD-GĪTĀ

2.77. The Bhagavad-Gītā provided the strongest support to Rammohun Roy when he argued the case for suttee-abolition, to convince the orthodox scholars of the Hindu community. It was mainly a scholarly debate, each side picking up quotations from the various Sanskrit texts, to support their respective points of view. The suttee-advocates depended largely on the later *smṛtis*, namely Angiras and Harita, whereas Rammohun Roy's arguments utilized the most authoritative scriptures of the Hindus, namely, the Upaniṣads and Bhagavad-Gītā. In fact, the quotations from the Bhagavad-Gītā were more numerous and they covered more of the issues raised during the debate.

2.78. The suttee-advocates wanted widows to perform the act of burning themselves, fortified by the belief that this act of theirs would bring in gains and they would go to heaven. Rammohun Roy was able to establish, on the authority of the Bhagavad-Gītā, that "acting with a desire for worldly or heavenly gains" was spiritually inferior to *niṣkāma* karma or "acting without the desire for worldly or heavenly gains". Utilizing this basic teaching of the Bhagavad-Gītā, Rammohun Roy was able to point out how the suttee-advocates had imposed false values on the society by declaring a suttee to be spiritually superior to a widow. In reality, the implication of the *niṣkāma* karma doctrine was that a widow leading an ascetic life, without hankering after heaven, was entitled to achieving eternal rest in God, and therefore was spiritually superior to a suttee who acted because of the desire for heaven.

2.79. Questions relating to oppressive and cruel behaviour of men towards women were raised by Rammohun Roy who told the suttee-advocates how such cruelty was linked with the latter's giving precedence to minor *smṛtis* in comparison to the basic scriptures like Bhagavad-Gītā. Underlying all this was the discriminatory attitude of the suttee-advocates towards women in spiritual matters, which, as Rammohun Roy explained, was against the teaching of the Bhagavad-Gītā. Rammohun Roy convincingly quoted Śrī Kṛṣṇa's assurance in the Gītā that women were entitled to the same spiritual progress as men, and further that those who sincerely tried to follow the spiritual path need have no fear of failure because God would help them. Therefore, all doubts of the suttee-advocates about the entitlement and capability of widows to lead a pious God-centred life were shown by Rammohun Roy to be unfounded, on the authority of the Bhagavad-Gītā.

2.80. The fact that the important role played by the Bhagavad-Gītā, in connection with the suttee-abolition efforts of Rammohun Roy, was relatively unknown, even amongst scholars, prompted Sharma to publish a paper on this subject in 1983. This is how he drew attention to the lack of knowledge on this subject, and also what Rammohun Roy did:

> It is common knowledge that Raja Rammohun Roy campaigned vigorously for the abolition of suttee, and was consulted by the Governor-General prior to the promulgation of the ordinance which banned this practice in 1829. It is, however, virtually unknown that Roy drew upon the Bhagavad-Gītā, among other texts, to present his case against the practice to his coreligionists.
>
> It is clear that Roy not only knew the Gītā but used it to forensic effect.[55]

2.81. Presenting the above paper along with others, in a book form in 1988, Sharma added: "That the Bhagavad-Gītā should have been made an instrument of social reform is significant in itself, it is also significant in that it set a precedent."[56]

2.82. Sharpe views this as the "first entry" of the Gītā "into the field of modern Indian politics."[57] Perhaps the word "politics" is intended to convey the general meaning of "social affairs". And it is generally agreed that Rammohun Roy was the first person to initiate the social application of the Gītā from 1818 onward (or rather from 1815 itself), a tangible success in which was achieved in 1829 when suttee was abolished. As to the first "political" application of the Gītā (in the sense of waging the struggle for political independence), the Indian society had to wait till 1897 (and for Bal Gangadhar Tilak).

2.83. Although Rammohun Roy did not specifically make use of the Lokasaṁgraha verses of the Gītā (viz. verses 20-26 of the third chapter),[58] Jha interprets Rammohun's approach "as conforming to the ancient Indian doctrine of Lokasaṁgraha (people's welfare)".[59] Rammohun utilized the general philosophy of *niṣkāma* karma, and Śrī Kṛṣṇa's teaching of "no-discrimination against women in spiritual matters", in an effort to get rid of an evil social custom. In the ultimate analysis, right knowledge and right belief constitute the foundation for social reform. To achieve this, Rammohuṇ Roy also utilized the Gītā-teaching of not being misled by 'fruit-promising' allurements advanced by ritualists. This helped Rammohun plead for karma-yoga based on buddhi-yoga (right action based on right knowledge) for the widows, and thus try to save them from being victimized and exploited by priests proclaiming a distorted version of the law of karma. Obviously the Gītā played a major role in helping Rammohun Roy overcome so many obstacles in the way of suttee-abolition.

CHAPTER THREE

Vivekananda: Institutionalizing the Karma-Yoga-Based Socio-Spiritual Approach

A BRIEF LIFE-SKETCH

Naren Prior to Meeting Sri Ramakrishna

3.1. Swami Vivekananda's pre-monkhood name was Narendra Nath Datta or Naren for short. The Dattas belonged to an aristocratic section of the Kṣatriya caste of Bengal, and they displayed several of the traditional characteristics of the Kṣatriyas, including a faith in leading an ostentatious life, in general, but also producing an occasional "Sannyāsin". For example, Naren's grandfather, a rich and cultured man, had abandoned wife and children, a high position, fortune, and society at the age of twenty-five, to retire into "the forest" and became a "Sannyāsin", and from that day had never been seen by the family. Naren's father Visvanath Datta, a solicitor in the Calcutta High Court, was known for his varied interests and activities, and being conscious of his own superior position in the society, he exhibited a broad outlook on social and cultural matters, including a feeling of indifference to caste. Naren's mother, Bhuvaneśwarī Devī, was a highly educated woman of regal majesty, whose heroic spirit had been nurtured on the great Hindu epics. During private conversation with his disciples in America, Vivekananda later acknowledged the deep influence of his mother and said, "It is my mother who has been the constant inspiration of my life and work."[1]

3.2. Born in 1863, Naren exhibited in his boyhood, talents in several fields, and the rich family circumstances enabled him to cultivate as many of them as he could possibly do in the early years of his life. The type of personality which Naren developed by 1880 (that is, before he met Sri Ramakrishna for the first time) has been described by Romain Rolland in the following words:

> The possessor of physical courage and the build of an athlete, he [Naren] was a past master in all physical exercises. He could box, swim, row and had a passion for horses. He was the favourite of youth and the arbiter of fashion. He danced the great religious dances with consummate art, and had a delightful voice, which later was to charm the ear of Ramakrishna. He studied vocal and instrumental music for four or five years under famous Hindu and Mussulman professors. He wrote tunes and published a documented Essay on the science and philosophy of Indian music. Indeed he was everywhere regarded as a musical authority. . . . At college he was distinguished for his brilliant intellect, embracing with equal zest the sciences, astronomy, mathematics, philosophy, and Indian and Western languages. He read the English and Sanskrit poets. He devoured the historical works of Green and Gibbon. He was fired by the French Revolution and Napoleon. From his childhood up he practised, like so many Indian children, the habit of meditation. At night he used to pore over the Imitation of Jesus Christ and the Vedānta. He loved philosophic discussions.[2]

3.3. A number of philosophic as well as practical questions arose in Naren's mind and he sought answers to such questions by consulting senior college students like Brajendra Nath Seal as well as leaders of the Brahmo Samaj, including Devendranath Tagore. The advice that Naren received through such consultations naturally varied, and each piece of advice seemed to provide partial help to Naren in his "search for truth." For example, Brajendra Nath Seal put forward the merits of rationalism, and he even spoke in terms of the "God of Reason." Romain Rolland describes how Brajendra's viewpoint could satisfy only Naren's "intellect" but not his "heart":

> Brajendra's rationalism was of a peculiar kind in that it claimed to be an amalgamation of the pure monism of the

> Vedānta, the Hegelian dialectic of the Absolute Idea, and the Gospel of the French Revolution: Liberty, Equality and Fraternity. He believed that the principle of individualism was "the evil", and Universal Reason "the good". . . . Brajendra's rationalism appealed to some sides of Naren's domineering nature, but the latter's tumultuous personality was not to be confined within such limits. Although his intellect certainly wished to accept (or impose) the sovereignty of universal reason and to make the foundation of morality an imperious negation of individualism, his life would not agree. . . . Naren's heart and senses looked for the living revelation, the realization of the Absolute, God-made man—some holy Guru, who could say to him, "I have seen Him, I have touched Him, I have been He."[3]

3.4. In comparison to Brajendra Nath Seal's philosophy of rationalism, the Brahmo Samaj spirit of "categorical reform" seemed to provide a way out of the orthodoxy and social divisiveness of the idol-worshipping Hindu. Naren joined the movement of young Brahmos in Bengal for the education and unity of the Indian masses without distinction of caste, race or religion. Some of them attacked orthodox Hinduism even more bitterly than did the Christian missionaries. Romain Rolland describes why the Brahmo spirit also failed to satisfy Naren's "heart":

> Naren's free and living intelligence quickly realised the unintelligent narrowness of the Brahmos, who were not free from cross-grained fanaticism, and Naren's spirit no less than his national pride was wounded by them. He could not subscribe to the abdication of Indian wisdom before the badly assimilated knowledge of the West. Although Naren continued to attend the meetings of the Brahmo Samaj, in his heart he was not at rest.[4]

3.5. As a last attempt to seek answers to the questions that made him live "in great turmoil of soul", Naren went to Devendranath Tagore and asked him: "Sir, Have you seen God?" Although Tagore recognized the depth of feeling and sincerity that prompted Naren to raise such fundamental issues, he gave no direct reply to his question and only said, "My boy, you have the eyes of a yogi. You should practise meditation."[5] Naren returned unsatisfied, and his inability to achieve the reconciliation of his mental struggles started showing up in the form of dreams, as he himself recalled in later days:

> From my youth up, every night just as I fell asleep, two dreams took shape. In one I saw myself among the great ones of the earth, the possessor of riches, honours, power, and glory; and I felt that the capacity to attain all these was in me. But the next instant I saw myself renouncing all worldly things, dressed in a simple loin-cloth, living on alms, sleeping at the foot of a tree; and I thought that I was capable also of living thus, like the Rishis of old. Of these two pictures, the second took the upper hand and I felt that only thus could a man attain supreme bliss. . . .And I fell asleep in the foretaste of that bliss. . . . And each night it was renewed. . . .[6]

3.6. Such was the condition of Naren in November 1880 when a friend of his, Surendranath Mitra, a rich gentleman converted to Christianity, asked Naren to sing a religious hymn, in the presence of Sri Ramakrishna who had by that time been widely recognized as a great spiritual leader.

Sri Ramakrishna Prior to Meeting Naren

3.7. Sri Ramakrishna, whose pre-sainthood name was Gadadhar, was born in 1836 in a poor Brahmin family of a Bengal village. His father, Khudiram Chattopadhyaya, had been deprived of all he possessed, because he had refused to bear witness to the advantage of the great landowner who was his neighbour. Khudiram died when Gadadhar was seven years old, and the latter had to depend on whatever his elder brother Ramkumar could earn as a teacher. Ramkumar tried to keep Gadadhar into school but without much success. Rather, the inner urge of Gadadhar's life was expressed in artistic emotions, so much so that a beautiful sight of snow-white cranes flying at the edge of a dark cloud made him lose his consciousness. Shortly thereafter, at the age of eight, Gadadhar was again seized with ecstasy when, playing the part of Śiva in the village festivities, he was carried away by devotional music and the sight of artistic images.

3.8. Poor family circumstances forced Ramkumar in 1855 to accept the paid office of a priest in a new temple, founded by Rānī Rasmani, a rich woman belonging to a low caste. This temple was dedicated to the Great Goddess, the Divine Mother, Kālī, and was located at Dakshineshwar, on the banks of the Ganga river near Calcutta. When Ramkumar died in 1856, his younger brother Gadadhar, the future Sri Ramakrishna, began his astounding career of spiritual disciplines and attainments, as a temple priest and devotee of Mother Kālī.

3.9. Of the total period of thirty years that Sri Ramakrishna spent at Dakshineshwar, the first half was devoted by him in personally verifying the efficacy of the diverse mode of *sādhanā* or spiritual discipline prescribed by the various religions. He was first initiated into the Tāntric mode of *sādhanā.* He practised it for two years, and passed successfully through all the stages till he was in a position to obtain from Mother Kālī answers to all his questions on many occasions. He then followed the mode of *sādhanā* laid down by the Vaiṣṇava cult, and is said to have obtained a vision of Śrī Kṛṣṇa. He was next formally initiated into ascetic life by Totāpurī, a great saint who had realized in his life the highest truths of Vedānta, and practised the Vedāntic *sādhanā.* Sri Ramakrishna was then initiated into the Sufi doctrine of Islam and followed all the rites prescribed by that religion. He ate and dressed like a Muslim, offered regular prayers to Allah, ceased to visit Hindu temples, and in three days, obtained the vision of God. Later, he practised similar *sādhanā* according to Christian rites, and on the third day obtained the vision of Jesus Christ. The significance of all these religious experiences has been summarized by Majumdar:

> Sri Ramakrishna made his own life a laboratory for the synthesis of different systems of religion—a wonderful synthesis of higher forms of spiritual discipline with rituals and ceremonies—of *sākāra* (God with form) with *nirākāra* (God without form); of Vedānta with devotion; of rationalism with emotion and intuition; of asceticism with social and domestic life.[7]

3.10. Another great distinguishing characteristic of Sri Ramakrishna's spiritual attainments was the spontaneity and depth of feeling with which he wanted to serve the poor. In 1868, when he travelled to holy cities like Varanasi and Allahabad with Mathur Babu, the master of his temple, the sight of human suffering aroused so much sympathy in his heart that he compelled his rich companion to do his best to alleviate at least a part of such suffering. Romain Rolland has described how Sri Ramakrishna's insistence on "sharing the fate" of the poor creatures brought about a change in Mathur Babu as well:

> When Sri Ramakrishna arrived at Deoghar with his rich companion, (Mathur Babu), he saw its almost naked inhabitants, the Santhals, emaciated and dying of hunger: for a terrible famine was ravaging the land. He told Mathur Babu that he must feed these unfortunates. Mathur Babu objected that he was not rich enough to support the misery of the whole world. Ramakrishna thereupon sat down among the poor creatures and wept, declaring that he would not move from thence, but would share their fate. Croesus [Mathur Babu] was obliged to submit and to do the will of his poor priest.
>
> During the summer of 1870 Mathur Babu made the mistake of taking Ramakrishna in the course of another journey to one of his estates at the time of the payment of dues. The harvests had failed for two years running and the tenants were reduced to extreme misery. Ramakrishna told Mathur Babu to remand their dues, to distribute help to them and to give them a sumptuous feast. Mathur Babu protested but Ramakrishna was inexorable.
>
> "You are only the steward of the Mother," Ramakrishna said to the rich proprietor. "They are the Mother's tenants. You must spend the Mother's money. When they are suffering, how can you refuse to help them? You must do so."
>
> Mathur Babu had to give in.[8]

3.11. Swami Shivananda recalls how Sri Ramakrishna set a unique example of the most humble service that he himself rendered to a pariah:

> Sri Ramakrishna, a Brahmin, went to a pariah's house and asked permission to clean it. The pariah, overcome by the

proposal, a criminal one in the eyes of an orthodox Hindu, which might have exposed his visitor and himself to the worst reprisals, refused to allow it. So Ramakrishna went to his house at night when all were asleep and wiped the floor with his long hair. He prayed: "O Mother, make me the servant of the pariah!"[9]

Naren and Sri Ramakrishna Together

3.12. Although Naren's singing of a religious hymn at Surendranath Mitra's house in November 1880 drew Sri Ramakrishna's attention, the latter had the capacity to peep into the "depth of Naren's unsatisfied soul", and he asked Naren to come and see him at Dakshineswar. At their next meeting, Naren's song moved the master deeply, and he started the process of obtaining Naren's participation in his mission, to which Naren initially resisted. In later years, Naren recalled this occasion and described it thus:

> He (Sri Ramakrishna) said, 'Ah! you have come so late. Why have you been so unkind as to make me wait so long? My ears are tired of hearing the futile words of other men. Oh! how I have longed to pour out my spirit into the breast of somebody fitted to receive my inner experiences!. . . .' He continued thus, sobbing the while. Then standing before me with folded hands he said, "Lord, I know that you are the ancient sage Nara, the incarnation of Nārāyaṇa, reborn on the earth, to take away the misery of humanity". I was amazed. "What have I come to see?" I thought. "He ought to be put in a straitjacket! Why, I am the son of Visvanath Datta. How dare he speak thus to me?". . . . But I remained outwardly unmoved and let him talk.[10]

3.13. A few minutes later, when the Master and Naren joined the group of friends assembled in the larger room, Naren heard the Master say (and these words were an answer to his own nocturnal strivings), "God can be realized. One can see Him and speak to Him as I speak to and see you. But who takes the trouble to do so? People will shed tears for a wife, children, or possessions. But who weeps for the love of God? Yet if a man weeps sincerely for Him, He will manifest Himself to him."[11]

3.14. Naren gradually felt that Sri Ramakrishna was "worthy of respect," but the former also wanted to be on his guard to escape the latter's "eccentric behaviour". The type of conflict between his "intellect" and "heart" that Naren had earlier experienced in his relations with Brajendranath Seal, now seemed to reappear, but in a reverse form, as Romain Rolland describes:

> Naren was struck by the incomprehensible power of Ramakrishna. It attracted him, as a magnet attracts iron, but he himself was made of stern metal. His reason would not submit to domination. If in his recent relations with the rationalist Brajendra Seal it had been his heart that strove against his intellect, now his intellect mistrusted his heart. He was resolved to maintain his independence, and to accept nothing from the Master except what could be rigorously controlled by his own reason. The uncritical faith of the others roused his contempt.[12]

3.15. Although several important developments took place to bring Naren and the Master closer and closer, a special mention needs to be made of what happened after Naren's father suddenly died in early 1884, leaving the family heavily indebted and facing starvation. In spite of the B.A. degree, Naren could not get any job and was hard put to it to maintain his widowed mother and younger brothers. At last, unable to bear the distress of the family, and in sheer desperation, he fell at the feet of Sri Ramakrishna and requested him to approach Mother Kālī on his behalf. Then, in Majumdar's words:

> Ramakrishna asked Naren to go himself and ask the favour of the deity. Naren went to the temple, but as soon as he stood before Kālī, he found in her the Mother Goddess in a living visible form. He forgot the worldly affairs and, prostrating himself before her, prayed that he might be endowed with true knowledge and a spirit of devotion and renunciation. When on his return he was questioned by Ramakrishna, he remembered that he had forgotten to pray to the Mother to remove his misery. He was sent back, and again a third time, but with no better result. . . . He was assured by Ramakrishna

that his family would not be wanting in bare necessities of life, and so it turned out, as Naren could secure some jobs.

3.16. Sri Ramakrishna gradually prepared Naren to be the head of the group of sincere devotees who would carry out the Master's Mission after he himself passed away. He never concealed his feelings about Naren's future destiny. When Naren implored the Master to show him the way to *nirvikalpa samādhi*—the attainment of final bliss after sundering all earthly ties—he was administered a sharp rebuke. "Fie on you!" exclaimed Sri Ramakrishna, "I never thought you so mean as to be anxious for your own salvation only whereas you have powers to do much good to mankind." At his insistent request the Master one day gave him a glimpse of it and said, "Just as a treasure is locked up in a box, so the realization of the supreme bliss will be locked up and the key shall remain with me. You have work to do."[14]

3.17. Sri Ramakrishna also taught Naren that the proper way of doing good to mankind was to view it as worship to God, and that it was sheer arrogance if any feeling of superiority were to be associated with compassion. As the Master put it, "Compassion! Who are you to be compassionate? God alone can have compassion for the mortal. But service to man should be done as worship to God—Jīva is none else than Śiva." Naren understood what the master had in mind, and he told his friends, "Today I have heard a new Truth of great significance. In time I shall broadcast this for humanity."[15]

3.18. A mysterious incident symbolizing the transmittal of special powers from Sri Ramakrishna to Naren, as confirmed by Vivekananda himself, has been described by Majumdar as follows:

> Knowing that his end was imminent, the Master, in order to endow Naren with the spiritual wealth which he himself had acquired after years of superhuman efforts and unprecedented austerities, called him to his side only three or four days before his *mahāsamādhi.* Having seated him in front and looking intently into the eyes of his dear disciple, he fell into a deep trance. Naren felt the powerful impact of a tremendous

force passing into his own body and soon lost all body consciousness. When, after a while, Naren came to himself, the Master was found shedding tears. When interrogated, Sri Ramakrishna softly replied, 'Oh Naren, today I have given you my all and have become a *fakir* (beggar). By the force of the power transmitted by me, great things will be done by you; only after that, will you go to whence you came.[16]

3.19. Naren also learnt from the Master the supreme lesson that it is more "glorious to help even one man" than to be freed from the cycle of birth and death. In the pre-Ramakrishna Hindu tradition as commonly understood (or rather misunderstood), personal salvation or Mukti was viewed as the highest attainment, and taking birth in the *saṅsāra* (for whatever reason) was considered a symbol of imperfection. Sri Ramakrishna, by his own example, helped revive the social service-oriented Hindu view, which was close to the Bodhisattva ideal of putting the salvation of all above one's own salvation. In the closing days of his worldly life, Sri Ramakrishna permitted visitors to seek his guidance on spiritual matters, even though doctors wanted him to take complete rest. As Romain Rolland puts it: He never turned anybody away. He said, "Let me be condemned to be born over and over again, even in the form of a dog, if so I can be of help to a single soul !"

And again, "I will give up twenty thousand such bodies to help one man. It it glorious to help even one man !"

He even reproached himself for his ecstasies, because they took time that might otherwise have been given to others: "O Mother, stop me from enjoying them ! Let me stay in my normal state, so that I can be of more use in the world."

During his last days when his disciples protected him in spite of himself from the importunity of devotees, he said, "How I suffer because no one needs my help today !"[17]

3.20. Sri Ramakrishna also explained to Naren and to other disciples, the secret of reconciling worldly life with spiritual development, which, in the Bhagavad-Gītā, has been identified as the technique of non-attachment or renunciation of the egoistic feeling of doer-ship. One of the parables which Sri Ramakrishna used to clarify his teaching on this subject was the following:

> As a wet-nurse in a rich family brings up the child of her master, loving the baby as if it were her own, but knows well that she has no claim upon it; so think ye also that you are but trustees and guardians of your children whose real father is the Lord God in Heaven.[18]

Vivekananda Carrying on Sri Ramakrishna's Work

3.21. The work done by Vivekananda during the sixteen-year period (1886-1902), after the passing away of the Master, to put into effect Sri Ramakrishna's Mission, can be broadly divided into four significant stages, namely,

(i) Initial attempts in India from 1886 onward, culminating in the Kanyakumari resolve of 1892.
(ii) First visit to the West, including speeches at the Parliament of Religions, and subsequent work (1893-1896).
(iii) Founding of the Ramakrishna Mission (1897).
(iv) Strengthening of the organization and worldwide network of activities and relationships (1898-1902), till his departure from this world in 1902.

3.22. For purposes of the present study, the most significant point is that Vivekananda revolutionized the traditional image of Sannyāsins by making social service an integral part of their life. Although a formal shape to his new ideas was given by Vivekananda in 1897, all his activities from 1886 onward helped prepare the ground for introducing so radical a change. A first-hand observation of the miseries of the poor in the various parts of the country culminated in what is commonly called "The Kanyakumari Resolve of 1892", and about which Vivekananda himself wrote in a letter from America:

> At Cape Comorin, sitting in Mother Kumari's temple, sitting on the last bit of Indian rock, I hit upon a plan. We are so many sannyāsins wandering about and teaching the people metaphysics—it is all madness. Did not our Gurudeva use to say, 'An empty stomach is no good for religion'? That these poor people are leading a life of brutes is simply due to ignorance. Suppose some disinterested sannyāsins, bent on doing good to others, go from village to village, disseminating

education and seeking in various ways to better the condition of all down to the caṇḍāla, through oral teaching and by means of maps, cameras, globes and such other accessories—can't that bring forth good in time?. . . . We, as a nation, have lost our individuality, and that is the cause of all mischief in India. We have to give back to the nation its lost individuality and raise the masses. . .[19]

IDENTIFICATION OF THE SOCIAL PROBLEMS OF INDIA

3.23. Vivekananda's assessment of the social problems of India was realistic, rather than academic, because he wandered all over the country for years, with a staff and a begging bowl in his hand. This was done prior to his journey to the West. Initially, after the passing away of his Master, he had thought of going on a pilgrimage to the holy places like Varanasi, Ayodhya, Vrindavan, and Ashramas of Yogīs in the Himalayas. However, after a couple of years spent on such visits, he turned his gaze to the common people for whom the struggle for survival itself was the basic reality. Romain Rolland has emphasized the significance of these travels which provided him with a first-hand knowledge of the poverty, ignorance, disease and misery of the masses:

> He wandered, free from plan, caste, home, constantly alone with God. And there was no single hour of his life when he was not brought into contact with the sorrows, the desires, the abuses, the misery, and the feverishness of living men, rich and poor, in town and field; he became one with their lives; the great Book of Life revealed to him what all the books in the libraries could not have done (for after all they are only collections), which even Ramakrishna's ardent love had only been able to see dimly as in a dream—the tragic face of the present day, the God struggling in humanity, the cry of the peoples of India.[20]

3.24. What bothered Vivekananda even more than the poverty itself, was the gulf between the rich and the poor, between the strong and the weak, and further, the ugly sight of the strong dealing a death-blow to those who are comparatively weak, without any standard of morality. Is this a country or hell, he asked, a country where millions of people live on the flower of the Mohuā plant, and a million or two of *sādhus*, and a hundred million or so of Brahmins suck the blood of these poor people, without even the least effort for their amelioration? This is our native land, he bemoaned, where huts and palaces existed side-by-side:

> Worn-out huts by the very side of palaces, piles of refuse in the near proximity of temples, the Sannyāsin clad with only a little loin-cloth, walking by the gorgeously dressed, the pitiful gaze of lustreless eyes of the hunger-stricken at the well-fed and the amply provided![21]

3.25. With such a wide gulf between the rich and poor, asked Vivekananda, how can we have unity and fellow-feeling which are the secrets of national greatness? Born, as it were, a disunited mob, we cannot combine. All these dissensions pained Vivekananda and he remarked:

> If one of our countrymen stands up and tries to become great, we all try to hold him down, but if a foreigner comes and tries to kick us, it is all right. We have become used to such slavery, have we not?. . .
>
> We are intensely selfish. Not three of us can come together without hating each other, without being jealous of each other. Why should the Hindu nation with all its wonderful intelligence and other things have gone to pieces? I would answer you, Jealousy. . . . Because of this we also lack organization and coordination of wills.[22]

3.26. Oppression of the masses, according to Vivekananda, was a big factor leading to the downfall of the country. Another equally significant factor was tyranny over women. The way they were kept under conditions of servile dependence on men made them so weak as to be "good only to weep at the slightest approach of a mishap or danger."[23] Evil customs were particularly injurious to women-child marriage, big gap in the ages of husbands and wives, ill-treatment of widows, and so on. What pained Vivekananda was that evil customs were being adhered to in the name of religion: "A girl of eight is married to a man of thirty and the parents are jubilant over it. And if any one protests against it, the plea is put forward, our religion is being overturned".[24]

3.27. Vivekananda lamented that, in contrast to the death-defying message of the Hindu scriptures—fearlessness and strength—the modern Indian society lived in a perpetual sense of fear. Lack of self-confidence and moral strength, according to him, could be partly traced back to physical weakness, which was identified by Vivekananda as "the cause of at least one-third of our miseries":

> In spite of the greatness of the Upaniṣads, in spite of the boasted ancestry of sages, compared to many other races, I must tell you that we are weak, very weak. First of all is our physical weakness. That physical weakness is the cause of at least one-third of our miseries. We are lazy, we cannot work. . . . What we want is vigour in the blood, strength in the nerves, iron muscles and nerves of steel, not softening namby-pamby ideas.[25]

TRACING THE PROBLEMS BACK TO RELIGIOUS PERVERSION AND LACK OF EDUCATION

3.28. Of the many angles from which the social problems of India could be analysed—economic, political, sociological, historical, cultural, religious and spiritual—Vivekananda placed the greatest emphasis on the religious and spiritual. He based this on his interpretation of what has been the "nerve-centre" of India's life from time immemorial.

> We made our choice ages ago, and we must abide by it. . . .
>
> Each nation, like each individual, has one theme in this life, which is its centre, the principal note round which every other note comes to form the harmony. In India, religious life forms the centre, the keynote of the whole music of national life. . . . Social reform in India has to be preached by showing how much more spiritual a life the new system

will bring; and politics has to be preached by showing how much it will improve the one thing that the nation wants—its spirituality.[26]

3.29. One of the commonest ways of expressing the state of degradation, using philosophical terminology, is by summarising it as "Tamas" which is one of the three *guṇas* of Prakriti, the other two *guṇas* being "Rajas" and "Sattva". Tamas denotes ignorance, inertia; Rajas denotes incomplete knowledge, intense activity; Sattva denotes right knowledge, peace. While introducing the "Problems of Modern India" to the readers of the Udbodhana, the Bengali journal of the Ramakrishna Order dated 14 January 1899, Vivekananda used the expressions "drowned in utter Tamas", "under the cloak of austerity", "taking the plea of Sattva":

> Do you not see—taking this plea of Sattva, the country has been slowly and slowly drowned in the ocean of Tamas or dark ignorance? Where the most dull want to hide their stupidity by covering it with a false desire for the highest knowledge which is beyond all activities, either physical or mental; where one, born and bred in lifelong laziness, wants to throw the veil of renunciation over his own unfitness for work; where the most diabolical try to make their cruelty appear, under the cloak of austerity, as a part of religion; where no one has an eye upon his own incapacity, but everyone is ready to lay the whole blame on others; where knowledge consists only in getting some books by heart, genius consists in taking the name of ancestors: do we require any other proof to show that that country is being day by day drowned in utter Tamas?[27]

3.30. The linkage between religion and social conditions has to be understood as explaining both the positive and the negative aspects, in the sense that, while social progress in the past rested on religious maturity, a deterioration in the social situation at present could be traced back to religious perversion. Vivekananda linked India's doom to ritual-centred priestcraft, orthodoxy, fanaticism, superstitions, and religious intolerance. Having forgotten the true spirit of religion, said Vivekananda, the priestly class made fools of common people by pushing them blindly from one ritual to another, from one evil custom to another. Caste distinctions became more and more rigid, and religious orthodoxy took pride in laying down hard and fast rules as to who can marry whom and who can dine with whom. People discussed for years such meaningless questions as whether to take food with the right hand or the left. If such a country does not go to ruin what else will? asked Vivekananda.[28] Religious perversion also appeared in the ugly forms of exclusiveness and touch-me-not-ism. Vivekananda asked the perpetrators of such a tyranny as well as the sufferers to "come out of your narrow holes":

> Hide your faces in shame. A race of dotards, you lose your caste if you come out! Sitting down these hundred of years with an ever-increasing load of crystallised superstition on your heads, for hundreds of years spending all your energy upon discussing the touchableness or untouchableness of this food or that, with all humanity crushed out of you by the continuous social tyranny of ages—what are you? and what are you doing now?. . . . Kick out the priests who are always against progress, because they would never mend, their hearts would never become big. Come out of your narrow holes, and look forward ![29]

3.31. While the priestly class demanded blind adherence to evil practices in the name of tradition, a section of the city-dwellers took pride in aping the West and in denouncing India's past. No serious attempt was made to understand the good points in the spiritual tradition of the society. Kulandaival has summarized Vivekananda's views on the pitiable condition of such a blind imitator of the West:

> He laughs at the ancient sages. All Hindu thoughts to him are arrant trash, philosophy, mere childish prattle, and religion, the superstition of fools. He wants to imitate the West in his daily life and in his thought and actions. Anything coming from the West is good to him. This kind of imitation never makes for progress. It is a sign of aweful degradation of man. When a man begins to hate himself and is ashamed of his ancestors, the end has come.[30]

3.32. But how did we create these two degrading extremes—the superstitious priest and the city-dweller imitating the West? Vivekananda identified the root cause as the lack of proper education. By education, he meant, not the amount of information that is put in the brain and runs rot there, undigested, all through life. What he wanted was life-building, man-making, character-making assimilation of ideas. This was not possible, said he, because, we have no hold on the education of the nation, neither secular nor spiritual:

> The education that you are getting now is entirely negative. A negative education or any training that is based on negation, is worse than death. The child is taken to school, and the first thing he learns is that his father is a fool, the second thing that his grandfather is a lunatic, the third thing that all his teachers are hypocrites, the fourth that all the sacred books are lies! By the time he is sixteen, he is a mass of negation, lifeless and boneless. And the result is that fifty years of such education has not produced one original man in the three Presidencies.[31]

3.33. While Vivekananda lamented the lack of "man-making" education in general, he felt even more strongly that the women of India were neglected by denying to them education, status, and opportunities of development. The evil of sex-discrimination, according to Vivekananda, represented a negation of the Vedāntic doctrine of the divinity of all human beings, men and women alike. Viewing women as the emblem of Divine Mother, he cried in agony; "The emblem of the Divine Mother has been reduced to a slave to bear children. Why is it that our country is the weakest and the most backward of all countries? Because Shakti is held in dishonour here. There is no chance for the welfare of India unless the condition of women is improved. It is not possible for a bird to fly on one wing only."[32] In fact, Vivekananda's British disciple, Sister Nivedita, who was an educationist in England, was assigned the important task of opening a girls' school in Calcutta, where "real" education could be given.

3.34. Non-adherence to moral and social values, by large sections of the Indian society, was partly due to a wrong interpretation of the Hindu scriptures, and in particular of the Karma doctrine. Vivekananda had a chance to point this out when in February 1897, an enthusiastic preacher belonging to the society for the protection of cows came to Calcutta for an interview with him. Bengal was at that time in the grip of a famine, and hundreds of thousands of people were falling into the jaws of death. So Vivekananda suggested to the preacher that, since their society had plenty of resources, they could provide food to the starving people. The preacher's reply and Swami Vivekananda's comments thereon have been recorded by Sharatchandra Chakravarty:

> Preacher: No, we do not help human beings because this famine broke out as a result of their Karma, their sins. It is a case of "like karma, like fruit".
>
> Hearing the words of the preacher, sparks of fire, as it were, scintillated in Swamiji's large eyes; his face became flushed. But he suppressed his feelings and said: Those associations which do not feel sympathy for men and, even seeing their own brothers dying from starvation, do not give them a handful of rice to save their lives, while giving away piles of food to save birds and beasts, I have not the least sympathy for, and I do not believe the society derives any good from them. If you make a plea of karma by saying that men die through their karma, then it becomes a settled fact that it is useless to try or struggle for anything in this world; and your work for the protection of animals is no exception. With regard to your cause also, it can be said that the mother-cows through their own karma fall into the hands of the butchers and die, and we need not do anything in the matter.
>
> The preacher was a little abashed and said: "Yes, what you say is true but the Shastras say that the cow is our mother."
>
> Swamiji smilingly said, "Yes, that the cow is our mother, I understand; who else could give birth to such accomplished children?"
>
> The preacher did not speak further on this subject, perhaps he could not understand the point of Swamiji's poignant ridicule.
>
> After the departure of the preacher, Swami Vivekananda told his disciples: "Do you see how much abused the karma theory of our Hinduism has been?"[33]

PLAN OF ACTION BASED ON PRACTICAL VEDĀNTA

3.35. By January 1897 when Vivekananda returned from the West to India, he had made up his mind to initiate a plan of action based on an harmonization of spirituality and social service. The underlying views of Vivekananda can, in the terminology of the Gītā, be also called "the Karma-yoga-based socio-spiritual approach to India's problems". In a speech in Madras he announced:

> My plan is to follow the ideas of the great ancient Masters. They were the great originators of society. . . . Circumstances have become a little different, and in consequence the lines of action have to be changed. . . .
>
> The first work that demands our attention is that the most wonderful truths confined in our Upaniṣads must be brought out from the monasteries and scattered broadcast all over the land. . .
>
> One word more. This national ship, my countrymen, has been ferrying millions and millions of souls across the waters of life. But today, perhaps through our own fault, this boat has become a little damaged, has sprung a leak. If there are holes in this national ship, this society of ours, we are its children. Let us go and stop the holes. Say not one harsh word against this society. I love it for its past greatness. . . . I do not dare to put myself in the position of God and dictate to our society, "This way thou shouldst move and not that. Ours is only to work, as the Gītā says, without looking for results."[34]

3.36. By making special mention of the Upaniṣads and the Gītā, Vivekananda made it clear that his plan represented an harmonization of Vedānta and Karma-yoga, or "practical Vedānta" as he called it. He also called it "real worship", as he explained in his address at Rāmeśwaram temple: "It is in love that religion exists and not in ceremony, in the pure and sincere love in the heart. External worship is only a symbol of internal worship; but internal worship and purity are the real things. . . . This is the gist of all worship—to be pure and to do good to others."[35]

3.37. One of the ways in which Vivekananda brought out the distinction between the "monastery-based Vedānta" and "practical Vedānta" was how he identified the root cause of misery. Whereas in the former (i.e. monastery-based Vedānta) the root cause of misery is only "ignorance", Vivekananda (explaining practical Vedānta) specified "ignorance" as well as "wickedness" as being equally responsible for human bondage and suffering:

> You must be pure and help anyone who comes to you, as much as lies in your power. And this is good Karma. By the power of this, the heart becomes pure (*Citta-śuddhi*) and then Śiva who is residing in everyone will become manifest. If there is dirt and dust on a mirror, we cannot see our image. So ignorance and wickedness are the dirt and dust that are on the mirror of our hearts.[36]

3.38. Vivekananda's intention in putting as much emphasis on wickedness as on ignorance was to say that a true knowledge of Vedānta must be reflected in compassionate behaviour. He knew that many of the orthodox scholars who knew Vedāntic scriptures by heart were as much guilty of unkind treatment towards the low-caste, poor countrymen as other high-caste Hindus who were not scholars. "Practical Vedānta", according to Vivekananda, meant theoretical knowledge as well as practice:

> Raise once more that mighty banner of Vedānta for on no other ground can you have that wonderful love until you see that the same Lord is present everywhere. The nation is sinking, the curse of unnumbered millions is on our heads—the unnumbered millions to whom we have talked of Vedānta and whom we have hated with all our strength, to whom we have talked theoretically that we are all the same and all are one with the same Lord, without even an ounce of practice. . . . Throw away everything, even your own salvation, and go and help others. Ay, you are always talking bold words, but here is practical Vedānta before you. The first part of this is that you should go to the sinking millions of India, and take them by hand, remembering the words of Lord Kṛṣṇa:
>
> Even in this life they have conquered relative existence

whose minds are firm-fixed on the sameness of everything, for God is pure and the same to all, therefore such are said to be living in God. (*Gītā*, V. 19)[37]

3.39. On other occasions, Vivekananda gave the same message (Help the poor to the extent of giving up your own salvation) under the title of "unselfishness". There is an obvious parallel to the Bodhisattva ideal of Mahāyāna Buddhism which refers to "one who treads the Path not for his own salvation alone but for the salvation of all."[38] As Vivekananda explained his concept of "sharing with others":

Does one feel happy to taste of a good thing all by oneself? One should share it with others. Granted that you attain personal liberation by means of the realisation of the Advaita, but what matters it to the world? You must liberate the whole universe before you leave this body. Then only you will be established in the eternal Truth. Has that bliss any match, my boy? You will be established in that bliss of the Infinite which is limitless like the skies. You will be struck dumb to find your presence everywhere in the world of soul and matter. You will feel the whole sentient and insentient world as your own self. Then you can't help treating all with the same kindness as you show towards yourself. This is indeed practical Vedānta.[39]

3.39. Vivekananda characterized "unselfishness" as the test of religion. According to him, the philosopher, the worker, and the devotee, all meet at one point, that one point being "self-abnegation". Conveying the same idea from another angle, he characterised "selfishness" as the chief sin:

Selfishness is the chief sin, thinking of ourselves first. He who thinks, "I will eat first, I will have more money than others, and I will possess everything", is the selfish man. Similarly, he who thinks, "I will get to heaven before others, I will get Mukti before others", is the selfish man. The unselfish man says, "I will be the last, I do not care to go to heaven, I will even go to hell if by doing so I can help my brothers." This unselfishness is the test of religion. He who has more of this unselfishness is more spiritual, whether he is learned or ignorant, he is nearer to Śiva than anybody else.[40]

3.41. As another example of the terminological variation used by Vivekananda to convey the same message, he coined the famous phrase "Daridra-Nārāyaṇa" which meant that the service of the poor was the service of God. To Śiva-worhippers he said, "Jīva is Śiva," and explained it further:

> He who sees Śiva in the poor, in the weak and in the diseased, really worships Śiva; and if he sees Śiva only in the image, his worship is but preliminary. He who has served and helped one poor man, seeing Śiva in him, without thinking of his caste, or creed, or race, or anything, with him Śiva is more pleased than with the man who sees Him only in temples.[41]

3.42. By thinking of the poor man as God, said Vivekananda, the risk of arrogance on the part of the helper is minimized. By having faith in God, one gives up the fruits of work unto the Lord, and worshipping Him thus, one does not expect any reward from mankind for the work one does:

> So drive out of your mind the idea that you are doing something for the world; the world does not require any help from you. It is sheer non-sense on the part of any man to think that he is born to help the world; it is simply pride, it is selfishness insinuating itself in the form of virtue.[42]

3.43. Expecting no reward for the work done, as taught by the Gītā, is a relatively easier way of giving up attachment to the fruits of work. Not that the work will not bear fruit; in fact, the law of karma says that any action done cannot be destroyed until it has borne its fruit. A karma-yogin does take into account what effect his actions will have on others, but he does not hanker after deriving selfish gains thereform.

3.44. A favourite idea of Vivekananda was that we do good deeds in the world, apparently to help the world, but really to help ourselves:

> The main effect of work done for others is to purify ourselves; this forgetfulness of self is the one great lesson we have to learn in life. . . . Every act of charity, every thought of sympathy, every action of help, every good deed, is taking so much of self-importance away from our little selves and making us think of ourselves as the lowest and the least; and therefore it is all good. Here we find that jñāna, bhakti, and karma — all come to one point. The highest ideal is eternal and entire self-abnegation, where their is no "I", but all is "Thou", and whether he is conscious or unconscious of it, karma yoga leads man to that end.[43]

3.45. Within the range of deeds that can be done to help others, Vivekananda included a wide variety, providing material benefits as well as giving knowledge, both secular and spiritual. He recognised the changing needs of the society with the passage of time. Speaking in terms of the Hindu terminology of the four *yugas* or time-periods, he interpreted Vyāsa's words as: "What is needed in this Kaliyuga is giving, helping others, the highest of gifts is the giving of spiritual knowledge, the next is the giving of secular knowledge, next to that is the saving of life, and the last is giving food and drink."[44] However, leaving aside Vyāsa's order of priorities, Vivekananda said, on another occasion, "First bread and then religion": "What we want is not so much spiritually as a little of the bringing down of the Advaita into the material world. First bread and then religion. We stuff them too much with religion, when the poor fellows have been starving. No dogmas will satisfy the cravings of hunger."[45]

3.46. To pay attention to both the secular and the spiritual needs of the society is a special feature of practical Vedānta. Similarly, it seeks to harmonize science and religion. In a lecture delivered in England, Vivekananda declared:

> Science and religion will meet and shake hands. . . . When the science teacher asserts that all things are the manifestation of one force, does it not remind you of the God of whom you hear in the Upaniṣads: As the one fire entering into the universe expresses itself in various forms, even so that one

Soul is expressing itself in every soul and yet is infinitely more besides? Do you not see whither science is tending?[46]

3.47. Although in the interest of those who are in a position to serve others, Vivekananda advised them to do their utmost, but with humility, still from the viewpoint of the receivers of such service, and also in general, he stressed the importance of self-help and self-confidence. Commenting on the Gītā verse VI.5, he called "self-help" as the "greatest lesson":

> It is a tremendous error to feel helpless. Do not seek help from anyone. We are our own help. It we cannot help ourselves, there is none to help us. The Gītā says, "Thou thyself art thy only friend, thou thyself thy only enemy. There is no other enemy but this self of mine, no other friend but myself." This is the last and greatest lesson, and Oh, What a time it takes to learn it! We seem to get hold of it, and the next moment the old wave comes. The backbone breaks. We weaken and again gasp for that superstition and help. Just think of that huge mass of misery, and all caused by this false ideas of going to seek for help.[47]

3.48. "Self-confidence" was given so much importance by Vivekananda that, in practical Vedānta, it plays the same role as "faith in God". For achieving success in his plan of action (referred to in para 3.35), Vivekananda's main requirement was "men who believe in themselves". In fact, the essence of practical Vedānta was viewed by him to be a "man-making religion":

> What we want is muscles of iron and nerves of steel. We have wept long enough. No more weeping, but stand on your feet and be men. It is a man-making religion that we want. It is man-making theories that we want. It is man-making education all round that we want.
>
> Men, men, these are wanted: everything else will be ready, but strong, vigorous, believing young men, sincere to the backbone, are wanted. A hundred such and the world becomes revolutionized. The will is stronger than anything else. Everything must go down before the will, for that comes from God and

God Himself; a pure and strong will is omnipotent.[48]

INSTITUTIONAL COMMITMENT TO SOCIAL SERVICE—A NOVELTY ACHIEVED AFTER FRATERNAL RESISTANCE

3.49. Hindu tradition speaks of *bhaktas* and saints loving all creatures and helping the needy. But these were generally individual efforts without much organizational support. Also, many of these *bhaktas* felt as if they were being pulled in two directions, one represented by worship of God's image, reading of scriptures, meditation, and preaching to devotees, and the other represented by rendering service to the sick, the poor and the neglected. With the worsening economic and social conditions in India, the importance of rendering service was recognised by reform movements like Brahmo Samaj, but some of its leaders gave the impression that the inspiration for rendering service came mainly from Western influences including Christian missionaries. Therefore such movements could not arouse mass support all over the country on a long-term basis.

3.50. Ramakrishna Mission founded by Vivekananda in 1897 distinguished itself as a religious organisation in Modern India which adopted social service as one of its main goals and which drew the inspiration for this mainly from the Indian tradition. In fact, six sources of inspiration have been mentioned, namely, their Master Sri Ramakrishna, other *bhaktas*, wandering monks, the Upaniṣads, the Bhagavad-Gītā, and the Buddha. Although Vivekananda gave a concrete shape to the social service programme of the Ramakrishna Mission, he said he was only carrying out the teaching of his Master Sri Ramakrishna. The strong emphasis of Karma-Yoga in the entire approach of the Ramakrishna Mission is a clear indicator of the impact of the Bhagavad-Gītā. While Vivekananda based the doctrine of Karma-yoga mainly on the Gītā, he often referred to the Buddha as an 'Ideal Karma-yogin'.

3.51. Sri Ramakrishna was characterised by Vivekananda as one who saw God in every being, whose heart wept for the poor, for the weak, for the downtrodden. But Sri Ramakrishna did not thrust such ideas on his disciples. When the problem of awakening spirituality in the hearts of the common people was raised with the Master, he had said, "Religion is not for empty bellies."[49] Sri Ramakrishna had also declared: "The day when Naren comes in contact with suffering and misery, the pride of his character will melt into a mood of infinite compassion."[50]

3.52. In 1886, when Sri Ramakrishna had fallen seriously ill, his intimate disciples (twelve in number) organized themselves under the leadership of Naren to serve the Master with utmost care, love and veneration. This whole-hearted love of God and devotion to the Master and his ideas led to the formation of the brotherhood, which soon after the Master's departure from this world developed into a Maṭh (Monastery of the Ramakrishna Order). However, its members were often on move with no coordinated and systematic plan of work and it took Naren several years of wandering throughout India and of sharing the misery and privations of the oppressed classes before he was able to assert in 1892 that, to care for the poor and to raise them is the first duty of religion. Subsequently Vivekananda's coining of the phrase "Daridra-Nārāyaṇa" elevated the service of the poor to be equal in importance and value to the service of God, or in Vivekananda's words: "The only God that exists, the only God in whom I believe. . . .my God the miserable, my God the poor of all races."[51] Furthermore, Vivekananda constantly reminded his brother disciples (who wanted to carry out the teachings of the Master) that the only way to help the poor was through the spirit of *niṣkāma* Karma of the Gītā:

> Why should we expect anything in return for what we do? Be grateful to the man you help, think of him as God. Is it not a great privilege to be allowed to worship God by helping our fellowmen? If we were really unattached, we should escape all this pain of vain expectation, and could cheerfully do good work in the world.[52]

3.53. Following the successful visit to the West, and after witnessing the keen interest that the people in South India expressed in his plan of action, Vivekananda arrived in Calcutta in February 1897. At that time the central idea in his mind was to put into practice what he had so long preached, by making the monks devote themselves to an active life of service for the masses and thus to make the monastic organisation a potent instrument for social and spiritual regeneration. His vision of utilizing the energies of the monks for spreading education among the illiterate, helping them fight against poverty and disease, removing social evils and inequities, and raising them to a higher level of morality, meant an innovation in the monastic practices as commonly understood in those days. It was not surprising, therefore, that there were voices of dissent among his brother-disciples. Nikhilananda explains what lay behind this fraternal resistance to Vivekananda's plan of action:

> The dissenting monks were individualists, eager for their personal salvation. They wanted to practise austerities and penances, enjoy peaceful meditation, and lead a quiet life of detachment from the world. To them God was first, and the world came next. At least that was the way they had understood Sri Ramakrishna's teachings. These young monks thought that for one who had taken the monastic vows, the world was māyā; therefore all activities, including the charitable and philanthropic, ultimately entangled one in worldly life.[53]

3.54. Vivekananda knew that the narrow vision of the young monks, focusing on an exclusive search for *mukti,* could only be widened by giving clearer instructions and sincere assurances. Therefore, he repeatedly pointed out to his brother-disciples that to worry about personal liberation was unworthy of those who called themselves disciples of Sri Ramakrishna. Karma-yoga activities carried out with a sense of dedication to the Almighty was as efficacious a means of salvation as meditation and austerities. With so much of misery and ignorance prevailing in the society, the duty of Sri Ramkrishna's disciples, as Vivekananda explained to his colleagues, was to serve the needy as the visible manifestations of God. He also told them that he wanted to create a new brand of monks, who would take not only the traditional vow of personal salvation, but also a new vow of service to humanity.

3.55. After a good deal of clarification, Vivekananda's views prevailed, and he proceeded to give institutional shape to his plan of action. He explained his ideas at a representative meeting of the monks and lay devotees held at Calcutta on 1 May 1897. He was convinced, he said, that lack of organization was a serious defect in the Hindu society. He also cited the example of the Buddhist organization which spread that religion in large areas of the world. He therefore asked for the cooperation of all in order to organize the educational, philanthropic and religious activities which had hitherto been carried out in an unsystematic way. The meeting unanimously approved of Viveka-nanda's proposal, and in a subsequent meeting on 5 May 1897, formally established the Ramakrishna Mission with the following aims and methods of action.

> The aim of the Mission is to preach those truths which Shri Ramakrishna has, for the good of humanity, preached and demonstrated by practical application in his own life, and to help others to put these truths into practice in their lives for their temporal, mental and spiritual advancement.
>
> The duty of the Mission is to conduct in the right spirit the activities of the movement inaugurated by Shri Ramakrishna for the establishment of fellowship among the followers of different religions, knowing them all to be so many forms only of one undying Eternal Religion.
>
> Its methods of action are:
>
> (a) To train men so as to make them competent to teach such knowledge or sciences as are conducive to the material and spiritual welfare of the masses;
> (b) to provide and encourage arts and industries; and
> (c) to introduce and spread among the people in general Vedāntic and other religious ideas in the way in which they were elucidated in the life of Shri Ramakrishna.
>
> Indian Work Department and Foreign Department:
>
> The activities of the Mission should be directed to the establishment of *maṭhas* and *āśramas* in different parts of India for the training of Sannyāsins and such of the householders as may be willing to devote their lives to educate others, and to the finding of the means by which they would be enabled to

educate the people, by going about from one province to another.

Its work in the Foreign Department should be to send trained members of the Order to countries outside India to bring about a closer relation and better understanding between India and foreign countries.

The aims and ideals of the Mission being purely spiritual and humanitarian, it shall have no connection with politics.

Anyone who believes in the mission of Shri Ramakrishna, or who sympathises or is willing to co-operate with the above-mentioned aims and objects of the Association, is eligible for membership.[54]

3.56. Side by side with the setting up of the Ramakrishna Mission, Vivekananda also wanted to systematize the working of the Maṭha. Although the Maṭha (monastery) had nominally come into existence in 1886, it had to be shifted from one location to another and its functioning was guided largely by unwritten rules based on an implicit understanding of Vivekananda's wishes. In December 1898, when the Maṭha shifted to Belur on a permanent basis, Vivekananda strengthened its organisation by putting down in writing an elaborate set of rules. The Maṭha being a purely monastic institution, the rules provided for disciplined life and spiritual practices, and emphasized the needs of strength of character, self-reliance, and faith in the Master. For new monks also the training to be imparted in the Maṭha clearly reflected the wider vision of Vivekananda, as the following two rules show:

> This Maṭha is established to work out one's own liberation, and to train oneself to do good to the world in every way, along the lines laid down by Bhagavan Shri Ramakrishna. For the women too there will be started a similar Maṭha.
>
> The root of all misery in India is the wide gulf between the lower and upper classes. Unless this difference is made up, there is no hope of any well-being for the people. Therefore we must send preachers to all places to give the masses education and religious teaching.[55]

3.57. Although all the monks appeared to be satisfied with the way Vivekananda explained to them his new concept of religion, namely, the worship of God through the service of the needy, a lingering doubt was still bothering some of them whether the real formulator of this concept was Vivekananda or Sri Ramakrishna. They had heard Sri Ramakrishna speak time and again against preaching, excessive study of the scriptures, and charitable activities, and exhort aspirants to intensify their love of God through prayer and meditation in solitude. Therefore they regarded Vivekananda's activities as out of harmony with the Master's teachings. One of them said bluntly to Vivekananda, "You did not preach our Master in America; you only preached yourself". Vivekananda retorted with equal bluntness, "Let people understand me first; then they will understand Sri Ramakrishna".[56]

3.58. But things came to a climax one day at Balaram's house in Calcutta, when Jogananda, a brother-disciple whom Sri Ramakrishna had pointed out as belonging to his 'inner circle' of devotees, said that the Master had emphasized bhakti alone for spiritual seekers and that philanthropic activities, organizations, homes of service for the public good, and patriotic work were Vivekananda's own peculiar ideas, the result of his Western education and travel in Europe and America.

3.59. Vivekananda at first replied to it in good humour. But he suddenly flared up. "You think you have understood Sri Ramakrishna better than myself!. . . . Your Bhakti is sentimental nonsense which makes one impotent. Hands off! Who cares for your Ramakrishna? Who cares for your Bhakti and Mukti? Who cares what the scriptures say? I will go into a thousand hells cheerfully, if I can rouse my countrymen, immersed in Tamas, to stand on their own feet and be men inspired with the spirit of Karma-yoga. I am not a follower of Ramakrishna or anyone, I am a follower of him only who carries out my plans! I am not a follower of Ramakrishna or anyone, but him only who serves and helps others, without caring for his own Bhakti and Mukti."[57]

3.60. Nikhilananda describes what happened next:

> The Swami's voice was choked with emotion, his body shook, and his eyes flashed fire. Quickly he went to the next room.

A few moments later, some of his brother-disciples entered the room and found him absorbed in meditation, tears flowing from his half-closed eyes. After nearly an hour the Swami got up, washed his face, and joined his spiritual brothers in the drawing-room. His features still showed traces of the violent storm through which he had just passed; but he had recovered his calmness. He said to them softly: "When a man attains bhakti, his heart and nerves become so soft and delicate that he cannot bear even the touch of a flower: . . . . I cannot think or talk of Sri Ramakrishna long without being overwhelmed. So I am always trying to bind myself with iron chains of jñāna, for still my work for my motherland is unfinished and my message to the world not fully delivered. So as soon as I find that those feelings of bhakti are trying to come up and sweep me off my feet, I give a hard knock to them and make myself firm and adamant by bringing up austere jñāna. Oh, I have work to do! I am a slave of Ramakrishna, who left his work to be done by me and will not give me rest till I have finished it.[58]

3.61. So profound and convincing was the impression created by this incident that no protest was afterwards made against Vivekananda's plans and methods of work. The Karma-yoga-based socio-spiritual approach to India's problems formulated by Vivekananda was thus fully adopted by Ramakrishna Mission.

3.62. Although the right technique of rendering *sevā* is given by Karma-yoga, an ultimate answer to the question: "Why should we render *sevā* to the poor?" is provided by jñāna-yoga or bhakti-yoga. A common argument put forward by *bhaktas* in India is, that although a knowledge of the identity of Ātman in all beings does provide an intellectual base for *sevā*, this by itself is not enough because *sevā* also calls for a feeling of compassion. The *bhaktas* therefore feel that the rendering of *sevā* (service) with compassion is achieved more easily in the path of devotion, as compared to the path of knowledge. The Indian tradition seems to provide general support to this. Moreover, although monks of the Ramakrishna Mission combined Advaita Vedānta with *sevā,* they too have an element of Bhakti. In fact,

Vivekananda believed in a harmonious development of Karma, Bhakti and Jñāna, and in his final message to the disciples, he clearly gave priority to *sevā* over other aspects of these paths when he said: " Let the reading of the Vedānta and the practising of meditation and the like be left to be done in the next life! Let this body go in the service of others."[59]

3.63. As we mentioned in para 3.55, the Ramakrishna Mission, under Vivekananda's guidance, kept itself aloof from politics. Whatever might have been the reasons underlying this policy, it averted a likely threat of dissolution of the Mission by the British Government in 1916. Rolland gives a graphic account of what happened after Vivekananda's death and how the revolutionary political agitators (who tried to use the Gītā as a proof of their alleged link with the Ramakrishna Mission) placed the Mission on a collision course with the British Government:

> 1905, the year of the division of the Province of Bengal, marked the beginning of the Swadeshi movement and political unrest. The (Ramakrishna) Mission refused to take part in them. In 1908 it was obliged to make a rule not to receive strangers at night in its establishment, because it feared some were abusing its hospitality in order to prepare their political offensives. It transpired from the answers of political prisoners that more than one, disguised under the robe of a sannyāsin, had cloaked their designs under the name of its work and religion. Copies of the Gītā and Vivekananda's writings were found on several of them. . . .
>
> In 1916, the Governor of Bengal announced that revolutionaries were joining the Ramakrishna Mission in order to achieve their ends. Fortunately, friends in high places intervened and the danger of dissolution of the Mission was averted.[60]

EXEMPLARY DEDICATION AND WIDENING COVERAGE OF SERVICE ACTIVITIES

3.64. Practical Vedānta was the foundation on which the whole structure of the new organization was sought to be built by Vivekananda from May 1897 onward. Reference has already been made above to the opposition of some of the brother-disciples to this new mode of salvation propounded by Vivekananda. He, however, not only stuck to his guns, but even went to the other extreme of denouncing every other form of salvation. His retort to his critics, that he would follow this path even if it went against the teachings of Ramakrishna indicates the depth of his feeling in the matter. The same spirit of dedication was expressed by him in letters written to his friends. For example, in a letter to Mary Hale dated July, 1897 he expressed a feeling of satisfaction:

> Only one idea was burning in my brain—to start the machine for elevating the Indian masses, and that I have succeeded in doing to a certain extent. It would have made your heart glad to see how my boys are working in the midst of famine and disease and misery-nursing by the mat-bed of the cholera-stricken pariah and feeding the starving caṇḍāla, and the Lord sends help to me, to them, to all.[61]

3.65. However, difficult tests of the organization's capability to fulfil its mission against heavy odds were still to come. In April, 1898, when Vivekananda was in Darjeeling to recoup his health, news reached him of the outbreak of plague in Calcutta. On May 3 1898, Vivekananda reached Calcutta, although his health was not good. He thought he might be of help to his people. They were terror-stricken by the plague and dismayed by the plague regulations. It was as if a storm were about to burst over Calcutta. People were fleeing in panic. Troops were called to quell riots. Vivekananda grasped the gravity of the situation at once. On the day of his arrival at the Maṭha he drafted a plague manifesto in Bengali and in Hindi. He wanted to start relief operations immediately to help the afflicted. When a brother-monk asked him, "Swamiji, where will the funds come from?", he replied with a sudden fierceness of decision: "Why, we shall sell the newly-bought Maṭha grounds, if necessary ! We are sannyāsins; we must be ready to sleep under the trees and live on daily Bhikṣā (alms) as we did before. What ! Should we care for Maṭha and possessions when by disposing of them we could relieve thousands suffering before our eyes!"[62] Fortunately, this extreme step was not necessary, for Vivekananda soon received promises of ample funds for his immediate work.

3.66. When plague again broke out in 1899, the Ramakrishna Mission undertook relief work under the leadership of Sadananda, assisted by Sister Nivedita and others. About Sister Nivedita's part in the work, we have it on the authority of the historian, Sir Jadunath Sarkar, an eyewitness, "that when the sweepers had fled away, he chanced upon a white woman one day clearing the streets with broom and basket in hand. This was none other than Nivedita, whose courage and sense of civic duty spurred the local youths to take up the cleansing of the lanes and streets, following her example, and make their quarters free from the threat of the pestilence".[63]

3.67. Sadananda himself similarly set an unprecedented example. If the stench of garbage accumulated in a narrow lane repelled even the practised sweepers, he would non-chalantly snatch the basket and spade from one of them and set about removing the decomposed heap till the sweepers too would step forward to help him. At the end, he would congratulate them and embrace them warmly, regardless of their social distance and dirty bodies. Or if there was an uncared-for patient, he would hug him and nurse him to recovery.

3.68. The above incidents bring out in bold relief the ideal of service enunciated by Vivekananda and the exemplary spirit of his close associates, which showed the steadily growing strength of the new organization.

3.69. More than ninety years have elapsed since the Ramakrishna Mission faced the initial challenges of rendering service to the needy under the most difficult circumstances. The fact that this institution not only maintained the spirit of dedication but also widened the coverage of service activities is a tribute to Vivekananda and his followers. Although a detailed account of such developments is beyond the scope of the present study, it is of interest to note that the social work activities of the Ramakrishna Mission now cover as many as six broad areas, namely:

(i) Educational work
(ii) Health
(iii) Cultural activities
(iv) Rural uplift
(v) Tribal welfare
(vi) Youth movement

Indira Patel, after describing the work being done by the Ramakrishna Mission in each field, singles out 'the inculcation of the right attitude' as a special feature of the Mission's training:

> One point which should be made clear is that the Mission's centers enlist youths or disciples and train them as social workers, the only difference between the academic training and the training imparted in the Maṭha lies in the initial emphasis on discipline, both mental and physical, with a view to inculcating the right attitude over and above generating a sensitivity, so essential in all social work.[64]

MONKS AS PILLARS OF RAMAKRISHNA MISSION

3.70. Renunciation and service are, according to Vivekananda, the twofold national ideals of modern India. "To practise and preach these ideals"—this is how the work of Ramakrishna Mission can be described. Organizationally, the principal workers of the Mission are monks or sannyāsins. In a speech to newly initiated monks in Calcutta towards the end of April 1897 (that is, just a couple of days before the establishment of Ramakrishna Mission), Vivekananda spoke of the glory of renunciation.

"The real aim of sannyāsa is "*ātmano mokṣārthaṁ jagaddhitāya ca*", that is, for one's highest freedom and for the good of the world.[65] Without having Sannyāsa, none can really be a knower of Brahman—this is what the Vedas and the Vedānta proclaim. Don't listen to the words of those who say: We shall both live the worldly life and also be knowers of Brahman. That is the flattering self-consolation of crypto- plesasure-seekers. He who has the slightest desire for worldly pleasures, even a shred of some such craving, will feel frightened at the thought of the path you are going to tread; so, to give himself some consolation he goes about preaching that impossible creed of harmonizing Bhoga (enjoyment) and Tyāga (renunciation). . . . No freedom without renunciation. Highest love for God can never be achieved without renunciation. Renunciation is the word. *Nānyaḥ panthāḥ vidyate ayanāya,* that is, there is no way other than this. Even the Gītā says: *kāmyānāṁ karmaṇāṁ nyāsaṁ saṁnyāsaṁ kavayo viduḥ,* that is, the sages know sannyāsa to be the giving up of all work that has desire for its end."[66]

3.71. In a speech in California in January 1900, on the subject of "My life and Mission", Vivekananda explained that the Indian concept of Sannyāsa is as old as the Vedas. Gradually a regulation was established that every man and woman towards the end of their lives, must get out of social life altogether and think of nothing except God and their own salvation. This was to get ready for the great event—death. So old people used to become sannyāsins in those early days. Vivekananda pointed out how a big change in the functioning of sannyāsa was brought about by Buddha. He (Buddha) being a young sannyāsin did not sit and think of death, he went about preaching and helping people. So that, according to Vivekananda, was a great reform.

3.72. In the latter part of the same California speech, Vivekananda admitted that monastic systems in modern India have merits as well as defects. What he wanted was a balance between the monastics and the householders. Specially for purposes of preaching, he said, the monks are more suitable because of the long tradition:

> The whole national soul in India is upon monasticism. You go to India and preach any religion as a householder: the Hindu people will turn back and go out. However, if you have given up the world, they say: 'He is good, he has given up the world. He is a sincere man, he wants to do what he preaches.' What I mean to say is that monasticism represents a tremendous power. . . . The monk in India is greater than the prince. There is no reigning sovereign in India who dares to sit down when the yellow "robe" is there. He gives up his seat and stands. Now, that is bad, so much power, even

> in the hands of good men—although these monastics have been the bulwark of the people. They are the centers of knowledge and reform. But better methods need to be worked out. . . . What we can do is just to transform the monastic system, give it another form. This tremendous power in the hands of the Sannyāsins of India has got to be transformed, and it will raise the masses up.[67]

3.73. Monasticism transformed to serve the Indian masses—this is how Vivekananda conceived of the Ramakrishna Mission. It is only because the monastic institution exists in the country, said Vivekananda, that great men like Shri Ramakrishna are born here. He raised a question: Why is it that in spite of its faults, this noble institution stands yet supreme over all the other institutions of life? And he also provided an answer: It is because the true Sannyāsins forgo even their own liberation and live simply for doing good to the world. Emphasizing this to the newly initiated Sannyāsins at Calcutta, Vivekananda concluded his address:

> For the good of the many, for the happiness of the many is the Sannyāsin born. His life is all vain, indeed, who, embracing sannyāsa, forgets this ideal. The Sannyāsin, verily, is born into this world to lay down his life for others, to stop the bitter cries of men, to wipe the tears of the widow, to bring peace to the soul of the bereaved mother, to equip the ignorant masses for the struggle for existence, to accomplish the secular and spiritual well-being of all through the diffusion of spiritual teachings and to arouse the sleeping lion of Brahman in all by throwing in the light of knowledge. . . . So achieve the consummation of human life before you pass off. Arise, awake, and stop not till the goal is reached.[68]

ROLE OF THE BHAGAVAD-GĪTĀ

3.74. The Bhagavad-Gītā had a very significant role in the life and work of Vivekananda. Although he did not write a verse-by-verse commentary covering the Gītā as a whole, he quoted and explained selected verses from it. In fact, in his short opening address at the Parliament of Religions in Chicago in September

1893, he quoted a verse from the fourth chapter of the Gītā. Majumdar highlights the special relevance of what Vivekananda quoted from the Gītā, to the broad objective of the Parliament of Religions itself: "Vivekananda regarded the Parliament as a vindication, a declaration to the world, of the wonderful doctrine preached in the Gītā, and quoted the following verse: Whosoever comes to Me, through whatsoever form, I reach him; all men are struggling through paths which in the end lead to Me".[69]

3.75. The most significant elements from the teachings of the Gītā, which Vivekananda explained to his followers, listeners and readers, and himself utilized in his work, are contained in the 1896 publication entitled "Karma Yoga".[70] Various aspects of karma, including "The secret of work", "What is duty?", "We help ourselves, not the world", and so on, are discussed by Vivekananda, not only from a theoretical angle but also in relation to life in modern times. One of the main messages which he wants to convey is the supreme importance of being "ready to sacrifice himself for others", "expecting no personal gain in return":

> However much the various systems of philosophy and religion may differ, all mankind stands in reverence and awe before the man who is ready to sacrifice himself for others. . . When you give something to a man and expect nothing—do not even expect the man to be grateful—his ingratitude will not tell upon you, because you never expected anything, never thought you had any right to anything in the way of a return.[71]

3.76. Vivekananda spoke about Śrī Kṛṣṇa and the Gītā, again in the course of four lectures delivered in April-May 1900. He described Śrī Kṛṣṇa as "the most rounded man" he knew of, wonderfully developed equally in brain and heart and hand.[72] Every moment of Śrī Kṛṣṇa, said Vivekananda, was alive with activity, either as a gentleman, as a scholar, as a poet. This all-rounded and wonderful activity and combination of brain and heart, Vivekananda saw in the Gītā—"and nothing can approach it anywhere",[73] as he declared emphatically.

3.77. This tremendous activity of the man (Śrī Kṛṣṇa), said Vivekananda, and then that heart! Vivekananda recognised Śrī Kṛṣṇa as "the first man, way before Buddha, to open the door of religion to every caste."[74] Thereafter, Vivekananda compared these two great personalities: "Buddha's activity was on one plane, the plane of teaching. He could not keep his wife and child and become a teacher at the same time. Kṛṣṇa preached in the midst of the battlefield. . . . It means nothing to this man—the flying of missiles about him. Calm and sedate he goes on discussing the problems of life and death. He practised what he preached in the Gītā: He who in the midst of intense activity finds himself in the greatest calmness, and in the greatest peace finds intense activity, that is the greatest Yogī as well as the wisest man."[75]

3.78. The Gītā verses which Vivekananda explained in the course of the above-mentioned lectures occur mostly in the first six chapters. The ideas that he emphasized were essentially the main elements of "Karmayoga", but in some cases he introduced additional details. For example, he said, with reference to the opening statement of Śrī Kṛṣṇa in the second chapter: "The Gītā opens with this very significant verse: Arise, O Prince, give up this faint-heartedness, this weakness. Stand up and fight. . . . Not one step back, that is the idea. . . . Fight it out, whatever comes. Let the stars move from the sphere. Let the whole world stand against us. . . . Arise, awake, stand up and fight. Die if you must. . . ."[76]

3.79. Analysing the initial arguments of Arjuna in the Gītā, Vivekananda sensed in them an attempt "to cover this weakness with the flowery names of love and higher moral ideas." This is a common human weakness, said Vivekananda:

> Many a time comes when we want to interpret our weakness and cowardice as forgiveness and renunciation. There is no merit in the renunciation of a beggar. If a person who can give a blow forbears, there is merit in that. If a person who has, gives up, there is merit in that. We know how often in our lives through laziness and cowardice we give up the battle and try to hypnotise our minds into the belief that we

are brave. . . . Appropriately, the Gītā opens with a strong call to Arjuna to give up faint-heartedness, to give up weakness.[77]

3.80. Another section of the Gita highlighted by Vivekananda was the one containing the Lokasaṁgraha-verses of the third chapter (III. 20-26). He translated Lokasaṁgraha as "working for the good of others", and citing the example of Śrī Kṛṣṇa Himself, Vivekananda asked men of knowledge to help the ignorant and gradually bring them up:

> Even if you have known the secret that you have no duty, that you are free, says Śrī Kṛṣṇa, still you have to work for the good of others. Because whatever a great man does, ordinary people will do also. If a great man who has attained peace of mind and freedom, ceases to work, then all the rest without that knowledge and peace will try to imitate him and then confusion would arise.
>
> Behold, Arjuna, says Śrī Kṛṣṇa, there is nothing that I do not possess and nothing that I want to acquire. And yet I continue to work. If I stopped work for a moment, the whole universe would be destroyed. That which the ignorant do with desire for results and gain, let the wise do without any attachment and without any desire for results and gain.[78]

Vivekananda characterised this as "a very powerful idea— which has become the ideal in India".[79] Undoubtedly one of the powerful forces that had inspired him when he started the Ramakrishna Mission in 1897.

Chapter Four

Tilak: Orienting the Gītā to Swaraj and Lokasaṁgraha

A BRIEF LIFE-SKETCH

4.1. In an attempt to trace the likely causes of Tilak's revolutionary ideas in politics, a good deal of attention is often devoted to the fact that he was a Chitpāvan Brahmin of Maharashtra. Leaving aside the mythological links of this community with Parashurama, who preceded Rāma as an avatar of Viṣṇu, the historical records speak of the glory that the Chitpāvans attained in the eighteenth century, as Peshwas. Although Shivaji was the founder of the Marāthā power in the second half of the seventeenth century, a big expansion of the territory under the control and influence of the Marāthās occurred in the days of the Peshwas in the eighteenth century. Unlike Shivaji, the Peshwas were Brahmins. These Brahmins left their ancestral home in Konkan, and joined the army of Shivaji's grandson, and in course of time, assumed a commanding position. The most famous of the Peshwas was Bajirao Bhat, who defeated the Nizam of Hyderabad and conquered large areas of territory from the Moghul Emperor. Wolpert characterizes the Chitpāvan community as "unique among India's priestly class", because they assumed temporal as well as spiritual power over the people.[1] The reign of the Peshwas came to an end in 1818 when the British administration was established in this part of the country.

4.2. Bal Gangadhar Tilak (or Bal for short) was born at Ratnagiri in 1856. His grandfather Ramchandrapant not only taught him how to read and write but also told him about the events of the "Indian Mutiny or the first war of independence" which occurred in 1857 and in which the Maratha chiefs played a significant role.

4.3. Bal's father, Gangadhar, was a school teacher who used his great knowledge of Sanskrit, mathematics and grammar to write textbooks for students. Bal's mother, Parwatibai, was a very religious woman. Tahmankar has narrated how Bal mourned his mother's death when he was only ten:

"Bal's mother was never strong and, perhaps owing to the habit of frequent fasting, and the other penances which she practised, her health gave way and she died in 1866, soon after her husband was transferred from Ratnagiri to Poona. Bal who was then barely ten years old, has left behind a Sanskrit poem in which he mourns his mother's loss.[2]

4.4. Only six years after his mother's death, Bal lost his father and became an orphan at the age of sixteen. Recollections of this tragedy became prominent in Bal's mind when, forty years later, he was in Mandalay jail and his two sons practically became orphans when their mother (i.e. Tilak's wife) died at Poona. In his message to his nephew from Mandalay jail, Tilak said in 1912: "Let them (Tilak's sons) remember that I was left an orphan when I was much younger than either of them. Misfortunes should brace us for greater self-dependence. . . . See that their time is not lost in useless grief".[3]

4.5. After completing his Bachelor's and the Law degrees, Tilak started his career as a teacher in the New English school in Poona in 1880. This was a private school opened by a famous Marathi writer Chiplunkar, in partnership with Tilak, Agarkar and Namjoshi. All four colleagues wanted to proclaim a principle—that Indian education should be carried out by Indians and for Indians. Limaye characterizes the New English School as unique in the country at that time: "No school through the length and breadth of India perhaps can boast of a group of founders of such great personality. The rejuvenation of the land of their birth was their goal and they looked upon education, properly conceived and properly conducted, as the surest way leading to it."[4]

4.6. Although Tilak gained reputation as a teacher, he, along with his colleagues, also ventured into journalism. They launched two newspapers in 1881, the *Kesari* written in Marathi, and the

Mahratta in English. Tahmankar outlines the distinguishing features of the two newspapers:

> The tone and temper of the *Kesari* were democratic, its aim was popular education and public agitation. The *Mahratta* was to serve as the authoritative organ of educated public opinion in Maharashtra. It discussed comprehensively every question of high politics, and offered its readers a selection of the views of foreign and Indian journals and publicists on the questions of the day.[5]

4.7. The success of the two papers was immediate. By the end of 1882 *Kesari* had the largest circulation of any vernacular paper in the country, and the *Mahratta* was well on the way to becoming the leading organ of native public thought in western India. The two newspapers owed their success, according to Tahmankar, to virile impassioned writing, animated at all times by lofty patriotism and the courage of conviction.

4.8. The next important activity with which Tilak was closely associated was the establishment of the Deccan Education Society in 1884, and the founding of the Fergusson College in 1885. Parvate describes how the spirit of sacrifice that Tilak and his colleagues displayed in working for a private educational institution, at nominal pay, was appreciated by leading scholars:

> Dr. Bhandarkar spoke highly of the self-sacrificing and self-effacing venture of the young and patriotic founders of the Deccan Education Society and referring particularly to Tilak he said: This first class graduate in law would easily have become a Rao Saheb and amassed a fortune, had he chosen to serve private and personal ends only, instead of embarking on the career of an educationist in a private institution.[6]

4.9. However, Tilak's association with the Deccan Education Society came to a close in 1890, and there was, at the root of it, a conflict between him and Gokhale. According to Wolpert, "superficially, the cause of conflict was monetary, though actually more basic questions of the power and principle were involved."[7] Ideological differences between Tilak and Gokhale persisted thereafter—Tilak championing the cause of revolution, and Gokhale, the cause of reform. Acute differences between Tilak and Agarkar also arose due to their different outlook on social reform. Agarkar gave up the editorship of *Kesari*, with the result that both the *Kesari* and the *Mahratta* now belonged to Tilak and occupied much of his time.

4.10. In 1891, the Age of Consent Bill, which sought to put legal restriction on child marriages, saw Tilak and the social reformers argue strongly and present the opposing points of view. The social reformers, including eminent scholars like Dr. Bhandarkar, were in favour of collaborating with the British authorities in removing evil customs from the Hindu society. However, Tilak wanted the Hindus to introduce reforms on their own, without letting a non-Hindu government interfere in their religious and social affairs.

4.11. In 1893, Tilak gave to the traditional Gaṇapati festival of the Hindus a revivalist look, so as to make it an effective means of creating cultural enthusiasm, religious consciousness and social solidarity. In the traditional way of worshipping the Elephant God, Gaṇeśa, the festivities were mostly confined to households. By making this a public function, Tilak attracted large gatherings of people, by providing artistic displays and music, and this facilitated the giving of lectures, not only on religious topics but also covering other issues, including anti-British propaganda. Barnouw sees in this a "second aim", namely, Hindu solidarity vis-a-vis the Muslims, but he assesses this to be "less significant" than anti-British consciousness.[8]

4.12. Having successfully launched the Gaṇapati festival, which was mainly directed to revive the religious enthusiasm of the Hindu community, Tilak turned his attention to organising the enthusiasm of the people in secular matters. In 1895 he organised a public meeting in Poona and resolved to raise a memorial fund to rebuild Shivaji's tomb at Raigarh, which was then in a very dilapidated condition. Encouraged by a good public response, the 1896-celebrations of the Shivaji festival were on a grand scale, as Wolpert summarizes:

The festival had all the trappings of a typical Hindu religious celebration with songs, dances, gymnastic events, readings from the scriptures, and distribution of sweets and betel leaves. In addition, however, ballads exalting Shivaji's heroic deeds, and lectures on the highlights of Marāthā history were delivered. Symbolizing the joint political and religious character of the celebration, huge painted portraits of Shivaji and his Brāhmin guru Ramdas were carried side by side in procession up to the mountain fortress where Shivaji had been coronated "Chhatrapati" (Lord of universe) in 1674.[9]

4.13. The year 1897 can be characterised as bringing to the forefront the impact of the Gītā on Tilak's political views. Although Tilak's family background had acquainted him with the Gītā at an early age, this only exposed him to the traditional interpretation, the inadequacy of which he realised only when he made his own studies. This is how he recalled his boyhood exposure to the Gītā:

> When I was quite a boy, I was often told by my elders that strictly religious and really philosophic life was incompatible with the hum-drum life of everyday. . . . I was also told that Bhagavad-Gītā was universally acknowledged to be a book containing all the principles and philosophy of the Hindu religion. The question that I formulated for myself to be solved was: Does my religion want me to give up this world and renounce it before I attempt to, or in order to be able to, attain the perfection of manhood?[10]

4.14. Tilak's new interpretation of the Gītā, although still in his mind and not yet formulated in the form of a book, got linked with the Shivaji festival of 1897, and ironically resulted in Tilak's arrest, trial and imprisonment. When Tilak addressed a big public meeting in Poona, he portrayed Shivaji not only as a great national hero but also as an adherent to the Karma-yoga teachings of the Gītā. He further said, among other things, that since Shivaji murdered Afzul Khan for the good of the society, and not for selfish gain, his action was blameless, according to the Bhagavad-Gītā. A few days after this speech, a British Officer, Rand, was murdered in Poona by Damodar Chapekar, to take revenge for atrocities committed on the public, as Chapekar put it. Although the police found no direct connection between Tilak's speech (in Marathi) and Chapekar's action, the non-Marathi-speaking jury found Tilak guilty of sedition and he was sentenced to eighteen months' imprisonment.

4.15. After the 1897-trial and imprisonment, Tilak became, on the one hand, a recognized enemy of the British, and on the other, 'Lokamānya' (Revered by the People) in Indian public opinion. His advocacy of 'Extremist' ideas was reinforced by similar views of Bipin Chandra Pal and Lala Lajpat Rai, and the three of them became known as "Lal-Bal-Pal". After the Bengal partition of 1905, Aurobindo also joined the Extremist group.

4.16. The anti-partition agitation in Bengal lasted six years till the partition was annulled in 1911. This agitation got widespread support from all sections of the society, including those who believed in the cult of the bomb. One such person was Khudiram Bose whose bomb-throwing at Muzaffar Pore (Bihar) in April 1908 later became known as the Alipore Conspiracy Case. Tilak was one of the leaders arrested in the aftermath of this incident, and although no link could be established between him and the bomb-thrower, Tilak was sentenced to six years imprisonment and sent to Mandalay (Burma).

4.17. Two statements made by Tilak in 1908 have become inextricably linked with his name in Indian history. As Sarma puts it:

> Two of Tilak's utterances have justly become famous and are cherished by the nation. One is "Swarāj is my birthright and I will have it". And the other is his reply to the judge who convicted and transported him for six years in 1908:
>
> "In spite of the verdict of the jury, I maintain I am innocent. There are higher powers that rule the destinies of things, and it may be the will of Providence that the cause which I represent should prosper more by my suffering than by my remaining free".[11]

4.18. During the long imprisonment in Mandalay, Tilak had to undergo all sorts of hardships. When the news of his wife's death in Poona in 1912 reached Tilak in Mandalay, he wrote back:

> "I am used to take my misfortunes calmly, but I confess that the present shook me considerably."[12]
>
> The only bright side of this tragic story was that Tilak wrote his commentary on the Gītā, called *Gītā-Rahasya*, while still in Mandalay.

4.19. The years 1916-18 saw Tilak as the "Uncrowned king of India", and even the Secretary of State, Mr. Montagu, wrote in his diary: "He (Tilak) is the politician who probably has the greatest influence of any person in India."[13]

While Tilak was away in England, during most of 1919, the Gandhian era in India's freedom struggle began, and it was a significant coincidence, that the first All-India Non-cooperation movement under Gandhi's leadership started on 1st August 1920, just a few hours after Tilak breathed his last. As Sarma puts it: "Doubtless, it is Tilak's mantle that has fallen on Mahatma Gandhi, and not that of Gokhale, though the Mahatma regards Gokhale as his political guru."[14]

A PARADOXICAL COMBINATION OF POLITICS, RELIGION, PHILOSOPHY, AND OPPOSITION TO RULER-REFORMER-COLLABORATION

4.20. Tilak was perhaps the most controversial figure in the political history of modern India. Abundant praise as well as ridicule has been showered upon him. On the one hand, he has been described as 'the Father of the Indian Revolution', 'the Maker of Modern India', 'the First Great Mass Leader in the Freedom Movement', and so on. The popular title 'Lokamānya' itself means 'Revered by the People'. It was he who gave to the whole of India the famous slogan 'Swarāj is my birthright and I will have it'. On the other hand, his political opponents called him an 'Extremist' determined to destroy the Congress Organization if he cannot control it. The British government considered him to be the greatest enemy of the empire.

4.21. Similar disagreements exist about Tilak's role in the realms of religion, philosophy, and social reform. Panikkar gives him the primary credit for the rediscovery of the Bhagavad-Gītā as the political and social gospel of Hindu India:

> The revolutionary interpretation of the Bhagavad-Gīta was primarily the work of Bal Gangadhar Tilak, the father of Indian Nationalism. . . . It fulfilled the urgent need to endow the Hindu people as a whole with a new ethic and a message for social action and to discover a dynamic doctrine which, while providing Hindus with modern social ideals, could enable them to transform their society. . . . The philosophy of the Hindus, so long considered to be contemplative and world-denying, was interpreted by Tilak as a dynamic doctrine for action for the welfare of the world. . . . the *Gītā-Rahasya* gave to modern India a scripture which, at once orthodox and universally accepted, was also, so to say, a handbook of revolution.[15]

4.22. However, Tilak's activist interpretation of the Gītā has not found favour with orthodox Advaitins who follow Śaṁkara. For example, Mahadevan contends that if Karma were obligatory as Tilak holds, then many passages in the Gītā would be unintelligible. From an Advaitin's point of view, the very purpose of Śrī Kṛṣṇa's teaching was to lead Arjuna to a knowledge of the indestructible self, which is eternal and has neither birth nor death. The problems of temporal existence are insignificant from this lofty angle. In the divine command to "surrender all thy works to me", Mahadevan sees the need for renunciation on the part of one who seeks release.

4.23. Similarly opponents of Tilak's approach criticized him for being a reactionary in social and religious matters. For example, Paranjpye found fault with Tilak's concentration on politics and accused him of neglect of other aspects of national uplift work:

> In my opinion, Tilak's want of appreciation of this need of work among ourselves shows the bankruptcy of his statesmanship and the futility of the claim made for him as the greatest

national leader. He opposed the Age of Consent Bill, he attacked well-known social reformers like Justice Ranade and Dr. Bhandarkar, he did not allow the social conference the use of the Congress *mandap*, and he did not cooperate with the Plague Inoculation Team. He organized anti-Muslim festivals devoted to Ganesh and Shivaji. No attempt was made by him to look at the aspirations of the backward castes in a sympathetic spirit and he poured ridicule and abuse on those who inveighed against the caste system.[16]

4.24. What lay behind such conflicting assessments of Tilak's role? The choice of priority was certainly a key factor. Right from the start Tilak had contended that the lack of political freedom was the root of all the evils in the country. He therefore decided to pursue the difficult path of politics to the exclusion of everything else. He explained this further, in reply to Paranjpye's criticism:

> Without the power to shape our own destiny, our national regeneration in a larger sense cannot, in my opinion, be effected and I have throughout my career tried to preach and emphasize this view. When I opposed the Age of Consent Bill, I did so mainly on this ground. I did not then think, nor do I think now, that a legislature which is not wholly responsible to the public is competent to deal with social questions. Another point involved in that controversy was Dr. Bhandarkar's interpretation of certain Sanskrit texts. It is well known that Government obtained the opinions of their own Paṇḍits on the matter, and when they were found to be in my favour, Government eventually decided to be wrong with Dr. Bhandarkar than right with me.[17]

4.25. Tilak asked Paranjpye to recall how the Moderates (who called Tilak an Extremist), mostly led by Government servants and pensioners in those days, never thought of going beyond a mild and diffused criticism of some measures of official administration with a view to getting them dropped or improved. They did not then have the courage to put forward the ideal of self-government before the people, and to educate public opinion in accordance therewith. On the contrary, they tried to obstruct the political work of the "Extremists" by misrepresenting them and also by back-biting them whenever possible. Tilak particularly mentioned how the word "Swarāj" was mistranslated by the Moderates who formed an unholy alliance with the Anglo-Indians to overwhelm the Extremists, until the Grand Old Man of India, Dada Bhai Naoroji declared from the Congress platform that Swaraj should be our goal. Even then the Moderates, according to Tilak, were not prepared to declare this ideal for practical work, nor to accept any scheme for the realisation thereof.

4.26. Tilak also explained how his group "the Nationalists" wanted to build on old foundations. Reform based on utter disrespect for the old did not appeal to them as constructive work. They did not want to Anglicize their institutions and so denationalize them in the name of social and political reform. He reminded Paranjpye that the latter's colleagues (Moderates) favoured alien methods even in offering prayers to God. As against this, the Nationalists desired to emphasize and preserve the national sentiment by giving due credit to all that was good in the old system but without detriment to progress and reform needed for the national uplift. In Tilak's view, the festivals of Gaṇapati and Shivaji were means to keep and maintain a proper pride in the doings of the ancestors. The large gatherings in the festivals provided an opportunity to the Nationalists to talk indirectly on the current problems also.

4.27. Leaving aside the other points contained in Tilak's reply to Paranjpye, a recent American writer, William Holland, has observed that religion played an important role in India's freedom struggle because the nationalist movement was characterised by a strain of Hindu revivalism. Like all empires the British suppressed political meetings but they generally observed a hands-off policy with regard to religion. This provided a loophole which nationalists like Tilak exploited to the full for political purposes.

4.28. Tahmankar has cited several instances that reveal Tilak's sympathetic behaviour towards the weaker sections of the society. One of these relates to the Gaṇapati festival of 1894. While walking along with thousands of persons in the religious procession, Tilak saw a boy of seven or eight crying loudly from a window of a house while his mother was trying to pacify him. Tilak stopped to ask why the boy was crying. The mother told Tilak that her son wanted his Gaṇapati to be taken to the river for the immersion ceremony along with other Gaṇapatis, but she dared not let him do this as her family belonged to the untouchable class. Tilak was moved to tears; he could not bear to see an innocent child suffer. He went into the house, took the Gaṇapati idol and placed it by the side of his own and the boy joined the procession holding on to Tilak's hand.

4.29. Another instance cited by Tahmankar relates to a special conference for untouchables in Bombay where Tilak declared before an audience of more than seven thousand people:

> If God were to tolerate untouchability, I would not recognize Him as God at all. . . . Although I have appeared amongst you in person for the first time, believe me you have been in my mind all the time. I do not deny that it was the Brahman rule that introduced the practice of untouchability. This is a cancer in the body of Hindu society and we must eradicate it at all costs.[18]

4.30. Still another instance is the description that Tilak gave of his political ideal as "the Swaraj of oilmen and sellers of betel-nut leaves", by which he meant the toiling masses, irrespective of caste and creed.[19] What people like Paranjpye found paradoxical was that, on the one hand, Tilak had declared that he was for removing all caste distinctions regarding interdining and untouchability, still on the other, he refused to sign a manifesto condemning untouchability. Tahmankar therefore describes "Tilak's career. . . . as a whirlpool of controversy, sometimes about social reforms, sometimes about political ideals and ways and means of achieving them and sometimes about purely personal matters".[20] Wolpert's explanation of Tilak's attitude, which was found paradoxical by Paranjpye, runs as follows:

> While Tilak may sincerely have believed in the beneficence

of the many causes he so ably popularised, at times he appears to have been motivated less by his own faith in the inherent worth of a particular cause, than by the belief that championing it would prove most expedient in winning him the support of the majority of his fellow countrymen. Conversely, while he personally may not have believed that every social reform he condemned was in itself harmful or unnecessary, he appears to have been supremely aware of the fact that a potent method of achieving swift popularity was by criticizing unpopular innovations.[21]

4.31. Arvind Sharma, after comparing the approaches of Tilak and Rammohun Roy on the issue of British governmental interference in Hindu social life, has found "a basic identity" overpowered by "differences in detail". Sharma observes that the position of these two leaders "have, to a certain extent, been misrepresented" with the result that:

> In much of modern historiography about British India, Raja Rammohun Roy has the image of an ardent social reformer and Bal Gangadhar Tilak at least that of a social conservative, if not that of a social reactionary.[22]

4.32. Rammohun Roy's role as a social reformer has already been described in Chapter 2. He tried his best to create Hindu public opinion in favour of the social reform (suttee-abolition). He did not want the British government to assume the role of a law-maker on this issue, fearing that such an interference might assume undesirable forms in future. Rammohum Roy conveyed this "privately" to the Governor-General. However, the Hindu society was too slow to change its ways, and the British government did not want any delay in stopping the evil custom. Sharma summarizes "Rammohun Roy's attitude on the point of British government interference in Hindu social life as one of ex-ante objection but ex-post approbation".[23]

4.33. Sharma has concentrated his attention on the role of Tilak in the controversy surrounding the Age of Consent Bill. According to Sharma, the suttee-abolition legislation of 1829 and the Age of Consent Bill of 1891, both represent landmarks in the social history of India. The purpose behind the Age of Consent Bill (which represented close collaboration between the British authorities and the Indian social reformers) was to put legal restriction on child-marriages. Tilak proposed before a public meeting in October 1890 that Hindus voluntarily agree to marry their daughters at the age of sixteen (which was higher than the age of twelve suggested in the Bill), and their sons at the age of twenty. However, Tilak objected to the Bill publicly on the same ground on which Rammohun Roy had objected privately to suttee-legislation. Tilak explained this in many statements, two of which are:

> We would not like that Government should have anything to do with regulating our social customs or ways of living, even supposing that the act of Government will be a very beneficial and suitable measure. . . .
>
> This we have to admit if we look at the Age of Consent Bill. The Muhammadans forced the Hindus to grow beards after cutting off Hindus' locks of hair by taking a sword in one hand and a Koran in the other. So also our subjugation to others gives evidence that our brave English people have the power to send us to "our Father in Heaven" after making us drink red water (wine) instead of the sacred water of the Ganges.[24]

4.34. Tilak's biographer, Ram Gopal, has stated that Tilak performed the marriage of his daughters after they had attained the age of sixteen. In doing so, he was not guided by the Age of Consent Act but by his own suggestion of voluntary agreement among Hindus to raise the minimum age of marriage in Hindu society.

4.35. Tilak's biographer, Parvate, has given interesting details about a school devoted to female education, which initially received full support from social reformers, but when exposed by Tilak's newspapers *Kesari* and *Mahratta* as a proselytizing activity under the garb of education, fell into disrepute in the eyes of the social reformers also. Parvate's version (with some deletions) is reproduced below:

Ramabai Dongre established a school for Indian girls, particularly widows. It was a residential school and the inmates of the school were constantly thrown in the company of the Christian missionary teachers of the Sharada Sadan which she established in Poona. Tilak did not like it very much, but Ranade, Bhandarkar and Agarkar were very enthusiastic about it. They became members of its advisory committee. Tilak also enrolled his name among the sympathizers of the school after satisfying himself that the Indian girls were not compelled to attend Christian prayers and the education imparted to them was only secular. He soon discovered that the condition was not being observed and the institution was functioning as a proselytizing body. He brought this to the notice of Ranade and Bhandarkar. They protested against it. Ramabai explained that only four girls were learning the Christian scripture. The matter was referred to the headquarters of the missionary society in America. The society backed Ramabai and invested her with full powers to conduct the Sharda Sadan as she thought best. The *Subodha Patrika* and *Sudharak* wrote tauntingly about Tilak, questioned his motives and called him an opponent of women's education. Tilak paid them in the same coin through the columns of the *Kesari* and the *Mahratta*. Ultimately even the social reformers found that it was impossible to support Ramabai's activities and shield her against public resentment.[25]

FIRST POLITICAL IMPRISONMENT, IRONICALLY LINKED WITH THE GĪTĀ

4.36. Tilak's imprisonment in 1897 was the first instance when an eminent Indian political leader was put behind bars by the British administration, and ironically, this was linked, among other things, with Tilak's new interpretation of Karma-yoga. It can be viewed as a coincidence that the following two events occurred in Poona during 1897, and although there was no direct connection between these two, they were put together by the British authorities to justify Tilak's imprisonment:

(i) Occurrence of the deadly epidemic "plague" in Poona in the spring of 1897, appointment of Walter Rand as Chairman of Plague Committee, resentment among the residents of Poona against the offensive behaviour of Rand and the British soldiers working with him, Rand's murder by Damodar Chapekar on 22 June 1897, Damodar's arrest and trial and subsequent hanging.

(ii) Celebration of Shivaji festival in Poona on June 12, 1897 under the presidentship of Tilak, speech by Tilak in Marathi that Shivaji's killing of the Moghul General Afzul Khan in 1659 was not a sin according to his (i.e. Tilak's) interpretation of Karma-yoga, publication of Tilak's speech, together with other material, in the Marathi newspaper *Kesari* of which Tilak himself was the editor.

4.37. In order to help understand the plague-related events as well as the significance of Tilak's speech on Shivaji festival, some details of the Rand story need to be given, as also the ethical issues connected with the killing of Afzul Khan. First, the Rand story together with Tilak's role therein. Most of Tilak's biographers agree, that the chairman of plague committee, Rand, although a man of great energy and courage, unfortunately lacked the finer qualities of a good administrator and did not respect the feelings of the people for whose welfare he was working. He employed British soldiers to go round the city and inspect the houses where plague cases had occurred or were suspected. The soldiers used rough and ready methods, and ignorant of the Marathi language, showed contempt of the customs, sentiments and religious susceptibilities of the people. While removing people from the affected houses into segregation camps, they herded together indiscriminately in the same camp, all sorts of people—for instance, expectant and nursing mothers were crowed together with men. Before long, the people of Poona began to dread the reign of terror of Rand and his search parties more than the epidemic itself. Added to all these, Rand and his committee were guilty of the supreme sin of failure, for without a vaccine to prevent it, plague continued taking its toll.

4.38. Tilak saw Rand with a citizens' deputation to explain to him the growing resentment of the public and made suggestions for minimizing people's hardships. He also organized the establishment of a separate private hospital for the Hindus with the support of people of different persuasions and creeds.

4.39. In the meantime, a determined group of reckless young men was planning to avenge in its own way the humiliation and distress of the people of Poona. They chose 22 June 1897, the diamond jubilee of Queen Victoria's succession to the throne, which was being celebrated in a big way all over the country. That night, when Rand and his assistant were returning from the party, Damodar Chapekar shot them dead.

4.40. The authorities immediately put the city under a curfew and imposed a punitive police force on the citizens of Poona. A prize announced for providing information about the murderer attracted one of the acquaintances of Damodar, and on the basis of the information received by the police, Damodar was arrested, and put on trial, sentenced to death and hanged.

4.41. Secondly, the Afzul Khan-Shivaji encounter of 1659. The Moghul General Afzul Khan was sent at the head of a mighty Bijapur army to wipe out, once and for all, the guerilla force of Shivaji. Afzul's army advanced to Wai, hoping to engage Shivaji on the open plain, but by the time they arrived there, the Marathas were gone, retreating to Pratapgarh, a fort on a hill. Afzul knew that it would be unwise to launch a frontal assault against the lofty ramparts of Pratapgarh. Recognizing his general's dilemma, a Brahman in the Bijapur camp named Pantoji Gopinath suggested that he be sent to Shivaji to try to convince him of the wisdom of surrender before his forces were starved out of that retreat. Afzul agreed, and Pantoji was admitted to the fortress to confer with Shivaji, who then appealed to Pantoji's Hindu faith, and thereby won him over to the Maratha cause. Returning to the Bijapur camp, Pantoji told Afzul that Shivaji wanted to meet the Bijapur general, man to man, to discuss ways of settling the dispute. Afzul agreed to have his army at the base of the hill, and to advance alone to a level spot more than half way up to the fort, where he and Shivaji came together. What happened next is not firmly established but in the encounter Afzul was dead. The leaderless Bijapur army suffered a defeat and Maratha power was firmly established.

4.42. Ethical issues raised by historians in the Afzul-Shivaji encounter are: Who struck first? Did both of them come armed to destroy the enemy or was Shivaji the only one so armed? Was Afzul's murder an act of bravery or treachery or a little bit of both? Tilak's answer to these questions is contained in his speech at Shivaji festival, on 12 June 1897, relevant extracts from which are given in para 4.44 below.

4.43. Why was it necessary for the British authorities to link Rand's murder with Tilak's speech? Because the police authorities of Bombay failed to find any basis whatsoever to establish a direct connection between Tilak and Rand's murder. The only possible justification for arresting Tilak then appeared to rest on the argument suggested first by British-owned newspapers that his speech at the Shivaji festival, though apparently referring to an historical incident, was an attempt to excite feelings of disaffection towards British rule. The Governor of Bombay, Lord Sandhurst, did not initially accept the validity of such an argument. Not only did he refuse to order Tilak's arrest, he even sanctioned Tilak's election to the Legislative Council. But the clamour in the *Times of India* and other British-owned newspapers for Tilak's arrest became louder and louder. According to one report, the British community of Bombay threatened to ostracize the Governor socially if he persisted in his "policy of weakness". Similar threats had forced the liberal Viceroy, Lord Rippon, a few years earlier, to drop the idea of giving more powers to Indian magistrates. In the present case, too, Lord Sandhurst had to accept the validity of the argument suggested for Tilak's arrest and prosecution.

4.44. But what exactly had Tilak said about Shivaji's killing of Afzul Khan which could be interpreted as an incitement to a murderous attack against the British? The relevant portion of Tilak's speech of 12 June 1897 is reproduced below:

> Let us even assume that Shivaji first planned and then executed the murder of Afzul Khan. Was this act of the Maharaja good or bad? . . . . Did Shivaji commit a sin in killing Afzul Khan or how? The answer to this question can be found in the Mahābhārata itself. Shrimat Kṛṣṇa's advice in the Gītā is to

kill even our teachers and our kinsmen. No blame attaches to any person, if he is doing deeds without being actuated by a desire to reap the fruits of his deeds. Shri Shivaji Maharaj did nothing with a view to fill the small void of his own stomach (i.e. from interested motives). With benevolent intentions, he murdered Afzul Khan for the good of others. If thieves enter our house and we have not sufficient strength in our wrists to drive them out, we should, without hesitation, shut them up and burn them alive. God has not conferred upon the Mlecchas (the foreigners) the grant inscribed on a copper-plate (having long-term validity) of the kingdom of Hindustan. Shivaji Maharaj strove to drive them away from the land of his birth; he did not thereby commit the sin of coveting what belonged to others. Do not circumscribe your vision like a frog in a well. Get out of the Penal Code, enter into the extremely high atmosphere of the Shrimat Bhagavat-Gītā, and then consider the action of great men.[26]

4.45. Judge Strachey agreed that there was "no reason why a person (Tilak) should not discuss, in a proper moderate way, whether the assassination (of Afzul by Shivaji) was justified. But although there are subjects of legitimate comments and discussion, you will readily recognize that these are delicate subjects for a man of importance, a leader of the people; that is to say, he ought to be careful as to the spirit in which they are discussed in the audience. It is one thing to discuss it amongst philosophers, it is another thing to discuss it amongst an ignorant mob."[27]

4.46. Tilak's biographers have analyzed in detail whether there was any justification at that time to connect Damodar's act of "political terrorism" with Tilak's views on "ethical relativism" as understood by him from the Gītā and applied by him to Shivaji-Afzul encounter. Obviously, the political factor was more weighty than the legal. That is why, Tilak's speech in Marathi was not translated by a language expert for the benefit of the non-Marathi speaking jurors. Tilak protested, but to no avail. Wolpert summarizes how the trial ended with Tilak's imprisonment and subsequent political implications:

> Tilak's protest was as much political as it was linguistic. The trial had aroused widespread journalistic and popular interest, attracting vast crowds to Bombay's High Court, especially in its final days. . . . Tilak was sentenced to eighteen months of rigorous imprisonment." A poll of despair settled over his political opponents in Congress as well as on his followers. At the Amraoti Congress that year, the President Surendra Nath Banerjee said, "For Mr. Tilak my heart is full of sympathy, my feelings go forth to him in his prison-house. A nation is in tears.[28]

4.47. By his Sanskrit scholarship and defence of orthodoxy, as Wolpert puts it, Tilak had won the respect and approbation of the elders of his community. By his trial and imprisonment he won the reverence and love of the young and the unlettered to whom suffering and sacrifice were the supreme signs of greatness. From now on, Tilak was called 'Lokamānya' meaning 'revered by the people'.

4.48. Tahmankar is of opinion that Tilak's trial of 1897 and his consequent imprisonment was a turning point in the history of India's fight for independence and democracy. Highlighting this is his "Prelude" to Tilak's biography, he characterizes this trial as the first clash in a decisive struggle between History and Destiny. Tahmankar continues:

> Fate had placed in Tilak's hands the threads of India's fate, and the weaving of them was, over the next fifty years, to change the course of history. In him fate had made a good choice, for in his fingers the threads did not slip or waver as the complex pattern of India's independence was being worked out by the people.[29]

4.49. In those days the Indian Penal Code made no special provision for political prisoners. Tilak was, therefore, not entitled to any concessions, even by way of providing him with a vegetarian meal (free from onions and garlic). In less than two months, his weight came down from 135lbs to 110lbs, and when the news of his worsening health leaked out, people began to fear the worst. The news shocked European Sanskrit scholars and there was some talk in the universities of Oxford and Cambridge in favour of taking effective steps to get him released. Professor Max-Müller, the world's great authority on the Vedas, was in correspondence with Tilak when the latter published his first essay in the field of Vedic research. Professor Max-Müller, with the help of two sympathetic members of British Parliament, organized a petition to the Queen, signed by a number of influential men, asking for clemency for a learned scholar, Tilak. This, together with other considerations which the British government might have had, led to Tilak's release from prison, about six months before the completion of his term. Also, in due course of time, (nearly twenty-two years), political prisoners got recognition as a special category under the Indian Penal Code. The process of achieving this was set in motion because of Tilak's suffering as an ordinary prisoner during 1897-98.

SECOND IMPRISONMENT AND THE WRITING OF *GĪTĀ-RAHASYA*

4.50. In the eventful life that Tilak led, two aspects stand out prominently, namely, his new interpretation of the Karma-yoga doctrine, and his fight with the British authorities leading to his imprisonment. It was noted in para 4.36 that Tilak's brief explanation of Karma-yoga in 1897 practically became a cause of his trial and first political imprisonment. This cause-effect relationship between those two was, in a way, reversed in 1908 when his second imprisonment (which lasted six years) became a cause of his monumental elucidation of Karma-yoga. Wolpert draws attention to the fact that the doctrine of "ethical relativism", first propounded by Tilak prior to his imprisonment in 1897, was "reiterated and elaborated upon" in the Mandalay prison (where Tilak stayed during 1908-1914), the final outcome of which was *Gītā-Rahasya* (published in 1915).[30]

4.51. The chain of events leading to Tilak's trial of 1908 can be said to have begun when the Governor-General, Lord Curzon, announced the partition of Bengal as of 16 October 1905. On the grounds of administrative efficiency, a new province called Eastern Bengal and Assam was to be carved out of Bengal. The

British government knew that the idea of partitioning Bengal was bound to be extremely unpopular, but they went ahead nevertheless. The "Bengali Revolution" which followed, marked a new highpoint of united popular agitation in that province. The national slogan "Bande Mātaram" (Salutation to Mother India) which originally occurred in Bankim Chandra's novel *Ānandamaṭha* was suddenly on the lips of every agitator. Rabindranath Tagore also participated in making the following declaration.

> Whereas the Government has thought fit to effectuate the partition of Bengal, in spite of universal protests of the Bengali nation we hereby pledge and proclaim that we as a people shall do everything in our power to counteract the evil effects of the dismemberment of our province and to maintain integrity of our race. So God help us.[31]

4.52. The repercussions of the Bengal agitation rolled wave-like across the whole of British India. Mass protest meetings were held, and government was warned of the plan to boycott British goods if partition was actually carried out. "It was", declared Tilak, "a critical time. We must act and not only hold meetings".[32] Within a few months, three major planks emerged in the platform of militant nationalism: boycott, Swadeshi, and national education. Tilak called upon all the countrymen "to give the Bengalis all necessary help", and explained the significance of the three elements which constituted the new plan of action. He suggested that the idea of boycott be considered a sacred practice. To make it successful, he said, we must try to learn how much produce is imported from England, how to manufacture those goods in India, (Swadeshi), and if they cannot be manufactured here, whether we can import them from non-English places. He also supported the idea of establishing "a University of our own, independent of Government aid and subject to no other control but that exercised by the best cultivated independent intelligence in the country."[33] The principal idea underlying national education, was according to Tilak, to give such education to the children of the land as will make them good patriots, who will serve the national cause of freedom.

4.53. Although the Congress broke up in two, namely, the moderate and the Extremist wings in 1907 (called the "Surat Split" because it occurred at Surat), it had no adverse effect on Tilak's activities in support of boycott, Swadeshi, and national education. On May 2, 1908 he made, for the first time, in a speech at Akola, the famous statement: Swaraj is my birthright and I will have it".[34] Furthermore Sarma gives Tilak credit for being the first political leader to visualize the likely form of "non-cooperation with the foreign ruler", which would be a step beyond the Congress policy of boycott. Tilak spoke of such an idea, in Calcutta on January 2, 1907:

> What the new party wants you to do is to realize the fact that your future rests entirely in your own hands. If you want to be free, you can be free; if you do not mean to be free, you will fall and be for ever fallen. So many of you need not take arms, but if you have not the power of active resistance, have you not the power of self-denial and self-abstinence in such a way as not to assist this foreign government to rule over you? This is boycott and this is what is meant when we say, boycott is a political weapon. We shall not give them assistance to collect revenue and keep peace. We shall not assist them in fighting beyond the frontiers or outside India with Indian blood and money. We shall not assist them in carrying on the administration of justice. We shall have our own courts and when time comes we shall not pay taxes. Can you do that by your united efforts? If you can, you are free from tomorrow.[35]

4.54. Just as Rand's murder by Damodar Chapekar in 1897 resulted in Tilak's imprisonment, a similar tragedy occurred in 1908. In the midst of the agitation that was going on because of the Bengal partition, a young Bengali man, Khudiram Bose, threw a bomb, on 30 April 1908, into a carriage at Muzafferpore (now in Bihar, but at that time within the province of Bengal). He wanted to kill Kingsford, who, as Chief Presidency Magistrate, had ordered some young men to be severely flogged for a comparatively minor offence. Khudiram Bose threw a bomb at a carriage which resembled that of Kingsford, but really belonged to one Kennedy, with the result that the wife and daughter of the latter were killed. Khudiram Bose and many others were arrested. Since the trial was conducted at Alipore, it became known as the Alipore Conspiracy Case. Khudiram Bose was hanged. Tilak was arrested in Bombay on 24 June 1908, and charged with sedition for ideas expressed in two of his editorials in *Kesari*, dated May 12 and June 9, 1908.

4.55. A jury of seven Europeans and two Parsis tried Tilak's case. Tilak could find no barrister to argue his case the way he wished. He wanted to establish that the Anglo-Indian press was guilty of defaming India and Indian people, which was as much a libel, and the Government did not take any steps against them. When he asked Muhammad Ali Jinnah, barrister of Bombay, to serve as his counsel and to focus attention on the failings of the Anglo-Indian press, Jinnah, "refused to adopt any line, as a counsel, except what I considered best for his defence."[36] So Tilak decided to plead on his own behalf. Wolpert sees in this defence the echo of the 'Svadharma' doctrine of the Gītā:

> Lokamānya's statement deserves an honoured place in the history of his nation's struggle for independence. . . . In traditional Hindu terminology it may be viewed as an exposition of the dharma of the newspaper editor, who like every other person in Hindu society had his special duty or religion to perform because of his occupational status. Just as the king's dharma was to rule wisely, and the warrior's to fight valiantly, so the newspaper editor's was to speak his mind on topical issues without fear of reprisal. Tilak's statement moreover, was an explanation as well of the dharma of the juror, and of the political agitator.[37]

4.56. The seven European jurors found Tilak guilty, while the two Parsis did not. Assured that there was no possibility of making the verdict unanimous by sending the jury back, Justice Davar asked Tilak if he had anything to say before sentence was passed. What Tilak stated in reply, on July 22, 1908 has since become a famous declaration of the belief in the ancient Hindu doctrine of Tapas or willingness to suffer for a just cause:

> What I wish to say is that in spite of the verdict of the jury I maintain that I am innocent. There are higher Powers that

> rule the destiny of things and it may be the will of Providence that the cause which I represent may prosper more by my suffering than by my remaining free.[38]

4.57. What followed can be briefly summarised. Tilak was sentenced to deportation for six years. As the news of Tilak's conviction spread, mills in Bombay struck in sympathy for him. The cloth, grain, freight, and stock markets as well as the cotton exchange, all closed down. This was the first mass political strike in recent Indian history. The agitation against the partition of Bengal continued unabated, and finally the British Government had to annul the partition in 1911.

4.58. Although Tilak's imprisonment in Mandalay jail in Burma was a period of much suffering and pain to him (his wife died at Poona while he was far away), it did provide, at the same time, "compulsory time off" from the busy life that Tilak had led in India. He made the best use of it for writing *Gītā-Rahasya,* and this was facilitated by the permission to receive non-political books that was granted to him by the British authorities after some delay. Tilak himself highlighted this in a press interview that he gave in Poona after his release in 1914.

> Even before I was imprisoned, a conviction was growing on me that the meaning of the Gītā, adumbrated by all the many commentaries and expositions, was not the correct one. I had long wanted to give concrete shape to my ideas on the meaning of the Gītā, together with a comparative study of the eastern and the western philosophies. I could do that only at Mandalay. . . .
>
> I do not know what would have happened to me if I had not been allowed to have books, because the room and the compound had become my entire world for the duration of my imprisonment; outside the compound, there was, so to speak a big void. . . . In the case of books, there were three orders issued; when I complained to the government, I was allowed to have the books I wanted for writing Gītā-Rahasya.
>
> I have now written this book in Marathi; it took me four to six months to write but much time was spent in thinking out its plan and then again in revising it. The manuscript is

with the government—they did not give it to me at the time of my release.[39]

4.59. Tilak's ideas as contained in *Gītā-Rahasya* are consistent with a lifetime of thought and action. He also believed that, unlike Śaṁkara, Rāmānuja, and Madhva, he had no pre-conceived theory to substantiate: "I approached the book with a mind prepossessed by no previous ideas about any philosophy, and had no theory of my own for which I sought any support in the Gītā". It soon became clear to him that "the Gītā was preached to desponding Arjuna to make him ready for the fight—for the action".[40] Luckily for him, he found that the thirteenth century Maharashtrian philosopher, Jñānadeva, had also attacked the renunciatory interpretation of Śaṁkara. In a renowned commentary on the Gītā, the *Jñāneśvarī*, and in his *Amṛtānubhava,* Jñānadeva had rejected Śaṁkara's concept of an illusory and meaningless world and described the material universe and man as "natural expressions of Reality". Even the *Jīvanmukta,* or liberated soul, of Śaṁkara and Vedāntists, fails in Jñānadeva's opinion, to achieve the bliss of a devotee living in the material world. In *Gītā-Rahasya,* Tilak cites Jñānadeva's description of the devotee, as an elaboration of the Gītā-concept of a perfect man engaged in actions for the welfare of the society. Tilak also refers to the Maharashtrian poet Tukārāma who was deeply influenced by Jñāndeva. The fact that Jñānadeva had written his Gītā commentary in Marathi, to reach the masses, had a special appeal to Tilak. This is not to imply that *Gītā-Rahasya* (written in Marathi) agreed with *Jñāneśvarī* in all respects. Far from it, because Tilak's emphasis was on unselfish action for social welfare rather than on devotive action and compassionate behaviour for individual salvation.

NEW IDEAS ON SOCIAL ACTION AND LOKASAṀGRAHA

4.60. Since the draft of *Gītā-Rahasya* had to pass through the censorship of the British authorities, Tilak had to avoid references to what his new ideas could imply in terms of political action. He therefore confined himseif to discussions of a philosophic and religious nature, and talked of the needs of the society in a general way. But in earlier writings in *Kesari* and

Mahratta, and in his political speeches, there were ample indications that he considered political independence as the paramount need of the Indian society at that time. The arguments in *Gītā-Rahasya*, making no direct mention of foreign rulers, were aimed at refuting the socio-religious approaches of two broad groups of Indians, namely,

(a) the traditional interpreters of the Gītā who had accorded a lower status to Karma-yoga as compared to Jñāna and Bhakti, and
(b) the Indians who had received modern education and who felt that the Hindu society could be pulled out of the mess mainly by means of social reform and by borrowing the philosophy of social action from the Christians and other liberal thinkers of the west.

4.61. Out of a large number of issues which Tilak raised to achieve his objective, four main topics can be identified for purposes of summarizing his message:

(i) Dharma-Kṣetra or the field where the battle for dharma or righteousness is fought
(ii) Avatāra or God's incarnation to re-establish dharma from time to time
(iii) Niṣkāma Karma or action without attachment to fruits of a selfish nature
(iv) Lokasaṁgraha or the goal of the good of the society.

DHARMA-KṢETRA

4.62. This is the first word in the Gītā and its traditional meaning was 'the sacred field', which the place 'Kurukṣetra' was supposed to be. There is a story in the Mahābhārata according to which Indra gave a blessing to Kuru that all those who die on that field in war or while performing religious austerities would obtain heaven. As a result of this blessing, this place came to be called sacred. Another common interpretation was that Kurukṣetra became sacred because the Mahābhārata war was fought there to establish dharma and justice, and also because Lord Kṛṣṇa imparted the sacred teaching of the Gītā at that place. The word 'Kṣetra' in the Gītā occurs also in the thirteenth chapter, in the sense of 'human body' and Śaṁkara associated several meanings with 'Kṣetra', for example, that which is protected against injury, or that which perishes or wastes away, or that in which the results of actions get fulfilled as in a field. The word 'dharma' in the Gītā has two distinct aspects, namely, individual or particular, and social or universal. When Arjuna admits in the second chapter that he is confused about his dharma, he is referring to the individual aspect. However, when Śrī Kṛṣṇa explains the concept of Avatāra or incarnation, in the fourth chapter, and links it with the need to protect dharma, the emphasis obviously is on the social or universal aspect.

4.63. When Śri Kṛṣṇa refers to the conditions which call for divine intervention, he mentions 'the decline of dharma' as well as 'the rise of adharma'. Subsequently, in the sixteenth chapter, one of the main characteristics of those who follow the path of *adharma* is stated to be 'doing harm and bringing about the ruin of the world'. This is consistent with the etymological derivation of the word dharma, signifying that which holds the society together. Tilak emphasizes dharma as a moral law which maintains the society, and warns against the evil consequences of adharma:

> When this dharma ceases to be observed, the binding ropes of society may be said to have become loose, and when these binding ropes are loosened, society will be in the same position as the planetary system consisting of the sun and planets would be in the sky without the binding foce of gravitation or as a ship would be on the ocean without a rudder.[41]

4.64. What Tilak did was to ask every member of the society to generalize the predicament of Arjuna and raise the issues of dharma in relation to present-day problems. The significance of Tilak's call to view the whole society as *dharmakṣetra* has been highlighted by Thomas: "Tilak was the first Indian national leader to bring out the meaning of the righteous war (*dharmayuddha*) in the *dharmakṣetra*, for modern India. He boldly stated that not only one's immediate field of activity but the whole of India is the *dharmakṣetra* of modern Indians".[42]

Panikkar not only refers to Tilak's wider interpretation of *dharmakṣetra*, but also finds a parallel between Arjuna's spirit of unmanliness at Kurukṣetra and the inactivity which gripped the Indian society when Tilak wrote *Gītā-Rahasya:*

> To Tilak India was the *dharmakṣetra*—the field of righteousness— and the inactivity which seemed to have gripped India was but a reflection of the unmanliness that Arjuna felt on the field of battle. The Gītā helped Arjuna to get rid of his dejection. The same purpose it can now fulfil on this new field of righteousness. To Tilak it was clear that it was only through the message of the Gītā that India could save herself.[43]

AVATĀRA

4.65. The doctrine of Avatāra or God's incarnation arises from Śrī Kṛṣṇa's famous declaration in the fourth chapter of the Gītā: "Whenever dharma decays and unrighteousness prospers, I appear in successive ages for the purpose of destroying evil-doers and re-establishing the supremacy of the moral law". In pre-Tilak days the tendency was to interpret this doctrine literally as a promise of God to take human shape to set matters right. Like many other teachings of Hinduism it was perverted into a doctrine for the passive acceptance of the present conditions, howsoever bad, on the plea that when it suits God He will be born into the world and change things by His direct intervention. It became therefore in the hands of sectarian teachers another argument for passivity, reinforcing fatalism connected with an equally damaging interpretation of the law of Karma.

4.66. Tilak linked the concept of Avatāra with the repeated call of Śrī Kṛṣṇa to Arjuna "Matkarma Kuru" or "do my work". To those who believed in the Vedāntic declaration that "a knower of Brahman himself becomes Brahman", Tilak appealed for taking up in hand the same tasks as an Avatāra does, namely, to help the righteous and to prevent evil-doers from harming the society. Otherwise, said Tilak, such "Knowers of Brahman" are selfish:

> It is pure selfishness for a man to be engrossed in the happiness of meditation while there are millions of people to whom he is bound by an inseparable bond, the bond of the all-pervading self. . . . It is natural that noble sentiments of sympathy towards all beings must arise in the minds of people who know that there is only one Ātman in alll created beings and the trend of his mind must naturally be towards universal welfare.[44]

4.67. Panikkar believes that the Avatāra doctrine, together with the social interpretation thereof as initiated by Tilak, gradually led to the formulation of a doctrine of rejuvenation of society. Viewed from this angle, the Gītā foresees the inevitable decay of all institutions and the necessity at different times of revolutionary changes to restore the harmony of life. While the Gītā emphasizes that there are permanent social values, it does not give support to the doctrine that what exists is always the best and that change in itself is something to be resisted. It goes much beyond this. It emphasizes that social institutions are liable to decay and petrifaction when the original values are lost sight of and social chaos follows as a result of which the purposes behind social organization begin to be misunderstood or misinterpreted. At such times, qualitative change or revolution according to the Gītā is a divinely ordained process. Panikkar attaches great importance to this doctrine of change:

> This sublimation of the doctrine of change is one of the major contributions of the Gītā to modern India. To a static society held down by custom and tradition and suffocated by the accretions of ages, the teaching that change is divinely ordained when society has decayed came as a life-giving revelation. There it was provided in the most authoritative text that dharma requires to be restated in every age and society must be reorganized to suit new needs. No stronger weapon could have been put in the hands of those who desired to reshape Indian society and give it purpose and vitality.[45]

NIṢKĀMA KARMA

4.68. Tilak recognized, as did the other commentators, that the Gītā actually advocates at least three paths of conduct for the seeker of perfection: *niṣkāma* karma or unselfish work, jñāna or knowledge, and bhakti or devotion to a supreme being. The main question was thus of allocation of priority. The commentary of Śaṁkara, based on the philosophy of Advaita Vedānta, had declared jñāna and renunciation of action to be the ultimate truth of the Gītā. Rāmānuja's Viśiṣṭādvaita commentary had stressed bhakti or devotion as the central theme. Madhva's commentary following the Dvaita school of philosophy also arrived at a similar conclusion in support of bhakti. What Tilak attempted to show was that each of these commentators had twisted the meaning of some of the verses of the Gītā "to advocate a pet theory of his own". A forced interpretation of the Gītā was also important for the classical Vedāntist commentators because they wanted to show that the basic philosophy of the Gītā was the same as that of the Upaniṣads and the Brahma-sūtras—the three authoritative scriptures together being called *prasthāna-traya*. Tilak questioned the validity of such an approach, because, if the Gītā contained nothing different from the other two elements of the *prasthāna-traya*, what would be the point in mentioning the Gītā separately as an authoritative scripture in its own right?

4.69. The concept of *niṣkāma* karma is based on the universality of action, that no man alive is free from performing his dharma, directed towards his own release and the welfare of world. All human actions are motivated by the desire to attain happiness, whether material or spiritual. Tilak distinguishes between desires of two types: (a) desire for the fruit of our action, and (b) desire which motivates us to the right action. The device or skill, *kauśalaṁ*, of giving up only selfish desire for the fruit, which causes unhappiness, and of performing one's duty (right action) according to one's status in life is known as yoga or Karma-yoga. The Gītā, according to Tilak, asks us to give up only selfish desire or attachment to the fruit, but not all desires nor all actions:

> Actions in the gross material world, which are lifeless in themselves, are not by themselves the root cause of unhappiness. The true root of unhappiness is the hope for result, desire of attachment with which man performs those actions. It naturally follows that in order to prevent this unhappiness, it is quite enough if a person by controlling his mind, gives up attachment, desire or hope of result entertained by him towards the objects of pleasure. It follows logically that it is not necessary to give up all objects of pleasure or actions or desires as prescribed by the Sannyāsa school.[46]

4.70. Tilak stated that the concept of *niṣkāma karma* or *svadharma* may be specifically related to the four castes when such an arrangement existed, as in the Gītā period, but that it applies nevertheless to all persons in all societies, with or without caste. Thus, by implication, caste rules are not the final sources of duty in modern India: "that duty which has fallen on one's shoulders or which, being possible, may have been taken up by one as a duty, of one's own choice, becomes a moral duty."[47] He cited the example of the Brahman Madhavrao Peshava who was praised by Rāma Śāstrībuva for taking up the duties of a soldier instead of religious duties when Maratha affairs were in a crisis.

LOKASAṀGRAHA

4.71. While *niṣkāma karma* provides the technique of performing one's duty, Lokasaṁgraha provides the goal, the direction, and therefore also the content of actions that constitute the duty. Tilak was the first Gītā-commentator to have identified and highlighted this important concept which occurs in the third chapter of the Gītā. The compound word Lokasaṁgraha means social harmony and welfare as well as world preservation, because its two component words *loka* and *saṁgraha* have more than one meaning each. For example, *loka* denotes mankind or the world, and *saṁgraha* stands for protecting, keeping, regulating, etc. Lokasaṁgraha thus epitomizes, in the Gītā, the social and universal dimension of Śrī Kṛṣṇa's teaching. Panikkar has rightly described Lokasaṁgraha as the special contribution of the Gītā, even beyond what the Vedas and Upaniṣads had given in this field, and the credit for declaring this to the modern Hindus and to everyone else goes to *Gītā-Rahasya.* In Panikkar's words:

> Lokasaṁgraha or the welfare of the world as the motive and object of all action is the special contribution of the Gītā to Hindu religious and social thought. It follows naturally from the doctrine of unattached action which is the central theme of Kṛṣṇa's teaching. If action is to be selfless and is to be without reference to the fruits thereof (in relation to the actor) then the question naturally arises, why should anyone persist in a course of action? The old theories of yajña or sacrifice provided a simple answer: action is to please the gods and to derive worldly benefits through them. Since that was not *niṣkāma* karma or action without reference to the results for the actor, the Gītā rejected it and supplied the answer that the object of all action should be Lokasaṁgraha or the welfare of the world.
>
> The social theory behind the Loksaṁgraha doctrine of the Gītā is most important. The conception of a world order which it is the duty of the individual to uphold by dedicating his activity towards that end, runs all through the teachings of the Gītā. The earlier Vedic religion had no such conception. Nor did the later thinkers who built up the comprehensive structure of Upaniṣadic thought devote any attention to social development. For the first time the Gītā gives a social content to religion and emphasizes the welfare of the world as the purpose of all action. The doctrine of sacrifice is thus given a wholly different meaning in the Gītā, where action dedicated to God is called Brahmayajña.[48]

4.72. Tilak's elaboration of Lokasaṁgraha was intended to show to the social reform-oriented, educated Indians that their attempts at copying the West arose only because they had not understood their own scriptures properly. In the nineteenth century, the reformist thinkers were, to begin with, impressed by the social purpose and wide humanism of Christianity, and the earliest spiritual stirrings of educated India were towards a dilution of Hindu religion with Christian thought which was best exemplified by one of the phases of the Brahmo-samāj. Brown explains why, in Tilak's opinion, the Lokasaṁgraha approach was better suited to India than the social action philosophy borrowed from the west:

> Tilak rejects the Activism of the West adopted by his Brahman rival, Gokhale, who believed in gradual social reform as a precedent to swaraj or Indian independence. The Lokamānya insisted on the ousting of the British and upon self-rule as prerequisite to all else. He characterised Western-type Activism as devoted merely to improving worldly existence, whereas the karmayoga of the Gītā was devoted to self-realization through service to mankind. The Western Energism was thus rājasa or emotional while the Indian variety was sāttvika or intelligent.[49]

VIEWING HOUSEHOLDERS AS PILLARS FOR SOCIAL ACTION

4.73. Although Tilak himself broadly accepted the metaphysical concept of the Advaita philosophy of Śaṁkara, whom he called "a superman and a great sage," the Gītā-commentary of Tilak, being Karma-yoga-oriented, was so different from the jñāna-centred commentary of Śaṁkara. Furthermore, as part of his argument establishing the inadequacy of "jñāna without karma," Tilak also criticized Śaṁkara for removing the prohibition on Sannyāsa or renunciation as a stage of life. Tilak quoted *smṛti* texts to assert that, in the Kaliyuga, that is after the days of the Kauravas and the Pāṇḍavas, the path of renunciation was prohibited. In fact, five things were forbidden: cow slaughter, meat eating at the Śrāddha ceremonies honouring the ancestors; Agnihotra or maintenance of the perpetual sacred fire; niyoga or begetting offspring from another's wife; and sannyāsa. Of these, Śaṁkara retained the first four prohibitions, but removed that on sannyāsa, which according to Tilak was partly responsible for a lukewarm attitude to the philosophy of activism as taught by the Gītā. In Tilak's approach, the main responsibility for Lokasaṁgraha activities has to be borne by householders, not sannyāsins.

4.74. Tilak's contention was that, not only in Kaliyuga but even prior to that, warnings were given about the disadvantages likely to be caused to the society by a widespread recourse to sannyāsa. This practice (of renunciation) was encouraged by Buddhists and the Jains. In the Bhagavad-Gītā, only an attitude of renunciation concerning the fruit of action is recommended, not renunciation of worldly duties as such. This Gītā way of harmonizing the two ancient doctrines—pravṛtti or karma, and nivṛtti or renunciation—was, in Tilak's opinion, more beneficial to the society than that attempted by Smṛti writers through the scheme of four Āśramas.

4.75. Smṛti writers like Manu devised the scheme of four Āśramas, out of which the second Āśrama (Gṛhastha) would concentrate on Karma, and the fourth Āśrama (Sannyāsa) would concentrate on Jñāna. However, these writers had fully realised the fact that if there was an inordinate increase in the desire of the people to take up sannyāsa, the activity in the world would be adversely affected and society would ultimately be tamed. Therefore, Manu placed definite restrictions as to when Sannyāsa Āśrama could be entered into. In fact, he compared the Gṛhastha Āśrama to the sea and other three Āśramas to rivers. (Manu.6.90) Inasmuch as the state of the householder provides the other three states with food, Manu enjoined the performance of all worldly activities, including acts of valour and of universal welfare, during Gṛhastha Āśrama. He argued that in coming to birth, every man brings on his back three debts which he owes to Ṛṣis, his ancestors, and the Vedic deities. He must discharge these debts by fulfilling his obligations, namely, to the Ṛṣis by the study of Vedas; to the ancestors by the procreation of offspring; and to the deities by the performance of sacrificial ritual. If he takes to Sannyāsa without having discharged his obligations, he will go to perdition. Two visible signs as to when a man might be ready for Sannyāsa are indicated by Manu, namely, when a man's body becomes covered with wrinkles, and he has seen his own grand-children. (Manu.6.2.).

4.76. There are indications that in many cases the preconditions for taking to Sannyāsa were not observed. Tilak refers to a story in the Ādiparva of the Mahābhārata that Jaratkaru did not discharge his debt to the ancestors, and started austere religious practices preparatory to Sannyāsa, before marrying;

that as a result of his having thus destroyed his possible children, he saw his ancestors dangling in the air, and that, in performance of their injunctions he later married.[50] Tilak also mentions another story that occurs in the Bhāgavata. Nārada advised the sons of Dakṣa Prajāpati to take to the path of Sannyāsa before they had married. Dakṣa Prajāpati reprimanded Nārada for this unlawful and objectionable behaviour, and laid a curse on him.[51]

4.77. In later times, many instances of people taking to Sannyāsa as an easy way of escaping from worldly responsibilities must have occurred. Tulsidāsa in Rāmacaritamānasa refers to people who, after the death of their wife, and realising that they are unable to maintain themselves as householders, shave off their hand and become Sannyāsin (Uttarakāṇḍa, 99.3). It was in anticipation of such occurrences that the *Smṛti*-writers had made sannyāsa a *kali-varjya,* that is prohibited in Kaliyuga. Tilak's *Gītā-Rahasya* strongly supports such prohibition against Sannyāsa, which was, however, removed by Śaṁkara.

TILAK-GANDHI TRANSITION EXPRESSED IN THE TERMINOLOGY OF THE GĪTĀ

4.78. Tilak completed six years of imprisonment (which enabled him to write *Gītā-Rahasya)* and came back to Poona in 1914. During the same year (1914), Gandhi completed what he called the "Satyāgraha" struggle for the Indian community in South Africa, and sailed for England, on his way to India. During the next six years (1914-20), the leadership of India's freedom struggle, drawing support from the masses, witnessed a gradual transition from Tilak to Gandhi, not directly, but through intermediary roles played by Gokhale and Annie Besant. Both Tilak and Gandhi maintained the linkage between the freedom struggle and the Gītā, but there was a significant difference in their interpretation of the Gītā, as will be explained after describing how the process of transition unfolded itself.

4.79. Tilak's biographers have described the "gloomy" political situation which existed in India in 1914. The Bengal agitation had changed its course when the Government withdrew the earlier partition-scheme in 1911. Consequently:

> Boycott, political or economic, ceased to count as a factor in practical politics. . . . national schools and colleges were deserted. . . . Wholesale repression drove the movement underground, bringing terrorism in its train. The terrorists were vigorously hunted. Popular leaders found their way either to jail or to self-imposed exile. The Congress with its dwindling enthusiasm and attendance met only to register the growing depression of the moderate leaders. . . The octopus-like Press Act strangled all freedom of writing. National literature was mostly proscribed, especially all that described Mr. Tilak's personality or preached his principles.[52]

4.80. One of the steps that could start pulling the country out of the depression was a possible "reunion" between the Moderates and the Extremists who had broken apart at the Surat Congress session of 1907. Vigorous efforts in this direction were initiated by Annie Besant who, as a Theosophist leader, had acquired fame by her lectures on the Gītā and other speeches extolling the virtues of Hinduism. Her journalistic and political activities became predominant during the years 1914-18 when she joined the Congress and started writing vigorous articles in the weekly journal "The Commonweal" and the daily newspaper "New India", both started by her in 1914. She saw both Tilak and Gokhale at Poona in December 1914, but the approaches of these two leaders remained divergent, so much so that Annie Besant's efforts for bringing the Moderates and the Extremists together achieved success only after Gokhale's death in 1915.

4.81. Gandhi had such a high regard for Gokhale that he described him as his political guru. Gokhale had extended his moral support to the cause of Indians in South Africa and had even paid a visit to South Africa in 1912, although the verbal assurances which he received from the South African Government were forgotten as soon as he left, and Gandhi had to launch the next phase of his Satyāgraha to get those assurances fulfilled. On his return to India, Gandhi continued to view Gokhale as his "teacher in politics" and called on him at Poona in January 1915, shortly before Gokhale died.

4.82. Wolpert has made a detailed comparative study of Tilak and Gokhale, summarizing, in one word, their overall approaches as "Revolution" and "Reform", respectively:

> It is as champions of these two predominant motifs in India's recent response to the West, and as bearers of these revolutionary and reform traditions that I have come to think of Tilak and Gokhale. . . . The channels cut by each have gone deep into the soul of Indian life, . . . fertilizing its rich soil with the inspiration of their thought and the results of their action. . . . They were tenuously joined, thanks to the broad power of Gandhi's remarkable syncretic capacity.[53]

4.83. The contrast between Tilak and Gokhale has also been expressed in detail, in the *History of the Congress* written by the official historian, Pattabhi Sitaramayya, in the following words:

> Gokhale's prime concern was with the administration and its improvement, Tilak's supreme consideration was the nation and its up-building. Gokhale's ideal was love and service, Tilak's was service and suffering. Gokhale's methods sought to win the foreigner, Tilak's to replace him. Gokhale depended upon others' help, Tilak upon self-help. Gokhale looked to the classes and the intelligentsia, Tilak to the masses and the millions. Gokhale's arena was the council chamber; Tilak's forum was the village maṇḍap. Gokhale's medium of expression was English, Tilak's was Marathi. Gokhale's objective was self-government for which people had to fit themselves by answering the tests prescribed by the English, Tilak's objective was Swarāj which is the birth-right of every Indian which he shall have without let or hindrance from the foreigner. Gokhale was on a level with his age; Tilak was in advance of his time.[54]

4.84. In spite of all the differences between Tilak and Gokhale, one great common point, according to Wolpert, was that "both were exemplars par excellence of activisim":

> Tilak claims to have resurrected to its proper primacy the timeless doctrine of karma-yoga, "the religion of action". Such was the doctrine taught by our forefathers, he insisted, who never intended that the goal of life should be meditation alone. No one, said he, can expect Providence to protect one who sits with folded arms and throws his burden on others. God does not help the indolent. . . .
>
> This was indeed the essence of Tilak's philosophy, and by and large of Gokhale's as well, since both were exemplars par excellence of activism. In his fifth anniversary day address to the Servants of India Society in 1910, Gokhale had in this sense, anticipated Tilak's message by entreating his followers: Work, work, is the cry all around. If you devote the best that is in you in a selfless spirit, your duty will have been done.[55]

4.85. Now to pick up the thread of Annie Besant's efforts to bring the Moderates and the Extremists together. Gokhale's death in February 1915 weakened the bargaining position of the Moderates, and they received a further shock when Pherozeshah Mehta died in November 1915. In the mean time both Tilak and Annie Besant started, separately, the Home Rule movement, in different parts of India. For Tilak, Home Rule became a synonym for Swarāj, and his famous earlier slogan now took the form "Home Rule is my birth right and I will have it".[56] Annie Besant reinforced the religious nature of the Home Rule movement and was also able to attract large members of women participants, as she herself pointed out:

> Home Rule has become inextricably intertwined with religion, by the prayers offered in temples, and also by its being preached, up and down the country, by Sādhus and Sannyāsins . . . . The strength of this movement is rendered ten-fold greater by the adhesion to it of large numbers of women who bring to its help the uncalculating heroism, the endurance, and the self-sacrifice of the feminine nature. . . . That is why I have said that the two words "Home Rule" have become a Mantraṁ.[57]

4.86. The year 1916 not only saw a United Congress emerge again—thus ending nine years of division between the Moderates and the Extremists—but also nation-wide acclamation for Tilak, the author of *Gītā-Rahasya*, who suffered for the cause of Swaraj, lost his wife while he was in jail, but himself luckily survived the long imprisonment and this year attained the age of 60. As Parvate and Tahmankar say, separately:

> Common people looked upon him as a saint, a yogī who had not only digested but turned into his daily life the teaching of the Gītā, and the teaching of disinterested work for the good of humanity.[58]
>
> The *Gītā-Rahasya* (published in Marathi and translated into other languages,) established Tilak's reputation as a great thinker and philosopher. It would be true to say that the Rahasya invested Tilak with high spiritual authority, the extent and depth of which it is dificult to exaggerate.[59]

4.87. A special train—the "Home Rule Special"—was arranged for Tilak and his supporters, to travel from Bombay to Lucknow, for the Congress session held in December 1916. Newspaper correspondents have given a vivid description of how Tilak was honoured, garlanded and wildly cheered all along the route of the special train. Tahmankar summarizes:

> Previously he was respected for his learning, worshipped for his saintly character, and admired for his courage; now in 1916 he had become the apostle of national liberation and thousands of people, young and old, wanted to catch a glimpse of him. They waited for the special train in the cold, and in pouring rain. His long years of suffering for the country had raised his reputation all over India to the point where he was the people's guide and philosopher. . . .
>
> At Lucknow, thousands of admiring men and women besieged the carriage in which Tilak was taken in a procession to Chedilal Dharm Shālā, shouting his slogan: "Swarāj is my birthright and I shall have it". The Dharm Shālā became, as it were, "a temple for the Nationalists and the Lucknow people alike."[60]

4.88. During the same year (1916), the occasion of Tilak attaining sixty years of age was celebrated with a grand religious ceremony, and offering of a free meal to thousands of destitute and poor people. At a large public meeting, addresses of appreciation were presented to Tilak with a purse of Rs.100,000. As Tahmankar says, this was a unique gesture as in modern Indian political history, no leader had received from his followers such a magnificent gift in recognition of his services to the country. In his speech Tilak announced that the money would be devoted to the cause of Home Rule.

4.89. In November 1917, when the Secretary of State, Mr. Montagu, arrived in India, he received an "oriental welcome" from Tilak, as recorded in Mr. Montagu's dairy:

> I have been garlanded by the renowned Tilak who, till a few years ago, served a long prison sentence for being, at any rate indirectly, connected by his newspaper writings with the murder of an Indian official. . . . He is the politician who probably has the greatest influence of any person in India. . . His procession to Delhi to see me was a veritable triumphant one.[61]

4.90. For the Congress session to be held in Calcutta in December 1917, according to Tahmankar, Tilak voluntarily renounced the presidency which Bengal had offered to him, and himself sponsored Annie Besant as president. However, president or no president, Tilak was hailed at that session as the "uncrowned King of India", as Tahmankar describes:

"Tilak attended the Calcutta Congress presided over by Annie Besant. He took with him a petition signed by 1,200,000 men and women in support of the demand for Indian Home Rule. . . .

"It was a moving spectacle when the whole audience, 1,200 strong, rose as one man as Tilak entered the Congress pandal. His reception was unparalleled. The newspapers described him as the "Uncrowned King of India". His prestige never stood higher than in those days of the Calcutta Congress.[61]

4.91. For the 1918-session of the Congress, to be held in

December of that year, Tilak was elected President, but he had to decline the offer because he had made plans to visit England—a visit which lasted more than a year, starting from October 1918. Two things kept Tilak busy in England. First, Tilak filed a libel suit against Sir Valentine Chirol who, in his book "Indian Unrest", had made certain sweeping statements which appeared to be derogatory to Tilak. Secondly, he established personal contacts with political and other leaders in England and tried to create public opinion in favour of Indian Rome Rule. In this he succeeded, but the decision in the Chirol-libel case went against Tilak.

4.92. While Tilak was still away in England, the political situation in India deteriorated rapidly, symbolized by the Jallianwala Bagh massacre which occurred at Amritsar on 13 April 1919. Congress' attempts at formulating an appropriate response to this and other serious events brought Gandhi to the forefront of Indian politics, since he had, in the preceding four years, successfully conducted Satyāgraha campaigns to solve local problems in different parts of the country.

4.93. The Amritsar Congress of December 1919 marked the last appearance of Tilak on the national platform. This was also the occasion when the differences between the approaches of Gandhi and Tilak—both claiming to follow the Gītā—were publicly voiced. Wolpert summarizes how the controversy between the two leaders started at Amritsar:

> During their heated controversy in the Subjects committee, Gandhi was remembered as having at one point suggested to Tilak that Indian politics must be based on truth, to which Tilak replied: "My friend, truth has no place in politics."[63]

4.94. During January and February 1920, the controversy between Tilak and Gandhi was carried on, through the columns of *Young India*. Only parts of the two leaders' statements are quoted below, and they illustrate how the Gītā was interpreted by them in two different ways. Tilak's statement of 28 January 1920 compared the teaching of the Gītā with that of Buddha. According to Tilak's interpretation:

'Politics is a game of worldly people, and not of sādhus[saints], and instead of the maxim "akkodhena jine kodhaṁ" [non-anger wins over anger] as preached by Buddha, I prefer to rely on the maxim of Shri Krishna, "ye yathā māṁ prapadyante tāṁstathaiva bhajāmyahaṁ" [I worship those who offer worship to me in the same manner]. That explains the whole difference and also the meaning of my phrase "responsive cooperation". Both methods are equally honest and righteous but the one is more suited to this world than the other. Any further explanation about the difference will be found in *Gītā-Rahasya*.[64]

4.95. Gandhi's reply contains not only his own interpretation of the Gītā and the Buddhist text, but also an oft-quoted Sanskrit phrase used by Tilak in *Gītā Rahasya* and how Gandhi wanted to modify it in Sanskrit:

For me there is no conflict between the two texts quoted by the Lokamānya. The Buddhist text lays down an eternal principle. The text from the Bhagavad-Gītā shows me how the principle of conquering hate by love, untruth by truth, can and must be applied. If it be true that God metes out the same measure to us that we mete out to others, it follows that, if we would escape condign punishment, we may not return anger for anger but gentleness even against anger. And this is the law not for the unworldly but essentially for the worldly. With deference to the Lokamānya, I venture to say that it betrays mental laziness to think that the world is not for sādhus. The epitome of all religions is to promote Puruṣārtha [human affairs], and Puruṣārtha is nothing but a desperate attempt to become sādhu i.e., to become gentlemen in every sense of the term.

Finally, when I wrote the sentence about "everything being fair in politics" according to the Lokamānya's creed, I had in mind his oft-repeated quotation "shaṭhaṁ prati shāṭhyaṁ" [villainy toward a villain]. To me it enunciates bad law. . . . I pit the experience of a third of a century against the doctrine underlying "shaṭhaṁ prati shāṭhyaṁ". The true law is "shaṭhaṁ prati api satyaṁ" [even toward a villain, truth]."[65]

Parvate states that, "two or three weeks before his death",

Tilak told Khadilkar to the effect that shaṭhaṁ prati satyaṁ was the way to take humanity to a higher cultural level. However, his own temperament and habits of life did not fit him for the task. He had already practised the doctrine of shaṭhaṁ prati shāṭhyaṁ for long and had disqualified himself for a non-violent struggle. He was feeling consciously or subconsciously the need of such a guide".[66] Parvate adds that "Gandhiji answered that need in course of time.[67]

ROLE OF THE BHAGAVAD-GĪTĀ

4.96. Tilak was the first Indian leader to initiate the political application of the Gītā, to obtain mass support in the freedom struggle. In order to do this successfully, Tilak gave a new interpretation to the overall message of the Gītā as well as to the many terms and concepts that occur therein. To begin with, Tilak told his countrymen that Śrī Kṛṣṇa taught the Gītā not only to Arjuna but to all of them:

> The Gītā religion proclaims to everybody, though nominally to Arjuna, the following teaching; perform lifelong your several worldly duties according to your respective positions in life, desirelessly, for the universal good. (Lokasaṁgraha)[68]

4.97. Just as Tilak extended the meaning of "Arjuna" so as to include "everybody", he applied a similar generalization to "Kurukṣetra"—the place where the battle between the Pāṇḍavas and Kauravas was fought. The original Gītā speaks of Kurukṣetra as "Dharmakṣetra" or the sacred ground. Various commentators before Tilak had tried to explain why the term "Dharmakṣetra' was used in this context. Tilak adopted a new approach and boldly stated that the whole of India is the Dharmakṣetra for modern Indians. As Damodaran observes, "the attainment of freedom from the British rule was a religious mission for Tilak".[69] Faced with the oppression of the foreign rule, Tilak interpreted "dharma" as a relentless struggle against the British authorities and the forging of a national movement to restore the freedom and the glory of India. "Our life and our dharma will be in vain", said he, "in the absence of Swarāj".[70]

4.98. Two of the commentaries on the Gītā, which were most popular in pre-Tilak days, were those by Śaṁkara and Rāmānuja. While Śaṁkara placed emphasis on jñānayoga, and Rāmānuja on Bhakti-yoga, both of them pushed Karma-yoga in the background. Tilak disagreed with both of them and asserted that Karma-yoga represents the essence of the Gītā. He summarized his views in the following words:

> The conclusion I have come to is that the Gītā advocates the performance of action in this world even after the actor has achieved the highest union with the supreme Deity by Jñāna or Bhakti. This action must be done to keep the world going by the right path of evolution which the Creator has destined the world to follow. In order that the action may not bind the actor, it must be done with the aim of helping His purpose, and without any attachment to the coming result. This I hold is the lesson of the Gītā. Jñānayoga there is, yes. Bhaktiyoga there is, yes. Who says not? But they are both subservient to the Karmayoga preached in the Gītā. If the Gītā was preached to desponding Arjuna to make him ready for the fight—for the action—how can it be said that the ultimate lession of the great book is Bhakti or Jñāna alone? In fact there is blending of all these Yogas in the Gītā.[71]

4.99. The concept of *niṣkāma karma* , as propounded by Tilak as the main teaching of the Gītā, is based on the universality of action, that no man alive is free from performing his dharma, directed towards his own release and the welfare of the world. All human actions are motivated by the desire to attain happiness, whether material or spiritual. Tilak takes a realistic attitude towards the problem of happiness and unhappiness in this life, and towards the corresponding passions of desire and avarice. He analyses human experience and history and comes to the conclusion that man spends most of his life unhappy and discontented. But this discontentment is at the root of all human attempts to better his life. He writes, "In short, discontent is the seed of future prosperity, effort, opulence, and even Release; and it must always be borne in mind by everybody that if this discontent is totally annihilated, we will be nowhere, whether in this world or in the next."[72] The Gītā itself encouraged the desire of Arjuna which sprang from his discontentment. But that was a desire to know the manifestation of the Divine. In other words, this was a motivation proper to the dharma of Arjuna.

4.100. On the other hand, says Tilak, if a man's desire for something which ultimately is harmful for his well-being is not checked, he will end up in greatest unhappiness. Tilak makes an all-important distinction between dissatisfaction and its attendant desires. The principle he advocates is desireless action. His opinion is that we should distinguish between desires of two types, (a) desire for the fruits of our action and (b) desire which motivates us to the right action. He writes, "The device or skill [*kauśalaṁ*]of giving up only that hope which causes unhappiness and performing one's duties according to one's status in life is known as Yoga or Karma-Yoga."[73]

4.101. What Tilak emphasizes again and again is freedom from attachment to the results of action. Even when we perform our duties for the welfare of the world, it should not be result-motivated, but simply as our dharma. "Lokasaṁgraha is an important duty," writes Tilak, "but it must not be forgotten that the advice given. . . .that all acts should be performed being free from attachment, applies equally to Lokasaṁgraha."[74] The acts become meaningful and a source of happiness when they are performed with the desire of dedicating all of them, including the fruits thereof, to the Lord. Here, one can say that a desire is at work. This is a noble desire, or motivation, because it is not result-oriented. The peace and happiness which ensues from the act of dedicating every thing to the Lord is not tied to the fruit of the action. So long as man is not free from the acquisitive sense, he will remain a slave to his actions. Those who are enlightened perform their actions till death with the idea of dedicating them to Brahman. Tilak interprets this as the final culmination of all Yogas—Karma, Bhakti, as well as Jñāna.

4.102. What brought about a direct confrontation between Tilak and the British authorities was the former's belief and assertion that, according to the Gītā, no blame attaches to Shivaji due to the murder of Afzul Khan because Shivaji had to do this to protect his motherland. God Himself takes avatāra, argued Tilak, to destroy evil-doers and to protect virtuous people, and thus to bring about Lokasaṁgraha. Tilak explained this further to justify the philosophy of 'measure for measure':

> Under any circumstances, punishing evil-doers in the interest of general welfare, as was done by the Blessed Lord, is the first duty of saints from the point of view of Ethics. In enunciating the proposition "evil should be conquered by saintliness", the fact that the conquest of or the protection from evil is the primary duty of a saint, is first taken for granted; and the first step to be taken for attaining that result is mentioned. But, it is nowhere stated by our moral philosophers, that if protection against evil-doers cannot be obtained by saintliness, one should not give 'measure for measure', and protect oneself, but should allow oneself to become a victim of the evil-doings of villains; and it must be borne in mind that, that man who has come forward to cut the throats of others by his own evil-doings, has no more any ethical right to expect that others should behave towards him like saints. Nay, it is clearly stated in our religious treatises, that when a saint is thus compelled to perform some unsaintly Action, the responsibility of such unsaintly Action does not fall on the pure-minded saint, but that the evil-doer must be held responsible for it, as it is the result of his evil-doings (*Manu.*8.19 and 351); and the punishment, which was meted out by the Blessed Buddha Himself to Devadatta, has been justified in Buddhistic treatises on the same principle (*Milinda-Pra.*4.1.30-34).[75]

4.103. Tilak is the first commentator on the Gītā to write in such a detail on the importance of Lokasaṁgraha. It is true that Tilak's interpretation of Lokasaṁgraha was, from 1919 onward, modified by Gandhi in the sense that *ahiṁsā* was made an inseparable element thereof. However, Tilak's conflict with the British authorities had come to a head almost a quarter of a century prior to the Gandhi era. And Tilak's biographers as well as those associated with the English translation of his Marathi writings believe that Tilak put into practice what he thought was the real meaning of the Gītā. For example, Sukthankar, who translated Tilak's *Gītā-Rahasya* into English, says in the 'Translator's Preface:

> The late Lokamānya Bal Gangadhar Tilak was a spiritual and intellectual giant. He was a monumental figure in the history of India, and it is a question whether he was more a philosopher than a politician and statesman, inasmuch as his statesmanship and his political activities would appear to have been based on the Karma-Yoga and the principles of Ethics, which he believed to have been expounded in the Gītā. In fact, the Gītā and its teachings would seem to have been the guiding beacon of his life; and if one considers what he did for India, and compares it with what he has preached in the *Gītā-Rahasya,* one will come to believe that he has practised what he preached, (which few people do), and that his political activities were a concrete example of that 'universal welfare' (Lokasaṁgraha), which, according to him, was preached by the Gītā to be the basis of Karma-Yoga.[76]

CHAPTER FIVE

Aurobindo: Extending Lokasaṁgraha, with Modification, from Karmayoga to Pūrṇayoga

A BRIEF LIFE-SKETCH

5.1. A good deal of significance is often attached to Aurobindo's date of birth (15th August) as well as to his ancestry. When the date fixed for India's Independence (15 August 1947) happened to be the same as Aurobindo's seventy-fifth birthday, he himself felt that "this coincidence" was not merely "a fortuitous accident":

> August 15th 1947, is the birthday of free India. . . .
>
> August 15th is my own birthday and it is naturally gratifying to me that it should have assumed this vast significance. I take this coincidence, not as a fortuitous accident, but as the sanction and seal of the Divine Force that guides my steps on the work with which I began life, the beginning of its full fruition.[1]

5.2. Among Aurobindo's ancestors, the direct or indirect influences exerted on him by his own father, and by his mother's father, pulled Aurobindo in practically opposite directions. Majumdar has described in detail how the "strongly anglicized" father of Aurobindo gave "strict instructions" to provide for Aurobindo a thoroughly Western education to fit him for public service under the British Government:

> Aurobindo's father, K.D. Ghose, an England-returned medical officer, was so strongly anglicized that he sent Aurobindo to England at the age of eight. . . .

Aurobindo, as a child, spoke only English, and under the strict instructions of his father he was brought up in England in such a way that he knew nothing of India and her culture.[2]

5.3. In comparison to the strong and direct influence which Aurobindo's father tried to exert on his son in his childhood, (but without a long-lasting effect), the influence of Aurobindo's mother's father, Rajnarain Bose, can only be characterized as indirect and implicit, but ultimately proving more effective. Majumdar speaks of Rajnarain Bose "as the father of nationalism in Bengal", who "turned the tide" against Keshab's followers who might otherwise have "proved to be a highly denationalizing element in the body-politic, owing to their tendencies towards European ethics and theology":

> Rajnarain Bose held out before his countrymen a complete and comprehensive picture of nationalism, touching almost every aspect of life, in a prospectus which he issued in 1866 with a view to the establishment of a "Society for the promotion of national feeling among the educated natives of Bengal". The object of this Society was to resist the powerful tendency of imitating the west, by reviving old ideas, traditions and customs in every walk of life. . . . Rabindranath Tagore says in his autobiography that he and his elder brother joined a secret society founded by Rajnarain Bose and got from him their first inspiration to free India.[3]

5.4. What stirred the souls of "a large number of Hindus" was a public lecture delivered by Rajnarain Bose in 1872 (the year of Aurobindo's birth), in which the idea of basing Indian nationalism on the Hindu religion was vehemently formulated. The concluding lines of this lecture of Rajnarain Bose were: "I see in my mind the noble and puissant Hindu nation rousing herself after sleep, and rushing towards progress with divine prowess".[4]

5.5. Majumdar speaks of "the effect produced by this lecture of Rajnarain Bose" on many persons, including Bankim Chandra Chatterji who wrote: "Let there be a shower of flowers and sandal on the pen of Rajnarain Babu".[5] Although Rajnarain

Bose's influence on Aurobindo might be indirect, the way it was reinforced by Bankim Chandra Chatterji and others, made it more penetrating, and its full effect became visible in Aurobindo's views after about thirty five years. As Majumdar summarizes:

> Rajnarain Bose played a significant role in the birth of nationalism in Bengal. . . . but it was his daughter's son Aurobindo who became the high-priest of the new cult of nationalism.[6]

5.6. Karan Singh has given details of how Aurobindo "managed to get himself disqualified for ICS," and started, instead, to utilize his stay at Cambridge University for participating in the activities of the Indian Majlis:

> At Cambridge, Aurobindo passed the First Part of the Classics Tripos in the first division after two years, and also won college prizes for English and literary ability. He was working simultaneously for the I.C.S. examination and passed all its terminal examinations. Finally he passed the open competition with distinction, but did not qualify for the service because he did not pass the riding test. As he puts it, he 'felt no call for the I.C.S. and was seeking some way to escape from that bondage. By certain manoeuvres he managed to get himself disqualified for riding, without himself rejecting the service which his family would not have allowed him to do.'
>
> When he went to Cambridge he came into contact there with an organization known as the Indian Majlis founded in 1891. He took an active part in the activities of the Majlis, of which he also became Secretary. Along with several other hot-blooded young men he participated in its debates, and it seems that he delivered several speeches against British imperialism that can only be described as revolutionary.[7]

5.7. Sarma views Aurobindo's stay at Cambridge as a tussle between "his erring father" on the one hand, and "Mother India" on the other. Since Aurobindo was soon to switch over his interests from Europe to India, and in particular, from Greek to Sanskrit, Sarma quotes a poem written by Aurobindo during 1890-92, which shows that he had already heard "the call of Saraswatī" for quitting the "Athenian lanes" in favour of the "shores of the Ganges":

> For in Sicilian olive-groves no more
> Or seldom must my foot-prints now be seen,
> Nor tread Athenian lanes, nor yet explore
> Parnassus or thy voiceful shores, O Hippocrene.
> Me from her lotus heaven Saraswati
> Has called to regions of eternal snow
> And Ganges pacing to the Southern sea,
> Ganges upon whose shores the flowers of Eden blow.[8]

5.8. Aurobindo's stay in India from 1893 to 1950 constitutes three successive phases, namely,

(i) The Preparatory phase (1893-1905)
(ii) The Bengal-partition phase (1905-10)
(iii) The Pondicherry phase (1910-50)

Regarding the beginning of the preparatory phase, Aurobindo recalled later how he arrived in India only to hear of his father's death and find his mother too ill to recognize him. But another event happened to him the moment he touched Indian soil; the darkness which had encompassed him all of his years in England lifted, and he had his first spiritual experience. In Aurobindo's own words: "Since I set foot on the Indian soil on the Apollo Bunder in Bombay, I began to have spiritual experiences, but these were not divorced from this world but had an inner and infinite bearing on it, such as a feeling of the Infinite pervading material space and the Immanent inhabiting material objects and bodies."[9]

5.9. Aurobindo's first job in India was in the princely state of Baroda, in the secretariat to start with and later as Professor of English and French and also as Vice-Principal of Baroda College. It was during these twelve years that he laid the foundations for his future work by learning Sanskrit and several of the modern Indian languages and, above all, by assimilating the spirit of Indian civilization and Hindu religion. He wrote a series of strong articles attacking the moderate policies of the

Indian National Congress. He and his younger brother Barindra also tried to organize secret revolutionary groups in Bengal. Aurobindo's occasional practice of Yoga in this phase was motivated partly as a spiritual endeavour and partly to gain an inner power for political use.

5.10. During the Bengal-partition phase, Aurobindo shared the leadership of the Nationalists, or the Extremists, as they were called, with Tilak, Lajpat Rai and Bipin Chandra Pal. Like Tilak, Aurobindo attained fame not only as a great political leader but also as a journalist whose writings won mass support for the nationalist causes, and it was the same act of bomb-throwing by Khudiram Bose at Muzaffarpore (Bihar) in April 1908 which resulted in Tilak's trial in Bombay and Aurobindo's trial in Calcutta.

5.11. During 1908-1909, Aurobindo was kept in the Alipur jail as an under-trial prisoner for about a year. Aurobindo later characterized this period of detention in the jail as the most momentous period in his life. In jail he read the Bhagavad-Gītā and it deeply affected him. He also had a profound religious experience which totally altered the course of his life. He saw in a vision the familiar form of Śrī Kṛṣṇa of the Gītā. As Aurobindo recalled in his famous Uttarpārā speech delivered immediately after his acquittal in 1909:

> Then He placed the Gītā in my hands. His strength entered into me and I was able to do the Sādhanā of the Gītā. . . . It was Vāsudeva who surrounded me. I walked under the branches of the tree in front of my cell. . . . It was Sri Kṛṣṇa whom I saw standing there and holding over me His shade. In the court, it was not the Magistrate whom I saw. . . . it was not the Counsel for the prosecution that I saw, it was Śrī Kṛṣṇa who sat there. . . . He smiled and said, 'I am guiding, therefore fear not. Turn to your own work for which I have brought you to jail and when you come out, remember never to fear, never to hesitate. Remember that it is I who am doing this, not you nor any other. . . .[10]

5.12. Referring to Aurobindo's acquittal itself, Karan Singh notices "an ironic twist of destiny" by virtue of which the District and Sessions Judge trying the case was one Mr. Beachcroft who was at Cambridge with Aurobindo and had stood second to him in Greek. Furthermore, Aurobindo's lawyer, C.R. Das, had the keen vision to foresee that Aurobindo was no ordinary political prisoner but a remarkable person of high destiny. Accordingly C.R. Das's speech for defence, which was spread over eight days, concluded with a prophetic appeal to the judge in the following words:

> My appeal to you is this, that long after the controversy will be hushed in silence, long after this turmoil and agitation will have ceased, long after he is dead and gone, he will be looked upon as the poet of patriotism, as the prophet of nationalism and the lover of humanity. Long after he is dead and gone, his words will be echoed and re-echoed, not only in India, but across distant seas and lands. Therefore I say that the man in his position is not only standing before the bar of this court, but before the bar of the High Court of History.[11]

5.13. Aurobindo emerged from the Alipur jail with the firm conviction that he was merely an instrument in the hands of the Divine, and that the Divine power was intimately and irrevocably working in the national movement, the success of which was therefore assured whether or not he as an individual remained on the scene. This new consciousness transformed his approach to the political problems of the day, and soon to the very problem of political activity itself. Although he took to journalism again to carry forward the nationalist cause, the eight month period from June 1909 to February 1910 can be viewed as a preparation for his final withdrawal from active politics.

5.14. The weekly paper, the *Karmayogin,* which Aurobindo started editing in June 1909, clearly showed the impact of the Gītā. Not only was the name of the paper taken from the Gītā, its motto also was the famous Gītā aphorism '*Yogaḥ karmasu Kauśalaṁ,*' meaning 'yoga is skill in action'. The cover illustration showing Śrī Kṛṣṇa driving Arjuna's chariot at Kuruskṣetra, proved highly effective as a religious symbol. Besides writing on political, social, economic and cultural topics of the day, Aurobindo published a series of essays on 'the Ideals of the Karmayogin'. Comparing 'the Karmayogin' with the 'Bande Mātaram' (the paper with which Aurobindo was associated prior to his imprisonment), Karan Singh remarks: "While in the Bande Mātaram, the political outlook had been predominant and the spiritual an undercurrent, in the Karmayogin the roles were reversed."[12]

5.15. Parvate is of opinion that Aurobindo had envisaged the desirability, if not the feasibility, of winning India's independence through an unarmed revolution. In one of his speeches, Aurobindo had said, "On their fidelity to Swadeshi, to boycott, to passive resistance, rested the hope of a peaceful and spiritual revolution. On that it depended whether India would give the example unprecedented in history of a revolution worked only by moral force and peaceful pressure".[13] However, Aurobindo realized that neither he nor any of the other leaders who were in India at that time seemed capable of leading such a 'spiritual revolution'. Almost prophetically he wrote in the Karma-yogin on 31 July 1909 that the country 'must wait for the man who is to come':

> The party is there, not less pervading and powerful than before but in want of a policy and a leader. The first it may find, the second, only God can give. The men who have led hitherto, have been strong men of high gifts and commanding genius, great enough to be protagonists of any other movement; but even they were not sufficient to satisfy one which is the chief current of a world-wide revolution. Therefore, the Nationalist Party, custodians of the future must wait for the man who is to come, calm in the midst of calamity, hopeful under defeat, sure of eventual emergency of triumph and always mindful of the responsibility which they owe not only to India, but to the world.[14]

5.16. Aurobindo's final decision to quit politics and to make his contribution to the cause of the humanity in the spiritual field came with apparent abruptness in February 1910. Writing 'On Himself' he gives a first-hand account of how he 'suddenly received a command from above':

> Here are the facts of that departure. I was in the Karmayogin office when I received the word, on information given by a high-placed police official, that the office would be searched the next day and myself arrested. (The office was in fact searched but no warrant was produced against me; I heard nothing more of it till the case was started against the paper later on, but by then I had already left Chandernagore for Pondicherry.) While I was listening to animated comments from those around on the approaching event, I suddenly received a command from above, in a Voice well-known to me, in three words, "Go to Chandernagore". In ten minutes or so I was in the boat for Chandernagore. . . . Afterwards, under the same "sailing orders" I left Chandernagore and reached Pondicherry on April 4, 1910.[15]

5.17. The fact that 'the progress of humanity' remained Aurobindo's goal was confirmed by Aurobindo himself when he gave Romain Rolland the following reason for his withdrawal from 'mediocre politics':

> India possesses in its past, a little rusty and out of use, the key to the progress of humanity. It is to this side that I am now turning my energies, rather than towards mediocre politics. Hence the reason for my withdrawal. I believe in the necessity for tapasyā (a life of meditation and concentration) in silence for education and self-knowledge and for the unloosing of spiritual energies. Our ancestors used these means under different forms; for they are the best for becoming an efficient worker in the great hours of the world.[16]

5.18. During the Pondicherry phase of Aurobindo's life, the year 1914 is significant because Paul Richard, a French writer, came with his wife Mira Richard to Pondicherry to collaborate with Aurobindo in the starting of the philosophical journal, the *Ārya* (Review of the Great Synthesis). The aims of this journal were to give the reader:

(i) A systematic study of the highest problems of existence;

(ii) The formation of a vast synthesis of knowledge, harmonizing the diverse religious traditions of humanity, occidental as well as oriental. Its method will be that of realism, at once rational and transcendental, a realism consisting of the unification of intellectual and scientific disciplines with those of intuitive experience.

5.19. But soon after the journal *Ārya* was started, the First World War broke out and Richard and his wife returned to France. Aurobindo continued the journal, publishing therein the results of his meditations, thoughts and experiences. In the next six years he published many of his famous writings, including Essays on the Gītā, The Life Divine, The Ideal of Human Unity and new interpretations of the Upaniṣads. About his written works Aurobindo later said, "I have made no endeavour in writing, I have simply left the higher Power to work."[17]

5.20. In 1920, Mira Richard returned from France to join Aurobindo in the spiritual work she had envisioned as needed for the world. During the last ten years in Pondicherry, Aurobindo had progressed for himself, but he could not do much by way of helping others. With the help of Mira Richard (who became The Mother of the Āśrama), Aurobindo was able to give to the world the spiritual message representing the results of his *sādhanā.* With the Mother in charge of the Āśrama, Aurobindo found the proper atmosphere and time that he needed to fulfil his mission—to prepare the physical earth plane for the new supramental age, the kingdom of heaven on earth. He wrote thousands of letters to his followers and also completed the epic *Sāvitrī* (23,806 lines of inspired poetry).

5.21. Following his retirement into a secluded portion of the Āśrama, Aurobindo faced accusations of escaping the harsh world of reality and suffering, and of retreating into a pleasant, painless, non-abrasive seclusion. Aurobindo clarified and pointed out that such accusations arose out of an "illusion":

> But what strange ideas again! —that I was born with a supramental temperament and that I have known nothing of hard realities! Good God ! My whole life has been a struggle with

hard realities, from hardships, starvation in England and constant dangers and fierce difficulties continually cropping up here in Pondicherry, external and internal. My life has been a battle from its early years and is still a battle: the fact that I wage it now from a room upstairs and by spiritual means as well as others that are external makes no difference to its character. But, of course, as we have not been shouting about these things, it is natural, I suppose, for others to think that I am living in an august, glamorous, lotus-eating dreamland where no hard facts of life or Nature present themselves. But what an illusion all the same![18]

5.22. In the world-wide message that Aurobindo sent on 15 August 1947, he spoke of his "dreams", which clearly showed how deeply devoted he always was to the ideals of "individual perfection, perfect society, human unity, and spiritual regeneration of the world".

The first of these dreams was a revolutionary movement which would create a free and united India. India today is free, but she has not achieved unity. . . .

Another dream was for the resurgence and liberation of the people of Asia and her return to her great role in the progress of civilization. . . .

The third dream was a world-union forming the outer basis of a fairer, brighter and nobler life for all mankind. . . . The momentum is there. . . . A new spirit of oneness will take hold of the human race.

Another dream, the spiritual gift of India to the world has already begun. . . amid the disasters of the time more and more eyes are turning towards her with hope and there is even an increasing resort not only to her teachings, but to her psychic and spiritual practice.

The final dream was a step in evolution which would raise man to a higher and larger consciousness and begin the solution of the problems which have perplexed and vexed him since he first began to think and to dream of individual perfection and perfect society. This is still a personal hope and idea, an ideal which has begun to take hold both in India and in the West on forward-looking minds. The difficulties in the way are more formidable than in any other field of endeavour, but difficulties were made to be overcome.[19]

5.23. Aurobindo "withdrew from the physical body" on 5 December 1950. However, the Mother of the Pondicherry Āśrama continued implementing Aurobindo's ideas, two of which need speical mention, for purposes of the present study:

(i) Śrī Aurobindo International University Centre was started on 24 April 1951. It was later called 'Śrī Aurobindo International Centre of Education'.
(ii) Auroville, "the Cradle of a new World", was founded on 29 February 1968.

VIEWING POLITICS AS GOD'S WORK, WITH STRESS ON RELIGIOUS SYMBOLS

5.24. Although Aurobindo's direct involvement in the nationalist movement was only during five years (1905-10), he made a significant contribution to the freedom struggle by viewing it as "God's work" and by exhorting all his countrymen to plunge into the fight as "instruments of God." He told the people that the real leader of the movement was God, who was inspiring persons like Aswini Kumar Datta of Barisal (East Bengal) and Bal Gangadhar Tilak of Poona (the chief spokesman of the Extremist wing of the Congress in the country):

> It is God who rides on the wings of the hurricane, it is the might and force of the Lord that manifested itself and His almighty hands that seized and shook the roof so violently over our heads. . . . Repression is nothing but the hammer of God. . . . They do not know that great as he is, Aswini Kumar Datta is not the leader of this movement, that Tilak is not the leader—God is the leader. . . . It is because God has chosen to manifest Himself and has entered into the hearts of His people that we are rising again as a nation. . . It will move forward irresistibly until God's will in it is fulfilled. . .
>
> Nationalism is a religion that has come from God. . . . If you are going to be a nationalist, if you are going to assent to this religion of nationalism, you must do it in the religious

spirit. You must remember that you are the instruments of God.[20]

5.25. The enthusiastic acceptance which Aurobindo's approach received in the country, and particularly in Bengal, grew out of the mood of patriotic awakening and religious revival, stirred up by the partition of Bengal. Lord Curzon's scheme of dividing the province of Bengal into two, although formally announced on 20 July 1905, was to take effect from 16 October 1905. The entire Bengali community felt a strong concern about a matter directly affecting their province such as they had never experienced before. Hundreds of public meetings were held and all sorts of ways of putting pressure on the government were talked of. Four methods of protest found strong support, namely, boycott of British goods, greater use of Swadeshi or goods made within the country, starting institutions of national education not controlled by the government, and observing the partition day as a day of mourning. Patriotic feelings were aroused by these methods of protest. Side by side with these, the following four "religious symbols" became prominent, almost spontaneously or inspired partly by the occurrence of festivals and partly through religious literature:

(a) "Rākhī" not only as a traditional festival but also as a religious symbol highlighting the indelible unity of the Bengali race and the promise of mutual protection (of *Rakṣā*)
(b) "Pūjā", the most important Bengali festival symbolically remodelled so as to include a grand "yajña" ceremony and a mass prayer to the Goddess to give to Her devotees strength at this critical hour
(c) "Bande Mātaram" adopted from Bankim Chandra Chatterji's novel "Ānandamaṭh" as the symbolic war-cry of the peaceful fighters for the Motherland
(d) "Vivekananda" as a symbol of the new Hinduism, emphasizing "sevā" or service of follow-brethren as an essential feature of religion, and also "fearlessness" as the message of the upaniṣads and the Gītā.

5.26. Each of the above-mentioned symbols, and action programmes associated therewith, contributed, in its own ways, in giving a religious orientation to patriotic feelings and in making the people mentally prepared to listen to Aurobindo's declaration that the movement is God's work. Furthermore, Rabindranath Tagore's active association with these programmes was also of great significance. For example, Tagore himself issued to the public a letter in Bengali, indicating how the Rākhī festival was to be given a new shape, for affirming that the bond of union between East Bengal and West Bengal was "implanted by Providence":

> On the 30th of Āświn, Bengal will be partitioned by legislation. To prove, however, that God did not ordain the severance of the race, it is proposed that the day should be commemorated by an observance of Rākhī Bandhan", to indicate the indelible unity of the Bengali race. . . .
>
> The mantra to be uttered on the occasion of tying the sacred Rākhī thread on the arms of one another is: 'Brothers live united'. . . . Let that day be commemorated to indicate the indissoluble brotherhood between East Bengal men and West Bengal men, between rich and low, between Christians, Mohammedans and Hindus, born of soil. . . . The Rākhī ceremony will indicate that no monarch's sword, howsoever powerful, can cut asunder the bond of union implanted by Providence amongst people forming one and the same race.[21]

5.27. The Pūjā ceremony, held at the Kalighat temple on 28 September 1905, was also given a new shape, including prayers to the Goddess for averting the doom of partition, and the taking of a solemn vow to discard all foreign clothes. The *Amrita Bazar Patrika* of Calcutta highlighted the following aspects of the Pūja festival of that year:

> The gathering was estimated to be more than 50,000. It was not a gathering of boys, nor of illiterate people. It was a respectable and representative gathering of the Hindu inhabitants of Calcutta and the neighbouring places, including the landed Hindu aristocracy, barefooted and dressed in holy silken clothes. . .
>
> But it was not a mere matter of crowds. The feeling was

> intense. This vast assembly, consisting of all grades of society, was led to congregate before the Goddess on that auspicious day—the Mahālaya day—to offer up to the Goddess prayers for averting the doom of partition and to take a solemn vow to discard all foreign clothes. . . .
>
> The Pūjā was followed by the Homa (yajña) ceremony which was a grand sight, a huge fire was burning to which ghee and other offerings, incense, and sandalwood were incessantly supplied, accompanied by the offering of mantras by thousands of voices. They invoked the aid of the Goddess, the centre of all power, to give them strength at this critical hour. . . .
>
> The Brahmins in the temple uttered the following invocation in Sanskrit: 'Worship the motherland before all other deities, give up sectarianism, all religious differences, animosities, and selfishness; adopt one and all the pledge of serving the mother country and devote your lives to relieve her distress.
>
> Standing in front of the Mother in the temple, the following vow was taken in batches: I solemnly promise that to the best of my power I wil never use foreign articles, that I will not purchase such articles from foreign shops which are to be had at Indian shops, that I will not employ foreigners for work which could be done by my countrymen.[22]

Majumdar, the author of the *History of the Freedom Movement in India* looks upon this solemn vow as the first declaration of war against the British—and this paved the way for Aurobindo to make his own contribution thereto as a karmayogin.

5.28. The adoption of "Bande Mataram", meaning "Hail Mother", as a greeting and slogan, for use by the agitators, played a long-lasting role in reminding all Indians that worshipping and serving the motherland was the highest form of religious devotion. This greeting forms part of a hymn to Mother Goddess in the Bengali novel *Ānandamaṭha* written by Bankim Chandra Chatterji. This hymn is really a song addressed to the motherland, Bengal and India, conceived not only as a geographical unit, but as the fountain source of everything that is dear to man, namely, physical strength, spiritual devotion, knowlege, religion, feeling, perception.

"Who says that the Mother is weak and helpless? Harken to the war-cry from seven (later changed to thirty) crores of voices, backed up by weapons held in hands twice that number".

The novelist Bankim Chandra makes one of the characters in the novel utter a remark: "But this is not mother—it is a country", to which the singer of the hymn replies: "A patriot knows no other mother, no other object of devotion".[23]

5.29. The Congress adopted this hymn of Bankim Chandra Chatterji as the National Song. (After independence, Tagore's song "Jana-Gaṇa-Mana" was adopted as the National Anthem). The symbolic expression of patriotism by means of the greeting "Bande Mātaram" became such a strong force that British authorities took repressive measures to stop this practice. It was one such occurrence in Barisal (East Bengal) where the local leader Aswini Kumar Datta tried, for purposes of holding a conference, to arrive at a compromise with the British administration whose main demand was that "Bande Mātaram" should not be used in the streets by the processionists. However, the authorities started beating boys for saying "Bande Mātaram" even inside their homes and schools, with the result that, ultimately the conference organised by Aswini Kumar Datta, became, in the words of the Congress leader Surendranath Banerji, "a story of acts of repression, one of the darkest in the annals of the Government of East Bengal."[24]

It was mainly with reference to this incident that Aurobindo described Aswini Kumar Datta as an instrument of God (see para 5.24 above). Barisal provided one of the strongest evidences of how effective and powerful the slogan "Bande Mātaram" was during the freedom struggle. The great contribution of Bankim Chandra, whose novel was the original source of "Bande Mātaram" was recognized by Aurobindo in the following words: "He (Bankim Chandra) bade us leave the canine method of agitation for the leonine".[25] Even school-boys behaved like lions when they insisted on saying "Bande Mātaram".

5.30. Although Vivekananda himself had avoided direct involvement in political activities, his teachings relating to "sevā", "fearlessness" and "strength" were found to be particularly inspiring by the students and other groups of young patriots who were anxious to do something worthwhile for the motherland. Majumdar finds a parallel between what these young persons picked up from the writings of Bankim Chandra and Vivekananda. Bankim Chandra's message of religious devotion to motherland, and the action-generating call of Vivekananda based on the philosophical teachings of the Upaniṣads and the Gītā—these became the sacred canon of the young patriots of Bengal. To a group of young men who had asked Vivekaṇanda for advice, he had said, "Be strong, my young friends; that is my advice to you. You will be nearer to heaven through football than through the study of the Gītā. . . . You will understand the Gītā better with your biceps, your muscles, a little stronger."[26] On another occasion he had said, "Remember the soul-stirring death-defying Mantraṁ—Abhīḥ—fearlessness—and shake off age long vestiges of slave-mentality, superstition and inferiority-complex".[27]

5.31. Majumdar has highlighted Vivekananda's influence on the young patriots:

> The Bhagavad-Gītā, frequently quoted by Vivekananda and made popular by the Bengali translation with elaborate commentary by Bankim Chandra, taught them to look upon this body as a mere transient thing—a tattered garment to be put off by the soul for a new one—and to perform one's duty in a detached spirit, without looking for its result or reward, laying down life or killing others, if need be, with equanimity—for every man is merely the agent of God and doing His work.[28]

5.32. Many such messages were given by Vivekananda only three years prior to the partition of Bengal, and they were still fresh in the memories of the people. Aurobindo himself was inspired by Vivekananda's words, and he took the editor of the *Indian Patriot* to task "for forgetting the teachings of Vivekaṇanda. . . . What does he think was the cause of the great awakening in Bengal?"[29]

5.33. To the religious symbols which had assumed importance prior to Aurobindo's joining the anti-partition uprising, Aurobindo himself made a significant addition in the form of the "Kurukṣetra Battlefield". He presented this symbol on the title-page of his weekly journal *Karmayogin*. Although Tilak had already appealed to all Indians to consider the entire country as the new Kurukṣetra, the battlefield for Swarāj, a pictorial presentation of the Kurukṣetra Battlefield on the title-page of Aurobindo's weekly paper had a special appeal. The Kṛṣṇa-figure giving the Karma-yoga message to Arjuna provided an explanation as to why the journal itself was called *The Karmayogin*. Ursula King attaches great importance to Aurobindo's contribution in popularizing the Kurukṣetra picture as a religious symbol carrying a political message:

> This motif (a picture of Krishna at Kurukshetra) decorates the title page of Aurobindo's weekly review 'Karmayogin', published at the height of his political activity in Calcutta between 1909-10 and continued for some time, after his departure for Pondicherry, by Sister Nivedita. As the title explicitly states, the *Karmayogin* was 'A Weekly Review of National Religion, Literature, Science, Philosophy, etc. . . .'. Above the title is the picture of Krishna and Arjuna in a chariot, surrounded by Sanskrit quotations from the Bhagavad-Gītā referring, for example, to verses ii.50 ('Yoga is wisdom in work') and iii.30 ('Offer to me all thy works and rest thy mind on the Supreme'). Religious and political nationalism are closely intertwined in this review which preaches a new Karmayoga through the very effective vehicle of the ideal Karmayogin symbol.[30]

5.34. The activist message symbolized by the Kurukṣetra-title-page was explicitly and repeatedly stated by Aurobindo in the columns of his weekly journal *The Karmayogin*. A specimen of what he wrote is given below:

> The recurrent cry of Śrī Kṛṣṇa to Arjuna insists on the struggle: 'Fight and overthrow thy opponents !', 'Remember me and fight!'. . . The charioteer of Kurukshetra driving the car of Arjuna over that field of ruin is the image and description of Karmayoga; for the body is the chariot and the senses are the horses of the driving and it is through bloodshed and

mire-sunk ways of the world that Śrī Kṛṣṇa pilots the soul of man to Vaikuṇṭha.[31]

5.35. The appeal of the religious symbols turned out to be highly effective because the poetic and literary revolution in Bengal went hand in hand Aurobindo's spiritual fervour. Since Rabindranath Tagore was the greatest of all the patriotic poets in Bengali, Majumdar summarizes this simultaneous revolution in spiritualism and poetry, jointly serving the cause of nationalism:

> If Aurobindo was the high priest, Rabindranath was the great poet of the swadeshī movement. What Aurobindo achieved in the realm of thought by his fearless writings, Rabindranath conveyed to the masses by his songs, incomparable in diction and inimitable in the melody of its tune. . .
>
> The idea which had inspired Bankim Chandra to write the Bande Mātaram hymn, was expressed through the medium of charming poems and songs by Rabindranath. But Rabindranath did a great deal more. He sang the glories of ancient India and its culture and brought vividly before us the portraits of Shivājī and Guru Govinda Singh as nation-builders, and of Banda as a symbol of the stoic heroism. Many of his ballads touch upon the patriotism, chivalry and heroism of the Rājpūts and the struggle of the Marāṭhās and Sikhs for freedom. . .
>
> Aurobindo and Rabindranath proved that pen is mightier than the sword. . . . They are entitled to the chief credit for changing the swadeshī into a genuine national movement which swept the whole country.[32]

5.36. Before looking into the various elements that constituted Aurobindo's political activities as a Karmayogin, it may be appropriate to see how Aurobindo's entry into the Swadeshi movement has been perceived by Majumdar, the author of the *History of the Freedom Movement in India*:

> The chief traits of the new cult were enunciated, with something like a spiritual fervour, by Aurobindo Ghose who came to Bengal as the high priest of new nationalism shortly after the inauguration of the Swadeshi movement. These were:

(i) the elevation of patriotism into a religion, and transformation of religion into patriotism by conceiving the motherland not only as mother but as Supreme God whose service is the only way to salvation; and
(ii) belief in God as the leader of the movement, in complete freedom as the goal, and passive resistance as the method".[33]

These together with other details are presented in the next section.

POLITICAL ACTIVITIES AS A KARMAYOGIN

5.37. Even before Aurobindo came to Bengal from Baroda, to work whole-heartedly for the nationalist cause, the Congress was practically sub-divided (though not formally) into two groups, the Moderates and the Extremists. Gopal Krishna Gokhale was the recognized leader of the Moderates. On the Extremists side, three persons were the most prominent, namely, Bal Gangadhar Tilak, Lala Lajpat Rai, and Bipin Chandra Pal, and a popular abbreviated expression for the three together was "Lal-Bal-Pal". The differences between the two groups got accentuated over the issue of how to respond to the partition of Bengal. Boycott, Swadeshi, and national education constituted the core of the Extremists' approach, while the moderates were hesitant to go along with such "revolutionary" ideas that were so different from the policies followed by the Congress since its inception in 1885.

5.38. At the annual session of the Congress held at Banaras in December 1905, the differences between the two groups were somehow patched up because neither of them wanted an open split. (Such a split occurred at Surat in 1907.) Since Gokhale, the Moderate leader was Congress President at Banaras, the Extremist group got together, after the Congress session was over, and decided to form what they called a "Nationalist Party" within the Congress but determined to push forward its own radical programme. So, thereafter, the two terms "Extremists" and "Nationalists" practically became synonymous.

5.39. Throughout the year 1906, an acrimonious controversy was carried on by the spokesmen of the two groups, through their respective periodicals, as both looked forward to a decisive trial of strength in the forthcoming session of the Congress at Calcutta scheduled to be held in December 1906. However, public opinion seemed to be going the Extremists' way, and one of the factors responsible for bringing this about was the arrival of Aurobindo and his close association with the Nationalist journal "Bande Mātaram". Majumdar considers Aurobindo's joining the Nationalist movement as significant as the arrival of a "Prophet", and Karan Singh also calls Aurobindo "the Prophet of Indian Nationalism". Here are Majumdar's words:

> Above all, the Extremist party had an accession of immense strength when it was joined by Aurobindo, who proved to be a host in himself. Indeed the entry of this new personality in the Congress arena may be regarded as a major event in Indian politics. Aurobindo's articles in the Bande Mātaram put the Extremist party on a high pedestal all over India.He expounded the high philosophy and national spirit which animated the party, and also laid down its programme of action. But far more valuable to the Extremist party than even his discourses, was his striking personality. Fired with religious fervour, he preached nationalism as a religion, and he, the prophet of this new religion, infused by his precept and example, courage and strength into everyone that came in touch with him.[34]

5.40. The differences between the two groups lay in the specification of the political goal to be achieved as well as in the methods to be adopted for achieving it. Considering, first, the goal, the term "Swaraj" used by Tilak was generally accepted, but its interpretation was not the same. The Moderates viewed it as colonial self-government rather than complete independence. A common argument of the Moderates and their sympathizers was that, since Swaraj in any form is bound to be a long way off, the Extremists should accept colonial self-government as an interim goal at least, and retain the right to enlarge it to compete independence in due course of time. However, Aurobindo, voicing the revolutionary spirit of the Nationalists, characterized the "gradualism" of the Moderates as a sign of "fear", and viewed Swaraj as "the direct revelation of God to our people":

> Our ideal is that of swaraj or absolute autonomy free from foreign control. . . . There are some who fear to use the word 'freedom', but I always use it because it has been the mantra of my life to aspire towards the freedom of my nation. . . .
>
> Swaraj is the direct revelation of God to our people—not mere political freedom but a freedom vast and entire, freedom of the individual, freedom of the community, freedom of the nation, spiritual freedom, social freedom, political freedom. . . .
>
> Social freedom was part of the message of Buddha, Chaitanya, Nanak, Kabir, and the saints of Maharashtra. . . .
>
> Spiritual freedom the ancient Rishis declared to us, . . . but without political freedom the soul of man is crippled . . . If political freedom is absent, the community has no great ends to follow. . . . A slave can never be noble and broad-minded. He cannot forget himself in the service of his fellows. . . he cannot be "sarvabhūtahite ratah" or one whose mind is full of the will to do good to others. . . .[35]

It must be mentioned that the Sanskrit phrase "sarvabhūtahite ratah" is from the Gītā.

5.41. Considering, next, the methods to be adopted for achieving the goal, the Moderates believed that considerable progress was possible under the aegis of the British rule itself, because "the weakest links in the chain are our own incapacity and disunity".[36] The Moderates therefore favoured the spread of Western education, a larger share in jobs carrying greater and greater responsibility, removal of evil customs by reforming public opinion if possible and by legislation if necessary, and other peaceful methods of the same type. The Extremists scornfully described the method of petition as mendicancy, and Aurobindo strongly argued why the Moderates' method was bound to be infructuous, for the British administration would never sacrifice its vital interests which the uplift of India necessarily involved. Aurobindo characterized social reform, educational reform, industrial expansion, and all attempts towards the moral improvement of the race "without aiming first and foremost at political freedom", as "the very height of ignorance and futility".[37]

5.42. With a view to deriving political advantage from the revolutionary enthusiasm generated among the people because of the partition of Bengal, the Extremists emphasized the methods of boycott, Swadeshi, national education, and passive resistance. Detailed considerations on these brought to the forefront two related issues, namely, (i) whether the Indian society at that time had the capacity to implement these methods, and (ii) what view to take about the likelihood of violence erupting because of the use of these methods? Needless to say, the attitudes of the Moderates and the Extremists were wide apart, in all these matters. The Moderates strongly felt that it was the best policy at that time to continue the time-honoured method of constitutional agitation. Passive resistance and boycott, according to them, were impracticable, and more in the nature of propaganda than reality. As Gokhale put it:

> We owe it to the best interests of the country to resist this propaganda with all our resources. It means the sure destruction, or at any rate, the indefinite postponement of all these opportunities for slow but peaceful progress which are at present within our reach.[38]

5.43. The Extremists did not try to meet the specific arguments of the Moderates for they too knew that the public at large was not yet ready for radical measures. However, the Extremists believed that it was time they should come to regard politics more seriously and as part of their religion, with " the power of faith and will which neither counts obstacles nor measures time".[39] To Aurobindo, any talk of assessing possibilities of success or failure, or of counting losses and gains, as suggested by the Moderates, was a sign of weakness and insincerity. Using the simile of "a demon attacking my mother", he asked: "If a demon sits on the breasts of my mother and is about to drink her blood, shall I sit idle and coldly calculate whether I have the strength enough to fight it? My only duty is to rush to the rescue of my mother". "In a similar spirit", he observed, "the Indians should approach the political question—their prime duty was to save the Motherland. It was for them to rush headlong to achieve this goal without pausing to think of its probable success or failure".[40]

5.44. To Aurobindo, boycott was a part of passive resistance. The first principle of passive resistance, according to him, was to make administration under existing conditions impossible by an organised refusal to do anything which would help either British commerce in the exploitation of the country or British officialdom in the administration of it. Such boycott he wanted to apply to educational institutions as well because of their anti-national character and discouragement of patriotism. His plan, if accepted by Congress, would ask all countrymen to:

> refuse to send children to Government schools or to schools aided and controlled by the Government. . . . Refuse also to have any resort to the alien courts of justice. . . . Refuse similarly to go to the executive for help or advice or protection,. . . and ultimately, refuse to pay taxes.[41]

5.45. Aurobindc knew that even to think of any programme of passive resistance presupposed strength and fearlessness or what in the Hindu tradition were referred to as Kṣatriya-like qualities. To carry on a fight for independence, he said, we have to be guided by Kṣatriya-morality rather than Brahmin-morality, and also avoid any confusion between the two: "Politics is the ideal of the Kṣatriya, and the morality of the Kṣatriya ought to govern our political actions. To impose in politics the Brahmanical duty of saintly sufferance is to preach varṇa-saṁkara (or confusion)".[42]

5.46. While appealing for public cooperation, the Extremists made it clear that sacrifice would be an important element in the quest for freedom. They turned to the religious concept of yajña (sacrifice) and related it to the political plane. Just as offerings put into the sacrificial fire bear fruit only if they are pure and dedicated to the Deity with full faith and devotion, Aurobindo wanted his countrymen to be ready to sacrifice their all—even lives—in the struggle for freedom:

> Liberty is the fruit we seek from the sacrifice, and the Motherland, the Goddess to whom we offer it; into the seven leaping tongues of the fire of the yajña we must offer all that we are and all that we have, feeding the fire even with our blood and lives and happiness of our nearest and dearest; for the Motherland is a Goddess who loves not a maimed and imperfect sacrifice, and freedom was never won from the gods by a grudging giver.[43]

5.47. Although the religious nature of the sacrifice was intended to provide justification for the people to "offer all that they have" in the case of freedom, Aurobindo also justified the "battle" itself, and the use of "any and every means of self-preservation".[44] For this purpose, Aurobindo made extensive use of the Gītā. The national struggle was another Kurukṣetra, a righteous war against the British imperialists. Aurobindo exhorted all Indians to draw from the Gītā the inspiration to fight, and thus to fulfil their dharma in the battle for freedom: "The Gītā is the best answer to those who shrink from battle as a sin and aggression as a lowering of morality.[45]

> To shrink from bloodshed and violence under such circumstances is a weakness deserving as severe a rebuke as Śrī Kṛṣṇa addressed to Arjuna when he shrank from the colossal civil slaughter on the field of Kuruskṣetra. Liberty is the life-breath of a nation, and when the life is attacked, when it is sought to suppress all chances of breathing by violent pressure, any and every means of self-preservation becomes right and justifiable—just as it is lawful for a man who is being strangled to rid himself of the pressure on his throat by any means in his power.[46]

5.48. Aurobindo also helped organize, through his younger brother, Barindra, "secret societies with revolutionary intentions" for what are sometimes referred to as "terrorist activities". Ironically, members of these societies often carried with themselves copies of the Bhagavad-Gītā and selected writings of Vivekananda. Lizelle Raymond has described Barindra's role in this context in the following words:

> Barindra's work in Bengal was the organization in the villages—even the most remote—of a chain of Samitis, or youth organizations, which would meet under all kinds of pretexts, but with the real aim of providing a civic and political education and opening the eyes of the young to the 'affairs of the nation'. . . In smoky little grain shops, on the terraced roofs of private houses, young men would meet to hear about the lives of Mazzini and Garibaldi, to read exhortations from Swami Vivekananda, to listen to the warlike incidents of the Mahābhārata and to comments on the Bhagavad-Gītā. The number of samitis increased daily.[47]

5.49. V. Subramaniam considers "the expectation of immediate results" as a serious weakness of the violent revolutionaries in India. Militarily, the British administration was too strong to be shaken up by stray incidents of bomb-throwing. Aurobindo himself realized by 1910 the limitations of violent methods of political action, in the circumstances then prevailing in the country. In Karan Singh's words:

> Terrorist outrages were on the increase in 1909 as the Government had succeeded in stifling the Nationalist party, the one political body which offered a legal and peaceful outlet for the people's resentment. Government repression was also on the increase. In the *Karmayogin* Sri Aurobindo commented on the shooting and assassinations, and laid the blame squarely on the Government's repressive policy. Finally he came to the conclusion that as the Nationalists were powerless to stem the rising tide of terrorism sweeping over Bengal, they could only suspend their own strictly lawful and peaceful activities and let the Government deal as best as it could with the situation that its own policies had inexorably created. Thus on February 5, 1910, he wrote in the *Karmayogin*: 'We advise our fellow Nationalists also to stand back and give an unhampered course for a while to Anglo-Indian statesmanship in its en-deavours to grapple with this hydra-headed evil.[48]

5.50. Aurobindo's political activities as a karmayogin were marked by spiritualism, but the fine balance of political and spiritual elements could not be indefinitely maintained. When the spiritual element in Aurobindo's thinking became predominant, the importance that he had attached to current political problems abruptly receded. Karan Singh has analysed how the rising tide of spiritualism swept aside Aurobindo's interest in political activities:

> Aurobindo's whole concept of political action and theory was based on his spiritual vision, which did not desert him even in the midst of the most extreme and turbulent political controversies of the day. Then came the Surat session and his meeting with Lele, which marked a considerable advance in his spiritual practices and experiences. Soon after came his year of enforced seclusion at Alipur, where it seems that the spiritual tendencies and powers latent in his psyche rose with a dramatic upsurge to the surface. It is in the very nature of the spiritual call that it is imperative and overriding, and if it develops inevitably dominates the mind of the seeker to the virtual exclusion of other activities.[49]

IMPORTANCE OF LOKASAṀGRAHA IN "ESSAYS ON THE GĪTĀ"

5.51. Aurobindo's *Essays on the Gītā* belongs to the Pondicherry phase. These essays present a new interpretation of the Gītā, based on new ideas associated with Purushottama, Prakriti, and Sat-Chit-Ananda. For example, to begin with "Purushottama", Aurobindo attaches special importance to the fifteenth chapter of the Gītā which speaks of "Three Purushas" namely, the Kshara, the Akshara and the Purushottama:

> The idea of the Purushottama has been prepared, alluded to, adumbrated, assumed even from the beginning, but it is only now in the fifteenth chapter that it is expressly stated and the distinction illuminated by a name. . . .
>
> The Purushottama is the Lord in the Kshara (the mutable). He is in the heart of every creature and is manifested in his countless Vibhūtis. The Kshara, the personal, the Purusha

self-subjected to Prakriti, is only one aspect of the Purushottama.
Another aspect of the Purushottama is the Akshara, the impersonal, the inactive, the immutable Self of all . . .

The Purushottama is both Akshara and Kshara, and yet he is "other"—the third—because he is more and greater than either of these opposites. . . .

The seventeenth verse of the fifteenth chapter is the key-word of the Gītā's reconciliation of these two—Kshara and Akshara—apparently opposite aspects of our existence. The Gītā uses the expression "anya" meaning "the other", and says: But other than these two is that highest spirit called the supreme Self who enters the three worlds and upbears them, the imperishable Lord.

5.52. A practically significant implication (in terms of continued action) which results from viewing the Purushottama as "greater than the Akshara", has been stressed by Aurobindo in the following words:

When pursued through the Akshara alone, any attempt at liberation would become the seeking of the Indefinable, the Actionless, a thing hard for our nature embodied as we are here in Matter. . . . The Purushottama is the supreme Lord, Parameshwara, no aloof and unrelated Indefinable, but the origin and father and mother and first foundation and eternal abode of self and cosmos and Master of all existences and enjoyer of askesis and sacrifice. . . . The Purushottama is the cosmic spirit in Time and it is he that gives the command to the divine action of the liberated human spirit.[51]

5.53. The doctrine of three Purushas (rather than two) has been further extended by Aurobindo, on the authority of the seventh chapter of the Gītā, in such a way as to include the doctrine of two Prakritis (rather than one):

The opening verses of the seventh chapter initiate ideas that occupy all the rest of the book. . . . The Gītā makes that deep and momentous distinction which is the practical basis of all its Yoga, the distinction between the two Natures, the phenomenal Nature and the spiritual Nature. . . . The phenomenal Nature, called "aparā prakriti" or "lower nature" in the fifth verse, is the Sānkhya Prakriti of the three guṇas—sattva, rajas, tamas.

The spiritual Nature is designated by Śrī Kṛṣṇa, in the same verse, as "parā prakritirme" or "My supreme nature" . . . . And this "I" here is the Purushottama, the supreme Being, the supreme soul, the transcendent and universal spirit. The original and eternal nature of the Spirit and its transcendent and originating Shakti is what is meant by the Parā Prakriti. For speaking first of the origin of the world from the point of view of the active power of his Nature, Kṛṣṇa assevers, 'This is the womb of all beings', etad yonīni bhūtāni. (VII.6) And in the next line of the couplet, again stating the same fact from the point of view of the originating Soul, he continues, 'I am the birth of the whole world and so too its dissolution; there is nothing else supreme beyond Me. (VII.6-7) Here then the supreme Soul, Purushottama, and the supreme Nature, Parā Prakriti, are identified: they are put as two ways of looking at one and the same reality . . . The Spirit is the supreme Being in his infinite consciousness and the supreme Nature is the infinity of power or will of being of the Spirit.[52]

5.54. Aurobindo's views on Parā Prakriti as the infinite timeless conscious power of the self-existent Being, out of which all existences in the cosmos are manifested and come out of timelessness into Time, represent a synthesis of the Vedāntic concept of Sat-Chit-Ananda and the Tāntric concept of the Divine Mother or Shakti. In Aurobindo's harmonizing approach, "Chit" or consciousness is referred to as "chit-shakti" or consciousness-force, and the importance attached thereto is highlighted by Joan Price:

> Perhaps one of the most outstanding features of Sri Aurobindo's philosophy is the importance he places upon chit-shakti, the Divine Mother of the original Tāntric philosophy. . . . By this affirmation of Consciousness with Force, Śrī Aurobindo avoids absolute idealism. . . .
>
> Chit-Shakti is the Mother Force (feminine principle). . . . Because of the "Time" movement of the Consciousness-

> Force, the timeless eternal co-exists with the multiplicity of forms which are subject to time. . . . Chit-Shakti is beyond the three guṇas of the lower prakriti; it stands above the worlds and links the creation to the ever unmanifest. . . . It creates all these beings and contains and enters, supports and conducts all these million processes and forces, embodies the powers of these and makes them living and near to us.[53]

5.55. According to Aurobindo's interpretation, the main message of the Gītā, founded upon the concepts of Purushottama and Parā Prakriti, is irrevocably linked with action performed for purposes of lokasaṁgraha. Aurobindo summarizes this messages as a call from Śrī Kṛṣṇa to Arjuna in the following words:

> I am the eternal worker within you and I ask of you works. I demand of you not a passive consent to a mechanical movement of Nature from which in your self you are wholly separated, indifferent and aloof, but action complete and divine, done as the willing and understanding instrument of the Divine, done for God in you and others and for the good of the world. This action I propose to you, first no doubt as a means of perfection in the supreme spiritual Nature, but as a part too of that perfection. Action is part of the integral knowledge of God and of his greater mysterious truth and of an entire living in the Divine; action can and should be continued even after perfection and freedom are won.[54]

5.56. Although the Lokasaṁgraha-oriented action founded upon Purushottama and Parā Prakriti constitutes an important part of Aurobindo's interpretation of the Gītā, it is necessary to look into some of his other ideas as well. For example, Aurobindo explains why, in his opinion, the famous verse of the second chapter "Thou hast a right to action, but none to the fruits of action" is "only a preliminary word governing the first state of the disciple when he begins ascending the hill of Yoga":

> For the Gītā goes on to affirm emphatically that the man is not the doer of the action; it is Prakriti, it is Nature, it is the great Force with its three modes of action that works through him, and he must learn to see that it is not he who does the

work. Therefore the "right to action" is an idea which is only valid so long as we are still under the illusion of being the doer; it must necessarily disappear from the mind like the claim to the fruit, as soon as we cease to be to our own consciousness the doer of our works. All pragmatic egoism, whether of the claim to fruits or of the right to action, is then at an end.[55]

5.57. When Aurobindo characterizes "the call to action as a right" only a preliminary teaching of the Gītā, it does not imply that he is encouraging inaction. In fact, he attaches great importance to the activism of the Gītā which so strongly modifies the quietistic tendencies of the Sānkhya as well as of the old metaphysical Vedānta. Aurobindo quotes Śrī Kṛṣṇa's warning given in the third chapter of the Gītā, to the effect that none can stand even for a moment without doing work because everyone is made to do action helplessly by the modes born of Prakriti. He compares this teaching of the Gītā with that of the Tāntric Shaktas:

> The strong perception of the great cosmic action and the eternal activity and power of the cosmic energy, which was so much emphasized afterwards by the teaching of the Tāntric Shaktas who even made Prakriti or Shakti superior to Purusha, is a very remarkable feature of the Gītā. Although here an undertone, it is still strong enough, coupled with what we might call the theistic and devotional elements of its thought, to bring in that activism which so strongly modifies in its scheme of Yoga the quietistic tendencies of the old metaphysical Vedānta. Man embodied in the natural world cannot cease from action, not for a moment, not for a second; his very existence here is an action; the whole universe is an act of God, mere living even is His movement.[56]

5.58. Recognising that action cannot be avoided, Aurobindo discusses the relative importance of the "the call of social duty" and "divine obligation in response to the call of God". Among those who emphasized the significance of duty, Aurobindo includes Bankim Chandra Chatterji, while among those who gave precedence to God's work, he referes to Buddha. Duty, according to Aurobindo, is a relative term depending on one's position in the society. If there is a conflict between one's duty and moral conscience, says Aurobindo, the latter commands unconditional obedience. The Gītā, as interpreted by Aurobindo, calls us to ascend to this higher plane, which is a 'supreme poise', leaving behind the mainly practical, and the purely ethical. This ascent leads to the 'Brahmanic consciousness'. The attainment of this consciousness is, according to Aurobindo, the meaning of rising beyond the three guṇas, or of becoming triguṇātīta. Aurobindo points to the carama śloka of the Gītā (XVIII.66) and says that the call to abandon all duties and take refuge in the Supreme alone, negates the importance of duties which society and custom demand from an individual. He writes:

> If that (refuge in the Supreme) can only be attained by renouncing works and life and all duties and the call is strong within us, then into the bonfire they must go, and there is no help for it. The call of God is imperative and cannot be weighted against any other considerations.[57]

Thomas sees in this statement a great personal meaning for Aurobindo. He abandoned what he considered as his dharma at one time and went to Pondicherry in obedience to a divine call to "take refuge in the Supreme alone".[58]

5.59. However, the call of God and the call of social duty need not pull in different directions. Confusion can be avoided, either if both the calls pull in the same direction, or if one surrenders to the call of God and devotes oneself whole-heartedly to the action enjoined thereby. To act with a right will, fixed in the One, aware of the one self in all and acting out of its equal serenity, not running about in different directions under the thousand impulses of one's superficial mental self—this is what the Gītā calls the Buddhi-yoga. Aurobindo describes the process by which Buddhi can be firmly fixed in the calm self-knowledge of the Purusha, mentioning also the need to take refuge in the Lord:

> It is the upward and inward orientation of the intelligent will that we must resolutely choose with a settled concentration

> and perseverence. . . This cannot be done perfectly by the act of the intelligence itself, by a merely mental discipline; it can only be done by Yoga with something which is higher than itself and in which calm and self-mastery are inherent. And this Yoga can only arrive at its success by devoting, by consecrating, by giving up the whole self to the Divine, "to Me, "says Krishna; for the Liberator is within us, but it is not our mind, nor our intelligence, nor our personal will, —they are only instruments. It is the Lord in whom, as we are told in the end, we have utterly to take refuge. And for that we must at first make him the object of our whole being and keep in soul-contact with him. This is the sense of the phrase "he must sit firm in Yoga, wholly given up to Me". (II.61)[59]

5.60. After describing how the Yoga of the intelligent will culminate in the Brahmic status, Aurobindo devotes a good deal of attention to yajña and the "eternal connecting truth of God and the world and works", which also helps him explain the special significance of Purushottama. Aurobindo's contention is that, if the sacrifice were to be offered to the "impersonal Brahman", then there is a risk that works may be reduced to a minimum and the nature of the works may not receive the attention it deserves. On the other hand, if the sacrifice is offered to Purushottama, then there is a positive sanction for continuance in works, and the nature of the action also matters, with the result that the concept of Lokasaṁgraha comes to the forefront. This comparison between the sacrifice offered to the impersonal Brahman and that offered to Purushottama, is brought out in two successive paragraphs:

> The impersonal Brahman has no activity and no desires, no object to be gained, no dependence for anything on all this world of creatures; it exists for itself, in its own self-delight, in its own immutable eternal being. We may have to do works without desire as a means in order to reach this impersonal self-existence and self-delight, but, that movement once executed, the object of works is finished; the sacrifice is no longer needed. Works may even then continue because Nature continues, ... but then, works may well be whittled down and reduced to a minimum,. . . . and the nature of the

works also does not matter. . . .

But the Gītā insists that the nature of the action does matter and that there is a positive sanction for continuance in works, not only that one quite negative and mechanical reason, the objectless compulsion of Nature. There is still, after the ego has been conquered, a divine Lord and enjoyer of the sacrifice, and there is still an object in the sacrifice. . . Therefore, through the Impersonal, we have to arrive at the Purushottama, and he in his divine greatness possesses both the Akshara and the Kshara. He manifests himself in the movement and in all the action of cosmic Nature; to him even after liberation the sacrifice of works in Nature continues to be offered.[60]

5.61. Aurobindo believes that, for understanding the basis of the Gītā's philosophy of divine works, the Lokasaṁgraha—related verses of the third chapter are probably the most important. He translates Lokasaṁgraha as the holding together of the peoples. In his view, "this great march of the peoples towards a far-off divine ideal has to be held together, prevented from falling into the bewilderment, confusion and utter discord of the understanding which would lead to dissolution and destruction and to which the world moving forward in the night or dark twilight of ignorance would be too easily prone if it were not held together, conducted, kept to the great lines of its discipline by the illumination, by the strength, by the rule and example, by the visible standard and the invisible influence of its Best. The best, the individuals who are in advance of the general line and above the general level of the collectivity, are the natural leaders of mankind, for it is they who can point to the race both the way they must follow and the standard or ideal they have to keep to or to attain. But the divinised man is the Best is no ordinary sense of the word and his influence, his example must have a power which that of no ordinarily superior man can exercise. What example then shall he give? What rule or standard shall he uphold?"[61]

5.62. In order to indicate more perfectly his meaning, the divine Teacher, the Avatāra gives his own example, his own standard. Aurobindo says that the giving of the example of God himself to the liberated man is profoundly significant:

> The liberated man is he who has exalted himself into the divine nature and according to that divine nature must be his actions. But what is the divine nature ? It is not entirely and solely that of the Akshara, the immobile, inactive, impersonal self; for that by itself would lead the liberated man to actionless immobility. It is not characteristically that of the Kshara, the multitudinous, the personal, the Purusha self-subjected to Prakriti; for that by itself would lead him back into subjection to his personality and to the lower nature and its qualities. It is the nature of the Purushottama who holds both these together and by his supreme divinity reconciles them in a divine reconciliation which is the highest secret of his being, rahasyam hyetad uttamaṁ.[62]

5.63. Aurobindo attaches great importance to bhakti, "the love and adoration of the Purushottama", its role being to "rear the spirit towards some greatest highest perfection"—founded on the base of "equality, desirelessness and freedom of spirit".[63] Referring to the characteristics of the bhakta, as given in chapter XII of the Gītā, Aurobindo writes:

> Several formulas of this fundamental equal consciousness are given here. First, an absence of egoïsm, of I-ness and myness, nirmamo nirahaṁkāraḥ. The bhakta of the Purushottama is one who has a universal heart and mind which has broken down all the narrow walls of the ego. A universal love dwells in his heart, a universal compassion flows from it like an encompassing sea. He will have friendship and pity for all beings and hate for no living thing: for he is patient, long-suffering, enduring, a well of forgiveness. A desireless content is his, a tranquil equality to pleasure and pain, suffering and happiness, the steadfast control of self and the firm unshakable will and resolution of the Yogin and a love and devotion which gives up the whole mind and reason to the Lord, to the Master of his consciousness and knowledge. Or, simply, he will be one who is freed from the troubled agitated lower nature and from its waves of joy and fear and anxiety and resentment and desire, a spirit of calm by whom the world

is not afflicted or troubled, nor is he afflicted or troubled by the world, a soul of peace with whom all are at peace.[64]

5.64. Harmonizing karma, Bhakti and Jñāna, Aurobindo summarizes "the Message of the Gītā" as being a call centred on "Lokasaṁgraha":

> All becomes here by the power of the Spirit; all do their works by the immanence of God in things and his presence in the heart of every creature. The Creator of the worlds is not limited by his creations; the Lord of works is not bound by his works; the divine Will is not attached to its labour: for it is omnipotent, all-possessing and all-blissful. But still the Lord looks down on his creations from his transcendence; he descends as the Avatara; he is here in you; he rules from within all things in the steps of their nature. And you too must do works in him after the way and in the steps of the divine nature untouched by limitation, attachment or bondage. Act for the best good of all, act for the maintenance of the march of the world, for the support or the leading of its peoples. The action asked of you is the action of the liberated Yogin; it is the spontaneous output of a free God-held energy, it is an equal-minded movement, it is a selfless and desireless labour.[65]

5.65. Aurobindo is very particular about the spiritual attainment of any person who, according to his understanding of the Gītā, can really do acts for Lokasaṁgraha. As Betai summarizes Aurobindo's views on this topic, acts for real Lokasaṁgraha can be done only by a *muktātmā* or a liberated soul who has no egoism and who has gone beyond the three guṇas.[66] Aurobindo uses the term 'divine activity' for such acts. A *mumukṣu* or one who is still struggling to attain spiritual heights can, at the most, perform sāttvika karma but not the full karma-yoga of Aurobindo's interpretation. Aurobindo does not deny the practical importance of sāttvika karma, but he insists that the teaching of the Gītā goes beyond disinterested performance of duty. He clarifies this by means of giving examples of *muktātmā's*: "The Gītā teaching means the following of the divine life. The abandonment of all Dharmas, Sarvadharmān, to take refuge in the supreme alone, and the divine activity of a Buddha, a Ramakrishna, a Vivekananda is perfectly in consonance with this teaching".[67]

SOCIAL ASPECTS OF INTEGRAL YOGA, SUPERMIND, AND SPIRITUAL EVOLUTION

5.66. The ideas contained in *Essays on the Gītā* were extended by Aurobindo, in the light of his own Sādhanā, culminating in the formulation of his theory of Spiritual Evolution, in which the concept of Supermind has a crucial role. He also developed a new technique, called integral Yoga, or Pūrṇa Yoga, by means of which the Yogī rises to the Supra-mental plane and then descends back to the material plane to help others achieve a similar Spiritual Evolution as quickly as possible. Aurobindo wrote volumes to explain these and related ideas. For purposes of the present study, a selective approach has been adopted, with a view to showing that the Integral yoga of Aurobindo has important social implications, because Aurobindo had specifically stated the main objectives of his "quest for the truth" to include "the application of our ideas to the problems of man's social and collective life".[68]

Spiritual Evolution

5.67. In an attempt to give a brief and simple account of Aurobindo's theory of Spiritual Evolution, the Vedāntic concept of Brahman as the Omnipresent Reality can be viewed as the foundation. Accordingly, all this, both spirit and matter, is Brahman. Aurobindo accepts the three attributes of the Omnipresent Reality denoted by Sat-Chit-Ananda, but he brings in the Tāntric principle of Shakti to modify Chit as Chit-Shakti. The nature of the Reality is thus the transcendent Absolute manifesting itself as a universal Conscious-Force and creating individual multiplicities out of self-delight. And this is the reality that humanity is—the cause and aim of growth and creativity, as Aurobindo puts it:

> As the poet, artist or musician, when he creates, does really nothing but develop some potentiality in his unmanifested self into a form of manifestation, and as the thinker, statesman, mechanist only bring out into shape of things that which lay

> hidden in themselves, was themselves, is still themselves when it is cast into form, so is it with the world and the eternal.[69]

5.68. All creation or becoming, according to Aurobindo, is this self-manifestation. The Infinite Being emerges in the appearance of the finite soul, the Infinite Consciousness emerges in the appearance of a limited consciousness. Mind, Life and Body are an inferior consciousness and a partial expression. Aurobindo uses the term "Involution" to denote the emergence of Matter out of Spirit, and the process leading the Matter back to its source of origin—the spirit—is the the "Spiritual Evolution" Aurobindo views it as a continuation of the "Biological Evolution" which has seen the emergence of Life out of Matter, and of Mind out of Life. Whereas the Biological Evolution was a slow, natural process, Aurobindo believes that the Spiritual Evolution could be expedited by human effort. The special feature of Aurobindo's theory of Spiritual Evolution is the anticipated emergence of Supermind out of Mind. As Karan Singh puts it:

> The advent of the human race (in which Mind has a dominating role) is by no means the final phase of evolution. In fact it is an intermediate stage, and mankind is now poised on the threshold of the next leap forward in the evolutionary process. This step is the evolution of mind to Supermind, the luminous realm of Truth-Consciousness, which will be a development even more profound than the preceding step from animal to human consciousness.[70]

Ascent from Mind to Supermind

5.69. Since the upliftment of the mind to the Supramental level is the key to understand Aurobindo's theory of Spiritual Evolution, it is necessary to understand the main elements underlying such an upliftment. The most important difference between mind and Supermind is in the manner of apprehending Reality. While Supermind essentially gets a unitary picture of Reality, mind tends to break and cut asunder a whole into its parts. Since mind, by its very nature, must analyze everything in terms of its component parts, it is unable, in Aurobindo's view, to know Reality which is partless, indivisible and essentially one. Sometimes even mental awareness claims to have known objects in their wholeness. However, this is the result of a two-step process-first, breaking the original unity of the object of knowledge, and secondly, trying to synthesize the broken parts again into a whole. Such a 'whole' will look artificial, it cannot, according to Aurobindo, restore the original unity of the object.

5.70. But this difference between mind and Supermind itself, says Aurobindo, is a pointer to the fact that mind is nothing but an urge to realise the Supramental level. Even the fragmentary knowledge that it has, is possible on account of the fact that the spiritual aspect of Supermind is already present in mind. It is because Supermind has already descended into mind, that mind is capable of spiritual activities, howsoever fragmentary such activities might be. Mind has an inherent tendency to go beyond itself, an inherent urge to rise higher. Moreover, even when it analyses and dissects the objects of its awareness, it at once feels the need of organizing it back into a whole. All these are examples of spiritual activities and that shows that Supermind is somehow already present in the mind. That is why Aurobindo says that mind is actually a fall from Supermind. This fall or involution is, according to him, a necessary condition of creation, because it represents the descent of the Spirit. That makes it a precondition of evolution also, the most significant stage of which is the upliftment of mind to Supermind.

5.71. This transition of mind to Supermind is not abrupt or sudden. Mind, after all, belongs to the "lower level" (along with life and matter) while Supermind belongs to the "higher level" (along with Sat-Chit-Ananda). Aurobindo also uses the terms "lower hemisphere" and "higher hemisphere". Generalizing from his own experience, Aurobindo has mentioned four intermediary stages in the ascent from mind to Supermind, namely, Higher mind, Illumined mind, Intuitive mind, and Overmind. Each of these stages is marked with a progressive heightening and widening of consciousness, and a gradual replacement of the "imperfect reasoning intellect" by intuition and direct cognition of Reality. The ascent is a slope, not a staircase, because the various stages interpenetrate and modify one another, in a manner that cannot be appreciated by mere logic.

5.72. In the Higher mind, which marks the first stage on the ascent from mind to Supermind, Aurobindo envisages a recognition of the limited role of logic and rationality, and their replacement by "spirit-born conceptual knowledge". In the Higher mind, according to Aurobindo, there is no need of the analytical activities that mind normally performs, no logical motion step by step towards a conclusion, no mechanism of expressed or implied deductions and inferences—in short, no longer any need for this limping action of our reason, which pertains to the realm of ignorance. Higher mind is a self-aware activity towards integration, and Aurobindo describes its most characteristic movement as a "mass ideation"—a seeing of the inner relation of ideas with ideas. This is the initial attempt to break away from the bondage of logic and rational analysis and to enter into the realm of the ideal, or "higher thought" as Aurobindo calls it.

5.73. The next stage in the ascent from mind to Supermind is the Illumined mind which seeks to know Reality primarily by vision, and not by thought. Aurobindo attributes greater perceptual power to "inner sight" and "inner light" than to "thought":

> A consciousness that proceeds by sight, the consciousness of the seer, is a greater power of knowledge than the consciousness of the thinker. The perceptual power of the inner sight is greater and more direct than the perceptual power of thought . . . As the Higher mind brings a greater consciousness into the being through the spiritual Idea and its power of Truth, so the illumined mind brings in a still greater consciousness through a Truth-sight and Truth-light and its seeing and seizing power.[71]

5.74. Still greater than the power of vision is the power of "intuition", and so the next stage in the ascent from mind to Supermind is designated by Aurobindo as the Intuitive mind.

Aurobindo views Intuition as the beginning of real knowledge since it brings messages from the higher or spiritual realm.

When the consciousness of the subject meets with the consciousness in the object, it sees, feels and vibrates with the knowledge of that which it contacts. Intuition, according to Aurobindo, has a fourfold power—a power of revelatory Truth-seeing, a power of inspiration or Truth-hearing, a power of Truth-touch or immediate seizing of significance, and a power of true and automatic discrimination of the orderly and exact relation of truth to truth. Such a description of the power of intuition is reminiscent of what the Vedic Rishis had when they uttered the essence of the Vedāntic Truth. Aurobindo views Intuition as being capable of performing all the functions of reason and intelligence, with the difference that its grasp of the Reality is direct and immediate, and not dependent on any intermediate element as in reason. Aurobindo sees in Intuition the beginning of the process of Integration.

5.75. The process of ascent from mind to Supermind—or the vertical ascent, as in a graphic picture—is practically complete at the stage of the Intuitive mind. However, two more features are still needed before the Intuitive mind attains the status of the Overmind, which, according to Aurobindo, is "the highest power of the lower hemisphere". One of these two features adds to the vertical ascent "a vast horizontal expansion of consciousness so as to make it cosmic". Consequently, the knowledge of the Overmind becomes global, by going beyond the representations of consciousness in particular centres. As Aurobindo puts it: "The Overmind takes up all that is in the three steps below it and raises their characteristic works to their highest and largest power, adding to them a universal wideness of consciousness and force, a harmonious concert of knowledge, a more manifold delight of being".[72]

5.76. The second special feature of the Overmind is that it is in direct contact with the Supermind and hence is capable of receiving the light from the Supreme Truth-Consciousness. Aurobindo believes that mental effort alone, unaided by higher powers wherefrom spiritual light descends, cannot attain pure knowledge. No such barrier affects the Overmind, which, because of its closeness to Supermind, receives the light from above and thus establishes the real link between the lower hemisphere and the higher hemisphere. Taking into account both the special features mentioned above, a very special status is assigned to the Overmind which is described by Aurobinbo as a 'super-conscient cosmic mind in direct contact with the supramental consciousness.'[73]

5.77. The final leap from the Overmind to the Supermind is associated with the capability of apprehending the Supreme Truth—the Absolute—as a unity, which is also called 'the Integral view' by Aurobindo. Since Overmind is the highest stage in the lower hemisphere, it has all other features of Supramental consciousness, the only limitation being that the Overmind views every power of the Supreme 'as a separate reality' rather than the Unity lying behind it. Aurobindo illustrates the distinction between the 'separatist view' and the 'Integral view' by using the concepts of Prakriti and Purusha. While, to the Overmind, Prakriti and Purusha appear as irreconcilable and separate realities, they give way to a vision of Unity in the Integral knowledge that the Supermind has of the essentially non-dual character of Reality. Aurobindo uses poetical imagery while describing the nature of Supramental consciousness:

> In the comprehensive knowledge of the Supermind, there is no independent centre of existence, no individual separated ego much as we see in ourselves—the whole of existence is to its self-awareness an equable extension, one in oneness, one in multiplicity, one in all conditions and everywhere.[74]

Integral Yoga

5.78. Aurobindo used the term 'Integral Yoga" or "Pūrṇa Yoga" to denote the technique by which one can ascend to the Supramental plane and then descend back to the material plane with a view to helping others achieve a similar Spiritual Evolution as quickly as possible. Two of the most striking features of this Yoga, according to Lal's analysis are:

(i) the specific inclusion of both ascent and descent and (ii) aiming at sarvamukti or the collective liberation of the mankind.[75] As Aurobindo puts it:

> Our Yoga is a double movement of ascent and descent, one rises to higher and higher levels of consciousness, but at the same time one brings down their power not only into mind and life, but in the end even into the body. And the highest of these levels, the one at which it aims is Supermind. Only when that can be brought down is a divine transformation possible in the earth consciousness.[76]

5.79. Regarding Aurobindo's goal of collective human liberation, Karan Singh remarks that although this view has affinity with the Bodhisattva doctrine of Mahāyāna Buddhism and the traditional Hindu doctrine of Jīvanmuktas or Siddhas, "it has seldom been so clearly put forward as the spiritual goal as in the theory of Śrī Aurobindo". [77] Calling this a "unique feature" of Aurobindo's yoga, Karan Singh argues why it is "stunning in its daring ambition and immensity":

> Aurobindo is emphatic that his Yoga is not merely directed towards individual salvation but is for humanity as a whole. Whereas traditional religions offered the devotee individual liberation from the bondage of material existence and a rise into the luminous spiritual sphere, Śrī Aurobindo insisted that the ascent was only one aspect of the whole spiritual adventure. Having ascended the Yogi must again come down so that he can help the mass of humanity, and indeed all matter in whatsoever form, to rise. Thus conceived, his Weltanschauung is stunning in its daring ambition and im-mensity. He sought not mere individual liberation, not liberation for the entire human race, not even liberation for all living beings, but nothing less than a complete transformation of material consciousness itself, the creation of 'a new heaven and a new earth.[78]

5.80. Aurobindo uses terms like Supermen or Supramental men or Gnostic beings to refer to persons who, after ascending to the Supramental plane, descend back to the material plane and participate in the efforts to establish the Divine life on earth. Obviously, the 'Supermen' practising Integral Yoga have no desire to exercise dominance over others like those who are called by the same title by Nietzshe. In order to avoid terminological confusion, the term 'Gnostic beings'—meaning 'Men of knowledge'—may be preferable to use. Basant Kumar Lal speaks of the ability of the Gnostic being to create harmonic unity with all beings:

> The Gnostic being would be the consummation of the spiritual man, his whole way of being, thinking, living and acting would be governed by the power of a universal spirituality. That is so on account of the nature of supermind itself, which is essentially unitary in character. Its consciousness is integral and therefore it would also harmonise and unify apparent diversities. That is why the Gnostic being will always have this sense of integral unity. This sense is so keen that the supramental Gnostic being will have not only this integral sense in his own inner or outer life, but would be able to create a harmonic unity even with the still surviving mental beings.[79]

5.81. Embree also highlights "Aurobindo's concern with the social results of mystical intuition", and points out how Spiritual evolution is intimately linked with problems of harmony:

> Aurobindo envisages that the achievement of the state of Divine Life would lead to an enriched order of humanity. In particular, he views problems of existence to be essentially problems of harmony. Aurobindo's concern with the social results of mystical intuition is in rather striking contrast with that of many other mystics. As man developed, he argues, he would become "acutely aware of the discord and ignorance that governs his relations with the world, acutely intolerant of it, more and more set upon finding a principle of harmony, peace, joy and unity.[80]

5.82. Joan Price views the Gnostic beings playing the important role of trying to transform the values of the entire world, and of acting as a free force with respect for truth and peace in society:

Śrī Aurobindo sees the gnostic way of living as the perfected life on earth; it is a way of living that develops instruments of knowledge and action in the world for a higher consciousness in physical nature and in doing this, transforms the values of the entire world. . . .

Acting as a free force with respect for truth, the gnostic being would live in peace; music, arts and crafts would be expressions of beauty and truth, the life and body would know the joy of purity and self-mastery. The divine life, insists Sri Aurobindo, is not what is usually thought of as ascetic, sterile and dull. . . A hidden sweetness and laughter in things, a sunshine and gladness of life are also powers and expressions of the Spirit.[81]

5.83. A practical demonstration of how a community might follow Aurobindo's ideals can be seen in the Auroville experiment—a few miles from the Aurobindo Āśrama in Pondicherry. A four-point Auroville Charter gives an idea of what this 'Cradle of a New World' stands for:

1. Auroville belongs to nobody in particular. Auroville belongs to humanity as a whole. But to live in Auroville one must be a willing servitor of the Divine Consciousness.
2. Auroville will be the place of an unending education, of constant progress and a youth that never ages.
3. Auroville wants to be the bridge between the past and the future. Taking advantage of all discoveries from without and from within, Auroville will boldly spring towards future realizations.
4. Auroville will be a site of material and spiritual researches for a living embodiment of an actual Human Unity.[82]

5.84. Karan Singh finds in Aurobindo's Integral Yoga, important elements of Karma, Bhakti, Jñāna and Rāja Yogas as well as some of Tāntric principles. Reddy has stated that, while Hatha-yoga elements are practically excluded, the principle of self-surrender plays a crucial role. Furthermore, in Reddy's opinion, the activities of Gnostic beings signify the fulfilment of the Lokasaṁgraha ideal of the Bhagavad-Gitā, perhaps in a modified form—the modification being that a Pūrṇa-yogin, while helping others, gives a higher priority to spiritual matters with a universal outlook, while a Karma-yogin begins with secular and Swadeshi needs and builds up, step by step. In Reddy's words:

> Aurobindo's synthesis almost leaves out the Haṭhayogic process, allows partial entry to the Rājayogic way and fully incorporates the triune path of Karma, Jñāna and Bhakti, laying full stress on the utilization of the powers of soul in mind. And this ideal is sought to be accomplished by the principle of self-surrender, a giving up of the whole of one's being and nature into the being, consciousness, force and delight of the Supreme. While the object of yoga ordinarily is liberation, or liberation and union of the individual soul with the Divine, and that of Haṭhyoga is liberation coupled with enjoyment of cosmic action, that of Pūrṇa Yoga is the threefold truth of liberation and integral union with the Divine, free and unfettered enjoyment of his cosmic manifestation and of participation and collaboration with the Divine in the fulfilment of the spiritual purpose of his manifestation in humanity and in Nature. In the words of Sri Aurobindo, "The individual yoga then turns from its separateness and becomes a part of the collective yoga of the divine Nature in the human race. The liberated individual being, united with the Divine in self and spirit, becomes in his natural being a self-perfecting instrument for the perfect outflowering of the Divine in humanity."... This we see in a seed-form in the Gītā's vision of the lokasaṁgraha dharma.[83]

5.85. Before closing this section, it would be of interest to consider the terminological question as to why Aurobindo's technique is called Integral Yoga or Pūrṇa Yoga. Basant Kumar Lal, quoting Aurobindo, has attributed this to two main considerations, namely,

(i) that important elements of practically all forms of yoga have been incorporated, and
(ii) that the aim is so comprehensive as to include all round and total development, and complete transformation of every aspect of being, and active participation in the spiritual Evolution of all mankind.[84]

ROLE OF THE BHAGAVAD-GĪTĀ

5.86. Aurobindo was initially inspired by Karma-yoga of the Gītā, and later he found therein substantial elements of Pūrṇa-yoga also. In spite of the possibilities of such a varied interpretation of the Gītā, there are certain basic ideas to which Aurobindo drew pointed attention, and one of them was Śrī Kṛṣṇa's teaching on the non-avoidability of action. As Aurobindo put it:

> In order to indicate more perfectly his meaning, the Divine Teacher, the Avatāra gives his own example, his own standard to Arjuna. "I abide in the path of action", He says, "the path that all men follow: thou too must abide in action.[85]

5.87. Since the Sannyāsa attitude of renouncing action was still prevalent in those days, Aurobindo clarified his own position, by first translating Śrī Kṛṣṇa's message as follows:

> O Son of Prithā, I have no work that I need to do in all the three worlds, I have nothing that I have not gained and have yet to gain, but I still abide verily in the paths of action—varta eva ca Karmaṇi", and then commenting:
>
> The Sanskrit word "eva" implies, I abide in it and do not leave it as the Sannyāsin thinks himself bound to abandon work.[86]

5.88. The principle of non-avoidability of action is further emphasized by Aurobindo with reference to the doctrines of three Purushas and two Prakritis—including Purushottama and Parā Prakriti—which according to Aurobindo are "the greatest contribution of the Gītā to Vedānta and without which the Gītā would be meaningless, full of contradictions, and would not be God's word to man".[87] If Akshara, the Immutable, the Actionless, were the goal, then the liberated person would seek renunciation of action. However, says Aurobindo:

> The Purushottama is greater than Kshara, the Mutable, as also greater than Akshara, the Immutable. The Purushottama is the Supreme Lord who enters the three worlds and upbears them. It is He that gives the command to the divine action

of the liberated human spirit.[88]

5.89. The "Parā Prakriti" of the Gītā is interpreted by Aurobindo as "the Spiritual Nature, the Supreme Nature", and is distinguished from "Aparā Prakriti" or "the Phenomenal Nature of the three guṇas—sattva, rajas, tamas". Actions of the liberated person who is beyond the three guṇas—are brought about by the Spiritual Nature, and so do not create any bondage to Saṁsāra. As Aurobindo puts it:

> The Supreme Soul, Purushottama, and the Supreme Nature, Parā Prakriti, are identified in the Gītā; they are put as two ways of looking at one and the same reality. The Spirit is the Supreme Being in his infinite consciousness, and the Supreme Nature is the infinity of power or will of being of the Spirit.[89]

5.90. According to Aurobindo's interpretation, the main message of the Gītā, founded upon the concepts of Purushottama and Parā Prakriti, is irrevocably linked with action performed for purposes of lokasaṁgraha. In Panikkar's opinion:

> Aurobindo's commentary is primarily a work of religion, but in view of the author's training and background it has had a wide social significance. It emphasized the ethical nature of the Gītā's teachings, and tore down mercilessly the obscurantist interpretation that polemical writers had given to its social message... This new interpretation won immediate recognition as a masterly exposition of the permanent truth of the Gītā in the context of modern life and in the language of modern thought."[90]

5.91. As a Karmayogin, Aurobindo joined the uprising against Bengal-partition, "as the high priest of new nationalism", "the chief traits of the new cult"—according to Majumdar, being:

(i) the elevation of patriotism into a religion and transformation of religion into patriotism by conceiving the motherland not only as Mother but as Supreme God whose service is the only way to salvation; and
(ii) belief in God as the Leader of the movement, in

complete freedom as the goal, and passive resistance as the method.[91]

5.92. To the religious symbols which had assumed importance prior to Aurobindo's joining the anti-partition uprising, Aurobindo himself made a significant addition in the form of the "Kurukṣetra Battlefield and Kṛṣṇa teaching Karmayoga to Arjuna." According to Ursula King:

> Religious and political nationalism are closely intertwined in Aurobindo's weekly 'Karmayogin' which preaches a new karmayoga through the very effective vehicle of the ideal Karmayogin symbol.[92]

5.93. In the Alipur jail, Aurobindo saw "in a vision", Śrī Kṛṣṇa placing the Gītā in his hands—and this proved to be the most momentous event of his life. This vision provided to Aurobindo, a teaching in the meaning of Svadharma and how to act as an instrument of God. Within a few months, his "inner voice" told him that the Divine power, acting through "a man who is to come" would eventually bring about India's political freedom, and further that his own Svadharma was to follow the spiritual path and to serve humanity thereby.[93] In Sarma's opinion:

> The importance of the mission of Śrī Aurobindo lies not so much in his restatement of the integral spiritual ideal taught in the Ṛg Veda, the early Upaniṣads and the Gītā, and his clearing the air of imperfect ideals like quietism, illusionism and asceticism, as in his actual practice of Pūrṇa Yoga. . .[94]

5.94. The Pūrṇa-Yoga or Integral Yoga of Aurobindo has important social implications because he had specifically stated the main objectives of his "quest for the truth" to include "the application of our ideas to the problems of man's social and collective life".[95] Integral Yoga, according to Lal, includes Sarvamukti or the collective liberation of the mankind.[96] In Reddy's opinion, Integral Yoga seeks to fulfil the lokasaṁgraha ideal of the Bhagavad-Gītā in a modified form—the modification being that a Pūrṇa-yogin, while helping other, gives a higher priority to spiritual matters, with a universal outlook, while a Karma-yogin begins with secular and Swadeshi needs and builds up, step by step. In Reddy's words:

> The Integral Yoga combines individual liberation with cosmic action, integrates realisation with transformation. . . . The individual Yoga then turns from its separateness and becomes a part of the collective Yoga of the divine Nature in the human race. The liberated individual being, united with the Divine in self and spirit, becomes in his natural being a self-perfecting instrument for the perfect outflowering of the Divine in humanity. This we see in a seed-form in the Gītā's vision of the lokasaṁgraha dharma.'[97]

Chapter Six

Gandhi: Adopting Ahiṁsā to Achieve Lokasaṁgraha and Satya

A BRIEF LIFE-SKETCH

6.1. Mohandas Karamchand Gandhi (or Gandhi for short) was born at Porbandar (Gujarat) on 2 October 1869. His father (Karamchand) was the Prime Minister of the small princely state of Porbandar, and later, also of two more neighbouring states of Rajkot and Vankaner. Gandhi's mother had a long-lasting influence on his life, and about the things that remained fresh in his memory, Gandhi wrote:

> The outstanding impression my mother has left on my memory is that of saintliness. She was deeply religious. She would not think of taking her meals without daily prayers. Going to Haveli—the Vaishnava temple—was one of her daily duties. . . To keep two or three consecutive fasts was nothing to her. . ..[1]

6.2. Gandhi's schooling till High School was mainly at Rajkot. Two plays—The Filial Love of Śravaṇa, and the Devotion to Truth of Harish Chandra—which Gandhi witnessed during his boyhood left an indelible impression on his mind. The reason why he called his autobiography as "The Story of my Experiments with Truth" can be traced back to the ideal which the legendary Harish Chandra upheld under all circumstances: As Gandhi himself says:

> To follow truth and to go through all the ordeals Harish Chandra went through was the one ideal it inspired in me. I literally believed in the story of Harish Chandra. The thought of it all often made me weep. My common sense

tells me today that Harish Chandra could not have been an historical character. Still both Harish Chandra and Śravaṇa are living realities for me, and I am sure I should be moved as before, if I were to read these plays again today.[2]

6.3. Among other influences of a religious nature, which started in Gandhi's early life and which are highlighted by him in his autobiography, "toleration for all branches of Hinduism and sister religions" is attributed to his father's close and friendly ties with Shiva worshippers as well as Jain monks.[3] Chanting God's name—or Rāmanāma—was taught to Gandhi by his nurse, Rambhā, and his father's illness provided to him an opportunity to listen to the Rāmāyaṇa. Sarma summarized (in 1944) Gandhi's recollections in the following words:

> When he was a child, his nurse taught him Rāmanāma (uttering God's name) to cure his fear of ghosts and spirits. The seed sown by that good woman was not lost, for Rāmanāma is still looked upon by Gandhiji as an infallible remedy for all the ills of life. The boy also listened to the reading of the Rāmāyaṇa of Tulsīdās in the presence of his father during his illness. Naturally he was profoundly impressed and has come to regard Tulsīdās's book even today as the greatest book in all devotional literature. Also at this time a Gujarati stanza gripped his mind and heart, especially its concluding lines (which can be translated as):
>
> "But the truly noble know all men as one,
> And return with gladness good for evil done."
>
> Its precept that one should return good for evil became thenceforth the guiding principle of his life.[4]

6.4. At the age of eighteen Gandhi went to England to study law, but only after he had taken three solemn oaths—to obtain clearance from his mother for going abroad—that he would not touch wine, woman and meat during his stay in England. Gandhi has described how a strong pressure was put on him by "a friend and well-wisher" to break the vows regarding meat and wine, and also how "peer pressure" put him on the track of "close companionship and marriage with an English girl, as so many Indian boys used to do". But, says Gandhi: "Daily I would pray to God for protection and get it. Not that I had any idea of God. It was faith that was at work—faith of which the seed had been sown by the good nurse Rambhā. . . .

"Who dare harm whom God protects?"[6]

6.5. Gandhi's first reading of the Bhagavad-Gītā took place in England, through the translation by Edwin Arnold, entitled "The Song Celestial" and this opened his eyes in new directions. On one side, he became anxious to know more and more about his religion of birth—Hinduism—and on the other side he read the scriptures of other religions. Especially remarkable was the very first impression of the Gītā, of the second chapter in particular and there too of the Sthitaprajña-section. He read again and again verses II.62-63 which came to him in the following translation by Arnold:

> If one
> Ponders on subjects of the sense, there springs
> Attraction; from attraction grows desire,
> Desire flames to fierce passion, passion breeds
> Recklessness; then the memory—all betrayed—
> Lets noble purpose go, and saps the mind,
> Till purpose, mind, and man are all undone.

Gandhi wrote in his autobiography:

> The verses in the second chapter. . . made a deep impression on my mind and they still ring in my ears. The book struck me as one of priceless worth. The impression has ever since been growing on me with the result that I regard it to-day as the book par excellence for the knowledge of Truth. It has afforded me an invaluable help in my moments of gloom.[7]

6.6. Gandhi returned to India with a Law degree in 1891, to find that his saintly mother, whose memory kept him pure in England all these years, had passed away and that his brother had kept the news from him to save him from pain and sorrow in a foreign land. After he returned home, he tried to set up legal practice in Bombay. But he found it impossible to make both ends meet. So he went back to Rajkot to live with his brother and try his luck in the local court there. But he had a very unpleasant experience with the British Political Agent in whose Court he had to appear. Consequently he was in a state of profound depression, when a job offer came from Dada Abdullah and Co., a firm in Porbandar which had business in South Africa. He was asked whether he would go to South Africa to instruct the Company's Counsel in a big case. Gandhi accepted this job offer and sailed for South Africa in April, 1893.

6.7. The twenty-one years (1893-1914) that Gandhi spent in South Africa are the most important from the viewpoint of the development of his personality—how he decided to spend all his time for social causes, how religious influences—and particularly the Gītā —moulded his philosophy of life, and how he developed a new technique of social action—Satyāgraha. Accordingly, a separate section attempts to indicate the main elements of Gandhi's experiment with Satyāgraha in South Africa.

6.8. When Gandhi arrived in India from South Africa in the beginning of 1915, he had already attained considerable fame but it remained to be seen how and with which "group" he would make common cause. His "political guru" Gokhale advised him to take a year, seeing personally what was going on in different parts of the country, and then make the appropriate institutional connections. The conflict between the Moderates and the Extremists was still on but due to Gokhale's death and widespread dissatisfaction with the British, the Extremists led by Tilak moved to the forefront. On the issue of obtaining mass participation by common people in the activities of the Congress, Tilak and Gandhi broadly agreed. Tilak's new interpretation of the Gītā was the topic of the day, because he had explained how Gītā's Karma-yoga could be applied to the freedom fight. Tilak gave to Gandhi the Gujarati translation of his book—*Gītā-Rahasya,* originally written in Marathi during his long political imprisonment. Gandhi too had formulated his own views in South Africa, based on his unique interpretation of the Gītā. On the need for applying the Gītā to the political problems of the country, Tilak and Gandhi were equally enthusiastic. However, Gandhi's insistence on viewing truth and non-violence as the basis of all social and political activities, was considered entirely unrealistic by Tilak. Such differences between the two leaders began to be voiced in 1919.

6.9. The Tilak-Gandhi transition can be said to have begun with the 'Satyāgraha Pledge' that was taken throughout the country in April 1919, and completed in August 1920. In fact, the date fixed for starting the All-India non-cooperation movement under Gandhi's leadership—1 August 1920—happened to coincide with the date of Tilak passing away from this world. However, during the preceding four years, Gandhi had established the Satyāgraha Ashrama near Ahmedabad, and had attracted thereto persons like Vinoba—who was then a college student and was moved by the "eye-opening" speech of Gandhi at Banaras University. Jawaharlal Nehru, too, a young lawyer at that time, felt the arrival of Gandhi "like a powerful current of fresh air", as he later wrote in 1946:

> And then Gandhi came. He was like a powerful current of fresh air that made us stretch ourselves and take deep breaths; like a beam of light that pierced the darkness and removed the scales from our eyes; like a whirlwind that upset many things, but most of all the working of people's minds. He did not descend from the top; he seemed to emerge from the millions of India, speaking their language and incessantly drawing attention to them and their appalling condition. Get off the backs of these peasants and workers, he told us, all you who live by their exploitation; get ride of the system that produces this poverty and misery. Political freedom took new shape then and acquired a new content. Much that he said we only partially accepted or sometimes did not accept at all. But all this was secondary. The essence of his teaching was fearlessness and truth, and action allied to these, always keeping the welfare of the masses in view.[8]

6.10. Before venturing to present to the country, the new technique of Satyāgraha, it was necessary to see how the experiment conducted in South Africa would work out under Indian conditions which were obviously far more complex than those in South Africa. A separate section is therefore devoted to summarizing the main elements of 'small-scale applications of Satyāgraha in India during 1915-18'.

6.11. The Gandhian era in Indian politics began in 1919 and after twenty-eight years the goal of independence was achieved. However, for Gandhi himself, the experiments with Truth and Non-violence were always the first priority. When he found that, due to lack of training in the technique of Satyāgraha, mob violence had crept into the movement, he called it a 'Himalayan blunder' and called off the aGītātion. His long imprisonment on many occasions enabled him to write his own commentary (in Gujarati) on the Gītā, as he explained in the introduction thereto:

> During my incarceration, I was able to study the Gītā more fully. I went reverently through the Gujarati translation of the Lokamānya's great work. . . .
>
> It has been my endeavour, as also that of some companions, to reduce to practice the teaching of the Gītā as I have understood it. The Gītā has become for us a spiritual reference book. I am aware that we ever fail to act in perfect accord with the teaching. The failure is not due to want of effort, but is in spite of it. Even through the failures we seem to see rays of hope. The accompanying rendering contains the meaning of the Gītā message which this little band is trying to enforce in its daily conduct.
>
> My desire to leave to Gujaratis, through the mother tongue, whatever knowledge I may possess, ... does not mean any disrespect to other renderings. They have their own place. But I am not aware of the claim made by the translators of enforcing their meaning of the Gītā in their own lives. At the back of my reading there is the claim of an endeavour to enforce the meaning in my own conduct for an unbroken period of forty years.

6.12. Panikkar has summarized Gandhi's ideas as to how the non-violent fight for independence from a foreign rule had close links with the Gītā doctrine of swadharma:

It was the Mahatma's conviction that foreign rule, i.e. the imposition of an alien way of life and thought, was not merely sinful because it was an attack on the Dharma of the ruled but it was even more against the Dharma of the ruler. That is why all through the twenty-eight years of his fight against British rule and even when he denounced that rule as satanic, he claimed to be a true friend of the British, as they now accept him to have been. The very denunciation of British rule to be satanic is the clue to his approach and can in its full significance be understood only in terms of the Gītā doctrine of Swadharma, or the law of one's own nature.[10]

6.13. Parallel to the 'agitational' element in the Satyāgraha campaigns against the foreign rule, there was the 'internal growth' element to which Gandhi gave the meaningful name: Constructive Programme. Gandhi attached the greatest importance to the various activities which were included in the constructive programme. As of 1940, the importance of the following items was highlighted by Gandhi under this programme:

(i) Hindu-Muslim or communal unity
(ii) Removal of untouchability
(iii) Prohibition
(iv) Khādī
(v) Other village industries
(vi) Village sanitation
(vii) New or basic education
(viii) Adult Education
(ix) Uplift of women
(x) Education in hygiene and health
(xi) Propagation of rashtrabhasha (national language)
(xii) Cultivating love of one's own language
(xiii) Working for economic equality.[11]

6.14. To give an idea of the comprehensive view of the Indian situation which Gandhi had for purposes of bringing about an all-round development of the Indian society along non-violent lines, it is necessary to present the following list of organizations connected with the Constructive programme, as prepared by V.K.R.V. Rao:

(i) Sevāgrām Āśrama
(ii) Kasturba Hospital
(iii) Nai Talim Sangh
(iv) Khādī Research Institute
(v) Gandhi Sevā Sangh
(vi) Mahilā Āśrama
(vii) Bajajwadi
(viii) Shikshā Maṇḍala
(ix) Gandhi Gyān Mandir
(x) Village Industries Research Institute
(xi) Magan Sangrahālaya
(xii) Rashtra Bhāshā Prachār Samiti
(xiii) Leprosy Foundation
(xiv) Grām Sevā Maṇḍala
(xv) Go Sevā Sangh
(xvi) Maharogi Sevā Maṇḍala
(xvii) Paramdhām Āśrama
(xviii) Mātri Sevā Sangh[12]

6.15. Within six months of India's independence, Gandhi faced the assassin's bullet, on 30 January 1948, with the words 'He Rāma'. The closing days of Gandhi's life witnessed 'the worst trials and tribulations' as Betai puts it.[13] India's independence on 15th August 1947 was won at the cost of the country's partition which led to inter-communal disturbances on an unprecedented scale. Gandhi tried his best to restore peace and harmony, but could achieve only partial success. Faced with violence in so many places at the same time, he even expressed his agony in words like the following:

> There was a time when people immediately carried out whatever escaped from my lips. Truly, I was then the commander of a non-violent army. But today mine is a cry in the wilderness. . . .
>
> In this age perhaps I am the only believer in non-violence. I pray to God to give me enough strength so that at least I, if none else, may be able to practise non-violence. . .[14]

Betai remarks:

It is remarkable that absolute devotion to God, total surrender to His will, directing all one's activities and one's very self towards becoming an instrument in the hands of God—these were the most remarkable features of Gandhiji's utterings in these last days. And he had read just this in the Gītā."[15]

EXPERIMENT WITH SATYĀGRAHA IN SOUTH AFRICA

6.16. Gandhi's technique of waging "non-violent fights" for social and political causes took a concrete shape in South Africa during the years 1906-14, and his own spiritual, moral and mental preparedness for making such a "new experiment" can be traced back to the years 1903-6. Prior to that, in 1894, he had helped the Indian community in the Natal province of South Africa to set up the socio-political organization called "The Natal Indian Congress". The word "Congress" helped create a feeling of close relationship with the Indian National Congress which had started functioning in India in 1885. During the initial years of its existence, the Natal Indian Congress circulated pamphlets to draw attention of the authorities and the general public to the discriminatory treatment which the Indian community and particularly the "indentured" and "ex-indentured" labourers were receiving from the white population of South Africa. The indentured labourers were those Indians who had gone to Natal on an agreement to serve for five years, in the sugarcane, tea and coffee estates. These labourers were practically "slaves" of their employers for the period of their agreement. They were contemptuously called "coolies". Even after the expiry of five years, the ex-indentured labourers were subjected to special taxation and other restrictions if they wanted to go from one place to another in an attempt to find means of living. The success which the ex-indentured labourers had started achieving in the trading and other occupations aroused the jealousy of European colonists whose real intentions were to force "unwanted" groups of Indians back to India, by subjecting them to intolerable restrictions.

6.17. At the start of the twentieth century, when the Transvaal-part of South Africa also came under the British administration, the Asiatic department of Transvaal Government wanted all the Indians to obtain a "certificate" which would show, in particular, their photographs and finger-prints. Sarma describes how, in Gandhi's opinion, the draft Ordinance of the Transvaal Government amounted to treating Indians like "criminal tribes":

> When he (Gandhi) read the various sections of the draft Ordinance reeking with hatred to Indians, he shuddered. He saw that, if the Ordinance was passed and meekly accepted, it would spell absolute ruin for the Indians in South Africa. He said, it was better to die than to submit to such a law. Even the laws to which the indentured labourers were subject were a mere flea-bite compared to the drastic rules and penalties proposed for all free Indians, rich or poor, educated or uneducated. Gandhiji thought the Ordinance could only be compared to some of the drastic laws directed against criminal tribes in India and would not suffer in comparison. Under its provisions even women and children had to be registered.[16]

6.18. With a view to determining the Indian community's response to the discriminatory legislation, the Transvaal Indian Association called, in September 1906, a public meeting which was attended by three thousand men. On the advice of Gandhi, fully supported by leading members of the community, a resolution was drafted, stating that "we declare our solemn determination not to submit to the Ordinance, if it became law, and to suffer all penalties attaching to such non-submission". Sarma adds:

> Gandhi made a speech which will go down into history. He explained the consequences of taking a solemn oath, he announced that he himself was taking the oath and would not violate it, even if all others did and left him and he had to face the wrath of the Government alone, and asked every man in the hall to come to a decision for himself individually. Others also spoke to the same effect including the President. And at last all present, standing with upraised hands, took an oath with God as witness not to submit to the Ordinance if it became law. Thus was Satyāgraha born on the 11th September, 1906.[17]

6.19. But how did Gandhi, a coolie barrister as he was called, feel that, in 1906, he had the spiritual courage as well as moral and material support of the Indian community so as to recommend to them the breaking of a law, howsoever unjust it might be? Sarma attributes this to the taking of "significant steps" by Gandhi during the years 1903-6, which marked the adoption of a new philosophy of life:

> The first step was his intense study of the Bhagavad-Gītā which from 1903 became his infallible guide in conduct. . . It was in the company of his Theosophist friends that he read Pātañjali's Yoga-sūtras and the Bhagavad-Gītā in the original. These two books gripped his mind, and he wanted to put into practice the Gītā teaching—that one should be in the world, but not of it. He wanted to practise *aprarigraha* (not having any possessions) and *samabhāva* (treating all as equals). So he deliberately allowed his Life Insurance policy to lapse and wrote to his brother giving him all his savings up to that moment and telling him that all his future savings, if any, would be utilized for the benefit of the community.
>
> The second step was the launching of a weekly journal called 'Indian Opinion', in 1904, financed by himself and practically edited by himself. . . .
>
> The third step was the nursing of the poor Indians at the time of the plague epidemic. . . .
>
> The fourth step was the founding of the Phoenix Settlement near Durban. . . . It was agreed that all the people in this Settlement would maintain themselves by manual labour on the farm and draw the same living wage. . . .[18]

6.20. Now to the conduct of the Satyāgraha itself, the first phase of which started in September 1906. The Transvaal legislation making it obligatory for Indians to obtain a "certificate" by 31 July 1907 was called by the Indian community as "the Black Act" and they had decided not to submit to it and to suffer the consequences thereof, but not to resort to violence. In the beginning, this movement was described as "Passive Resistance". However, Gandhi saw that the English term "Passive Resistance" was misleading because it did not correctly indicate the nature of the Indian movement. Passive resistance was supposed to be the weapon of the work, who would use methods of violence, if and when they could use them. This term could not therefore be applied to the Indian movement, which had renounced all violence in thought as well as deed and which aimed at conquering untruth by truth, hatred by love, and violence by non-violence. Gandhi therefore offered a prize, through his journal 'Indian Opinion', for the person who would invent the most suitable Indian expression, in place of 'Passive Resistance'. Maganlal Gandhi suggested the word "Sadāgraha", and Gandhi himself modified it to Satyāgraha".

6.21. With a view to obtaining the Indian population's compliance with the "Black Act", the Transvaal Government opened many offices for receiving applications and for issuing "certificates". However, volunteers of the Indian community dissuaded the would-be applicants by picketing, so much so that only 500 certificates could be issued, as against a target of 13000. On the last day of registration, that is, 31 July 1907, a mass meeting of the Indian community was called at Pretoria, the capital of the Transvaal. The Government sent one of their officers to this meeting, to admonish the leaders not to break their heads against a stone wall. However, this type of warning only strengthened the resolve of the people who were determined not to be cowed down by threats, nor even by punishment.

6.22. Soon the Government sent a warning to Gandhi and to other leading members of the Indian community that they must either register themselves under the Act or leave the country or face arrest. Accordingly, Gandhi was arrested and sentenced to two months' imprisonment. This was his first experience of jail life. Within a week, more than a hundred Satyāgrahī prisoners joined Gandhi. With more and more Indians ready to go to jail, the Government offered a compromise, saying that if a majority of Indians registered voluntarily, and not by compulsion, the Black Act would be repealed. This compromise was accepted by the leaders of the Indian community, and all the Satyāgrahī prisoners were freed.

6.23. Gandhi had a hard time convincing a small section of the Indian community, composed of some Paṭhāns, about the reasonableness of the compromise agreement with the Government. Among these Paṭhāns, some mischief-monger spread a rumour that Gandhi had taken a bribe from the Government. One of the Paṭhāns became so angry with Gandhi that he struck him on his head with a heavy cudgel. Gandhi fainted and fell down. A British clergyman took him to his house and arranged for medical care. Gandhi issued a statement that he did not want the assailant to be prosecuted, but the police took its own course and got him sentenced to three months' imprisonment. In the meantime, the misunderstanding underlying this incident was removed and the Indian community was again united in its whole-hearted support to Gandhi over the issue of voluntary registration.

6.24. Now it was the turn of the Transvaal Government to repeal the Black Act, but General Smuts, the head of the Government, refused to honour the word that he had given at the time of the compromise. Gandhi, who had risked his life in making his countrymen register themselves voluntarily, was shocked, at this breach of faith. How could he face the Indian community after this, he asked himself. He addressed a letter to General Smuts, but there was no reply. He then consulted the other leaders of the community and announced that, unless the Government acted by a specific date (16 August 1908) the certificates collected by the Indians voluntarily would be burnt, and "they would humbly and firmly take the consequences".

6.25. General Smuts called this message of the Indians an ultimatum sent to the Government by people who had no idea of its power. But the Indians too were determined to meet the challenge, as Sarma describes:

> A public meeting was announced to be held two hours after the time limit, for the purpose of the ceremony of making a bonfire of the certificates. . . . On the mosque ground of Johannesburg every inch of available place was filled by Indians of all classes. An iron cauldron of the largest size available in the market was brought and set up on a platform in the grounds for the burning of the certificates. As the meeting was about to commence, a volunteer who had been

posted at the Telegraph Office arrived on a cycle with a telegram from the Government announcing their inability to change their minds. The telegram was read to the audience, who received it with cheers, and who re-confirmed their determination to continue the Satyāgraha struggle.[19]

6.26. The second phase of the Satyāgraha began in 1909 and many arrests were made. Gandhi spent three months in jail along with his son. When the jails became overcrowded with the Satyāgrahī prisoners, the Government tried the method of deporting them to India. But many of them were born and brought up in South Africa, and there was an outcry in India and England against their deportation. The prison authorities then opened road-side camps where prisoners had no protection against cold. Two young prisoners died because of these hardships. Still the community did not falter. The more cruel the Government, the firmer the resolve of the Satyāgrahīs. In one of the prisons, the Satyāgrahīs had to go on a hunger-strike for seven days to obtain the minimum facilities required for human subsistence.

6.27. During the latter part of 1909, a deputation of the South African Indians, including Gandhi, went to England to plead for their just cause. They received a sympathetic hearing by Lord Ampthill, a former Governor of Madras, who tried to persuade General Smuts to repeal the Black Act, but the latter refused to change his policy. Lord Ampthill thereupon said that he had nothing but congratulations to offer to those who were so willing to suffer for a principle and to carry on such a righteous struggle with such clean weapons.

6.28. During the third phase of the Satyāgraha, the problem of maintaining the families of the poor Satyāgrahī prisoners called for attention. What was needed was a large farming area in the Transvaal where these families could live together as members of a cooperative establishment, and maintain themselves by their own labour. The Phoenix settlement which Gandhi had started in 1906, was in Natal, nearly three hundred miles away. Luckily for the poor Indian community, a German architect and a friend of Gandhi, Kallenbach, who had a big farm of eleven hundred acres in the Transvaal region, lent the use of his farm for the Satyagrahī families without any rent. Gandhi called this "Tolstoy Farm", in recognition of what he had learnt from Tolstoy's writings about the importance of the concept of "bread-labour".

6.29. This phase of the non-violent struggle of the Indians in South Africa thus continued till 1912 when Gokhale, a prominent Indian leader held in high esteem by the British Government, accepted Gandhi's request and decided to visit South Africa. Both Indians and Europeans living in South Africa vied with one another in welcoming and honouring the great Indian statesman. Gokhale had long discussions with the ministers, and before leaving South Africa, he told Gandhi, "Everything has been settled. The Black Act will be repealed. The racial bar will be removed from the immigration law. The tax on the ex-indentured labourers will be abolished".

6.30. But nothing came out of the assurance given by the ministers to Gokhale. General Smuts announced that, as the Europeans in Natal objected to the repeal of the tax, the Government could not pass any legislation. Gandhi informed Gokhale, who expressed deep pain but saw no further use of his intervention. The only course left was for the Indians in South Africa to intensify the fight.

6.31. In March 1913, another intolerable grievance cropped up for the Indian community, necessitating the participation of Indian women also in the non-violent struggle. The Cape Supreme Court decided in a case that all marriages that were not celebrated according to Christian rites and registered by the Registrar of Marriages were outside the pale of legal marriages in South Africa. Thus according to this judgment, all Hindu, Muslim and Zoroastrian marriages were illegal, and therefore the married women of these communities and their children lost their legitimacy. Gandhi wrote to the Government but got no reply. He therefore invited the Indian women to come into line with men to offer Satyāgraha. Even women with babies in arms came forward to take part in the struggle. Kasturba Gandhi was among the women who were arrested and imprisoned, in this, the fourth, phase of the Satyāgraha.

6.32. The arrest of women and their imprisonment with hard labour aroused much sympathy in India and England. The Satyāgraha in South Africa entered its fifth phase when indentured labourers in Natal also started going on strike. Their employers retaliated by cutting off their light and water supply, driving them out of their quarters and even whipping them. Hundreds of them came to Gandhi and offered to do whatever he would advise.

6.33. Faced with five thousand indentured labourers who were thrown out of their quarters, the only solution that Gandhi could devise was to start a journey on foot to the Tolstoy Farm. This was the sixth phase of the Satyāgraha and it called for detailed planning and organization because the marchers, covering twenty miles a day for eight days, had to be provided with bread and sugar, and rules for sanitation and discipline had to be observed throughout the eight-day march. A large European bakery agreed to supply bread because its owner knew that the Satyāgrahī marchers were only seeking the minimum of justice through their unity and self-suffering.

6.34. As the marchers completed nearly half of their journey, observes Sarma, the Government felt more and more confused. It was the firmness of the Indians coupled with their peacefulness that distressed General Smuts. If they had taken to rioting or violence of any kind, they could have been easily shot down. But something had to be done before they reached their destination. Gandhi was arrested and sentenced to nine months' imprisonment. His friends Polak and Kallenbach were also arrested. The march of the indentured labourers of Natal was also stopped, and the Government made plans to deport them back to Natal by special trains.

6.35. The Satyāgraha entered its seventh phase when the indentured labourers of Natal, who were deported and treated as convicts, refused to work in mines. They were then whipped, kicked and maltreated in various ways. The strike now spread to all the mining centres, and the men came out in thousands.

The Government adopted a policy of blood and iron. Mounted policemen chased the strikers, brought them back and forced them to work. When the strikers resisted, fire was opened on them, killing some and wounding others. These atrocities were all reported by cablegrams to Gokhale, and the news spread throughout India. The Viceroy, Lord Hardinge spoke in favour of the Satyāgrahīs, and at Gokhale's request, Andrews and Pearson offered to intervene.

6.36. Upset by the attitude of the Viceroy of India, the South African government decided to get out of the awkward situation by appointing a commission to inquire into the grievances of Indians and make recommendations. An interim recommendation of the commission was to release Gandhi, Pollak and Kallenbach. Gandhi and Andrews saw General Smuts, and when a provisional agreement for redressing all the grievances of Indians was reached, the Satyāgraha was suspended. After some time, the commission recommended compliance with all the demands of the Satyāgrahīs, and the necessary legislation was enacted by the South African Government in June 1914. Thus ended, successfully, Gandhi's first experiment with Satyāgraha, which passed through seven phases and lasted eight years.

6.37. In Spratt's opinion, the Satyāgraha in South Africa could be called a 'model', not only because it was the first use of the new technique but also because it stayed very close to the 'principles': "It was conducted against very heavy odds by poor and ignorant people—the majority indeed were illiterate—but there was hardly an instance of breach of the principles. . . ."[20]

6.38. Perhaps the greatest testimony of Gandhi's success as a Satyāgrahī was the change of heart that was apparently brought about in the "so-called opponent", viz. General Smuts. Verma quotes how Smuts became deeply conscious of the virtues of sincerity, unselfishness and humanism that he found in Gandhi, Smuts wrote:

> However often we may differ from him, we are conscious all the time of his sincerity, his unselfishness, and above all of his fundamental and universal humanity. He always acts as a

great human, with deep sympathy for men of all classes and all races and especially for the under-dog.[21]

SMALL-SCALE APPLICATIONS OF SATYĀGRAHA IN INDIA DURING 1915-18

6.39. The feasibility of applying the Satyāgraha technique to Indian conditions was tested by Gandhi, mainly on five occasions during the years 1915-18. The most well-known of these was the Champaran Satyāgraha of 1917. However, there were two occasions prior to Champaran when Gandhi had prepared the concerned groups of people to be ready to offer Satyāgraha if the issues were not settled through negotiations. Although the need to actually use the Satyāgraha weapon did not arise in either of these two cases, because the problems were solved prior to reaching that stage, Gandhi still considers the first of these two occasions as "heralding the advent of Satyāgraha in India."[22] In view of this, a brief account of two of the five "tests" of Satyāgraha, conducted by Gandhi during the years 1915-18, namely the first and the third, is given below.

6.40. The first occasion was in 1915, on the issue of the customs barrier at Viramgam, between British India and the Kathiawad States, due to which all the railway passengers travelling on that route had to suffer hardships. Motilal, a voluntary social worker of that area and tailor by profession requested Gandhi to do something to end the trouble. Gandhi asked him, "Are you ready to go to jail?" "We are ready to march to the gallows", was the firm reply of Motilal. Gandhi went to Rajkot, collected all the necessary information about the customs barrier at Viramgam and opened correspondence with the Government. He also dropped a hint in his speeches at various places that the people should be prepared, if necessary, to offer Satyāgraha at Viramgam.

6.41. Gandhi's speeches were duly reported to the Government of Bombay, by the police (C.I.D.). When Gandhi saw the Governor of Bombay, he was told that the Government of India was responsible for the customs barrier and that he should turn to them for relief. Gandhi then met the Viceroy, Lord Chelmsford, and placed the facts before him. The Viceroy was astonished, for he knew nothing about the matter. He at once called for the papers and within a few days thereafter the customs cordon was removed.

6.42. Prior to the favourable decision of the Viceroy, Gandhi was asking the people of Kathiawad States to be ready to pursue the matter, without fear but peacefully. In general the attitude of the Government to public grievances was extremely unsympathetic in those days. Therefore getting ready for a showdown with the Government was not a small thing. Although in the end Satyāgraha was not actually offered, the imminent possibility of its being offered was probably an important factor in obtaining redress. Gandhi therefore regarded the Viramgam Customs Case as "heralding the advent of Satyāgraha in India".[23]

6.43. As already pointed out, the main test of the Satyāgraha technique took place in connection with the Champaran struggle of 1917 when Gandhi had to actually offer Satyāgraha on behalf of the poor farmers who were being exploited by indigo planters. For the last hundred years, every Champaran tenant was bound by law to plant three out of every twenty parts of his land with indigo for his landlord. This system was known as 'tīnkaṭhiā', and it worked as a great hardship for thousands of poor farmers. At the Congress session of December 1916, Gandhi was requested to go to Champaran and to do something to relieve the distress of the people.

6.44. Gandhi thought it necessary to make an unbiased inquiry into the grievances of the Champaran farmers. For this, he thought it was his duty, before starting the inquiry, to know the planters' side of the case. He interviewed both the Secretary of the Planters' Association and the Commissioner of the Tirhut Division. Both of them resented his 'intrusion', as they called it, and said that an outsider like him had no business to come between the planters and their tenants, and advised him to leave the place at once.

6.45. Gandhi ignored the advice of the Secretary and the Commissioner and went to Motihāri, the headquarters of the Champaran district. A legal notice was then served on him, ordering him to leave Champaran. Gandhi refused to leave till his inquiry on behalf of the riots was finished. He then received a summons to take his trial the next day for disobeying the order.

6.46. The news of the summons served on Gandhi spread like wild fire, and huge crowds gathered together in Motihāri and followed Gandhi wherever he went. The people had now lost all fear of the authorities. They yielded obedience to Gandhi and not to the police. The officials did not know how to proceed with the case. The Government pleader pressed the magistrate to postpone it, but Gandhi requested him not to do so, as he wanted to plead guilty.

6.47. In the Court of the Magistrate, Gandhi read a statement in which he said, he had come to Champaran on a pressing invitation from the ryots, who had some grievances against the indigo planters. He had come to study the situation and, if possible, to assist the Administration in doing justice. He had no other motive. He could not believe that his coming would in any way disturb public peace or cause loss of life. As a law-abiding citizen his instinct was to obey the order of the Magistrate. But his sense of duty to those who had invited him compelled him to stay. Amidst this conflict of duties he would throw the responsibility of removing him on the Administration. Therefore he decided to submit without protest to the penalty of disobedience.

6.48. Gandhi's statement concluded with the words: "I have disregarded the order served on me, not for want of respect for the lawful authority, but in obedience to the higher law of our being, the voice of conscience".[24]

6.49. About twenty-five years after Gandhi had made this famous statement before the Champaran magistrate, he recalled the wider political significance thereof and told Louis Fischer: "That day in Champaran became a red-letter day in my life. This was my first act of civil disobedience against the British. It became the method by which India could be made free".[25]

6.50. The Champaran magistrate was taken by surprise to hear Gandhi's statement and he did not know what to do, because the apparently simple matter had grown into such a big issue as to call for a political decision by the Lieutenant-Governor. The only thing that the magistrate could do was to postpone judgment. Gandhi wired the details of the situation to the Viceroy, to Madan Mohan Malviya and to other friends. The result was that, before Gandhi could appear before the court to receive the sentence, the magistrate wrote to him that the Lieutenant-Governor had ordered the case to be withdrawn.

6.51. The Collector then wrote to Gandhi that he might conduct the proposed inquiry and that all the necessary help would be given to him by the Government officials. The planters were much displeased, but Gandhi's inquiry went on. At his suggestion, the Lieutenant-Governor appointed a committee to go into the whole question. The committee's findings were in favour of the ryots. A bill to abolish the 'tīnkaṭhiā' system was introduced. It was fiercely opposed by the planters, but owing to the firmness of the Lieutenant-Governor, the century-old burden on the poor farmers was removed. This was the first occasion in India on which Satyāgraha, actually offered, brought relief to the people. After this and two more 'tests', Gandhi offered to apply the Satyāgraha-technique to All-India political problems, from 1919 onwards.

MASS SCALE APPLICATIONS OF SATYĀGRAHA IN INDIA DURING 1919-48

6.52. For purposes of applying Satyāgraha against the foreign rule in India, Gandhi attached great importance to the technique of non-violent non-cooperation by the masses. This implied chiefly the withdrawal of cooperation from a government that, in the non-cooperators' view, was extremely unjust, oppressive or corrupt. The purpose of non-cooperation was to put so much pressure upon the government that the act of governance itself might become impossible. As Gandhi put it:

> I believe, and every body must grant, that no government can exist for a single moment without the cooperation of the

people, willing or forced, and if people suddenly withdraw their cooperation in every detail, the government will come to a standstill . . . Cooperation with a just government is a duty; non-cooperation with an unjust government is equally a duty.[26]

6.53. In September 1920, Gandhi moved the resolution on non-cooperation at the special session of the Indian National Congress. Lala Lajpat Rai, a close colleague of the late B.G. Tilak, presided over this session. However, Bipin Chandra Pal, another close colleague of Tilak, supported by C.R.Das, opposed Gandhi's move, and put forward an amendment to the effect that a mission should be sent to England to lay India's grievances before the British Prime Minister and explain the temper of the Indian people. After a long discussion among the Congress delegates—numbering nearly three thousand—Gandhi won by a majority of two to one. By this resolution the Congress adopted the policy of progressive non-violent non-cooperation until the atrocities committed in the Punjab were acknowledged and corrective action taken to set them right and a policy of leading the country to Swarāj was announced.

6.54. A seven-point scheme of non-cooperation was specified, indicating what the countrymen were advised to do to put into effect the Congress resolution, namely:

(i) surrender of titles, honorary offices and nominated seats in Local Bodies
(ii) refusal to attend Government levies, durbars and other official and semi-official functions
(iii) gradual withdrawal of children from schools and colleges owned or aided by Government, and the establishment of national schools
(iv) gradual boycott of British courts by lawyers and litigants and the establishment of private arbitration courts
(v) refusal on the part of the military, clerical and labouring classes to offer themselves as recruits for services in Mesopotamia
(vi) withdrawal by candidates of their candidature from the so-called 'Reformed Councils ' and refusal on the

part of voters to vote for any candidate thereto
(vii) boycott of foreign goods.[27]

6.55. Nehru believes that the full impact of the comprehensive scheme of withdrawal of cooperation went so deep as to shake up the very foundations of the British rule in India:

> Realising that the main props of British rule were fear, prestige, the cooperation, willing or unwilling, of the people, and certain classes whose vested interests were centred in British rule, Gandhi attacked these foundations. Titles were to be given up and though the title-holders responded to this only in small measure, the popular respect for these British-given titles disappeared and they became symbols of degradation. New standards and values were set up and the pomp and splendour of the viceregal court and the princes, which used to impress so much, suddenly appeared supremely ridiculous and vulgar and rather shameful, surrounded as they were by the poverty and misery of the people. Rich men were not so anxious to flaunt their riches; outwardly at least many of them adopted simpler ways, and in their dress, became almost indistinguishable from humbler folk.[28]

6.56. The last item in the seven-point scheme of non-cooperation was 'boycott of foreign gods'. Although, on paper, it sounded like what the Nationalist Party had preached at the time of Bengal partition nearly fifteen years earlier, the actual events of the 1920's proved to be far more revolutionary. Khādī—the hand-spun and hand-woven cloth—became a symbol of Swadeshi. On this issue, too, there was an initial opposition to Gandhi's ideas by some of the leaders, but soon the impact of Khādī on the society—and particularly the villages—was so great as to dispel all doubts. Gandhi pleaded the cause of khādī in repeated statements like the following:

> Khādī is a controversial subject. Many people think that in advocating Khādī I am sailing against a head wind and am sure to sink the ship of Swarāj and that I am taking the country to the dark ages. But the proof of the pudding is in the eating. For me nation-wide spinning is a yajña. It is the

symbol of unity of Indian humanity, of its economic freedom and equality and, therefore, ultimately, in the poetic expression of Jawaharlal Nehru, "the livery of India's freedom".[29]

6.57. Nehru found in Khādī and other Swadeshi activities, a practical programme of uniting the urban and rural areas, and of enabling educated people like himself to establish bonds of sympathy with the poorest of the villages:

> Gandhi sent us to the villages, and the countryside hummed with the activity of innumerable messengers of the new gospel of action. The peasant was shaken up and he began to emerge from his quiescent shell. The effect on us was different but equally far-reaching, for we saw, for the first time as it were, the villager in the intimacy of his mud-hut, and with the dark shadow of hunger always pursuing him. We learnt our Indian economics more from these visits than from books and learned discourses. The emotional experience we had already undergone was emphasized and confirmed and henceforward there could be no going back for us to our old life or our old standards, howsoever much our views might change subsequently.[30]

6.58. While non-violent non-cooperation as one type of Satyāgraha was tried by Gandhi in the 1920's, he adopted in 1930 the second type of Satyāgraha, namely, Civil Disobedience. Iyer has tried to clarify the subtle difference between these two types of Satyāgraha:

> Non-cooperation was conceived in a much wider context as an instrument of social action. . .
>
> Civil disobedience is more difficult than non-cooperation because it presupposes the habit of willing obedience of laws without fear of their sanctions. . . .
>
> Gandhi's emphasis was on Ahiṁsā in non-cooperation and on Tapas in civil disobedience, although both concepts contained elements of self-suffering and non-violence.
>
> Non-cooperation made fewer spiritual demands on its users. . . . Civil Disobedience called for a spirit of Tapas or self-suffering, which in practice only a few were capable of exemplifying. . . .[31]

6.59. Gandhi himself, while tracing the expression 'civil disobedience' to Thoreau, explained how the Indian experiment was wider in terms of application and stricter in regard to the emphasis on non-violence:

> Civil disobedience is civil breach of unmoral statutory enactments. . . .
>
> The expression was, as far as I am aware, coined by Thoreau to signify his own resistance to the laws of a slave State. He has left a masterly treatise on the duty of Civil Disobedience. But Thoreau was not perhaps an out and out champion of non-violence. Probably, also, Thoreau limited his breach of statutory laws to the revenue law, i.e., payment of taxes, whereas the term Civil Disobedience as practised in India covered a breach of any statutory and unmoral law. It signified the resister's outlawry in a civil, i.e., non-violent manner. He invoked the sanctions of the law and cheerfully suffered imprisonment. It is a branch of Satyāgraha.[32]

6.60. In 1930, Gandhi picked up the issue of breaking the "Salt Tax Law" because this hurt the poorest of the Indians relatively more deeply. He envisaged a twenty-four-day march from his Ashrama to the sea coast—known as the Dāṇḍī March—so that he could explain the idea personally to hundreds of thousands of people and the message of civil disobedience could thus spread all over the country. Before starting the march, he addressed thousands of people who had gathered near Ahmedabad to receive his message: "Our case is strong, our means the purest and God is with us. There is no defeat for the Satyāgrahīs till they give up truth. I pray for the success of the battle which begins tomorrow."[33]

6.61. The twenty-four-day march by seventy-nine volunteers generated unprecedented enthusiasm and big support for the cause which Gandhi represented. The marchers reached Dāṇḍī on 5 April 1930, and next morning, Gandhi broke the salt law by picking up the salt from the sea-shore without paying tax, and added: "Now that the technical or ceremonial breach of the salt law has been committed, it is now open to anyone who would take the risk of the prosecution under the salt law to manufacture salt, wherever he wishes and whenever it is convenient".34

Sarma summarizes the events that followed:

> This was the signal for huge demonstrations with tens of thousands of men and women in all the important towns of India. The whole country was ablaze with the fire of Civil Disobedience. The salt law was broken in many places. And there were picketings of foreign cloth shops and drinking booths by Satyāgrahī women. All these were, of course, followed by arrests on a vast scale.[35]

6.62. In order to make the mass-scale Satyāgraha movements as effective as possible, Gandhi carried on his "mass education" through writings, speeches, personal advice, and continuous field level training of volunteers by local leaders. For example, he made it clear time and again that the following psychological and sociological conditions must be fulfilled to bring the Satyāgraha movements as close as possible to the moral standards envisaged in his idealistic formulation:

(i) The Satyāgrahī is not to harbour any hatred in his heart against the opponent because in the long run hatred is a waste of energy.
(ii) The issue for which Satyāgraha is launched should be a true and substantial one, i.e., the cause must always be legitimate and just.
(iii) The Satyāgrahī must be prepared to undergo all kinds of humiliations, persecutions and sufferings. In the end he must be ready to lay down his life. Hence Satyāgraha can be practised only by the stout in heart.[36]

6.63. Prior to the launching of the Civil Disobedience campaign of 1930, Gandhi also laid down the following "Important Rules for the Satyāgrahī"—the ideal image of whom was drawn so as to be like the Sthitaprajña of the Gītā :

(i) A Satyāgrahī will harbour no anger.

(ii) He will suffer the anger of the opponent.
(iii) In so doing he will put up with assaults from the opponent, never retaliate; but he will not submit, out of fear of punishment or the like, to any order given in anger.
(iv) When any person in authority seeks to arrest a civil resister, he will voluntarily submit to the arrest.
(v) If a Satyāgrahī has any property in his possession as a trustee, he will defend it, even at the cost of his life.
(vi) A Satyāgrahī will neither swear nor curse.
(vii) A Satyāgrahī will never insult his opponent.[37]

6.64. Nehru has described how the Congress organization, in response to Gandhi's call, condemned terroristic activities, and appealed to the countrymen to willingly accept pain and suffering inflicted by the British administration through imprisonment and other repressive measures:

> "Gandhi brought about a complete change in the Congress organization. . . .
>
> Action was to be the basis, and more specifically, action using peaceful methods. Thus far the alternatives had been just talking and passing resolutions, or terroristic activity. Both of these were set aside and terrorism was especially condemned as opposed to the basic policy of the Congress. A new technique of action was evolved which, though perfectly peaceful, yet implied non-submission to what was considered wrong and, as a consequence, a willing acceptance of the pain and suffering involved in this. Gandhi was an odd kind of pacifist, for he was an activist full of dynamic energy. There was no submission in him to fate or anything that he considered evil; he was full of resistance, though this was peaceful and courteous.[38]

6.65. The 1930's and 1940's also saw increasing attention paid by Gandhi as well as the Congress to tackle the problem of untouchability and of inter-communal harmony. Whenever the situation became critical, Gandhi staked his life, by announcing "fasts" till the leaders of the various groups would get together and agree to "reasonable solutions". Nehru has highlighted how the fight was simultaneously on two fronts—"against the foreign rule" and "against our own social evils":

> The call of action was twofold. There was, of course, the action involved in challenging and resisting foreign rule; there was also the action which led us to fight our own social evils. Apart from the fundamental objective of the Congress—the freedom of India—and the method of peaceful action, the principal planks of the Congress were national unity, which involved the solution of the minority problems, and the raising of the depressed classes and the ending of the curse of untouchability.[39]

6.66. Regarding the efforts made by Gandhi to establish inter-communal harmony during the last six months of his life, M.M. Verma writes:

> Perhaps, even Gandhi did not realize the great heights to which he had attained in his last phase. . . .
>
> 15 August 1947 saw Gandhi trying to quell riots in Calcutta. He spent the day in fasting and prayer, and while India woke into freedom, Gandhi was peaceless. . . .[40]

And similar views have been expressed by Louis Fisher:

> The fact that Gandhi's fast restored Calcutta to its senses and peace, the fact that his presence reduced the mass killing in Delhi to occasional outbursts, the fact that his fleeting visit to Dr. Zakir Hussain's Okhla Academy gave it immunity to violence, the fact that hardened bandits laid their arms at his feet, the fact that Hindus would listen to Koran verses and that Moslems would not object to hearing the holy words of Islam from the mouth of a Hindu—all this remains to inspire or haunt those whose actions would suggest that they have forgotten it. It is the seed of conscience and the source of hope.[41]

ADOPTING THE GĪTĀ-IDEALS IN THOUGHT, WORD AND DEED

6.67. A practical application of the Karma-yoga teaching of the Gītā, as Gandhi interpreted it, meant the voluntary acceptance and enthusiastic fulfilment of the duties that naturally came one's way—Swadharma. He believed that if pursued with a sense of detachment and unselfishness, a life of Karma-yoga could lead to the attainment of *moksha*. A life of dedicated service to one's kind in the spirit of the Gītā, believed Gandhi, would not generate an attitude of aggressive or self-righteous altruism; rather it would lead to a progressive expansion of the human self till it came to comprehend the whole of mankind. The Gītā further insisted on cultivating an attitude of equanimity. A state of perfection, in the terminology of the Gītā, was represented in the personality of a Sthitaprajña or a Bhakta or a Trigunatita. This also meant, in Gandhi's words, an ideal Satyāgrahī".[42] As he put it, "For me the road to salvation lies through incessant toil in the service of my country and humanity. I want to identify myself with every thing that lives. I want to live at peace with both friend and foe. So my patriotism is for me a stage on my journey to the land of eternal freedom and peace".[43]

6.68. When Gandhi was in South Africa, there were, besides the Gītā, two other strong influences on his philosophy of life, namely Ruskin and Tolstoy. Ruskin's "Unto this last" impressed Gandhi so much that he translated it into Gujarati under the title "Sarvodaya". Gandhi listed three main ideas put forth by Ruskin:

(i) The good of the individual is contained in the good of all
(ii) A lawyer's work has the same value as the barber's, as all have the same right of earning their livelihood from their work
(iii) A life of labour, i.e. the life of the tiller of the soil and the handicraftsman is the life worth living.[44]

To Tolstoy, Gandhi gave credit for enunciating convincingly the "Bread Labour Law", namely that "God created man to work for his food and said that those who ate without working were thieves".[45]

6.69. After Gandhi returned to India and made a deeper study of the Gītā, in consultation with his Ashrama-residents and particularly Vinoba, the ideas underlying "Sarvodaya" were found to be included in the comprehensive Gītā-ideals of sarvabhūtahitaṁ', 'Swadharma', and 'yajña'. As V.P. Verma also states: "Literally Sarvodaya means the good of all living beings and thus it has almost the same meaning as the concept of sarvabhūtahita advocated in the Bhagavad-Gītā. Similarly, Gandhi's interpretation of 'yajña' included 'bread-labour' as well as the need to do it in a spirit of service".[46] As Gandhi put it: "The Gītā says that anybody who eats without performing yajña, in Tolstoy's language 'bread-labour', is a thief, and he eats sin. But body-labour becomes yajña only when it is undertaken in a spirit of service, not of indulgence as it may easily become when it is done only to develop the animal in man".[47]

6.70. Betai is of opinion that, with the passage of time, as Gandhi explained the meaning of the Gītā-ideals more and more to the nation, the comprehensive nature of these ideals became clearer to him as well.

> The Gītā grips his mind as his guide in matters of religion and conduct and the same is destined to become in later life his guide for all matters spiritual. Of course, the reading of the scriptural works of different religions continues. 'Unto This Last' of Ruskin leaves a permanent impression on his mind, but, as it becomes clear in the years that follow, the influence of Hinduism is enhanced and the influence of the Gītā grows deeper and deeper. Gandhiji is now a man of his own natural heritage, environment, cultural background and religious as also spiritual leanings and here the Gītā is his guide.[48]

6.71. Gandhi's technique of Satyāgraha, which began on a rather modest scale in South Africa in 1906, gradually became an All-India movement, affecting hundreds of millions of people. Since the Indian society was deeply divided because of differences in religions, castes, languages, political ideologies, etc., it was an extremely difficult task to present a united front in the non-violent agītātion against the British Rule. Furthermore, Gandhi's move was not only against the foreign administration but also against evil customs and traditions that had plagued the Indian society for centuries. Orthodox sections of the society, interpreting religious books in their own way, opposed social reforms. The foreign administrators, following the policy of 'Divide and Rule', exploited inter-religious and inter-caste differences and adopted policies which came in the way of Indian unity. Gandhi's followers had to undergo suffering in the form of imprisonment, police violence and repression. To sustain a non-violent movement under such circumstances, Gandhi had to present a series of programs, and not be disheartened by set-backs and difficulties. Only a true Karmayogin following the Gītā-ideals in thought, word and deed could carry on the non-violent fight on so many fronts for so many years. That is why Gandhi compared an ideal Satyāgrahī with the Sthitaprajña —the term used in the Gītā for a Karmayogin who is able to maintain steady wisdom under the most difficult circumstances. In fact, the Sthitaprajña verses of the Gītā (II. 54-72) constituted part of the evening prayer which Gandhi conducted as a public function everyday.

6.72. Many of the common people of India were poor and illiterate but the long cultural tradition had so moulded their thinking that they instinctively placed their confidence in a person whose image was like that of a saint—a person trying to do good to the society or "Sarvabhūtahite rataḥ" in the language of the Gītā, and having no selfish designs (*niṣkāma*), and willing to undergo suffering (tapasyā) for a just cause. The Indian tradition is full of stories showing the victory of dharma over adharma, of truth over falsehood, of the devas over asuras —in fact, victory of unarmed monkeys over armed demons. In the Mahābhārata, Śrī Kṛṣṇa gave the choice to Arjuna and Duryodhana—either take all the army of Yādavas or take Śrī Kṛṣṇa himself who would guide but not fight. Arjuna immediately chose Śrī Kṛṣṇa and not his army. Only in a society where such stories had become a part of non-formal education and cultural tradition, could Gandhi talk convincingly that 'There is no such thing as defeat in non-violence; the end of violence is surest defeat'.[49]

6.73. The cause of ending foreign rule appeared to the Indian society to be intrinsically just, although some people thought the country was not fully prepared for independence right away. From the practical point of view, it was necessary to focus attention on what can be called 'secondary causes'. For example, the first All-India Satyāgraha of 1919 was directed against two Bills which would have given the British authorities emergency powers, and which according to the draft Satyāgraha pledge, were characterised as "unjust, subversive of the principle of liberty and justice and destructive of the elementary rights of individuals".[50] The fact that Gandhi lived in an Ashrama wholly devoted to the cause of doing good to the society helped in establishing his credentials as a selfless worker who sought no personal gains. Furthermore, the Ashrama rules and regulations, enjoining spiritual discipline and tapasyā on all its members, made it clear that Gandhi was willing to undergo suffering for a just cause. The essence of the non-violent aGītātion was to make people willing to undergo similar tapasyā . As Sarma puts it:

> Gandhi drafts a brief appeal to the nation to observe a twenty-four hours' fast and a complete all-India hartal, to regard the day to be fixed by the leaders as a day of national humiliation and prayer and to hold meetings on that day in all cities, towns and villages throughout India and pass resolutions praying for the withdrawal of the hateful Act. The date that was fixed at first was 30 March 1919, but it was subsequently changed to 6 April. The appeal went home to the hearts of the people and, though the notice was short, there was a complete suspension of work throughout India on that date, and in all big cities monster meetings such as were never witnessed within living memory were held.[51]

6.74. Similarly, for the Satyāgraha campaign of 1930, Gandhi chose a 'secondary cause' represented by 'Tax on Salt', the burden of which fell relatively more heavily on the poor. And the technique for arousing countrywide awareness included a twenty-four-day march, from the Satyāgraha Ashrama to Dāṇḍī on the sea-coast. Furthermore, Gandhi's spirit of sacrifice for a just cause was reflected in his declaration that he would not come back to his Ashrama till Swarāj was won. Even a leader like Motilal Nehru (father of Jawaharlal Nehru) saw in Gandhi's march a parallel to the epic of Rāmāyaṇa and said: "Like the historic march of

Ramachandra to Lanka, the march of Gandhi would be memorable, and the places he passes through would be sacred".[52]

6.75. Sarma has given further details as to how Gandhi utilized the Dāṇḍī-march to explain the non-violent way of carrying on the fight:

> There were 79 volunteers to march with Gandhi and the distance to be covered was 223 miles. Thousands of men, women and children stood as spectators on either side of the road. . . . Gandhiji preached his gospel of non-violence to the assembled crowds. . . . At Borsad he said, "The British rule in India has brought about moral, material, cultural and spiritual ruination of this great country. I regard this rule as a curse. I am out to destroy this system of government. . . . Sedition has become my religion. Ours is a non-violent battle. We are not out to kill anybody, but it is our dharma to see that the curse of this government is blotted." At Bhatgam he turned the searchlight inwards and severely castigated the people for the luxuries they provided for him and his followers and said, "To live above the means befitting a poor country is to live on stolen food. Nor did I bargain to set out on this march for living above our means.[53]

6.76. Gandhi knew that unless something concrete was offered to the poor people to reduce the pangs of hunger, mere exhortation for making sacrifice and for observing non-violence would sound hollow. Therefore, the 'Constructive Programme'. which included work-opportunities (howsoever inefficient in the strict economic sense)—in hand-spinning, hand weaving, and other village industries—became the backbone of the entire movement. As M.M. Verma puts it:

> The constructive programme carried Gandhi's message to the Indian peasants and created among them consciousness of their rights. It provided an opportunity to the rank and file to do some work for social reconstruction. It produced common bonds of fraternity. . . .
>
> Constructive activities are not only an evidence of the sincerity of Satyāgrahīs but they also show to the masses, as

> mere words cannot, the potentiality of Satyāgraha for ending all exploitation and elevating their status. Constructive work also goes a long way to convince the opponent of the non-violent intentions of Satyāgrahīs. . . .
>
> Constructive work has to be quiet, solid and substantial. It is a direct personal service of the masses—suffering for them, organizing them, educating them in the ways of non-violence and thus bringing about a peaceful atmosphere of solemn determination. Constructive work is thus collective purification effort through service. It is mass effort and mass education.[54]

6.77. Removal of untouchability was another important element of Gandhi's constructive programme. He coined a new term "Harijan"—meaning "God's men"—for the so-called 'untouchables' in the Hindu society. Some Harijan leaders fell into the trap of the British policy of 'Divide and Rule' and expressed support for "separate electorate for the Harijans". Gandhi warned them that such an arrangement would perpetuate the evil custom of untouchability. He even announced that he would give up his life—by fasting unto death—unless the Harijans are considered equal citizens like everybody else and their representation assured by a system of reservation, within a joint electorate system. On the seventh day of Gandhi's fast, the proposal for separate electorate for Harijans was dropped by mutual agreement, enabling Gandhi to issue the following statement:

> The hand of God has been visible in the glorious manifestation throughout the length and breadth of India during the past seven days. The cables received from many parts of the world blessing the fast have sustained me through the agony of body and soul that I passed through during the seven days, but the cause was worth going through that agony. The sacrificial fire once lit shall not be put out as long as there is the slightest trace of untouchability still left in Hinduism.[55]

6.78. Orthodox Hindus tried to justify untouchability by interpreting some of the old books in their own way. The situation was similar to the arguments put forward by the Suttee-advocates who had opposed Rammohun Roy's suttee-abolition efforts in the 1820's. Faced with such claims on behalf of the protagonists of untouchability on religious grounds, Gandhi adopted a similar course as Rammohun Roy had done more than a century ago, namely, to take the help of the Bhagavad-Gītā. Betai summarizes the success achieved by Gandhi on the untouchability-front, through the authoritative support of the Gītā:

> The Gītā told him that all men are equal, all men deserve the supreme blessings of God, the Gītā bars no one from divine attainment that he calls self-realization. This spirit that he derived from the Gītā made him a life-time servant of and upholder of the rights of the untouchables in particular and the down-trodden of the society in general. He rightly opined that untouchability is a blot on Hindu society and religion and he prided in calling himself a Bhangi. Eradication of untouchability is one of the greatest works of Gandhiji and for this he derived justification from the Gītā.

6.79. 'Uplift of women' constitutes another important plank in Gandhi's constructive programme. The fact that the Gītā makes no distinction between man and woman strengthened Gandhi's belief in the need to provide equal opportunities to women. He always wanted India's womanhood to rise to realise its due status, work and duty in society. He wanted women to have due education. He wanted them to become real partners in the lives of their husbands and family; he wanted women to play a leading role in the Satyāgraha movements and in the reconstruction of the country. So many of his activities were guided by these ideas.[56]

6.80. Another important cause for which Gandhi fasted several times, and ultimately faced the assassin's bullet, was inter-religious harmony, in general, and Hindu-Muslim unity in particular. In his prayer meetings, verses from various scriptures—including the Gītā and Koran—were recited. Louis Fischer attaches great significance to 'the fact that Hindus would listen to Koran verses and that Moslems would not object to hearing holy words of Islam from the mouth of a Hindu'.[57] Gandhi's argument was that, even after the partition of the country, Muslims in the 'secular state of India' should feel safe and equal to all other citizens. He helped restore communal harmony in Calcutta by undertaking a fast in September 1947 till the city's leaders pledged to keep peace. In January 1948, just a couple of weeks before his assassination, Gandhi's fast in Delhi helped restore inter-communal goodwill—and this was acknowledged by Pakistani Minister Zafrullah Khan who said that 'a new and tremendous wave of feeling and desire for friendship between the two Dominions is sweeping the subcontinent in response to the fast'.[58]

6.81. J.H. Holmes wrote to Gandhi, 'I count these last months to be crown and climax of your unparalleled career. You were never so great as in these dark hours'.[59] Betai attributes this capability to face all calamities—like the Sthitaprajña of the Gītā—to Gandhi's adherence to the Gītā as a child adheres to its mother. Betai summarizes some of the happenings of the closing days of Gandhi's life:

> In those days he invoked the help of the Gītā again and again. . . So fearless was he that when Lady Mountbatten came to congratulate him when he was saved from the bomb-explosion on 20 January 1948, he could reply in perfect equanimity of spirit and perfect fearlessness: "On this occasion, I have shown no bravery. If somebody fired at me pointblank and I faced bullet with a smile, repeating the name of Rama in my heart, I should indeed be deserving of congratulations".[60]

And indeed this is what happened when Nathuram Godse fired at him on 30 January 1948. And this proved to be the final evidence in support of the statement that Gandhi tried to live by the Gītā-ideals—as he interpreted them—in thought, word and deed. As Sarma puts it:

> There is perfect harmony between Gandhiji's life and his teaching. In fact, his whole life is an embodiment of his teaching. His greatest contribution to the thought of our age is contained in the word 'Satyāgraha', which he invented. If his writings are an exposition of this new dharma, he is himself an incarnation of it. He is not only the author of

Satyāgraha but also an ideal Satyāgrahī. Therefore his character, as revealed by his actions, is an important for us as his writings.[61]

6.82. Ursula king has summarised what might be called the general assessment of the people in regard to Gandhi's effort to be an ideal Karmayogin:

> The ideal Karmayogin is for Gandhi the person who chooses the way of selfless action and sacrifice as path to God. The central importance of this message for Gandhi and the way it presupposes a substantial reinterpretation of the Bhagavad-Gītā has been commented in detail by Agehananda Bharati and will not be further discussed here. It may be mentioned, however, that a further development has taken place in that today Gandhi himself is often seen as the ideal Karmayogin. The newly understood Karmayoga taught by the Krishna of the Bhagavad-Gītā has found concrete and permanent historical expression in the person and work of Gandhi. Hindu religious teaching today makes use of the ideal Karmayogin symbol by applying it both to the classical Krishna and the contemporary Gandhi. Not only Hindus but others, too, refer to Gandhi as Karmayogin; for example, in a recent study of mysticism and contemporary spirituality, a western author describes Gandhi as a 'true mystic of action, a true karmayogin'. This shows the wide diffusion of the Karmayogin ideal and implies an even further transformation of its meaning. One may also note that no other representative of modern Hinduism illustrates the originality as well as the dilemma of the Karmayogin symbol more strikingly than Gandhi does.[62]

DEBATE ABOUT GANDHI'S DERIVATION OF AHIṀSĀ FROM THE GĪTĀ

6.83. Tilak started applying the Gītā to political issues in 1897, and Aurobindo's intensive study of the Gītā began in 1908. However, Aurobindo's political activities came to a close when he went to Pondicherry in 1910. Tilak died in 1920. So the longest and most significant direct application of the Gītā to India's freedom struggle was carried out by Gandhi, say from

1919 till 1947. But whereas Tilak and Aurobindo had quoted the Gītā to justify the use of force if necessary, Gandhi's interpretation was just the opposite. This can be called a qualitative difference between Gandhi on the one hand, and Tilak and Aurobindo, on the other. Gandhi made a distinction between violence and fearlessness; in fact he told people that fearlessness is mentioned in the Gītā as the first virtue of *daivī sampat.* He was against all forms of violence, "not on grounds of efficacy, but on grounds of moral indefensibility". His application of the ethical principles, especially the teachings he derived from the Gītā, elevated the national movement to a higher plane. His theory that the end could not be separated from the means, as Nehru observes, has been one of his greatest contributions to India's public life. Nehru continues, "The idea is by no means new, but this application of an ethical doctrine to large scale public activity was certainly novel".[63]

6.84. Gandhi's derivation of Ahiṁsā from the Gītā was far from easy because the Gītā teaching was given on the battlefield of Kurukṣetra, and the entire Mahābhārata speaks of the war between the Pāṇḍavas and the Kauravas. Gandhi tries to bypass these difficulties by taking the view that the Mahābhārata and Gītā are largely allegorical. He raises a question; Who are Dhṛtarāṣṭra and Yudhiṣṭhira and Arjuna? And who is Kṛṣṇa? Were they all historical characters? And does the Gītā describe them as such? He then proceeds to answer the question thus: I regard Duryodhana and his party as the baser impulses in man, and Arjuna and his party as the higher impulses. So the Mahābhārata as a grand religious work describes the battle of life, the battle between right and wrong, the battle between truth and untruth, the battle between Dharma and Adharma. The persons described therein may be historical, says Gandhi, but the author of the Mahābhārata has used them merely to drive home the religious theme, namely, that Truth outweighs everything else on earth.

6.85. Gandhi argues that in spite of describing warlike situations in great detail, the author of the Mahābhārata has not established the necessity of physical warfare; on the contrary he has proved its futility. He has made the victors shed tears of sorrow and repentance, and has left them nothing but a legacy of miseries.

6.86. Gandhi admits that the Gītā was not written to establish Ahiṁsā, nor was it necessary to do so because Ahiṁsā was an accepted and primary duty even before the Gītā age. He has argued out his view of the main lesson of the Gītā, namely, Anāsakti or selfless action. He then continues: The Gītā had to deliver the message of renunciation of fruit. But the Gītā has indirectly accepted the principle of Ahiṁsā. In order to follow the doctrine of detachment or renunciation of the fruit of action, man has to accept the principle of Ahiṁsā. When there is no desire for fruit, says Gandhi, there is no temptation for Hiṁsā.[64]

6.87. Why then did Vyāsa choose a war-story to indirectly convey the principle of Ahiṁsā, and did he not realise the inconsistency? It appears that in those days, even though Ahiṁsā was one of the basic virtues of Hinduism, a participation in a war for dharma by Kṣatriya rulers was considered a normal occurrence. The Mahābhārata has, on several occasions, distinguished between the right conduct for ascetics on the one hand and Kṣatriya rulers on the other. However, Gandhi says that such distinctions arise out of limitations of poets, but need not apply to Śrī Kṛṣṇa's teachings in the Gītā because the ideal shown there can be reached by all.

6.88. Gandhi further argues that Parameshwara who is deeply concerned about maintaining orderliness in society cannot possibly teach Hiṁsā to His devotee. The singer of the Gītā is God the supreme in the form of Kṛṣṇa who is known as Pūrṇa Avatāra as also Yogeśvara. What can He teach other than Ahiṁsā when He is expounding before Arjuna, and through him to humanity at large, the ideal of religion, ethics and spiritual attainment of life? If we study the whole of the Gītā and examine its descriptions of Sthitaprajña, Brahmabhūta, Bhakta and Yogī, says Gandhi, we can reach only this conclusion that Kṛṣṇa of the Gītā was the very incarnation of Ahiṁsā, and that the observance of Ahiṁsā is part of the nature of persons attaining perfection.

6.89. Gandhi draws a distinction between the way of violence historically adopted by kings and the way of non-violence used by the people. History as we know it, says Gandhi, is a record of the wars of the world. How kings played, how they became enemies of one another, how they murdered one another, is found accurately recorded in history, and if this were all that had happened in the world, it would have ended long ago. If the story of the universe had commenced with wars, not a man would have been found alive today. The fact that there are so many men still alive in the world shows that it is based not on the force of arms but on the force of truth or love. Therefore, the greatest and most unimpeachable evidence of the success of Ahiṁsā is to be found in the fact that, in spite of all the wars. the world still lives on.

6.90. Gandhi does not attach much importance to a superficial, occasional statement (like that of Arjuna in the beginning of the Gītā) expressing anxiety about the horrors of war, because, as Betai puts it, "Arjuna's refusal to fight is not non-violence. It is not the result of genuine awakening and enlightenment, but a flash as if of future happenings, through his attachment and sorrow".[65] Śrī Kṛṣṇa as an avatāra dispels Arjuna's ignorance and attachment and asks him to fight for the protection of dharma, only as an instrument in the hands of God. Gandhi comments: "God the supreme is above violence and non-violence. I believe in Kṛṣṇa, but my Kṛṣṇa is the Lord of the Universe, the creator, preserver and destroyer of us all. He may destroy because He creates."[66]

This shows that, in Gandhi's opinion, participation in God's work does not include participation in destroying the wicked, because a human being (as a person) should not have the arrogance to label another human being as wicked. However, Gandhi does envisage non-cooperation with those who, in our opinion, are committing injustice and violence. This is one of the practical ways of applying what Gandhi calls "Satyāgraha", representing soul-force or non-violent resistance.

6.91. Gandhi admits that the Hindu Ṛṣi who said that 'Violence vanishes before Ahiṁsā' must have done so on the basis of his own experience or that of other Rishis. The more violent the aggressor, the firmer the practice of Ahiṁsā required to bring about an abandonment of violence. Cultivation of the virtue of the Ahiṁsā to such an extent may need long practice. Also, a non-violent person is willing to lay down one's life in an attempt to win over the heart of the aggressor. Hindus read from ancient scriptures the glorious example of the seer Dadhīci who laid down his life to protect the society, of king Shibi who risked his life to save the life of a dove, of Prahlād and Sudhanvā who went through untold ordeals, and of Muni Nārada who won over a robber by his non-violence. In the middle ages, the history of Vaiṣṇava saints provides many examples of evil appearing on the path of good but melting away by the love of the saints. Śrī Chaitanyadeva, an apostle of Vaiṣṇavism, remained calm and offered his love to the ruffian who violently struck him. Similar instances of the use of non-violence by great personalities are available from Buddhist and Jain literature also.

6.92. Scholars including Tilak, Radhakrishnan and Rajagopalachari feel that Gandhi is "stretching" the ordinary meaning of the Gītā verses to read the message of Ahiṁsā therein. Also, there are differences of opinion as to whether ethical standards suitable for individuals in their private lives could be extended to collective conduct. For example, Tilak says, "A mere high religious ideal does not prove very useful in practical politics."[67] Iyer characterizes Tilak as a relativist and Gandhi as an absolutist. Regarding the difference between Radhakrishnan and Gandhi, Betai says:

> Radhakrishnan agrees that the Gītā preaches Ahiṁsā, but it is not Ahiṁsā of Gandhiji's ideal and definition. He means to suggest that when a man of action takes to an attitude of saṁnyāsa and does his works in perfect detachment, as a duty, as social service, and as work of God, be it the worst of its kind, it is Ahiṁsā. Here he accepts that there can be niṣkāma hiṁsā but wants to suggest that niṣkāma hiṁsā is Ahiṁsa.
>
> Gandhiji would not agree with Radhakrishnan here.[69]

Similarly, Rajagopalachari does not like Gandhi's ideas of interpreting the Gītā and the Mahābhārata only as an allegory and then deriving the doctrine of Ahiṁsā therefrom. He suggests, instead, that "We should forget the battle scene when we study the Gītā as a scripture of sanātana dharma. . . . The Gītā as a scripture of Hinduism stands apart from the Mahābhārata."[70]

6.93. Whatever might be the academic differences between Gandhi and other interpreters of the Gītā, the vast "practical experiments" with Ahiṁsā which Gandhi conducted and the ultimate attainment of India's political independence under Gandhi's leadership, did help in putting forth the Ahiṁsā doctrine as a bold, new technique for the modern age. Ursula King goes so far as to say that "Hindu religious teaching today makes use of the ideal Karmayogin symbol by applying it both to the classical Krishna and the contemporary Gandhi. . . .[71] The continued usage and widespread presence of this symbol are a sign of the creativity of Hinduism and of its religious activity, sensitive to the needs of modern men."[72]

6.94. Since Lokasaṁgraha epitomizes the needs and goals of humanity and the world, a gradual recognition of Ahiṁsā as a yugadharma (or dharma relevant to present age) would help appreciate the complementary nature of the contributions made by Tilak and Gandhi towards interpreting the Gītā for meeting India's critical needs. P.M. Thomas expresses his own agreement with Raj Krishna's statement to the effect that Tilak tried to supply the philosophical proof and Gandhi the practical demonstration that action for the welfare of the world could be direct means of liberation.[73] Perhaps this observation can be elaborated further by saying that Tilak's scholarship helped focus attention on Lokasaṁgraha, while Gandhi's life-long experiments raised the possibility for Ahiṁsā to be gradually recognized as the basic means for achieving that goal.

6.95. Gandhi's experiments represented an attempt to extend the application of Ahiṁsā in two directions, namely, from the Ṛṣis and saints to common people, and from individual application to mass scale application. Although the main political party accepted Gandhi's leadership for the national struggle, to many of the leaders Ahiṁsā was only a practical tool for a limited purpose, and not necessarily a long-term ideal having religious or spiritual significance for the rest of their lives. Among common people, the level of understanding of the new doctrine remained vague, and they acted mostly out of their faith in Gandhi as a Mahātmā or great soul. Of course, hundreds of thousands participated actively in non-violent programmes like non-cooperation with the foreign rulers and civil disobedience of unjust laws, and many faced bullets without retaliation. However, a serious failure occurred when communal riots took place after political independence was won. On the whole, the mass scale application of Ahiṁsā can be considered a partial success, which in itself was unique in the entire history of the world. An inference to be drawn is that it was easier to inspire people by Ahiṁsā against a foreign ruler, than to keep them united and peaceful for solving socio-economic-religious problems of day-to-day life.

6.96. It is clear that Gandhi's derivation of Ahiṁsā from the Gītā reflected his own deep conviction and faith in the Gītā. It is also clear that common people following Gandhi had their own limitations in understanding the Ahiṁsā doctrine and in putting it into practice. In spite of all this, how can we account for the degree of success that was achieved in applying the Gītā to India's freedom struggle? The main points can be listed as follows:

(a) In the Gītā, the Pāṇḍavas representing the forces of the good fought for a just cause against the Kauravas which represented the forces of the evil. The similarity of this fight with the freedom struggle against a foreign ruler was easy to understand.

(b) It was possible to generate a sense of unity in practically the whole of the society because the target of attack was a foreign power.

(c) Even those who did not want to mix up religion and politics supported the cause of the freedom struggle on secular grounds.

(d) Gandhi's emphasis on the use of non-violent means won the support of those who did not favour assassination of British officials. Of course, many such supporters had doubts whether non-violent methods would succeed.

Reassurance came from the Indian scriptures which declared that adherence to truth and non-violence was ultimately bound to succeed.

6.97. Howsoever limited might have been the results of Gandhi's experimentation with mass-scale Ahiṁsā, in today's atmosphere of terrorism connected with fundamentalistic ideologies of different types, it would be a safe policy to insist that all the Lokasaṁgraha activities (and particularly, those of a non-governmental nature) must be non-violent. From this viewpoint, the Gandhian interpretation of the Gītā assumes great significance, because even terrorists killing their opponents often claim that they have no selfish interest to serve. Non-violence can supplement the criterion of selflessness, as a further check to terrorism. More and more thinkers and social reformers all over the world are accordingly being attracted to this new technique. For example, Sissela Bok as well as Devaki Jain (in separate articles) envisages widespread application of Ahiṁsā with small groups, to begin with, and its gradual extension to wider issues and territories:

> I am most interested in the Gandhian alternative. Gandhi, far from denying the presence of violence in the world, meant to carve out spaces, territories in human interaction, where violence would nevertheless not be used .... Once these territories have thus been carved out, they can be enlarged, extended, and become models for others. ...[74]
>
> A women's united platform need not be completely issue-based, but could well be methodology-based (for example, based on the way of non-violence).[75]

6.98. An interesting and novel application of the non-violent approach to the protection of forests in India has been made by the "Chipko movement" (Chipko means hugging). In the Himalayan hills area, when all efforts for preventing the cutting of trees failed, ordinary women and men "hugged" the trees and flung their bodies before the axes. These people were inspired by Gandhi's example. A local organization called "Lakshmi Ashram" helped organise the people to bring about socio-economic change through peaceful methods. Radha Bhatt writes about the success achieved, not only in the Chipko movement but also in other activities aimed at protecting the environment, saving cultivated land and drinking water supply:

> The hill-people's action gave birth to the famous non-violent ecological movement known in India and throughout the world as "Chipko". Similar action was taken by the women of Khirakot when they fought against the businessman and the government who had started a soapstone quarry on their village land, which had spoiled their village forest, their cultivated land, their drinking water, and the footpaths to their fields. They succeeded. . . . But where are the roots of this non-violence? I believe they are rooted deep in the culture and religion of our people.[76]

6.99. Before concluding this brief account of the possibilities of continued practical use of Gandhian, non-violent methods, broadly denoted by the term 'Satyāgraha', it is necessary to refer to the controversy, which has often arisen in India, as to whether such methods can or should be resorted to in a democracy. Gandhi himself had warned against the risk of Satyāgraha turning into durāgraha (evil force), particularly if the underlying goal, though outwardly the good of others, was, at the heart of it, selfish gain:

> Satyāgrahīs must not transgress the limits prescribed by wisdom and appreciation of their own capacity. Satyāgraha offered on every occasion, seasonable or otherwise, would be corrupted into durāgraha. And if any one takes to Satyāgraha without having measured his own strength and afterwards sustains defeat, he not only disgraces himself but he also brings the matchless weapon of Satyāgraha into disrepute by his folly.[77]
>
> A satyāgrahī has to be unattached to the attainment of the object of Satyāgraha. . . . Satyāgraha cannot be resorted to for personal gain, but only for the good of others.[78]

6.100. Santhanam argues that general Satyāgraha against a democratic government cannot be justified, but he also allows for some marginal cases. He thinks that individual Satyāgraha has a definite place in a democracy as a corrective against the misuses of political power and as a safeguard for the preservation of the democratic spirit.[79] Gadgil is emphatic that mass civil disobedience, violent or even non-violent, in a constitutional democracy, is bound to result in anarchy.[80]

However, Barve is equally emphatic that, even in a democracy, a non-violent conflict on a mass scale cannot be avoided when there is no other alternative.[81]

After analyzing both sides of the controversy, Iyer feels that a mutually acceptable, general criterion for the legitimacy and the limits of Satyāgraha in the Indian democratic system is "peculiarly difficult to give":

> At the extremes there is an element of truth on both sides, which could be put equally in the language of democracy and of Satyāgraha.
>
> The democrat is right to be concerned about the danger of anarchy and irresponsible disobedience engendered by the resort to Satyāgraha especially in a community in which law-abiding habits have not taken deep root and constitutional procedures are unfamiliar to the majority. The satyagrahī is also justified in insisting on the right to Satyāgraha even in a democracy, for it is all too easy to denounce all appeals to natural law in the name of *raison d'tat,* legal sovereignty or paternalistic state action. It is between these two extreme positions—the pre-requisites of effective government and the claims of conscience—that it becomes peculiarly difficult to give a general criterion for the legitimacy and the limits of Satyāgraha in a democratic system.[82]

ROLE OF THE BHAGAVAD-GĪTĀ

6.101. Gandhi's main contribution in regard to the application of the Gītā to social and political causes was that he developed the Satyāgraha-technique based on Ahiṁsā. Many scholars who go merely by the words of the Giīā argue that "Mass scale Ahiṁsā" was Gandhi's own philosophy and that he linked it with the Gītā to obtain widespread support of the people. However, Gandhi's portrayal of an ideal Satyāgrahī as the Sthitaprajña of the Gītā does establish the Gītā as the main reference book to understand the full implications of the Gandhian technique.

6.102. The Sthitaprajña verses of the Gītā (II. 54-72) had appealed to Gandhi when he started reading Edwin Arnold's translation at the age of twenty, as a student of Law in England. His decision to put into practice the Gītā-teaching was taken in South Africa at the age of thirty-four. According to Sarma, this decision was the first of several steps that Gandhi took in 1903 and which, three years later, enabled him to launch his first experiment with mass-scale Satyāgraha:

> The first step was his intense study of the Bhagavad-Gītā, which from 1903 became his infallible guide in conduct. . . . He wanted to put into practice the Gītā-teaching—that one should be in the world, but not of it. . . .[83]

6.103. While Gandhi was busy experimenting with mass-scale applications of Ahiṁsā to deal with issues of social injustice, discrimination and exploitation, Tilak, undergoing political imprisonment due to his agitation for Swarāj, completed his commentary on the Gītā, emphasizing Karma-yoga and Lokasaṁgraha as the main teaching thereof. Faced with an oppressive foreign rule, Lokasaṁgraha or the good of the society called for an effective application of the Gītā-teaching to win Swarāj or political independence. What the freedom-fighters were urged to do was niṣkāma karma or to carry on the freedom struggle as a duty, without expecting any personal rewards. While Lokasaṁgraha and niṣkāma karma constituted common elements in the approaches of Tilak and Gandhi, differences between the two leaders arose over the issue of the role of Ahiṁsā. Tilak summarized his approach by a Marathi phrase meaning "peacefully if possible, but otherwise by force".[84] Gandhi ruled out the use of physical force, and claimed that non-violence, if properly practised, was more effective than violence. As he put it, "There is no such thing as defeat in non-violence; the end of violence is surest defeat."[85]

6.104. Panikkar has explained how the Lokasaṁgraha ideal stressed by Tilak was supplemented by the Ahiṁsā doctrine of Gandhi, and further, how the unique combination of Ahiṁsā and Lokasaṁgraha resulted in an exemplification of the image of a Sthitaprajña in the personality of Gandhi:

> To Gandhiji, it was not sufficient that the ideal should be Lokasaṁgraha or the welfare of all. It was even more important that the means should be ethically right. For action to be Brahma Yajña or sacrifice or dedication to God, it must be pure and uncontaminated not merely by unselfishness but by anything which injures others. His doctrine of Ahiṁsā or non-violence was therefore not the creed of pacifism or a denial of force, but an emphasis that the force of action should not be such as to injure the true nature of another's law of life—of the Swadharma of the opponent.[86]
>
> If activism was what Tilak emphasized, it is the Sthitaprajña doctrine—that of selfless service—that Gandhiji taught by his commentary on the Gītā. Gandhi's exposition of the Gītā was not a learned one. It was not a work of objective scholarship like that of Tilak, or of inspired interpretation like that of Aurobindo. Gandhiji believed in selfless action for the good of the world and he found that doctrine stated with unambiguous lucidity and authority in the Gītā. He was in fact the embodiment of the Gītā ideal of the equable mind devoted to action meant for the benefit of all—the Sthitaprajña who unmoved by anger or by fear had his feet planted firmly in the world and directed all his action to the benefit of the world. He was the true Karmayogin and his commentary on the Gītā is therefore a statement of his personal credo.
>
> Gandhiji's special contribution to the integral teachings of the Gītā is not selfless action for the welfare of the world but the emphasis on the means. There was a suggestion in Tilak's Gītā-Rahasya that the Karmayogin's action, as it was dedicated to God, was above moral laws so long as the object was clearly understood to be the common weal. It is this unexpressed doctrine of Tilak that Gandhiji sought to set right by his commentary on the Gītā and the practical interpretation he gave to it through his own life.[87]

6.105. The need for a Sthitaprajña to lead the country to Swarāj was, in a prophetic but indirect way, expressed by Aurobindo also, when he wrote the following, before leaving for Pondicherry:

> The Party is there, not less pervading and powerful than before but in want of a policy and a leader. The first it may find, the second, only God can give. The men who have led hitherto, have been strong men of high gifts and commanding genius, great enough to be protagonists of any other movement; but even they were not sufficient to satisfy one which is the chief current of a world-wide revolution. Therefore, the Nationalist Party, custodians of the future must wait for the man who is to come, calm in the midst of calamity, hopeful under defeat, sure of eventual emergence of triumph and always mindful of the responsibility which they owe not only to India, but to the world.[88]

6.106. Apart from the Sthitaprajña-ideal of perfection, which Gandhi also expressed in terms of realization of Truth (Satya), another concept of the Gītā which helped Gandhi strengthen the social aspect of the teaching was "Yajña". Gandhi valued the Gītā-approach of modifying the meaning of Yajña and himself carried such modification still further so as to make it increasingly relevant to present social conditions and to serve the cause of Lokasaṁgraha. Tilak and Aurobindo had done something similar, but had not made practical applications thereof to the same extent. The Gandhian interpretation of Yajña carried with it a twofold process of change. On the one hand, it meant identifying new approaches and productive activities (like Khādī and village industries) which if undertaken in a spirit of Yajña could help the society. Secondly, Gandhi also suggested the abandonment of the traditional way of performing a Yajña, for example, burning of wood. Although fire was the symbol of yajña in Vedic times and is still so considered by religious organisations like Arya Samaj, the Gītā envisaged the possibility of using fire in a symbolic sense (IV.24). Gandhi tried to create public opinion in favour of subjecting every religious practice to the test of relevance in modern times. He gave the following comment on the yajña-related verses of Gītā:

> I cannot understand the idea that one can perform a yajña by lighting a few sticks. It does not do to say that doing so purifies the air. There are many other ways of purifying the air. Why should we at all pollute the air? But this is not the

> aim behind a yajña. When the Āryans first came to this country, they tried to civilize the non-Āryan races. Maybe the idea of yajña was originally conceived for the uplift of the latter. There were big forests in those days, and it may have been regarded as everyone's duty to help in clearing these forests, for it was a social necessity. And because the work was regarded as a duty, it came to be looked upon as a means of attaining mokṣa. Innumerable ceremonies were devised, all of which required the lighting of fire. In burning wood in this age, we misuse the capital of our forefathers, or we show ourselves witless pedants by understanding the thing in a literal sense.[89]

6.107. Gandhi is very emphatic that verses III.9 to III.16 which speak of the origin of yajña and of the importance of continuing in motion the wheel of yajña, should be interpreted in such a way as to solve the most pressing problems of today's society. He raises the question: What is meant by saying that mankind was created along with Yajña?, and he suggests an answer: Just as we cannot escape the cycle of birth, old age and death, so also bodily labour is our lot in life from which there is no escape. In a country like India, extremely backward that it was, he saw not only laziness and a dislike for physical labour and lack of care to do one's own small jobs on one's own, he also saw that a sense of hatred for physical labour even for one's own needs existed in the society, and so he wanted that dignity of labour should be established. He also felt that for removing the grave sin of untouchability, the sense of dignity of labour and self-dependence as also keenness for service should be emphasized. He therefore took the view that labouring enough for one's food has been classed in the Gītā as a Yajña. He suggested similarly that the wheel of yajña, in verse III.16 should in today's conditions mean the spinning wheel. Whereas in old days cutting down trees and burning wood had become a yajña, at the present time, said Gandhi, spinning and other village industries have become a yajña. If water was scarce and we had to fetch it from a distance of two miles, fetching water would be yajña.

6.108. When Gandhi was in South Africa, there were, besides the Gītā, two other strong influences on his philosophy of life, namely Ruskin and Tolstoy. Ruskin's "Unto This Last" impressed Gandhi so much that he translated it into Gujarati under the title "Sarvodaya". To Tolstoy, Gandhi gave credit for enunciating convincingly the "Bread Labour Law", viz. that God created man to work for his food and said that those who ate without working were thieves. However, after Gandhi returned to India and made a deeper study of the Gītā, in consultation with his Ashrama-residents and particularly Vinoba, the ideas underlying "Sarvodaya" and "Bread Labour" were found to be included in the comprehensive Gītā-ideals of 'Sarvabhūtahitam', 'Swadharma', and 'Yajña'.

6.109. Removal of untouchability was another important social mission of Gandhi for which he took the help of the Gītā. Orthodox Hindus tried to justify untouchability by interpreting some of the old books in their own way. Gandhi achieved success by adopting a similar course as Rammohun Roy had done more than a century ago—namely, by quoting the Gītā in support of his stand that all human beings are equal in the eyes of God.

6.110. Another important cause for which Gandhi fasted several times, and ultimately faced the assassin's bullet, was inter-religious harmony, in general, and Hindu-Muslim unity in particular. The Gītā, advocating a reconciliatory approach in religious matters, was particularly helpful to Gandhi in this matter.

6.111. The secret of Gandhi's success was that he tried to live by the Gītā-ideals—as he interpreted them—in thought, word and deed. As Sarma puts it:

> "There is perfect harmony between Gandhiji's life and teaching. In fact, his whole life is an embodiment of his teaching. . . . He is not only the author of Satyāgraha but also an ideal Satyāgrahī".[90]
>
> And Gandhi had equated the ideal Satyāgrahī with the Sthitaprajña of the Gītā.

§ 110. Another [illegible] Gandhi [illegible] [illegible] religious [illegible] [illegible] Hindu-Muslim [illegible] [illegible] the Gita [illegible] in the matter.

[illegible] Gandhi [illegible] Sarvodaya [illegible]

Chapter Seven

From Roy to Gandhi: Expanding the Social Role of the Gītā

7.1. The socio-religious and/or political activities of the five prominent persons included in this study—spanning the one hundred and thirty-five-year period (1815-1950)—are marked with diversity as well as continuity. Elements of diversity are obvious from the fact that the focus of activity shifted from socio-religious reform to social service and socio-spiritual re-awakening and further to socio-ethical revolution and political independence. Underlying currents of continuity—denoted by expressions like reformism, patriotism, Hindu renaissance—could be identified. However, a more specific thread of continuity, from Roy to Gandhi, is that each of them used the Bhagavad-Gītā as an important source of inspiration and new ideas, to achieve success in the social movement of the day.

7.2. There was no compulsion or imposition associated with the invoking of the Gītā by any of the persons included in this study. Hinduism being basically an unorganized religion, allowing for choices in many matters including preference for a scriptural text—any leader of social movement could make use of the Vedas, the Upaniṣads, the Gītā, the Rāmāyaṇa, the Purāṇas and so on—either singly or in groups. The fact that the Gītā was utilized to help push forward a variety of social movements over such a long time-period, can best be explained by the statement that this particular book was able to provide answers to questions that vitally affected the success of the social causes from time to time. The case study of each of the five leaders included in this study helps illustrate this statement.

RAMMOHUN ROY

7.3. Starting with Rammohun Roy, what sort of questions confronted him when he wanted to create public opinion in favour of abolishing the evil custom of suttee? The priests had joined hands with narrow-minded, avaricious elements in the society and had provided a religious cover to what was basically a property-grabbing device. By declaring that the suttee, who burnt herself with her dead husband's body, would go to heaven, an impression had been created as if the custom was intended to benefit the widow herself. If Rammohun Roy had argued that this talk of going to heaven was only a superstition, he would probably have been ex-communicated from the Hindu society as an anti-religious non-entity. A basic question confronting Rammohun Roy, therefore, was: could he present any Sanskrit quotation from any of the scriptures, to prove that going to heaven by burning herself was not in the best interests of the widow?

7.4. Rammohun Roy was a great Sanskrit scholar, and he knew the Vedas, the Upaniṣads, the Gītā, and presumably other scriptures as well. After opting for early retirement from the East India Company job in 1815, he started exploring ways for bringing about socio-religious reforms. The most effective answer to the above-mentioned question regarding suttee, that he could formulate in 1818 was: To burn herself with the desire to go to heaven is spiritually inferior to *niṣkāma* karma of the Gītā —which means, in this case, staying alive as a widow and performing one's worldly duty, without hankering after the fruit i.e. selfish gains. And Rammohun was able to make this answer generally acceptable because, as he put it, the Gītā is "the essence of all śāstras".[1]

7.5. The suttee-advocates had to admit that Rammohun's answer, deriving authority from the Gītā, did prove that, in principle, staying alive as a widow and performing acts according to the teaching of the Gītā, was spiritually superior to becoming a suttee. However, they still wanted to establish that, in practise, the suttee was superior. So their next argument was: Granted that *niṣkāma* karma is the best, because it is the way to the highest spiritual bliss, but women are in general inferior to men and there are great risks that a widow may not be able to practise *niṣkāma* karma for the rest of her life. So, in practice, it is better for her to burn herself with her husband's body and attain heaven (without running the risk which is involved in opting for *niṣkāma* karma).

7.6. Rammohun Roy found, in the Gītā, a suitable answer to the above argument also. He asserted that, according to the Gītā, women as well as men have the same entitlement to the highest spiritual bliss, and also that it is contrary to the Gītā's teaching to cast doubts on a widow's capability to practise *niṣkāma* karma. Furthermore, said Rammohun, the Gītā provides for a safeguard for those who try their best to practise *niṣkāma* karma but are unable to attain spiritual perfection within the present life—the safeguard being that their upward journey towards perfection will be continued in their next life and so on till the goal is reached. In this way, arguing from the standpoint of a believer in the Hindu scriptures, Rammohun Roy was able to answer all the questions raised by the suttee-advocates.

7.7. Furthermore, Rammohun had to show a way out of wrong beliefs even though no direct question was raised about them. He noticed, as a rational analyst, that the superstitious beliefs which the suttee-advocates and priests had imposed on the Hindu society represented a distorted version of the so-called 'law of karma'. While an important objective underlying this law was probably to warn evil-doers that they could never escape the evil consequences of their misdeeds, the orthodox priests had encouraged fatalism and a passive acceptance of existing conditions, howsoever bad. 'If you follow priests' advice, you will go to heaven, and don't worry about the harm apparently being done now (like burning yourself)'— this was the type of reasoning that the priests had imposed on ignorant people. In the ultimate analysis, right knowledge and right belief constitute the foundation for social reform. To achieve this, Rammohun made use of the Gītā-teaching of not being misled by 'fruit-promising' allurements advanced by ritualists.[2] Thus Rammohun pleaded for Karma-yoga based on Buddhi-yoga (i.e. right action based on right knowledge) for the widows, and tried to save them from being victimized and exploited by a distorted version of the law of karma.

7.8. Rammohun Roy's arguments, based on the authority of the Gītā (and also supported by quotations from the Upaniṣads), were so convincing that even the suttee-advocates replied: "What you have said we shall carefully consider".[3] In any case, the British Government was able to assert thereafter that the suttee-custom was not in accordance with authoritative Hindu scriptures. Although the decision to impose a legal ban on suttee was taken by the Governor-General in 1829, Rammohun Roy has been rightly given due credit for making serious efforts for this cause from 1815 onward. Rammohun also became a pioneer in making the first social application of the Gītā in modern history.

7.9. Although Rammohun Roy invoked mainly the Gītā to bring about social reform, he depended on the Vedas and the Upaniṣads for formulating the charter for Brahmo Samaj, which was Rammohun's contribution in the field of religious form. In orther words, the two-pronged reformist movement in India—covering social and religious issues separately—pioneered by Rammohun Roy, adopted a multi-scriptural approach, wherein the choice of scripture depended on specific needs of the two movements.

VIVEKANANDA

7.10. Vivekananda's movement (named after his Master Sri Ramakrishna), which took a concrete shape more than sixty years after Rammohun Roy, had a broader and more co-ordinated vision. Rather than formulate separate programmes for social and religious reforms, an integrated view, aiming at socio-spiritual re-awakening of the country, was adopted. Although the underlying approach was still multi-scriptural, a serious effort was made to combine the Vedānta of the Upaniṣads, and the Karma-Yoga of the Gītā, under a new philosophy called "Practical Vedānta".

7.11. The Ramakrishna Mission, established by Vivekananda in 1897, although non-political, was still revolutionary in certain respects. Monks were to be the pillars of the new organization, but their motto marked a clear departure from the tradition inasmuch as it stressed 'social service' as the best way to Mokṣa (Liberation). Vivekananda coined a new Sanskrit phrase for this, namely, 'ātmano mokṣārthaṁ jagaddhitāya ca", meaning 'for one's mokṣa as well as for the good of the world'.[4]

7.12. Vivekananda's ideas were so revolutionary that some of his own colleagues (i.e. brother-disciples of Sri Ramakrishna) initially expressed what could be called 'fraternal resistance'. However, when the depth of Vivekananda's feelings and commitment to the new ideal became clear, then a united front emerged. In this way, Vivekananda succeeded in ensuring that the Ramakrishna Mission adopted the karma-yoga-based socio-spiritual approach to India's problems.

7.13. One of the social service activities of the Ramakrishna Mission was to render help to the poor, and particularly at the time of calamities like famines and epidemics which were quite frequent in Bengal at that time. Vivekananda suggested to an orthodox Hindu preacher belonging to the society for the protection of cows, that since their society had relatively more resources, they could also participate in famine-relief activities. The preacher not only refused to help starving human beings but also added that such starvation was the result of their karma. This was a clear indication that the perverted view about the law of karma, which Rammohun Roy had come across in the early decades of the nineteenth century was still prevalent in the last decade of that century. Vivekananda therefore made special efforts to educate the society in the Karma-yoga doctrine, which was one way of removing from the people's mind "the wrong interpretation of the law of karma", as he put it.[5]

7.14. The strong emphasis of Karma-yoga in the entire approach of the Ramakrishna Mission is a clear indicator of the impact of the Gītā. While Vivekananda based the doctrine of

Karma-yoga mainly on the Gītā, he often referred to the Buddha as an 'Ideal Karma-Yogin'.[6]

7.15. Vivekananda's emphasis on 'social service' as an important element in socio-spiritual re-awakening in the country, strengthened further by dedicated work done by the Ramakrishna Mission over the years, gradually moulded the approach of many 'political or social reform groups' also, as noted recently by Madeleine Biardeau. She made a special study of social service groups in India during the eighties, with a view to identifying their sources of inspiration. Her findings confirm Vivekananda's great contribution in bringing into prominence the social role of the Gītā:

> The term 'sevā', service, is one that recurs quite frequently in the names of many political or social reform groups. . . .
>
> Undoubtedly the influence of Vivekananda who had been so impressed in his travels to the West by charitable institutions, and of his Ramakrishna Mission as well, lent great credence to the idea of selfless service. It is nevertheless more than likely that all of this took place within pre-existing ideological frames of reference, and that the Bhagavad-Gītā was its greatest source of inspiration.[7]

TILAK

7.16. Another significant expansion of the social role of the Gītā—in the form of its being got linked with India's freedom struggle—was initiated by Tilak, in the same year (1897) in which the Ramakrishna Mission was established by Vivekananda. But how did Tilak manage to use the Gītā for political purposes? He did this by depicting the seventeenth century Marāṭhā leader, Shivaji as a great national hero whose ideals should be followed by all Indians, and by asserting that Shivaji's adherence to the Karma-yoga teachings of the Gītā was an important factor contributing to his (i.e. Shivaji's) success against the enemies of the Motherland. What made Tilak's public speeches "seditious" in the eyes of the British authorities was the way in which he applied his interpretation of the Gitā doctrine of *niṣkāma* karma to an ethically controversial act of Shivaji.

7.17. Speaking at the largely attended Shivaji Festival in Poona on 12 June 1897, Tilak said, among other things, that, according to the Bhagavad-Gītā, Shivaji did not commit any sin by murdering the enemy's General, Afzul Khan (when the two of them met to discuss terms for avoiding battle), because Shivaji did this for his Motherland and not for any selfish gain. It so happened that, ten days later, a British officer, who had antagonized the public by his harsh treatment, was murdered by a young Indian man (Chapekar) of the same city, Poona. Although the police could not establish any direct link between Tilak and Chapekar, an "indirect" blame was somehow put on Tilak, because of his above-mentioned speech, which was also published in the Marathi paper that he edited.

7.18. Indian historians generally agree that Tilak being sentenced to imprisonment for eighteen months because of his speech of 12 June 1897 marked a turning point in the freedom movement. He was the first important political leader to be jailed, and since there was no separate category of "political prisoners" in those days, he was locked up along with criminals and harshly treated. Even his demand for a simple vegetarian meal, free from onion and garlic, was refused and he might have died in the jail had Professor Max-Müller and other European Sanskrit scholars (who had seen Tilak's writings) not sent a petition to the Queen of England. Tilak's release, six months in advance of the due date (based on the original period of his sentence), saved his life. But the fact that he aroused mass scale patriotic feelings by linking the freedom struggle with the Gītā, and also that he was willing to suffer untold hardships in the process of sticking to his beliefs, made him "Lokamānya" (Revered by the People) in Indian public opinion.

7.19. Two of the most well-known Gītā-commentators in pre-Tilak days had interpreted this scripture from a non-activist angle. For example, Śaṁkara had picked up Jñāna-yoga (leading to renunciation of karma) as the central message of the Gītā, and Ramanuja had similarly emphasized Bhakti-yoga as the main teaching—both pushing Karma-yoga in the background. Tilak used his deep knowledge and an activist approach of life, to explain in detail, and forcefully, that the essence of the Gītā is Karma-yoga, centred on the ideal of Lokasaṁgraha (the good of the society). Tilak's ideas had a strong appeal to Indian activists as well as scholars. For example, Panikkar agrees with Tilak that, because of the Lokasaṁgraha ideal—which puts forth the notion of social responsibility, or of giving the highest priority to the good of the society—the Gītā has greater relevance as well as practical applicability to present-day needs and conditions, even in comparison to the Vedas and the Upaniṣads. Here are Panikkar's words:

> The social theory behind the Lokasaṁgraha doctrine of the Gītā is most important. The conception of a world order which it is the duty of the individual to uphold by dedicating his activity towards that end, runs all through the teachings of the Gītā. The earlier Vedic religion had no such conception. Nor did the later thinkers who built up the comprehensive structure of Upaniṣadic thought devote any attention to social development. For the first time the Gītā gives a social content to religion and emphasizes the welfare of the world as the purpose of all action.[8]

7.20. Subramaniam also agrees that Tilak's pioneering work helped give the Gītā "the status of the bible of India's national struggle", and further that the activism derived from the Gītā by Vivekananda and Tilak was more appropriate to the needs of the country, than that derived from the Vedas by Dayananda:

> By the turn of the (twentieth) century, a number of factors were combining to give the Gītā the status of the bile of India's national struggle. . . . This was the time when Tilak's new interpretation of the Gīta, equating it with Karma-yoga was firing the imagination of the Indian intelligentsia and of the nationalists in particular. . .
>
> The Gītā's activism was a more controlled philosophical activism than the aggressive natural Aryan activism of the Rig-Veda glorified by Dayananda. In its original context, the Gītā served to revive Arjuna's drooping spirits and a precedent for a partially activist interpretation existed already in the great Marathi commentary Jñāneshwari. And just recently,

Vivekananda had increased that stress with his lectures on Karma-Yoga, his highly activist conduct and his activist approach to all things religious and social.[9]

7.21. Tilak's success in obtaining mass support for the freedom struggle was, to a considerable extent, due to a new interpretation that he put on several of the terms in the Gītā. For example, he told his countrymen that Arjuna was only the "nominal" listener of the Karma-yoga teaching, for in reality that message is for "everybody".[10] Similarly, referring to the place—Kurukṣetra or dharmakṣetra—where the battle between the Pāṇḍavas and the Kauravas was fought, he said, the whole of India is the "dharmakṣetra" for modern Indians.[11] As Damodaran observes, 'the attainment of freedom from the British rule was a religious mission for Tilak', and he appealed to all his countrymen to have the same 'mission' and to be ready to make sacrifices therefor.[12] 'Our life and our dharma will be in vain", said he, "in the absence of swarāj".[13] He declared, "Swarāj is my birthright and I will have it".[14] The long prison sentences that he underwent "as the greatest enemy of the empire" added further weight to his appeal to the countrymen. His wife died at their home in Poona, while he was in the Mandalay jail in Burma. Tilak's famous commentary on the Gītā—called *Gītā-Rahasya*—was written during his six-year stay in the jail, and published after his release, in 1915.

7.22. Tilak interpreted the Avatāra, doctrine of the Gītā to justify his own philosophy of "measure for measure":

> Under any circumstances, punishing evil-doers in the interest of general welfare, as was done by the Blessed Lord, is the first duty of saints from the point of view of Ethics. In enunciating the proposition "evil should be conquered by saintliness", the fact that the conquest of or the protection from evil is the primary duty of a saint, is first taken for granted; and the first step to be taken for attaining that result is mentioned. But, it is nowhere stated by our moral philosophers, that if protection against evil-doers cannot be obtained by saintliness, one should not give 'measure for measure', and protect oneself, but should allow oneself to

become a victim of the evil-doings of villains. . .[15]

7.23. Since Tilak advocated strong agitational methods against the British rule, he was called a Revolutionary or even an Extremist. The dominant group in the Indian National Congress at that time being that of Reformists or Moderates, Tilak's battle was as much against the British as against the Reformists. Tilak criticized the social reform-oriented, educated Indians and said that their desire to borrow the social action philosophy from the West arose only because they had not understood the Gītā properly. The moderates like Gokhale called Tilak a social reactionary because he (Tilak) did not support social reform legislation—Tilak's argument being that a foreign government, totally unrepresentative of the Indian people, should not be allowed to interefere in socio-religious matters of the Hindus. Brown explains how Tilak rejected the criticism levelled against him by the Moderates:

> Tilak rejects the Activism of the West adopted by his Brahman rival, Gokhale, who believed in gradual social reform as a precedent to swaraj or Indian independence. The Lokamānya insisted on the ousting of the British and upon self-rule as pre-requisite to all else. He characterised Western-type Activism as devoted merely to improving worldly existence, whereas the Karma-yoga of the Gītā was devoted to self-realization through service to mankind. The Western Energism was thus rājasa or emotional while the Indian variety was sāttvika or intelligent.[16]

7.24. Although Tilak highlighted the Lokasaṁgraha-oriented Karma-yoga of the Gītā (and rejected Śaṁkara's emphasis on Jñānayoga), his (Tilak's) acceptance of the Advaita philosophy put him essentially in the same metaphysical camp as Śaṁkara. Tilak's criticism was directed against the system of Sannyāsa (in the revival of which Śaṁkara played an important role), because, as he (Tilak) put it, the Sannyāsa system misguided people towards renunciation of their worldly duties. Tilak believed that the system of renouncing the world of work was encouraged by the Buddhists and the Jains, whereas, in the Bhagavad-Gītā, only a mental attitude of renunciation concerning the fruit of action is recommended, not renunciation of worldly duties as such. In Tilak's approach, the main responsibility for Loksaṁgraha activities has to be borne by householders, not Sannyāsins. In this respect, Tilak's views differ from those of Vivekananda, because the Karma-yoga-based socio-spiritual activities of the Ramakrishna Mission are carried on under the leadership and active supervision of, as well as participation by, Sannyāsins.

AUROBINDO

7.25. The political application of the Gītā, initiated by Tilak, was carried further by Aurobindo. Although Aurobindo's direct involvement in the nationalist movement was of a rather short duration (1905-10), several factors contributed to its being regarded as highly significant. For one thing, Aurobindo joined the movement at the time of Bengal-partition, which had aroused strong patriotic feelings and inspired large numbers of people "to do something" at such a critical time. The new atmosphere ensured greater popular support to Extremists or Nationalists, as they were called, led so far by Bal Gangadhar Tilak, Lala Lajpat Rai, and Bipin Chandra Pal—or Lal-Bal-Pal, for short. Aurobindo's joining hands with them, and also with the Nationalist journal "Bande Mātaram" is considered as significant as the arrival of a "Prophet"—the most important factors being Aurobindo's 'personality' and capacity to lead. Here are the words of Majumdar, author of the *History of the Freedom Movement in India:*

> Above all, the Extremist party had an accession of immense strength when it was joined by Aurobindo, who proved to be a host in himself. Indeed the entry of this new personality in the Congress arena may be regarded as a major event in Indian politics. Aurobindo's articles in the Bande Mātaram put the Extremist party on a high pedestal all over India. He expounded the high philosophy and national spirit which animated the party, and also laid down its programme of action. But far more valuable to the Extremist party than even his discourses, was his striking personality. Fired with religious fervour, he preached nationalism as a religion, and he, the prophet of this new religion, infused by precept and

example, courage and strength into everyone that came in touch with him.[17]

7.26. As a political activist, the message that Aurobindo got from the Gītā was that of Karma-yoga, but the underlying philosophy of Aurobindo was not exactly the same as that of Tilak. Whereas Tilak was an Advaita Vedāntist, Aurobindo believed in Śrī Kṛṣṇa as the Purushottama, who, according to Aurobindo, is even higher than the Akshara of the metaphysical Vedānta. In practical terms, while Tilak's emphasis was on performing one's worldly duty without the desire for fruit, Aurobindo believed in surrendering his entire self to Śrī Kṛṣṇa, the Purushottama and in acting according to "the inner voice", as an instrument of God. This is how Aurobindo described the "vision of Śrī Kṛṣṇa "that he had in the Alipur jail during 1908-9:

> Then He (Śrī Kṛṣṇa) placed the Gītā in my hands. His strength entered into me and I was able to do the Sādhanā of the Gītā. . . . It was Vāsudeva who surrounded me. I walked under the branches of the tree in front of my cell. . . It was Śrī Kṛṣṇa whom I saw standing there and holding over me His shade. In the court, it was not the Magistrate whom I saw. . . . it was not the Counsel for the prosecution that I saw, it was Śrī Kṛṣṇa who sat there. . . . He smiled and said, 'I am guiding, therefore fear not. Turn to your own work for which I have brought you to jail and when you come out, remember never to fear, never to hesitate. Remember that it is I who am doing this, not you nor any other. . . .[18]

7.27. An important activity that Aurobindo started in June 1909, after his acquittal from the Alipur Conspiracy Case, was the editing of a new weekly journal "Karmayogin". Not only was the name of the paper taken from the Gītā, its motto also was the famous Gītā aphorism 'yogaḥ karmasu kauśalaṁ', meaning 'yoga is skill in action'. The cover illustration showed Śrī Kṛṣṇa driving Arjuna's chariot at Kurukṣetra. Although Tilak had already appealed to all Indians to consider the entire country as the new Kurukṣetra, the battlefield for swaraj, a pictorial presentation of the Kurukṣetra Battlefield on the title page of Aurobindo's weekly paper had a special appeal. Ursula King attaches great importance to Aurobindo's contribution in popularizing in Kurukṣetra picture as a religious symbol carrying a political message:

> Aurobindo's weekly review 'Karmayogin' (was) published at the height of his political activity in Calcutta between 1909-10. . . Religious and political nationalism are closely intertwined in this review which preaches a new Karma-yoga through the very effective vehicle of the ideal Karmayogin symbol.[19]

7.28. Aurobindo also helped organize, through his younger brother, Barindra, 'secret societies with revolutionary intentions' for what are sometimes referred to as 'terrorist activities'. Ironically, members of these societies often carried with themselves copies of the Bhagavad-Gītā and selected writings of Vivekananda. However, a serious weakness of the violent revolutionaries in India was, as Subramaniam puts it, "the expectation of immediate results".[20] Militarily, the British administration was too strong to be shaken up by stray incidents of bomb-throwing. Aurobindo himself realised by 1910 the limitations of violent methods of political action, which he described as 'hydra-headed evil'.[21] This change of attitude was also linked with the rising tide of spiritualism in Aurobindo's thinking, because of which, in February 1910, he 'suddenly received a command from above' to quit politics, and to make his contribution to the cause of the humanity in the spiritual field.[22]

7.29. Parvate is of opinion that Aurobindo had envisaged the desirability, if not the feasibility, of winning India's independence through an unarmed revolution. In one of his speeches, Aurobindo had said, "On their fidelity to Swadeshī, to boycott, to passive resistance, rested the hope of a peaceful and spiritual revolution. On that it depended whether India would give the example unprecedented in history of a revolution worked only by moral force and peaceful pressure".[23] However, Aurobindo realized that neither he nor any of the other leaders who were in India at that time seemed capable of leading such a 'spiritual revolution'. Almost prophetically he wrote in the Karmayogin on 31 July 1909 that the country 'must wait for the man who is to come, calm in the midst of calamity, hopeful under defeat. . .'.[24]

7.30. The fact that 'the progress of humanity' remained Aurobindo's goal at Pondicherry also, was confirmed by Aurobindo himself when he gave Romain Rolland the following reason for his withdrawal from 'mediocre politics': "India possesses in its past, a little rusty and out of use, the key to the progress of humanity. It is to this side that I am now turning my energies, rather than towards mediocre politics. Hence the reason for my withdrawal. . . ".[25]

7.31. Aurobindo's *Essays on the Gītā* belong to the early years of the Pondicherry phase when he was in the process of moving from the status of a Karmayogin to that of a Pūrṇayogin. The Gītā's teaching on Karma-yoga had, by then, been elucidated by Vivekananda as well as Tilak. Aurobindo presented his own version, founded upon the concepts of Purushottama and Parā Prakriti, and on the doctrine of complete self-surrender to the Divine Will. The importance of performing action for purposes of Lokasaṁgraha, and as an instrument of the Divine, is conveyed by Aurobindo in his own unique style. Panikkar says that 'this new interpretation won immediate recognition as a masterly exposition of the permanent truths of the Gītā in the context of modern life and in the language of modern thought.[26]

7.32. As a Pūrṇayogin, Aurobindo's views contain not only what he found in the Gītā but also the results of his own Sādhanā. According to Aurobindo, the main objectives of his "quest for the truth" include "the application of our ideas to the problems of man's social and collective life".[27] In Reddy's opinion, Pūrṇayoga or Integral Yoga seeks to fulfil the Lokasaṁgraha ideal of the Gītā in a modified form—the modification being that a Pūrṇayogin, while helping others, gives a higher priority to spiritual matters, with a universal outlook, while a Karma-Yogin begins with secular and swadeshī needs and builds up, step by step.[28]

GANDHI

7.33. The final study in the present selection pertains to Gandhi, in whose life and work, Thomas discerns "the culmination" of the movement which began with Rammohun Roy.[29] Gandhi began applying the Gītā to social problems in 1906. The occasion was the launching of a Satyāgraha campaign in South Africa, in protest against the enactment of legislation which was intended to impose taxes and other hardships on the Indians on racial grounds. The legislation called "the black Act" by the Indians, would have adversely affected thirteen thousand Indians, most of whom were poor labourers, either indentured or ex-indentured. When the Government paid no attention to petitions and representations, the Indian community declared that they would not submit to the Black Act and would be willing to undergo punishment, as a non-violent way of expressing their non-cooperation. The Satyāgraha struggle lasted eight years. Mass scale arrests were made and prisoners were treated harshly. Ultimately, the story of the non-violent battle of the poor Indians for a just cause won suport from some influential British leaders in India and England, and under their pressure the Government in South Africa withdrew the discriminatory legislation in 1914—signifying the success of Gandhi's experiment with Satyāgraha.

7.34. Gandhi attributed several significant elements of this movement to the Gītā. He said that he found the underlying doctrine of Ahiṁsā from the description of the Sthitaprajña in the Gītā —i.e. of a Karmayogin who gives priority to doing good to the society, without expecting any selfish gains. Another important feature of the Sthitaprajña, which Gandhi as the chief organiser of a long drawn-out struggle found extremely useful, was Samatva—the capacity to remain calm and unperturbed under the most difficult circumstances.

7.35. Before venturing to present to India herself, the new technique of Satyāgraha, it was necessary for Gandhi to see how the experiment conducted in South Africa would work out under Indian conditions which were obviously far more complex than those in South Africa. Five 'tests' of Satyāgraha , mainly on local issues, were successfully conducted by Gandhi during 1915-18, the most important being the one undertaken on behalf of poor farmers of Champāran (Bihar) who were being exploited by indigo planters. The underlying issues in the other four tests were:

(i) Hardships suffered by railway passengers at the customs barrier at Viramgam (Gujarat)
(ii) Demand to abolish the system of indentured emigration of labourers from India to other British colonies
(iii) Demand of the mill-workers of Ahmedabad to refer the dispute over working conditions to arbitration
(iv) Demand of the farmers of Kaira district (Gujarat) for suspension of revenue collection due to crop-failure.

7.36. In 1919, the Jallianwala Bagh massacre in Punjab created a crisis, and the Congress leaders could not agree on how to respond. When Gandhi proposed that the technique of Satyāgraha based on Satya and Ahiṁsā be adopted for carrying on the struggle, the main opposition was voiced by Tilak. The argumentation between Tilak and Gandhi was essentially on the question as to which one of them represented the Gītā-teaching on the subject of Satya and Ahiṁsā more accurately. Wolpert summarizes how the differences between these two leaders were publicly voiced at the Congress session of December 1919: "During their heated controversy in the subjects Committee, Gandhi was remembered as having at one point suggested to Tilak that Indian politics must be based on truth, to which Tilak replied, 'My friend, truth has no place in politics'."[30]

Two weeks thereafter, Gandhi re-stated his Satyāgraha-approach: "We believe that nothing but the strictest adherence to honesty, fair play and charity can advance the true interests of the country".[31]

7.37. The upshot of the Tilak-Gandhi controversy that began in 1919 and came to a close in 1920 (due to Tilak's death), can be stated in the terminology of the Gītā as follows: While Lokasaṁgraha and *Niṣkāma* Karma constituted common elements in the approaches of Tilak and Gandhi, differences between them arose mainly over the issue of the role of Ahiṁsā. Tilak summarized his approach by a Marathi phrase meaning, 'peacefully if possible, but otherwise by force'.[32] Gandhi ruled out the use of force, and claimed that non-violence, if properly practised, was more effective than violence. As events developed, the Lokasaṁgraha ideal stressed by Tilak was supplemented by the Ahiṁsā doctrine of Gandhi, and the unique combination of Lokasaṁgraha and Ahiṁsā resulted in an exemplification of the image of a Sthitaprajña in Gandhi.

7.38. The degree of support which Gandhi's Satyāgraha-proposal received from the Congress and the country in 1919-20 was partly due to the spade-work already done by Tilak and Aurobindo for linking the Gītā with the freedom struggle. Keeping this in mind, an objective way of appreciating Gandhi's role in making a political application of the Gītā in India is to view it as being complementary to that of Tilak and Aurobindo, and particularly Tilak. This is Panikkar's opinion also:

> To Gandhiji, it was not sufficient that the ideal should be Lokasaṁgraha or the welfare of all. . . . There was a suggestion in Tilak's Gītā-Rahasya that the Karma-Yogin's action, as it was dedicated to God, was above moral laws so long as the object was clearly understood to be the common weal. It is this unexpressed doctrine of Tilak that Gandhiji sought to set right by his commentary on the Gītā and the practical interpretation he gave to it through his own life.[33]

7.39. Apart from the Sthitaprajña-ideal of perfection, which Gandhi also expressed in terms of realization of Truth (Satya), another concept of the Gītā which helped Gandhi strengthen the social aspect of the teaching was "Yajña". Gandhi valued the Gītā-approach of modifying the meaning of Yajña and himself carried such modification still further so as to make it increasingly relevant to present social conditions and to serve the cause of Lokasaṁgraha. Tilak and Aurobindo had done something similar, but had not made practical applications thereof to the same extent. The Gandhian interpretation of Yajña carried with it a twofold process of change. On the one hand, it meant identifying new approaches and productive activiteis (like Khādī and village industries) which if undertaken in a spirit of Yajña could help the society. Secondly, Gandhi also suggested the abandonment of the traditional way of performing a Yajña, for example, burning of wood.[34] Whereas in old days cutting down trees and burning wood had become a yajña, at the present time, said Gandhi, spinning and other village industries have become a yajña. If water was scarce and we had to fetch it from a distance of two miles, said Gandhi again, fetching water would be yajña[35]

7.40. The insistence on Ahiṁsā was not the only point of difference between Gandhi on the one hand, and Tilak and Aurobindo, on the other. Another point of difference was related to the question, whether social reform should await the attainment of Swaraj. Tilak and Aurobindo wanted to concentrate all the attention on driving out the foreign rulers, with the result that they antagonized the social reform-oriented Moderates like Gokhale. Gandhi's comprehensive approach included working on both the fronts simultaneously—namely, against the foreign rulers, and against social evils. The term 'constructive programme' denoted a large number of socially useful activities, including, for example, removal of untouchability, and inter-religious harmony.

7.41. Removal of untouchability was an important social mission of Gandhi for which he took the help of the Gītā. Orthodox Hindus tried to justify untouchability by interpreting some of the old books in their own way. Gandhi achieved success by adopting a similar course as Rammohun Roy had done more than a century ago—namely, by quoting the Gītā in support of his stand that all human being are equal in the eyes of God. As a critical point on this issue, Gandhi had to undertake a fast also.

7.42. Another important cause for which Gandhi fasted several times, and ultimately faced the assassin's bullet, was inter-religious harmony, in general, and Hindu-Muslim unity in particular. The Gītā, advocating a reconciliatory approach in religious matters, was particularly helpful to Gandhi in this matter.

7.43. Ursula King has summarized what might be called the general assessment of the people in regard to Gandhi's efforts to be an ideal Karmayogin:"

> . . .no other representative of modern Hinduism illustrates the originality as well as the dilemma of the Karmayogin

symbol more strikingly than Gandhi does. . . .

The newly understood Karma-yoga taught by the Krishna of the Bhagavad-Gītā has found concrete and permanent historical expression in the person and work of Gandhi. Hindu religious teaching today makes use of the ideal Karmayogin symbol by applying it both to the classical Krishna and the contemporary Gandhi.[36]

7.44. The five case studies taken together clearly show that the social role of the Gītā, which began with a specific issue (sutteeabolition) connected with the work of Rammohun Roy from 1815 onwards, underwent a big expansion during the next one hundred and thirty-five years. Vivekananda used the Gītā to lay stress on social service and socio-spiritual re-awakening of the country. Tilak initiated the political application of the Gītā, which was taken further by Aurobindo also. Gandhi, by introducing a new technique of social action and socio-ethical revolution (the technique derived from the Gītā, as he put it), carried to a "culmination" the work initiated by Rammohun Roy, and to which Vivekananda, Tilak and Aurobindo had made significant contributions. The expanding social role of the Gītā drew strong support from, and got intimately linked with, Lokasaṁgraha, the social ideal underlying *Niṣkāma* Karma.

Part Two

Lokasaṁgraha: The Social Ideal of the Gītā

Chapter Eight

Why the Social Ideal Remained Neglected for so Long

8.1. Whereas Part One of this study described 'how' selected leaders of social movements in India applied the Karmayoga teaching of the Gītā to socio-religious and political problems of the country, the more substantive and theoretical question as to 'why' such applications could possibly be made is discussed in Part Two. More specifically, the main objective of Part Two is to show that in addition to the individual goals of 'Preyas' and 'Śreyas'—i.e. the 'Pleasant' and the 'Good'—the Bhagavad-Gītā also contains the social goal of 'Lokasaṁgraha'—the 'Good of the Society'.

8.2. A question is often raised whether the Hindu scriptures emphasize only the ultimate individual goal—Śreyas or Mokṣa—or they also simultaneously attach noticeable importance to intermediate goals—Preyas at the individual level, and Lokasaṁgraha at the social level. The Kathopaniṣad, which first spoke of Śreyas and Preyas, presented the former as the choice of the wise and the latter as the choice of the unwise.[1] The Gītā took a more balanced view. Although it did not use the term 'Preyas', it recognised the importance of its components—Artha and Kāma—i.e. Wealth and Pleasure—provided they are in conformity with Dharma.[2] This can be called a conditional acceptance of the significant role of Preyas for an individual—representing a sort of modification of the Upaniṣadic view. This process of modification was taken a step further when the Gītā also stressed the importance of the social ideal, Lokasaṁgraha—a term not found in the Upaniṣads.[3]

REASONS FOR NEGLECT OF LOKASAṀGRAHA

8.3. There are certain reasons why the social ideal of the Gītā—Lokasaṁgraha—did not, for a long time, catch hold of the readers' attention as prominently as some of the other teachings. For one thing, the concept of Prasthāna-traya and the way it was traditionally interpreted often tended to ignore such of the ideas and terms of the Gītā as were not found in the other two 'authoritative scriptures', viz. the Upaniṣads and the Brahmasūtras. These three scriptures—the Upaniṣads, the Brahmasūtras, the Gītā—were collectively called Prasthāna-traya, and attempts were made to prove that their philosophical views are the same. A fear was expressed by Sarma in the early fifties that since the term 'Lokasaṁgraha' does not occur in the Upaniṣads, it might not receive due attention from a 'casual reader': "Svadharma, Lokasaṁgraha, and yoga are the three important terms which may be said to sum up the message of the Gītā. A casual reader is apt to lose sight of the middle term, especially as it is a term not mentioned in the Upaniṣads."[4]

8.4. Writing in a similar vein, Vinoba and his brother Balkoba, identified 'sthitaprajña' and 'Lokasaṁgraha' as two of the most important terms of the Gītā, neither of which occurs in the Upaniṣads.[5]

8.5 Tilak explained in detail how the traditional attitude towards Prasthāna-traya resulted in the relative neglect of the activist message of the Gītā:

> Some people think that, as the Upaniṣads are generally in support of Sannyāsa, there will arise a mutual opposition between the three parts of the Prasthāna-traya, if the Gītā is explained as being in support of Action; and the authoritativeness of the three parts will be endangered. . . .
>
> As the Upaniṣads support the path of Sannyāsa, and the Gītā supports the path of Karmayoga, these two parts of the Prasthāna-traya can be seen to be mutually co-operative like two hands, instead of being mutually antagonistic. . .
>
> If the Gītā did not contain anything more than the Upaniṣads and the Brahmasūtras, there would be no point in including the Gītā in the Prasthāna-traya.[6]

8.6. Panikkar gives Tilak credit for pointing out that the Lokasaṁgraha doctrine of the Gītā went beyond what the Vedas and the Upaniṣads had said about the social ideal:

> The social theory behind the Lokasaṁgraha doctrine of the Gītā is most important. The conception of a world order which it is the duty of the individual to uphold by dedicating his activity towards that end, runs all through the teachings of the Gītā. The earlier Vedic religion had no such conception. Nor did the later thinkers who built up the comprehensive structure of Upaniṣadic thought devote any attention to social development. . . . Tilak's exposition of the more activist doctrines of the Gītā struck the intelligentsia with the force of a new message. . . .[7]

8.7. The Prasthāna-traya tradition was not the only barrier that Tilak had to cross to bring Karma-yoga and Lokasaṁgraha to the forefront of Indian religious and philosophic thinking. The non-activist interpretations of the Gītā made by the most eminent, ancient commentators, viz. Śaṁkara and Rāmānuja, also needed to be 'challenged' with the help of an alternative version displaying a similar standard of traditional scholarship. More specifically, Śaṁkara had picked up Jñānayoga (leading to renunciation of karma) as the central message of the Gītā , and Rāmānuja had similarly emphasized Bhakti-yoga as the main teaching—both pushing Karma-yoga in the background. Brown gives Tilak credit for using his deep knowledge and an activist approach to life, to write a commentary that 'found strong support among his compatriots':

> Tilak accuses other commentators, including Saṁkara and Rāmānuja . . . of distorting the text so as to force an interpretation consistent with the views of each cult. But Tilak himself, being free of any cult, believes he is able to give a scientific analysis of the true import of the Gītā. . . . The Lokamānya has found strong support for his views among his compatriots.[8]

8.8. Even before Tilak took in hand the challenging task of removing the barriers that had kept the Karma-yoga doctrine in the background, Vivekananda had started emphasizing, in his talks, the activist message of this scripture. Without entering into deep interpretational controversies of the type that Tilak considered necessary for his mission of shaking up old notions, Vivekananda picked up the social service component of Karma-yoga to revolutionize the concept and practice of Sannyāsa. The complementary roles of Vivekananda and Tilak in making Karma-yoga the centre-piece of socio-religious thinking in the country, in the beginning of the twentieth century, have been highlighted by Subramaniam:

> This (the turn of the century) was the time when Tilak's new interpretation of the Gītā, equating it with Karmayoga was firing the imagination of the Indian intelligentsia and of the nationalists in particular. . . And just recently, Vivekananda had increased that stress with his lectures on Karmayoga, his highly activist conduct and his activist approach to all things religious and social.[9]

8.9. Once the ice was broken by Vivekananda and Tilak, the process of bringing into prominence the Lokasaṁgraha-centred Karmayoga was carried further by Aurobindo, Gandhi and others. Gandhi's contribution was particularly significant because he made Ahiṁsā—non-violence—an inseparable part of Lokasaṁgraha. This was an important modification of Tilak's approach, as Panikkar explains:

> To Gandhiji it was not sufficient that the ideal should be Lokasaṁgraha or the welfare to all. It was even more important that the means should be ethically right. For action to be Brahmayajña or sacrifice or dedication to God, it must be pure and uncontaminated not merely by selfishness but by anything which injures others. . . .
>
> There was a suggestion in Tilak's Gītā-Rahasya that the Karmayogin's action, as it was dedicated to God, was above moral laws so long as the object was clearly understood to be the common weal. It is this unexpressed doctrine of Tilak that Gandhiji sought to set right by his commentary on the Gītā and the practical interpretation he gave to it through his own life.[10]

8.10. So much about the problem of imposition of non-activist ideas from other scriptures by traditional interpreters, which suppressed the Lokasaṁgraha teaching of the Gītā for such a long time. Another consideration, which probably Sarma had in mind (reference para 8.3 above) relates to the internal structure and style of the Gītā itself. As will be clarified a little later, Śrī Kṛṣṇa introduces the subject of Lokasaṁgraha at, what can be called, the 'second stage of the Karma-yoga teaching'—to which a 'casual reader' referred to by Sarma (in para 8.3. above), might not pay full attention.

8.11. In order to recognize the existence of the 'first' and the 'second' stages of the Karma-yoga teaching, it is necessary to recall that the Gītā, being a synthesis of Brahmavidyā and Yogaśāsta —i.e. metaphysics and ethics—sets forth the essential principles of a spiritual religion. All the ideas are presented here as a 'saṁvāda', that is, in the form of conversation between Śrī Kṛṣṇa and Arjuna. The conversational style, being different from that of a systematic monologue, puts forth the various elements of the teaching as answers to questions—say, in instalments—rather than in a pre-arranged 'lump sum' fashion.

8.12. The conversation between Arjuna and Śrī Kṛṣṇa naturally takes place in the form of a series of questions and answers. The first point in Arjuna's initial question is—admitting that the Kauravas have committed crimes and are determined to fight, why should not the Pāṇḍavas, realizing the huge loss involved in the destruction of the family, think of a unilateral solution, like 'refusing to fight'. This is accompanied with Arjuna's suggestion that he better run away from the battlefield and live on bhaikṣyam or charity. Śrī Kṛṣṇa briefly talks about Sāṅkhya philosophy, and then presents the 'first stage' of the Karma-yoga teaching.

8.13. Verse nineteen of the third chapter can be said to mark the end of the 'first stage' of the Karma-yoga teaching. While details will be presented later, a brief glimpse of what Śrī Kṛṣṇa said can be given here. He ruled out escapism and emphasized that Karma in unavoidable, and that even the minimum goal of life, *śarīrayātrā* or maintenance of physical life, cannot be achieved without karma. (III.8). Śrī Kṛṣṇa then takes up the next point in Arjuna's question, namely his desire for obtaining śreyas or 'good', and release from sin and grief. Śrī Kṛṣṇa explains that the root cause of grief and bondage is not karma but attachment to the fruits thereof, and that, therefore, Arjuna must act without attachment. (III.19) Śrī Kṛṣṇa's assurance that everything which Arjuna was looking for—freedom from sin, release from grief, and even the ultimate goal of śreyas—can be achieved by performing *Niṣkāma* Karma, could be considered as marking the completion of the first stage of the Karmayoga teaching.

8.14. We may ask: "Why then does the conversation proceed to the next stage?" The answer to that is provided by Śrī Kṛṣṇa himself when he tells Arjuna (in part, explicitly, and to some extent, implicitly): "Your vision is narrow because you do not look beyond your own good or that of your near and dear ones, svajanaṁ. But you have to take into account the society and the world, the Loka. (III.20) By all means strive for your limited personal goals, but also keep in mind the larger social and world goals, of preserving dharma and order, and of achieving harmony, unity and universal welfare, Lokasaṁgraha.

8.15. It can be considered significant that Arjuna representing an ordinary human being is initially depicted as too much engrossed in narrow personal and family problems, and that the teaching on Lokasaṁgraha (the social ideal) is conveyed by Śrī Kṛṣṇa almost entirely on his own initiative. On most of the other occasions in the Gītā, Arjuna asks a question to which Śrī Kṛṣṇa gives a reply. We can interpret this as an indirect evidence that the subject of Lokasaṁgraha is so important that, even without Arjuna's asking, Śrī Kṛṣṇa includes it in his teaching, and he cites his own practical example of working for Lokasaṁgraha and warning of a grave crisis in the world if he did not do so. A practical distinction between *Niṣkāma* Karma and Lokasaṁgraha is that, while the former provides the technique of work, the latter provides the content of work and its goal. However, from the viewpoint of a 'casual reader' referred to by Sarma (reference para 8.3 above), there is a risk that he or she might stop at the first stage of the teaching and obtain only partial knowledge of Karmayoga—and miss out on Lokasaṁgraha which forms part of the second stage of the Karmayoga teaching.

TWO ASPECTS OF DHARMA AND CRISIS—OF WHICH THE SECOND LIABLE TO BE IGNORED

8.16. Although Arjuna, taking a narrow view, asked about Śreyas, and Śrī Kṛṣṇa, presenting a broader vision, spoke also of Lokasaṃgraha, a key-word used by both of them was 'Dharma'. Obviously, Arjuna used the word 'dharma' in its individual aspect, as a way leading to Śreyas. Śrī Kṛṣṇa, while doing full justice to Arjuna's query, went further and stressed also the social and universal aspect of dharma which was closely linked with Lokasaṁgraha. Thomas draws attention to the two aspects of Dharma in the Gītā:

> The concept of dharma has two distinct aspects, namely individual or particular, and social or universal. . . .
>
> The very context in which the discourses are given is the confusion of Arjuna about his dharma (II.7). This is the individual aspect of dharma. . . .
>
> The universal aspect (of dharma) is taken up most directly when Kṛṣṇa argues that the purpose of avatāra (incarnation) is to protect dharma (IV.8).[11]
>
> Commenting on the purpose of avatāra (IV.8), Tilak clarifies that "Lokasaṁgraha (III.20) is only another name for the work which the Blessed Lord does by being incarnated in this manner.[12]

8.17. Among the first words used by Śrī Kṛṣṇa, while addressing Arjuna, were the following: "Engulfed in a crisis (viṣame samupasthitaṁ) (II.2), give up faint-heartedness and stand up to fight".

But what was the nature of this crisis? Arjuna took a narrow view as if it was only a 'personal crisis' for himself—how to choose between duty and family-loyalty. But basically, the unlawful usurption of the entire kingdom by the Kauravas—who were durbuddhiḥ (I.23) or evil-minded, and ātatāyinaḥ (I.36) or felons—was a social crisis. Obviously, people's welfare (Lokasaṁgraha) could not be expected from the Kauravas.

8.18. Aurobindo, in his *Essays on the Gītā*, speaks of the world as a 'theatre' on which two 'struggles' are continuously going on—the inner struggle and the outer struggle:

> In the inner struggle the enemies are within, in the individual, and the slaying of desire, ignorance, egoism, is the victory. . . .
> But there is an outer struggle between the powers of the Dharma and the Adharma in the human collectivity. . . . This outer struggle too the Avatāra comes to aid, directly or indirectly, to destroy the reign of the Asuras, the evil-doers, and in them depress the power they represent and to restore the oppressed ideals of the Dharma.[13]

8.19. Aurobindo continues: "The Avatāra comes to bring nearer the kingdom of heaven on earth in the collectivity, as well as to build the kingdom of heaven within, in the individual human soul. . . ."[14]

Although, following the above line of thought, the Gītā could be invoked to tackle both types of crises—the individual crisis as well as the social crisis—the way of seeking an answer in Lokasaṁgraha was undoubtedly for the social crisis. This has been illustrated, with reference to modern times, in Part One of this study, which describes how leaders of social movements in recent history applied Karmayoga centered on Lokasaṁgraha to face situations of social and political crises.

8.20. Klostemaier also envisages the 'need' to turn to the Gītā, especially in times of crises and confusion":

> Many Indians, and increasingly many non-Indians, too, have considered the Gītā not only a book to be read and studied but a guide to living. A need for such guidance is felt, especially in times of crises and confusion like ours, when the institutions are no longer able to provide orientation and when there are no longer commonly accepted values and standards. Clearly, the Gītā is a book of crisis.[15]

8.21. Klostermaier continues:

> A direct modern Western reference to the Bhagavad-Gītā occurred in a context, in which to call it historical is almost an understatement—it may better be called apocalyptic. In the course of his trial, J. Robert Oppenheimer, who was accused of passing atomic secrets to the Soviet Union, described the thoughts that passed through his mind when he witnessed the first atomic test explosion in the desert of new Mexico:
>
> On the sight of the fireball two ancient verses (of the Gītā) came to my mind:
>
> Of a thousand suns in the sky if suddenly should burst forth the light, it would be like unto the light of that Exalted One. (XI.12).
>
> Death am I, cause of destruction of the worlds, matured and set out to gather in the worlds there. (XI.32)[16]

8.22. Klostermaier has clarified that his statement about the prophetic dimension of the Gītā does not imply the universal applicability of the dharma taught by the Gītā to tide over the crisis. Nevertheless, the statements given above do suggest the need to create public awareness of the Gītā-concept of Lokasaṁgraha, in the hope that practical steps to face the crisis might follow such awareness at the grassroots level. Reasons which led to the neglect of Lokasaṁgraha in the past might, otherwise, cause a similar damage again. Out of the two aspects of both Dharma and crisis, there is a continuing risk that 'casual readers' of the type referred to by Sarma (para 8.3), might not pay full attention to the second aspect, i.e. to the social issues of the day.

SEQUENCE OF PRESENTATION

8.23. In order to be faithful to the sequence of stage-by-stage conversation, as occurring in the Gītā, we first present in Chapter Nine the Karma-yoga teaching relating to the ultimate individual goal (Śreyas), i.e. the technique of *Niṣkāma* Karma. We then explain in Chapters Ten to Thirteen the teaching on social and environmental goals, that is Lokasaṁgraha.

8.24. Chapter Ten begins with a presentation of the various meanings which the two component words 'Loka' and 'saṁgraha' have, deriving therefrom the wide range of meanings of the compound word 'Lokasaṁgraha' itself. An important source for such derivations is highlighted, namely Śrī Kṛṣṇa's statement that He Himself works for Lokasaṁgraha. Thereafter, attention is drawn to some other related terms in the Gītā—like sarvabhūtahitaṁ meaning the good of all beings—which help elucidate the social ideal of the Gītā.

8.25. Chapter Eleven looks into some of the practical implications of Lokasaṁgraha. What sorts of considerations assume importance when the main object of one's karma is Lokasaṁgraha? Putting together the views of the several Lokasaṁgraha-interpreters (including the author of this study), as many as ten aspects of 'karma for Lokasaṁgraha' are presented in this chapter. A related point of interest is how the widening of goals—from Śreyas to Lokasaṁgraha—goes hand-in-hand with a shift from what Hiriyanna calls 'self-regarding virtues' (like mental discipline) to 'other-regarding virtues' (like compassion).[17]

8.26. Chapter Twelve examines the relationship between Lokasaṁgraha on the one hand, and some of the important Gītaconcepts used for duty-specification, on the other, namely:

— svadharma
— yajña-dānaṁ-tapas, often spoken of as a trio.

Following the discussion on 'duty-prompted Lokasaṁgraha'—called by us as the first stage of Lokasaṁgraha'—we move on to 'spontaneous Lokasaṁgraha'—also called as the second stage of Lokasaṁgraha. The conceptual difference between the two is traced to the Gītā verse VI.3.

8.27. Hindu scriptures including the Gītā speak in terms of four puruṣārthas or goals of life, namely, Artha (Wealth), Kāma (Pleasure), Dharma, Mokṣa. This ultimate goal, Mokṣa, is denoted by several terms, one of which is Śreyas.[18] But what sort of relationship does Lokasaṁgraha have with each of the four puruṣārthas? This important question is taken up for discussion in Chapter Thirteen.

8.28. Our presentation of Lokasaṁgraha as belonging to stage two of the conversation between Śrī Kṛṣṇa and Arjuna links it primarily with Karma-yoga. Such a linkage is faithful to the original text of the Gītā because Lokasaṁgraha is explicitly mentioned in the Karmayoga chapter of the scripture, in verses III.20 to III.26. However, we show in Chapter Thirteen that the linkage between Lokasaṁgraha on the one hand, and Bhaktiyoga or Jñānayoga on the other, is equally strong if we take into account implicit references by means of other terms which convey the spirit (though not the letter) of Lokasaṁgraha. As already mentioned, terminological variants of Lokasaṁgraha are presented in Chapter Ten. However, linkages of the social ideal with bhakti and Jñāna are explored in Chapter Thirteen.

8.29. The closing chapter (Fourteen) summarizes the main results achieved in Part Two of this study. Lokasaṁgraha, the social ideal of the Gītā, although recognized only after a long period of neglect, can, in the twentieth century, be said to have come to the forefront amongst socio-religious thinkers.

8.30. An important difference, relating to the coverage of other writers' views, as between Parts One and Two of this study, needs to be mentioned. Since Part One descried how selected leaders of social movements applied Karma-yoga to socio-religious and political problems of their times, only the activists' views on the Gītā (supplemented by the opinions of their biographers and critical analysts) could be included therein. However, Part Two being more theoretical, references are made to views, on the Gītā, of academicians and scholars as well, along with those of activists. Statements made without any reference can, therefore, be considered as representing the personal viewpoint of the author of this study.

CHAPTER NINE

Arjuna's Search for Śreyas and Śrī Kṛṣṇa's Teaching on Niṣkāma Karma

9.1. One of the most important statements of Śrī Kṛṣṇa in the Gitā is: na cāśuśrūṣave vācyaṁ (XVIII.67) which has been translated by Tilak as well as Gandhi to mean "do not mention this teaching to one who has no desire to listen to it." In fact, Śrī Kṛṣṇa observed this principle himself, and during the course of his conversation with Arjuna, he either responded to Arjuna's questions or picked up the right moment when Arjuna was keen to listen. But it is of special significance to understand the initial question of Arjuna, and even more so, what really lay behind this question.

9.2. Although Arjuna's request to Śrī Kṛṣṇa to move his chariot between the two armies starts in verse I.21, and a statement of his unease and inability to fight begins in verse I.28, the first questions that Arjuna asks are contained in verses I.36 to I.39:

> What pleasure can be ours, O Kṛṣṇa, after we have slain the sons of Dhṛtarāṣṭra? Only sin (pāpam) will accrue to us if we kill these felons (ātatāyinaḥ). (I.36)
>
> So it is not right that we slay our kinsmen, the sons of Dhṛtarāṣṭra. Indeed, how can we be happy, O Mādhava, if we kill our own people? (I.37)
>
> Even if these whose minds are overpowered by greed, see no wrong in the destruction of the family and no crime in treachery to friends. (I.38)
>
> Why should we not have the wisdom to turn away from this sin, O Janārdana, we who see the wrong in the destruction of the family? (I.39)

9.3. The fact that the Kauravas were his kinsmen was known to Arjuna even prior to this moment, and he also knew that his teacher Droṇa and venerable grand-uncle Bhīṣma were on the side of the Kauravas. But the actual sight and the imminence of the battle suddenly raised a doubt in Arjuna's mind whether his duty to fight for a just cause should really have priority (in a moral sense) over his family ties. If those in front of him had not been his teacher, elders, kinsmen and friends, such a conflict between duty and family ties would not have arisen.

9.4. Arjuna uses the term "ātatāyinaḥ" (felons) for the Kauravas because they had committed so many crimes. Chidbhavananda lists some of these crimes, because of which, the felons, according to Hindu tradition, were punishable by death, no sin attaching to one who killed them: "The Kauravas had secretly set fire to the residence where the Pāṇḍavas were expected to be sleeping; they had surreptitiously tried to poison their food and had attempted murder of the Pāṇḍavas who were legitimate heirs to the throne; deceitfully they had tried to deprive the Pāṇḍavas of their kingdom, wealth and wife."[1]

9.5. Arjuna also knew that all possible attempts had been made to avoid the war, including Śrī Kṛṣṇa's mediation efforts and Pāṇḍavas' willingness to accept only a small part of the kingdom, the whole of which legitimately belonged to them. However, the insatiable greed of the Kauravas had left no choice to Pāṇḍavas other than fighting a war for their just right.

ATTACHMENT: THE CAUSE OF CONFUSION

9.6. What then lay behind Arjuna's plea that he would incur sin (pāpam) if he killed Droṇa, Bhīṣma and the Kauravas? Radhakrishnan argues that Arjuna's plea for escapism was a product of tamas and rajas guṇas which prompted him to give up his duty due to ignorance and fear of physical suffering:

> Arjuna takes up a pacifist attitude and declines to participate in a fight for truth and justice. . . . He does not raise the question of right or wrong of war. He has faced many battles and fought many enemies. He declares against war and its horrors because he has to destroy his own friends and relations

(svajanam). It is not a question of violence or non-violence but of using violence against one's friends now turned enemies. His reluctance to fight is not the outcome of spiritual development or the preponderance of sattvaguṇa but is the product of tamas and rajas gunas.

9.7. How the three guṇas (sattva, rajas, tamas) influence one's understanding of one's moral duty (to which Radhakrishnan has referred above) is explained in the eighteenth chapter of the Gītā. For example, sāttvika buddhi, according to verse XVIII.30, clearly understands what ought to be done and what ought not to be done, what is to be feared and what is not to be feared, what binds and what frees the soul. The next verse XVIII.31 characterizes rājasī buddhi as that by which one knows in a mistaken way the right and the wrong, and what ought to be done and what ought not to be done. Similarly, verse XVIII.32 describes tāmasī buddhi as that which, enveloped in darkness, conceives as right what is wrong and sees all things in a perverted way, that is contrary to the truth.

9.8. Linking ignorance or confusion about one's duty to tāmasī or rājasī buddhi is one way of diagnosing Arjuna's problem. Another, related way is to link it with the concept of attachment which is used extensively in the Gītā. Attachment clouds one's vision and shakes one's determination to stick to one's duty. Vinoba links Arjuna's confusion about his dharma with his attachment to his own people (svajanam):

> Was Arjuna moved by the spirit of non-violence, as Asoka was to be later? No, this was only attachment to his own people. Arjuna's attachment confused him and overshadowed his devotion to duty. It was then that he thought of philosophy. When a man with a sense of duty is caught in illusion, even then he cannot bear to face the naked fact of his lapse from duty. He usually covers it up with an inquiry into principles. Arjuna was just in this plight. He wanted to evade his duty because his vision was clouded by illusion, moha.[3]

ASKING FOR INSTRUCTION ON ŚREYAS

9.9. Whatever might be Śrī Kṛṣṇa's analysis of the underlying cause of Arjuna's confusion, Arjuna himself was under the impression that his pleas to turn away from the sin was based on wisdom. He continued to talk for a while in a tone of self-righteousness. "A desire to listen", which, according to Śrī Kṛṣṇa as mentioned in para 9.1. above, is a prerequisite for a disciple, was still not visible in Arjuna. Therefore, the first words which Śrī Kṛṣṇa spoke were in the form of a counter-question: Whence has come to thee this dejection of spirit in this hour of crisis? Cast off this petty faintheartedness and arise. Arjuna wonders whether it would be better for him to take to sannyāsa and to subsist on bhaikṣyam (begging). But immediately thereafter he realizes his weakness and ignorance, presents himself as a śiṣya (pupil), and asks for instruction on śreyas (good);

> My very being is stricken with the weakness of sentimental pity. With my mind bewildered about my duty, I ask thee. Tell me, for certain, what is śreyas. I am thy pupil; teach me, I am seeking refuge in thee. (II.7)
>
> I do not see what will drive away this śokam (sorrow) which dries up my senses, even if I should attain rich and unrivalled kingdom on earth or even the sovereignty of the gods. (II.8)

9.10. These two verses have a special significance in understanding the approach of the Gītā. Arjuna, who was so far a kinsman and friend of Śrī Kṛṣṇa, now becomes a disciple. This frame of mind is a prerequisite to any search (jijñāsā) for knowledge. In verse IV.34 also, humble reverence, inquiry, and service, are mentioned as necessary qualifications of a disciple. Having established the appropriate relationship between himself and Śrī Kṛṣṇa, Arjuna asks for instruction on Śreyas, the good. The two goals, śreyas (good) and preyas (pleasant), are highlighted in the dialogue between Yama and Nachiketā in Kaṭhopaniṣad. Ranganathananda explains:

> The term preyas means that which is pleasant, immediately attractive; the term śreyas means that which conduces to true welfare, which is ultimately beneficial. Ethics and religion divide all objects and experiences into these two cat-

egories. "Even a purely materialistic ethics, which believes only in pleasure and self-interest, makes a distinction between preyas and sreyas made here, between pure self-interest and enlightened self-interest, between short-sighted selfishness and far-sighted selfishness. But it is only in systems of spiritual ethics and philosophy, which believe in a non-physical spiritual reality in man, that this distinction between śreyas and preyas becomes significant. To all such, catering merely to the sensate man is preyas, and what helps the manifestation of the spiritual man is śreyas.[4]

9.11. Although Arjuna asks for instruction on śreyas, it does not imply that the Gītā-teaching leads one only to śreyas, to the exclusion of preyas. In fact, an attempt has been made in the Gītā to harmonize śreyas and preyas. According to Tilak's interpretation, even Yama, in Kaṭhopaniṣad, in spite of giving priority to śreyas over preyas, by granting three blessings, enabled Nachiketa to obtain both:

> In the phrase used for blessing, one says: śāntiḥ puṣṭis tuṣṭiś cāstu, that is, may there be peace along with material happiness and contentedness (in proper proportions). The same is the moral of the Kaṭhopaniṣad. . . . When Yama asked Nachiketā to ask for (three) blessings, Nachikta did not in the first place ask for the blessing of Brahmajñāna, but first said: My father has got angry with me; may he become propitious to me. Secondly teach me the science of agni, that is, of all sacrificial ritual which will give me material opulence. When he had acquired these (two) blessings, he asked for the third one, saying: teach me the knowledge of the Ātman. But when Yama suggested that he would give him additional happiness instead of this third blessing, Nachiketa insisted: now explain to me that Brahmajñāna which will lead to śreyas, instead of aspiring for more of the knowledge of sacrificial ritual than was necessary for obtaining preyas. In short, as stated in the last mantra of this upaniṣad, Nachiketā obtained both.[5]

9.12. After mentioning śreyas in verse II.7, Arjuna also asks Śrī Kṛṣṇa in verse II.8, to show him the way to obtain release from śokām (sorrow). It is obvious from Arjuna's statement that he is anxious to know the root cause of śokam, and how the fundamental issues of happiness and unhappiness can be tackled.

TEACHING ON SAMATVA OR EVEN-MINDEDNESS

9.13. Since Arjuna was afraid of incurring sin (*pāpam*) in killing his own people, Śrī Kṛṣṇa begins his teaching by philosophically examining the questions: 'What is death', and 'what is killing'. Our focus in this book being more on ethics than on metaphysics, we shall only present a brief summary of this part of the teaching. Man is an aggregate of the body and the ātman, says Śrī Kṛṣṇa. Out of these, the ātman, which becomes perceptible as 'I', as a result of ahaṁkāra, is permanent and immortal. It is today, it was yesterday, and it will also be tomorrow. Therefore, the words 'to kill' or 'to die' cannot, according to Śrī Kṛṣṇa, be properly applied to the ātman, and there is no room for lamentation in that matter. Then remains the body. That, of course, is admittedly non-permanent and desctructible and will come to an end, if not today or tomorrow, at the latest after a hundred years. But, says Śrī Kṛṣṇa again, the ātman, after getting out of one body, acquires later on another body in accordance with the previous karma, and so it is also not proper to lament over the loss of a body. In short, whether one looks at the matter from the viewpoint of the body or the ātman, lamentation on account of death, according to Śrī Kṛṣṇa, is unwise.

9.14. But what about the experiences of pain and pleasure in day-to-day life? The Gītā ideal of samatva or even-mindedness (which is repeated in several places) is first presented in verses II.14 and II.15:

> Contacts between bodily organs and their objects in the external world, O Arjuna, give rise to cold and heat, pleasure and pain. They come and go and do not last for ever; these learn to endure, O Arjuna. (II.14)
>
> "The main who is not troubled by these, O Arjuna, who remains the same in pain and pleasure, who is wise, makes himself fit for eternal life. (II.15)

9.15. On this reference to samatva in the context of metaphysical knowledge, Radhakrishnan makes the following observation: To be subject to grief and sorrow, to be disturbed by the material happenings, to be deflected by them from the path of duty that has to be traversed, niyatam karma, shows that we are still victims of avidyā or ignorance.[6]

9.16. The next reference to samatva occurs in the context of svadharma, which in the case of Arjuna meant his duty as a kṣatriya, traditionally understood as assigned by the society within the system of four varṇas. Leaving aside, for the time being, the question whether svadharma in general conveys meanings other than varṇa-dharma, the appeal to Arjuna's sense of svadharma was re-inforced from two perspectives. First, he was reminded that customary tradition associated social honour, earthly sovereignty, heavenly bliss, and śreyas, with the performance of svadharma. Secondly, Arjuna was told by Śrī Kṛṣṇa that if he could perform his traditional svadharma according to the (new) Gītā-technique of samatva, then he need not have the fear of incurring sin (even if he killed his svajanam). Verses II.31 to II.37 reiterate the traditional beliefs, but it is in verse II.38 that a harmonization of svadharma and samatva is presented, and this can be considered as a basic, new teaching of the Gītā.

9.17. In order to bring out the Gītā-technique of first taking up a traditional concept and then modifying it, the verses II.31 to II.38 are presented below in parts, the first part consisting of three verses:

> Further, having regard for thine own duty, thou shouldst not falter; there exists no greater śreyas for a kṣatriya than a battle enjoined by duty. (II.31)
>
> Happy are the kṣatriyas, O Arjuna, for whom such a war comes of its own accord as an open door to heaven. (II.32)
>
> But if thou doest not this lawful battle, then thou wilt fail thy duty and glory and will incur sin. (II.33)

9.18. There is a pointed reference here to śreyas which Arjuna is seeking. According to tradition, protection of right by the acceptance of battle, if necessary, is his social duty, and not renunciation. His dharma is to maintain order by force and not to become an ascetic by shaving off the hair and by thinking of subsisting on bhaikṣyam. Furthermore, Śrī Kṛṣṇa points out to Arjuna that the latter's argument about incurring sin if he kills his svajanam, is one-sided, because if he does not do his duty of fighting, then too he will incur sin. (II.33) Subsequently, Śrī Kṛṣṇa shows a way out of this dilemma by explaining that, whereas the sin from non-performance of duty is unconditional, the sin in killing svajanam is conditional and can be overcome by samatva. (II.38)

9.19. In the second part of our presentation of the svadharma verses, we take the next four verses, namely, II.34 to II.37:

> Besides, men will ever recount they ill-fame, and for one who has been honourd, ill-fame is worse than death. (II.34)
>
> The great warriors will think that thou hast abstained from battle through fear and they by whom thou wast highly esteemed will make light of thee. (II.35)
>
> Many unseemly words will be uttered by thy enemies, slandering thy strength. Could anything be sadder than that? (II.36)
>
> Either slain thou shalt go to heaven, or victorious thou shalt enjoy the earth; therefore arise, O Arjuna, resolved on battle. (II.37)

9.20. Some scholars express surprise that sensibility to criticism by society has been mentioned in the above verses as a factor in decision-making. But, as we stated earlier, verses II.31 to II.37 mainly reflect traditional views, prior to the incorporation of the samatva-element which occurs in verse II.38.

9.21. We conclude our presentation of the svadharma verses by quoting verse II.38 which modifies the traditional views so significantly that samatva becomes the main focus of attention. In fact, the general validity of the traditional concept of svadharma representing varṇa-dharma has been questioned by scholars like Sarma,[7] but samatva as a central teaching of the Gītā has been recognised by all the commentators, and it is because of this recognition that verse II.38 is quoted so frequently: "Treating alike pleasure and pain, gain and loss, victory and defeat, then get ready for battle. Thus thou shall not incur sin." (II.38)

TEACHING ON ANĀSAKTI OR NON-ATTACHMENT

9.22. Although the teaching on samatva given in verse II.38 does refer to some of the questions raised by Arjuna, for example, whether he could take to sannyāsa for obtaining śreyas and release from sorrow, Śrī Kṛṣṇa feels it necessary to look into the matter more deeply. One of the basic questions is: what is the root cause of sorrow? Secondly, what practical steps are needed to arrive at the state of samatva or even-mindedness? Discussions of practical issues like this (laying stress on action) are covered in the Gītā under the wisdom of yoga; and this has been distinguished from the wisdom of sāṁkhya (which lays stress on knowledge).

9.23. What is the root cause of sorrow? The Gītā presents in verses II.62 and II.63 a chain of unhappiness and destruction starting from attachment (saṅgaḥ) to objects of pleasure:

> When a man dwells in his mind on the objects of sense, attachment to them is produced. From attachment springs desire and from desire comes anger. (II.62)
>
> From anger delusion, from delusion loss of memory, and from loss of memory, the destruction of intelligence, and from the destruction of intelligence he perishes. (II.63)

9.24. In practical life, attachment to objects of pleasure is rooted in feelings of mine-ness (mamatva) and egotism (ahaṁkāra) which exist in the mind of the doer, and because of which the doer harbours a desire for personal benefits by arguing like this: "whatever action is performed by me is done with the desire that I should get the benefit, because the action is mine". If there is any obstruction in the way of getting such benefit, the chain of misery starts. And if the obstruction looks like the handiwork of another person, it gives rise to anger or even hate, and this leads to evil action which leads to self-destruction. Because of the common occurrence of such cases in life, the Gītā uses a flexible terminology, and terms like saṅga or āsakti (attachment), phalāśā (desire for fruit), and kāma (desire), convey the same idea.

9.25. The above analysis is in the context of Karma-yoga which prescribes that all lawful actions included in one's svadharma should be performed, but without entertaining any selfish desire for the fruit thereof. The jñāna-yoga analysis carries the chain of misery a step further, beyond desire or attachment, to avidyā or ignorance of the real nature of things. It is often argued then, quoting Mahābhārata (Santi.240.7), that: "Karmaṇā badhyate janturvidyayā tu pramucyate" that is, a living being is bound by karma and, is released by vidya. So, according to the doctrine of the sannyāsa school, Jñāna is the only means of liberation from the chain of avidyā-kāma-karma. However, the Karma-yoga doctrine, while recognizing the usefulness of vidyā, regards karma as unavoidable, and envisages the possibility of obtaining śreyas as well as freedom from śoka, by means of non-attachment to the fruits of karma.

9.26. Upadhyaya thinks that starting the chain of misery from either ignorance or attachment or desire need not imply a significant difference in ethical standards:

> Karma forces leading to the cycle of birth and rebirth are generated by ignorance and the consequent craving or desire for worldly affairs. The Gītā as well as Buddhism regards ignorance and desire as the cause of deluded actions which are responsible for the continued chain of existence. . .[8] In both of them, attachment, hatred and delusion (rāga, dveṣa and moha) are regarded as the basic roots of all actions, by abandoning which one's actions are said to become free from all defilements and one is said to realise the supreme serenity."[9]

9.27. Tilak has explained that the Karma-yoga approach does not imply the giving up of all desires; rather it adopts the skilful middle path between the extremes of desire and contentment:

> Giving up all kinds of thirst, and with it, all actions, in order

to escape the evil effect of thirst or discontent is not the pure (sāttvika) path. Thirst or discontent about a good or beneficial matter is the seed of future prosperity; and therefore one has to carefully consider what thirst or discontent causes unhappiness. One should adopt the skilful middle path of giving up only that particular hope, thirst or discontent which produces unhappiness, and it is not necessary for that purpose to give up all kinds of action whatsoever.[10]

9.28. To adopt the skilful middle path (VI.17) between the extremes of desire and contentment, calls for mental discipline. The Gītā commends the true spirit of inward detachment, not outer renunciation of action. Verse III.7 is one of the many verses which convey this teaching: "He who controls the senses by the mind, O Arjuna, and without attachment engages the organs of action in the path of work, he is superior." (III.7)

9.29. The importance of the mental discipline which enables one to acquire the spirit of inward detachment has been traced by Tilak to Upaniṣads also:

"mana eva manuṣyāṇaṁ kāraṇaṁ bandhamokṣayoḥ.
bandhayā viṣayāsaṅgī mokṣe nirviṣayam smṛtaṃ"
(Maitry up. 6.34; Amrtabindu 2)

that is: "the mind of a man is the only cause for his being bound (by karma) or being released; when the mind is enslaved by objects of pleasure, it is bound, and when it goes beyond those objects, that is, when it becomes unattached, that is release."

9.30. Two of the most famous verses of the Gītā, one containing the teaching in terms of giving up the desire for the fruit of action and the other in terms of non-attachment, are II.47 and III.19, respectively:

To action alone hast thou a right and never at all to its fruits; let not the fruits of action be thy motive; neither let there be in thee any attachment to inaction. (II.47)
Without attachment, perform always the work that has to be

done, for man attains to the highest by doing work without attachment. (III.19)

9.31. Gandhi called his Gujarati translation of the Gītā as Anāsaktiyoga, emphasizing non-attachment to the fruit of one's action as the central teaching. He believes that renouncing the fruit of action or being non-attached to it mean the same thing:

> How is one to be free from the bondage of action, even though he may be acting? The manner in which the Gītā has solved the problem is to my knowledge unique. The Gītā says: 'Do your allotted work but renounce its fruit—be detached and work—have no desire for reward and work.' This is the unmistakable teaching of the Gītā. He who gives up action falls. He who gives up only the reward rises.[11]

9.32. Gandhi also clarified that renouncing the fruit does not imply doing the work carelessly or unscientifically; nor does it imply any insistence on throwing away the fruit when it comes as a natural consequence of effort:

> Renunuciation of fruit in no way means indifference to the result. In regard to every action one must know the result that is expected to follow, the means thereto, and the capacity for it. He who, being thus equipped is without desire for the result and is yet wholly engrossed in the due fulfilment of the task before him is said to have renounced the fruits of his action.
>
> Again let no one consider renunciation to mean want of fruit for the renouncer. The Gītā reading does not warrant such a meaning. Renunciation means absence of hankering after fruit. As a matter of fact, he who renounces reaps a thousandfold.[12]

VIRTUES NEEDED FOR ATTAINING RELEASE FROM SORROW

9.33. When Śrī Kṛṣṇa tells Arjuna that attachment to objects of pleasure is the root cause of sorrow, he actually implies a chain of unhappiness and destruction. (Reference para 9.23 above).

We can also call it a chain of vices, which includes attachment, desire, anger, delusion, loss of memory, and destruction of intelligence. Although this looks like a negative approach to the teaching of dharma, such lists of vices (which one is asked to avoid in one's life) are popular in the Hindu tradition. Vices highlighted in different contexts vary, and in the Gītā itself, there are several lists, long and small, to which we shall refer from time to time.

9.34. Corresponding to the above chain of vices, Śrī Kṛṣṇa also tells Arjuna about a chain of virtues which starts from mental discipline and non-attachment, and which, not only goes up to the state of release from sorrow, but also beyond, up to the state of steadfast wisdom:

> A man, who has mental discipline and is free from attachment and aversion, who lets the senses move among worldly objects, but keeps the senses under control, he attains serenity of mind. (II.64)
>
> And in that serenity of mind, he attains the state of end of all sorrow, and soon thereafter the state of steadfast wisdom. (II.65)

9.35. The above chain of virtues includes mental discipline, non-attachment, freedom from aversion, normal participation in worldly activities, sense control, and serenity of mind. Identifying a list of virtues in this way represents a positive approach to the teaching of dharma. Like the lists of vices, the lists of virtues are also very popular in the Hindu tradition, and their content also varies from one context to another. In the Gītā itself, there are several lists of virtues, long and small, to which we shall refer on different occasions.

9.36. The Gītā has laid down that evil or virtue, which we ascribe to any particular action of a person, does not lie in the action itself, but depends on the frame of mind of the person who does it. That is why mental discipline (or mental tapas) marks the beginning of the chain of virtues. Upadhyaya stresses this while explaining the ethics of the Gītā: "The supremacy of inner will over outer action is emphasized in the Gītā quite clearly. Śrī Kṛṣṇa says: Far inferior, indeed, O Arjuna, is mere action to the discipline of intellect. (II.49)"[13]

9.37. Although the term "mental discipline" is very comprehensive, the aspect which is highlighted in the above chain of virtues is its expression in the form of non-attachment and freedom from aversion. In the Hindu tradition, all the dualities affecting one's feelings (pleasure and pain, praise and blame, cold and hot) are considered a primary cause of bondage, and rāga-dveṣa (attachment and aversion) are the foremost among all the dualities. To go beyond these dualities (or to be nirdvandva) is one of the main characteristics of the supreme state of samatva (or even-mindedness). (IV.22)

9.38. The next virtue in the chain is the ability to let the senses move among worldly objects, but keeping the senses under control. Upadhyaya sees in this "the avoidance of the two extremes, namely, self-indulgence and self-mortification."[14] On the one hand, the intellect and the mind have to be withdrawn from distracting desires, but, on the other hand, the practice of forceful repression or the stifling of the senses has to be avoided.

9.39. Vinoba has made a detailed study of the Gītā verses dealing with the virtue of leading a normal worldly life with senses under control. He says that the method of combining freedom and restraint, which a tortoise adopts, should not be difficult for a human being:

> The Gītā argues in verse II.58 that if a creature like the tortoise can protect itself in this manner, can a man not do so? When a tortoise sees no danger, it puts its appendages out and freely moves about, but at the first indication of danger, it draws in its limbs into the shell. Similarly, let your senses range freely when there is no apprehension of danger, but come away from a place that seems dangerous to you (from the ethical point of view).[15]

9.40. Vinoba distinguishes between the crude and subtle aspects of sense-control, the crude referring to the physical control of the outer senses and the subtle referring to the control of the desire or the taste which lies at the root of those senses. Both kinds of control need to be practised, but they have to draw upon different sources of strength:

> Examine your desires and determine for yourself with the help of your own intelligence, which are good desires and which are bad. Our own opinion is proof enough for us. To determine the nature of some desires, the assistance of science can be taken. For example, when you desire to eat something sweet, eat fruits instead of candy. In this way, a bad desire can be eliminated when a good one is put in its place. This method of overcoming desires through purification is the safest and the best. . .[16]

The Gītā tells us that knowledge and perseverence give us the strength required to restrain the senses. But even after one has gained control over the outer senses in this way, one's mastery is not secure until one has likewise won control over emotional impulses.[17] Verse II.59 expresses this by saying that the objects of sense turn away from the embodied soul who abstains from feeding on them, but the taste for them remains. Even the taste turns away when the Supreme is seen. This is the first reference to Bhakti or devotion in the Gītā.[18]

9.41. Serenity of mind marks the culmination of the chain of virtues. Chidbhavananda defines serenity of mind as "eschewing depresssion and confusion and being established in a blissful calmness.[19] . . . It is a form of samādhi for the mind to be fixed in purity and tranquillity, while making benign use of the senses."[20] Tilak also stresses this point, namely, that "the serenity of mind referred to here is not the result of giving up action, nor the objects of sense; it is acquired while moving about among the objects of the senses with an unattached frame of mind, that is, without entertaining any selfish desire for the fruit of action."[21]

9.42. Arjuna's question as to how to attain the state of release from all sorrow is thus answered. And in so doing, it is clarified that the concept of release from sorrow is not one-sided, because a person in the state of steadfast wisdom "neither grieves nor desires, neither rejoices nor hates". (II.56-57) In short, it can be viewed as a state of samatva or even-mindedness. Śrī Kṛṣṇa had already referred to samatva in two different contexts, one linked with metaphysical knowledge and the other for modifying the traditional appeal for svadharma. While coming back to samatva through the defining characteristic of Karma-yoga (namely, non-attachment to the fruit of action), the Gītā elevates samatva to be synonymous with yoga: "Fixed in yoga, do thy work, O Arjuna, abandoning attachment, with an even mind in success and failure, for evenness of mind is called yoga." (II.48)

Even-mindedness in success or failure enables one to concentrate all attention on the performance of one's duty, and this leads to efficiency or skill in action, which is another way of characterization of yoga in the Gītā: "One who has achieved buddhi-yoga casts away even here both good and evil. Therefore strive for yoga, yoga is skill in action." (II.50)

Radhakrishnan remarks that such a person "is rid of selfishness and therefore is incapable of evil."[22]

KARMA-YOGA AND THE HARMONIZATION APPROACH

9.43. In the preceding paragraphs we have summarized the initial teaching of Śrī Kṛṣṇa in conjunction with the questions which Arjuna had raised. We now proceed to analyse this teaching with a view to demonstrating that a unique characteristic of the Gītā is the harmonization approach. This will consist in showing the following: Two concepts which are often considered mutually incompatible, are harmonized to yield a modified new concept, which tries to combine the best elements of each unmodified concept, the assumptions being that there is something worthwhile in each concept, and also that neither concept by itself is perfect for all situations. By and by, we shall describe harmonization of several pairs of concepts, but to start with, we shall describe how the Vedic karma-kāṇḍa and the Upaniṣadic sannyāsā-oriented teaching has been harmonized in the karma-yoga of the Gītā.

9.44. In the opinion of scholars like Tilak, the Vedic religion at the time of the Gītā was divided into two main divisions, namely karma-kāṇḍa and Jñāna-kāṇḍa. Karma-kāṇḍa originally meant the worship of the Vedic deities by sacrificial ritual (yajña) in the belief that the worshippers would obtain children and grand-children, and cows, horses and other wealth in this life, and a happy state after death by the grace of these deities. It was also believed that the whole community would benefit from the sacrificial ritual because the prayers to the deities were not only for personal good but also for the good of the community. At the back of it was the belief in "Ṛta", the Vedic principle that the universe is governed by the cosmic order. Detailed instructions about the performance of the rituals were given in the Brāhmaṇas which constituted an important section of the Vedas. But as the ritual prescribed for the various sacrifices was different in the different Brāhmaṇas, doubts arose as to which one was correct. Therefore Jaiminī made a collection of explanatory rules for bringing about harmony between these mutually contradictory instructions. The rules laid down by Jaiminī are known as Mīmāṁsā-sūtras or the Pūrva-Mīmāṁsā, and therefore the ancient karma-kāṇḍa later on acquired the name of the Mīmāṁsaka-Mārga. For our present purposes, the important point to note is that, according to Jaiminī, the highest goal of life is attained by remaining in the state of a householder, and by performing yajña.

9.45. With the passage of time, according to Tilak again, the importance given to Brāhmaṇas shifted to Upaniṣads which regarded sacrificial ritual as inferior in comparison to the knowledge of Brahman. The religious path described in the Upaniṣads is known as Jñāna-kāṇḍa. Yet, as the different Upaniṣads contain certain ideas which are not wholly consistent with one another, it was also necessary to harmonize them. This was done by Bādarāyaṇācārya in his Vedānta-sūtras or Brahma-sūtras or the Uttara-Mīmāṁsā. Although some Upaniṣads like Īśa contain ideas on karma which can transform karma-kāṇḍa into Karma-yoga, the other Upaniṣads like Bṛhadāraṇyaka emphasize Jñāna to such an extent that they even contain renunciatory statements like the following:

> The scients of yore did not have any desire for children; they used to say: 'as we see that the whole world is nothing but

our atman, why should we have any other generation?' and without entertaining the desire for wealth, children, heaven, and the other spheres, such scients used to renounce those things and roam about the world begging for alms. (Br. Up. 4.4.22)

9.46. A shift in the emphasis from Karma-kāṇḍa to Jñāna-kāṇḍa marked, according to Tilak, a decline in the desire for prosperity and wealth, not only for individuals but also for the community. The path of Sannyāsa, that is, of knowledge of Brahman coupled with apathy towards wordly life thus became preponderant in the time of the Upaniṣads. Activistic teachings contained in Upaniṣads like the Īśa, and advice such as "do not cut off the line of progeny" contained in Taittirīya Upaniṣad (1.11.1) were considered only a minority view.

9.47. Faced with two types of doctrine, one putting stress on Pravṛtti or karma and the other putting stress on Nivṛtti or Sannyāsa or renunciation, both claiming their origin in Vedas or Upaniṣads, two types of attempts at bringing about harmony between them were made in ancient India, as described by Tilak.[23] First, Smṛti writers like Manu devised the scheme of four Āśramas, out of which the second Āśrama (Gṛhastha) would concentrate on karma, and the fourth Āśrama (Sannyāsa) would concentrate on Jñāna. We have already described in Part One (para 4.75) what Manu said about the relative importance of Gṛhastha Āśrama within the overall scheme of four Āśramas. However, critical comments occur in the Mahābhārata and the Bhāgavata (reference Part One, paras 4.76-77), indicating that, in many cases, the pre-conditions set by Manu for taking to Sannyāsa were not observed. Because of this, and other considerations, Tilak believed that the scheme of four Āśramas devised in the Smṛtis had only limited applicability, and it carried within itself the risk of loss of society.[24]

9.48. Tilak further believes that the second type of harmonization presented in the Gītā, by changing Karma-kāṇḍa into Karma-yoga, by restricting Sannyāsa (Jñāna-kāṇḍa) to a mental attitude, and by supplementing both of them with the additional easier doctrine of Bhakti, is better than the above-mentioned scheme of the Smṛtis. The Gītā accepts the main doctrines of the Upaniṣads about the importance of Jñāna, and also that Karma-kāṇḍa alone can only take one to heaven for a limited time but not to genuine Release. However, the Gītā regards the performance of karma as worldly duties to be unavoidable for the maintenance of the individuals as well as the society and the world. The new technique of the Gītā to have Karma done without causing bondage is "Non-attachment to the fruits of Karma", and this is facilitated (in Bhakti Yoga) by dedicating all karmas and their fruits to Śrī Kṛṣṇa in a spirit of devotion.

9.49. Karma-yogins, following the Gītā, divide all actions into two categories, namely Kāmya or those based on selfish desires, and Niṣkāma or those inspired by the good of the society. They make a Sannyāsa of Kāmya Karma, and perform the Niṣkāma Karma in the spirit of dedication to Śrī Kṛṣṇa. This, according to Tilak, is the Bhāgavata Dharma, known also as Nārāyaṇīya Dharma, since Ṛṣi Nārayaṇa as an incarnation of the Para-Brahman initially propounded it to another Ṛṣi Nara, and later on Śrī Kṛṣṇa who was the incarnation of Nārāyaṇa taught it to Arjuna who was the incarnation of Nara.[25] The Bhāgavata Dharma teaches that all the actions appropriate to the state of a householder should be performed desirelessly till death, and that escapism under the guise of Sannyāsa cannot be considered as an option. The Gita has re-affirmed this repeatedly, for example, verse XVIII.7 says that the Sannyāsa of any duty that ought to be performed is not right.

9.50. Upadhyaya has also described in detail what he calls "the Bhagavad-Gītā Technique of Compromise and Reconciliation". Unlike Tilak, he links the Sannyāsa-path with early Buddhism rather than with the Upaniṣads, but his account of the harmonization between Pravṛtti and Nivṛtti, as brought about by the Gītā is similar: Upadhyaya starts this section of his book like this:

> In the light of the above account of the one straight path of renunciation or knowledge (sannyāsa or jñāna) preached by early Buddhism, we can now see how the Gītā in keeping

with its synthetic character tries to evolve a compromise between the tenets of renunciation (nivṛtti or sannyāsa) and worldly action (pravṛtti), and advocates a triple path consisting of disinterested action (karmayoga), devotion (bhakti yoga) and knowledge (jñāna yoga). Evidently, in so doing, it makes certain adjustments, additions and alterations which differentiate its position from that of early Buddhism.[26]

9.51. Upadhyaya notes that the Gītā establishes its ethical precepts on the basis of its metaphysical and theological concepts of the all-pervading Self and God. For the purpose of reconciling different tenets, the Gītā gives its own definition of renunciation, namely, that it consists in giving up only the inner desire or attachment, while carrying on the active life of the world. Upadhyaya continues:

> The Gītā represents the tenet of the Bhāgavata dharma in its true spirit, embodying a philosophy of action based on devotion, and compromising it at the same time with the doctrine of knowledge or renunciation.[27]

9.52. In his *Essays on the Gītā,* Aurobindo also describes the role of Karma-yoga of the Gītā as a ground for the reconciliation between the two extremes, Vedist and Vedāntist, as he calls them:

> Here then are the two ideals, Vedist and Vedāntist, standing as if in all their sharp original separation and opposition, on one side the active ideal of acquiring enjoyments here and the highest good beyond by sacrifice and the mutual dependence of the human being and the divine powers, and on the other, facing it, the austerer ideal of the liberated man who, independent in the Spirit, has nothing to do with enjoyment or works or the human or the divine worlds, but exists only in the peace of the Supreme Self, joys only in the calm joy of the Brahman. The Karma-yoga verses of the Gītā create a ground for the reconciliation between the two extremes; the secret is not inaction as soon as one turns towards the higher truth, but desireless action both before and after it is reached.[28]

9.53. The above description, following Tilak, Upadhyaya, and Aurobindo, presents the Karma-yoga of the Gītā as a harmonization of Pravṛtti and Nivṛtti, or in other words, of Vedic Karma-kāṇḍa and Upaniṣadic Jñāna-kāṇḍa. Several other instances of harmonization attempted in the Gītā will be referred to in the following chapters.

Chapter Ten

Lokasaṁgraha: A Broad Social Goal, Supplementing Individual Śreyas

10.1. Verses III.20 to III.26 (which explicitly introduce Lokasaṁgraha or universal welfare) mark the beginning of the second stage of the teaching of Śrī Kṛṣṇa. Prior to that He answers Arjuna's question as to how he can obtain Śreyas, and release from sin and grief. We can say that the attainment of individual goals in life (not extending beyond svajanam or own people) is the main subject of teaching in the first stage.

A THREE-WAY EXTENSION

10.2. Before we study the seven Lokasaṁgraha verses in detail, we may remark that, when Śrī Kṛṣṇa moved on from a reply to Arjuna's question on śreyas, to his own self-chosen topic of Lokasaṁgraha, it was not merely a routine change of topic, but a significant widening or extension of the teaching. We plan to highlight, in this chapter, three aspects of this extension:

(a) In addition to the individual goal of Śreyas, wider goals ranging from social harmony and social responsibility to world preservation are introduced.

(b) The purpose of karma or human action gets a new meaning from Śrī Kṛṣṇa's statement that He Himself works for Lokasaṁgraha, and further that if He did not do so, the world would be destroyed. Following this exemplification of Lokasaṁgraha, the importance, for human beings, of setting an example, for the society, by their own conduct is stressed, care being taken that there is no ahaṁkāra or egotism.

(c) The meaning of samatva highlighted so far was "even-mindedness in success or failure". The need for a wider meaning of samatva as "even-mindedness towards all people" is indicated. Alternatively, terms like ātmaupamya or sāmya are mentioned. (For these and other terms like sarvabhūtahitam, which can be used in conjunction with Lokasaṁgraha, we have to search all over the Gītā, and need not remain confined to the Lokasaṁgraha verses).

We now take up these aspects one by one.

GOALS OF LOKASAṀGRAHA—SEVERAL VARIANTS

10.3. Lokasaṁgraha is a compound word of two component words, loka and saṁgraha. The first word 'Loka' denotes, in different contexts, either human beings or the world. The second word, 'saṁgraha' similarly has more than one meaning, ranging from 'keeping together' to 'protecting' as also to 'regulating'. Śaṁkara defined the world Lokasaṁgraha as 'weaning people from the tendency to take to the path of wrong.' Vivekananda translated Lokasaṁgraha as 'working for the good of others', and added that this is "a very powerful idea—which has become the ideal in India".[1]

10.4. Tilak has suggested two meanings, one referring to mankind and another referring to various worlds. Since he is the first commentator to highlight, most forcefully and with a detailed explanation, the concept of Lokasaṁgraha in the Gītā, his opinion about both the meanings is noteworthy. First, taking loka to mean mankind, Tilak writes:

> The last and the most important direction of the Blessed Lord to Arjuna in support of the doctrine of karma-yoga is centred on Lokasaṁgraha. . . . Taking all the meanings of saṁgraha as given in dictionaries, Lokasaṁgraha means 'binding men together, and protecting, maintaining and regulating them in such a way that they might acquire that strength which results from mutual cooperation, thereby putting them on the path of acquiring merit while maintaining their good condition. . . . (After looking at Śaṁkara's definition) it will

be clear that my interpretation of Lokasaṁgraha as 'making wise, those persons who behave recklessly as a result of ignorance, and keeping them together in a happy state, and putting them on the path of self-amelioration' is neither strange nor without authority.[2]

10.5. Tilaka compares his first meaning of Lokasaṁgraha to the concept of the 'welfare of society' which he says 'has become a very important science at the present time in western countries'. Tilak also says that 'the words 'welfare of a nation' have been used in the same sense in the Manusmṛti (7.144).'

10.6. Secondly, Tilak interprets loka in a wider sense so as to include the world not only of humans but also of gods, etc. Taking the comprehensive meaning of saṁgraha as above, Tilak explains:

> I must now make it clear that the world 'Loka' in Lokasaṁgraha does not indicate only mankind. It is true that the word Lokasaṁgraha ordinarily means the benefit of human beings, as man is superior to the other created beings in the world. Yet, in as much as the Blessed Lord also desires that the bhurloka, satyaloka, pitṛloka, devaloka and the several other loka or worlds, which have been created by him should also be properly maintained and go on in a proper way, I must say that the world 'Lokasaṁgraha' has, in this place, the comprehensive meaning that the activities of all these various spheres should go on properly in the same way as those of mankind. (Lokasaṁgraha = lokānām saṁgrahaḥ, i.e., the maintenance of various worlds.) . . . Furthermore, all these worlds should not only be maintained, but should also become mutually beneficial.[3]

10.7. One of the arguments given by Tilak in support of his wider interpretation is that the verse III.20 of the Gītā, which explicitly introduces Lokasaṁgraha for the first time, quotes King Janaka as an ideal karmayogī, and further that Janaka himself in Mahābhārata refers to the benefit of gods, etc. in addition to the benefit of human beings. To help appreciate this argument, we first give a translation of the Gītā verse III.20, and then shall refer to Mahābhārata:

> It was even by Karma that Janaka and others attained to perfection. Thou shouldst do Karma also, keeping an eye to Lokasaṁgraha. (III.20)

10.8. The most commonly quoted statement of Janaka, as a firm indication of his non-attachment, is: mithilāyām pradīptāyām na me dahyati kiñcana, that is, even if the capital of my kingdom is burnt, there is nothing in it that is mine that is burnt. But Tilak says that this only tells half the story, and he completes the story in the following words:

> From the point of view of Lokasaṁgraha, the main question is why Janaka was still carrying on the activities of ruling, though he had no selfish interest or advantage and had become perfectly non-attached to his kingdom. Janaka himself says: 'all these activities are for the benefit of the gods, the ancestors, all creatures, and my guests, but not for myself'.[4]

10.9. Tilak further argues that since verses III.11 and III.12 of the Gītā also refer to devas, the inclusion of devaloka in Lokasaṁgraha is justified. This is an appropriate point to refer to Gandhi's interpretation of devas in these verses because it has a bearing on his definition of Lokasaṁgraha. Gandhi says: The term 'gods' in verses III.11 and III.12 must be taken to mean the whole creation of God. The service of all created beings is the service of the gods and the same is yajña.[5] Continuing in the same vein, he defines Lokasaṁgraha as welfare of humanity, and links it with his concept of yajña.[6]

10.10. Aurobindo translates Lokasaṁgraha as 'the holding together of the peoples'. Regarding the seven Lokasaṁgraha-verses of Gītā (III.20-26), Aurobindo writes in his *Essays on the Gītā*: "There are few more important passages in the Gītā than these seven striking couplets".[7]

Aurobindo finds in the Karma-yoga ideal set by Janaka, a message that works have to be done with the same desirelessness after the liberation and perfection. However, as he moves from the status of a Karmayogin to that of a Pūrṇayogin, his concept of Lokasaṁgraha undergoes a modification. As a Pūrṇayogin, he opposes all kinds of pragmatic tendencies concerned much more with the present affairs of the world than with any high and far-off spiritual possibilities. He rejects any idea of a large moral and intellectual altruism in the concept of Lokasaṁgraha, and states that what the Gītā means is "a spiritual unity with God and with this world of beings who dwell in him and in whom he dwells.[8]

10.11. Radhakrishnan interprets Lokasaṁgraha as maintenance of the world. He sees in this concept a call to rise above narrow visions that seek comfort in merely doing duty to family, neighbours, city or the state. He says:

> Lokasaṁgraha stands for the unity of the world, the interconnectedness of society. . . .[9]
>
> The emphasis of the Gītā on Lokasaṁgraha, world-solidarity, requires us to change the whole pattern of our life. We are kindly, decent men who would be shocked and indignant if a dog is hurt, we would fly to the protection of a crying child or a maltreated woman and yet we persist in doing wrong on a large scale to millions of women and children in the comforting belief that by doing so, we are doing our duty to our family or city or the state. The Gītā requires us to lay stress on human brotherhood.[10]

10.12. Vinoba interprets Lokasaṁgraha as 'keeping people together, and on the right path'. He says that the Karma-Yoga technique of getting rid of selfishness by the method of diffusion will be successful only if the process of purification of desire is carried on simultaneously:

> A personal, individual desire may be given a general, social application in order to cross over from attachment to non-attachment. By this method desire can be progressively enlarged and diffused. But what if the desire itself be impure? That will bring about not only the downfall of the individual but also a social decline. A desire is not purified merely by extension to society.[11]

10.13. Dandekar includes within Lokasaṁgraha, not only 'the stability, solidarity and progress of society' but also 'an active awareness of one's social obligations'. He characterizes the Gītā-ideal of 'social integrity' as significantly different from the 'individualistic' view of the Upaniṣads. Here is an extract from Dandekar's essay on the Bhagavad-Gītā:

> The Upaniṣadic attitudes towards life and society is fundamentally individualistic. The Gītā, on the other hand, teaches that man has a duty to promote Lokasaṁgraha or the stability, solidarity, and progress of society. Society can function properly only on the principle of the ethical interdependence of its various constituents. As an essential constituent of society, therefore, man must have an active awareness of his social obligations. . . .[12]

10.14. Raju believes that *Niṣkāma* karma of the Gītā can best be translated as involving 'the principal of duty for duty's sake', and he warns against misinterpreting it as 'motiveless or aimless action'. In the opinion, both Lokasaṁgraha and individual salvation constitute the 'double aim' of the Gītā. Here is an extract from Raju's 'Philosophical Synthesis in the Bhagavad-Gītā':

> The teaching (of the Bhagavad-Gītā) involves a double aim:
>
> 1. The processes of the human world must be kept going. They should not be hindered, but furthered. When evil prevails and the good suffers, the Brahman takes on the appropriate incarnation, destroys evil, and protects the good. But why should the Brahman, which is eternally perfect and for which there is nothing to be desired, take the trouble of incarnating itself as a mundane being, go through the stages of birth, growth, and death ? Why should the incarnation, that knows that it is the same as the eternal brahman, take the trouble of acting in this world ? If it does not act, the world does not survive . . . Sustaining the world (is) Lokasaṁgraha. . . .
> 2. The second aim of the teaching is salvation. It is through action without any self-centered motive that one attains salvation. . . .[13]

10.15. Arapura interprets Lokasaṁgraha in a comprehensive sense, to cover the objective of preserving the world. There are threats to life itself due to environmental pollution caused by toxic substances, deforestation, and improper handling of wastes of all types. Scientific discoveries (including nuclear energy) are being misused, according to Arapura, to such an extent that human civilization which took thousands of years to build might be subjected to sudden, mass destruction. Additional health hazards are also due to uncontrolled increase in the population in those areas which already suffer from inadequacy of resources, malnutrition, poverty, and natural disasters. Above all, social institutions are finding it difficult to cope with the shocks of family break-up, mental tensions and neglect of children. In the face of all these threats, says Arapura, the world community stands in need of stabilizing influences that can be exerted by religious and moral ideas and grass-root organizations based thereon. Arapura believes that the Gītā-concept of Lokasaṁgraha needs to be spelt out in such a way as to enable an ethical input (howsoever small) in the formulation of an inter-disciplinary effort for world preservation and human welfare.[14]

10.16. Rangacharya has tried to summarize the different interpretations of Lokasaṁgraha as follows:

> This word has been somewhat variously interpreted to mean the accomplishment of the good of the world so as to prevent it from going astray, the inducement offered to the world so as to make it adopt the life which we consider to be good for it. . . . This could be called 'guidance and control of the world' or 'taking the world along with one'.[15]

10.17. Obviously, Rangacharya's summarization cannot include all the ideas that have been associated with an umbrella-like term like Lokasaṁgraha, by the various Gītā-interpreters. Also, much depends on the degree of emphasis or priority. Although Rangacharya does mention 'taking the world along with one', we would like to make an explicit mention of the concept of social responsibility. Dandekar has used a similar expression, namely 'social obligations'. While clarifying the ideal of Lokasaṁgraha to Arjuna, Śrī Kṛṣṇa had explained, 'If I do not act, the world would be ruined'. Any person using a similar approach will need to ask himself or herself: what will be the impact of my action or inaction on the society ? The 'social responsibility' concept arising from this approach is significantly different from what is called 'individualism', which gives a person freedom to act so long as other people's freedom is not endangered. Undoubtedly, the Lokasaṁgraha concept of social responsibility has a larger domain of awareness of social obligations than individualism. Of course, it should be made clear that the above-mentioned emphasis on social responsibility has nothing to do with social tyranny associated with the Indian caste system. At any rate, the words 'Loka' and 'saṁgraha', being free from divisive as well as discriminatory notions of all types, can probably serve present-day needs as well.

EXEMPLIFICATION THROUGH GOD'S OWN WORK

10.18. Verses III.22-24, in which Śrī Kṛṣṇa points to his own example as working for Lokasaṁgraha, are extremely important for understanding, among other things, the meaning and scope of the word 'karma'. Detailed comments and interpretations have been given by several scholars, but we begin by presenting a simple translation of the three verses:

> There is not for me, O Arjuna, any work in the three worlds which has to be done nor anything to be obtained which has not been obtained; yet I am engaged in karma. (III.22)
>
> For if ever I did not engage in karma unwearied, O Arjuna, men in every way follow my path. (III.23)
>
> If I should cease to work, these worlds would fall in ruin and I would be the creator of disordered life and destroy these people. (III.24)

10.19. Verse III.22 contains a strong warning to those who have a narrow view about the purpose of karma, namely that it will help them obtain something which they do not have and want to obtain. In fact, Arjuna himself had taken this stand when he argued that since he was willing to give up his claim on the kingdom, he saw no harm in withdrawing from the battle and in taking up sannyāsa. Śrī Kṛṣṇa emphasizes in this verse that the real purpose of karma is not to satisfy any narrow, selfish desire, because if it had been so, then He need not have performed any karma.

10.20. Although Śrī Kṛṣṇa implicitly refers here to His karma as preserver of the universe (IX.18, XV. 13) (including the unceasing movement of the sun, the moon, the earth, etc. as also nature's processes and laws which are guided by divine intelligence and will) Gandhi says that even the actions of the avatāra narrated in Hindu scriptures present a great ideal:

> Kṛṣṇa served the people all his life, a real servant of the people. He could have led the hosts at Kurukṣetra, but he preferred to be Arjuna's charioteer. His whole life was an unbroken Gita of karma. . . . As a child he was a cowherd and we still know him by the name of Gopāla, cowherd. . . Kṛṣṇa knew no sleep nor idleness. He kept a sleepless vigil over the world.[16]

10.21. Writing in a similar vein, Vinoba presents further details of what Śrī Kṛṣṇa did as a karmayogin:

> In Mahābhārata war, everybody at sunset leaves the field for evening prayer, but Lord Kṛṣṇa unyokes the horses from the chariot, gives them water, rubs them, removes the burrs from their bodies, and feeds them from his yellow garment which he has filled with grain. . . .
>
> At the Pāṇḍavas' Rājasūya sacrifice, Śri Kṛṣṇa clears the leaf-plates after the feast. . . .
>
> So the saints have pictured a karmayogī God who rubs horses, takes cows out to graze, drives a chariot, cleans dishes and mops up floors.[17]

10.22. Vivekananda also, speaking about Śrī Kṛṣṇa and the Gītā, described Śrī Kṛṣṇa as 'the most rounded man' he knew of, wonderfully developed equally in brain and heart and hand.[18] Every moment of Śrī Kṛṣṇa, said Vivekananda, was alive with activity, either as a gentleman, as a scholar, as a poet. This all-rounded and wonderful activity and combination of brain and heart, Vivekananda saw in the Gītā—"and nothing can approach it anywhere,"[19] as he declared emphatically.

10.23. This tremendous activity of the man (Śrī Kṛṣṇa), said Vivekananda, and then that heart ! Vivekananda recognised Śrī Kṛṣṇa as "the first man, way before Buddha, to open the door of religion to every caste."[20] . . . Moreover, said Vivekananda, Kṛṣṇa preached in the midst of the battlefield. . . . It means nothing to this man—the flying of missiles about him. Calm and sedate he goes on discussing the problems of life and death. He practised what he preached in the Gītā: He who in the midst of intense activity finds himself in the greatest calmness, and in the greatest peace finds intense activity, that is the greatest Yogī as well as the wisest man."[21]

10.24. For Aurobindo, too, while he was politically active, Śrī Kṛṣṇa of the Bhagavad-Gītā was the ideal Karmayogin, engaged in overthrowing the evil-doers. A specimen of what Aurobindo wrote in his weekly journal 'The Karmayogin' is given below:

> The recurrent cry of Śrī Kṛṣṇa to Arjuna insists on the struggle: 'Fight and overthrow thy opponents !', 'Remember me and fight !'. . . The charioteer of Kurukṣetra driving the car of Arjuna over that field of ruin is the image and description of Karmayoga; for the body is the chariot and the senses are the horses of the driving and it is through bloodshed and mire-sunk ways of the world that Śrī Kṛṣṇa pilots the soul of man to Vaikuṇṭha'.[22]

10.25. Verse III.23 refers to the "ideal-establishing" role of an avatāra. In particular, the importance of avoiding tandra, or "a mixture of Tāmasic vices like idleness, procrastination and indifference to duty" as Chidbhavananda puts it,[23] is stressed. The ideal-establishing role of an avatāra is highlighted when Śrī Rāma is addressed as maryādā-purushottama. In Hindu tradition, all the avatāras represent the continuity of dharma, and no exclusiveness is intended when we refer to one of them.

10.26. Verse III.24 is a very forceful statement of Śrī Kṛṣṇa's role as the preserver and protector of the universe, the dharma, and the people. It is obviously linked to verse IV.8 in which three broad functions which an avatāra performs are specified: "For the protection of the good, for the destruction of the wicked, and for the establishment of righteousness, I come into being from age to age." (IV.8)

10.27. Although it might appear from verse IV.8 that, after an avatāra has established righteousness, the wicked wait for some time and then reassert themselves till the next avatāra puts them down, verses III.23-24 make it clear that there is no such discontinuity in the functioning of God for Lokasaṁgraha. Whether or not a popularly recognized avatāra is visible, the divine process of preservation and protection of the universe and the dharma is continuously in operation.

10.28. A question is often raised, 'If God himself is continuously working for Lokasaṁgraha, why do we see so much destruction and unrighteousness?' Gandhi's replies to such questions spring from his faith in the existence of an invisible law:

> I have found that life persists in the midst of destruction and, therefore, there must be a higher law than that of destruction. . . .
>
> Superficially we are surrounded in life by strife and bloodshed, life living upon life. But some great seer, who ages ago penetrated the centre of Truth, said: It is not through strife and violence, but through non-violence that man can fulfil his destiny and his duty to his fellow-creatures. It is a force which is more positive than electricity and more powerful than even ether. At the centre of non-violence is a force which is self-acting.[24]

10.29. Tilak says that some of the followers of sannyāsa school try to justify their escapist attitude by arguing that since Parameśvara has created the world and is busy maintaining it also, why should they worry about Lokasaṁgraha? Although the hollowness of such arguments can be exposed in many ways, we quote below how Tilak finds the escapist attitude inconsistent with knowledge:

> If a man of knowledge becomes uniform with Parameśvara as a result of jñāna, how will he escape the necessity of performing that action which is performed by the Parameśvara? Besides, whatever the Parameśvara has to do, has to be done by Him

through the medium of scients. Therefore, active noble sentiments full of sympathy towards all created beings must arise in the mind of the man who has had the direct realization of the form of the Parameśvara in the shape of the feeling that there is only one ātman in all created beings; and the trend of his mind must naturally be towards Lokasaṁgraha.[25]

EXEMPLARY HUMAN CONDUCT ALSO ESSENTIAL

10.30. Sadācāra or good conduct is mentioned in Manusmṛti (II.6) as one of the four roots of dharma, the other three being the Vedas, the smṛtis (or dharma-śāstras), and acceptability to the individual. In the same section of Manusmṛti, sadācāra is viewed as those rules of conduct which, having been fixed by revered people, have been passed on from generation to generation. However, the need for change and adjustment (as exemplified by the well-known Gita phrase 'deśe kāle ca pātre ca' (XVII. 20) meaning adjustment to place, time and person) has been recognised in Hindu scriptures. Mishra says that a significant point of which the ancient Indian seers were fully aware was: "that there are eternal values of life, which form the basic foundation of social structure, as well as, there are changing values which depend upon the need of the time."[26]

10.31. In the Gītā after Śrī Kṛṣṇa told Arjuna of the importance of having Lokasaṁgraha as an important goal of life, he also advised Arjuna about setting an example to others by his good conduct: "Whatsoever a great man does, the same is done by others as well. Whatever standard he sets, the world follows." (III.21)

10.32. Commenting on this verse, Radhakrishnan also refers to the destabilizing modern tendency not to attach much importance to the concept of "great men":

> Common people imitate the standards set by the elect. Democracy has become confused with disbelief in great men. The Gītā points out that the great men are the pathmakers who blaze the trail that other men follow. The light generally comes through individuals who are in advance of society. They see

the light shining on the mountain heights while their fellows sleep in the valley below. They are, in the words of Jesus, the "salt", the "leaven", the "light" of human communities. When they proclaim the splendour of that light, a few recognize it and slowly the many are persuaded to follow it.[27]

10.33. In the Mahābhārata, Yudhiṣṭhira tells Yakṣa: "mahājano yena gataḥ sa panthāḥ" (Vana. 312.115), i.e. dharma is the path followed by venerable persons (although Arvind Sharma interprets mahajana as meaning masses). In the context of Lokasaṁgraha, the underlying teaching of the Gītā verse III.21 is that mere theoretical knowledge about what is good and what is real is not enough unless this knowledge is reflected in one's conduct. Gandhi is perhaps one of the best examples in modern India, of a person who believed in practising a virtue (say, non-violence) before preaching it. The following quotations from his writings stress this point:

> Non-violence cannot be preached. It has to be practised. . . Your ahiṁsā to be effective, must shine through your speech, your action, your general behaviour. A votary of ahiṁsā must cultivate a habit of unremitting toil, sleepless vigilance, ceaseless self-control. . .
>
> 'Enmity vanishes before ahiṁsā' is a great aphorism. It means that the greatest enmity requires an equal measure of ahiṁsā for its abatement. Cultivation of this virtue may need long practice, even extending to several births. . . .[28]

10.34. Vivekananda deduced from Śrī Kṛṣṇa's exemplification of Lokasaṁgraha, a message of 'loving the world, but without attachment':

Kṛṣṇa says:

> Look at Me, Arjuna! If I stop from work for one moment, the whole universe will die. I have nothing to gain from work; I am the one Lord, but why do I work ? Because I love the world. . . .
>
> God is unattached because He loves; that real love makes us unattached. . . . Do you ask anything from your children

> in return for what you have given them ? It is your duty to work for them, and there the matter ends. In whatever you do for a particular person, a city, or a state, assume the same attitude towards it as you have towards your children—expect nothing in return. If you can invariably take the position of a giver, in which everything given by you is a free offering to the world, without any thought of return, then will your work bring you no attachment. Attachment comes only where we expect a return.[29]

10.35. Since Lokasaṁgraha means bringing about a unity of purpose and cooperative effort in the society for a just cause, Śrī Kṛṣṇa asks the wise men not to be content by their own actions, but also to encourage others to act as well:

> Let the man of knowledge not unsettle the minds of the ignorant who are attached to action. The enlightened man doing all works in a spirit of yoga, should set others to act as well. (III.26)

10.36. The underlying message here is not to push people around, against their will; nor is it to perpetuate their ignorance. The plea is in favour of a slow and steady effort to educate common people and to encourage them to follow voluntarily the example of the wise. Ultimately, each individual has to choose one's own path, as the Gītā teaches in verse VI.5 which says that: "Let a man lift himself by himself; let him not degrade himself; for the self alone is the friend of the self and the self alone is the enemy of the self."

10.37. Tilak explains that a karmayogin who has attained steadfast wisdom puts in his efforts for the welfare of all (without entertaining any desire for fruit) with a twofold objective, namely, their material happiness as also their spiritual advancement:

> Giving merely material happiness to otherpeople will not be the sole objective of a sthitaprajña. His activities will be directed towards purifying the minds of all the persons forming a society, and thereby enabling them to ultimately reach the metaphysically perfect state he himself has reached.[30]

10.38. The word 'joṣayet' (meaning to encourage or induce) occurring in verse III.26 has led Aurobindo to find much support here for his special interpretation of the Gītā:

> To act for Lokasaṁgraha, impersonally, for the keeping and leading of the peoples on the path to the divine goal, is a rule which rises necessarily from the oneness of the soul with the Divine, the universal Being, since that is the whole sense and drift of the universal action. . . .
>
> Oneness with God, oneness with all beings, the realisation of the eternal divine unity everywhere and the drawing onwards of men towards that oneness are the law of life which arise from the teachings of the Gītā. There can be none greater, wider, more profound. Liberated oneself, to live in this oneness, to help mankind on the path that leads towards it and meanwhile to do all works for God and help man also to do with joy and acceptance all the works to which he is called, kṛtsnakarmakrit, sarvakarmāṇi joṣayan, no greater or more liberal rule of divine works can be given.[31]

10.39. By adopting the approach of the Gītā, underlying the world joṣayet, Gandhi achieved considerable success in obtaining mass support for his Satyāgraha movements based on the technique of ahiṁsā, which for him was a matter of deep conviction and practice, but which initially appeared to be beyond common people's capacity. Iyer has quoted Spratt's analysis (written in 1939) of how the struggle by the Indian community in South Africa under Gandhi's leadership in the early years of the twentieth century was a model of what Satyāgraha ought to be:

> It was conducted against very heavy odds by poor and ignorant people—the majority indeed were illiterate—but there was hardly an instance of breach of the principles. It dragged on in all for eight years: the longest fight Gandhi has ever conducted. People became disheartened. At one time he could count upon only sixteen followers. But in the end the "law of growth" prevailed. Almost the whole community again entered the fight, and satisfactory terms were obtained. He was left with an apparently immovable faith in the capacity

of ordinary poor people to undergo these trials and to observe the principles; and a no less indestructible faith in the efficacy of the method.[32]

LOKASAMGRAHA NO OBSTACLE TO ŚREYAS—EVEN DESIRE FOR LOKASAMGRAHA NO OBSTACLE

10.40. Perhaps the most dramatic instance of actually facing the argument that 'Lokasaṁgraha might jeopardize śreyas', occurred in the life of Vivekananda. In 1897, when Vivekananda proposed that the monks devote themselves to an active life of service for the masses, there were voices of dissent among his brother-disciples. Nikhilananda explains what lay behind this fraternal resistance to Vivekananda's plan for promoting Lokasaṁgraha:

> The dissenting monks were individualists, eager for their personal salvation. They wanted to practise austerities and penances, enjoy peaceful meditation, and lead a quiet life of detachment from the world. To them God was first, and the world came next. At least that was the way they had understood Sri Ramakrishna's teachings. These young monks thought that for one who had taken the monastic vows, the world was māyā; therefore all activities, including the charitable and philanthropic, ultimately entangled one in worldly life.[33]

10.41. Vivekananda knew that the narrow vision of the young monks, focusing on an exclusive search for mukti, could only be widened by giving clearer instructions and sincere assurances. Therefore, he repeatedly pointed out to his brother-disciples that to worry about personal liberation was unworthy of those who called themselves disciples of Sri Ramakrishna. Karmayoga activities carried out with a sense of dedication to the Almighty were as efficacious a means of salvation as meditation and austerities. In the terminology of this chapter, what Vivekananda told the dissenting monks was that, Lokasaṁgraha, instead of being an obstacle to śreyas, was actually the best way leading thereto. With so much of misery and ignorance prevailing in the society, the duty of Sri Ramakrishna's disciples, as Vivekananda explained to his colleagues, was to serve the needy as the visible manifestations of God.

10.42. After a good deal of clarification, Vivekananda's views prevailed, and the Karma-yoga-based socio-spiritual approach to the country's problems was fully agreed to by all the members of the Ramakrishna Mission. Vivekananda coined the famous Sanskrit phrase 'ātmano mokṣārthaṁ jagaddhitāya ca', which meant that each monk of the Mission was to pursue two goals, viz. one's highest freedom and the good of the world. In fact, using the terminology of this chapter, an alternative version for Vivekananda's phrase could be 'ātmanaḥ śreyorthaṁ Lokasaṁgrahāya ca'—the meaning of which is the same as before because mokṣa and śreyas, on the one hand, and jagaddhita and Lokasaṁgraha, on the other, are synonyms.

10.43. Gandhi also believed that, if pursued with a sense of detachment and unselfishness, a life of Lokasaṁgraha-centred Karma-yoga could lead to the attainment of mokṣa or śreyas. According to Gandhi, a life of dedicated service to one's kind in the spirit of the Gītā would not generate an attitude of aggressive or self-righteous altruism; rather it would lead to a progressive expansion of the human self till it came to comprehend the whole of mankind. As Gandhi put it:

> For me the road to salvation lies through incessant toil in the service of my country and humanity. I want to identify myself with every thing that lives. I want to live at peace with both friend and foe. So my patriotism is for me a stage on my journey to the land of eternal freedom and peace".[34]

10.44. Among the protagonists of the Sannyāsa School—leaving aside revolutionary thinkers like Vivekananda—it was the common belief that karma could only lead to citta-śuddhi or purification of mind, but not to mokṣa, which, they thought, was attainable only by jñāna i.e. knowledge. Another view of theirs was that, after achieving a state of perfection, karma could, or rather should, be given up. Activist interpreters of the Gītā—Vivekananda, Tilak, Aurobindo, Gandhi, and others—helped refute both these beliefs, by asserting convincingly that Lokasaṁgraha-activities led one to mokṣa and were to be carried on even after attaining perfection.

10.45. So much about Lokasaṁgraha not being an obstacle in the path to śreyas. But what about the desire for Lokasaṁgraha? According to Sannyāsa School, all desires, like all karma, led to bondage. Tilak explained in detail how the Gītā did not support this view. More specifically, Tilak said that *niṣkāma* Karmayoga (in spite of being translated as the technique of desirelessness) did not imply the giving up of all desires. Tilak clarified that Hindu scriptures, including the Gītā, want to encourage the desire for right knowledge, for the company of saints, for listening to scriptures, etc. because such desires do not cause bondage to saṁsāra.[35] In the Gītā, for example, Arjuna says in verse X.18: "Relate to me again in detail, O Kṛṣṇa, of thy power and manifestation; for I am not satisfied with hearing thy nectar-like speech." And Śrī Kṛṣṇa fully approves of such desire on Arjuna's part. In fact, Śrī Kṛṣṇa advises Arjuna in verse XII.9: If, however, thou art not able to fix thy thought steadily on me, then have the desire to reach me by the practice of concentration, O Arjuna."

Śrī Kṛṣṇa attaches so much importance to Lokasaṁgraha that he asks Arjuna in verse III.25 to act "without any attachment, but with the desire for Lokasaṁgraha": "As the unlearned act from attachment to their work, so should the learned also act, O Arjuna, but without any attachment, with the desire for Lokasaṁgraha." (III.25)

10.46. A fine distinction is made in verse III.25 between having the desire for Lokasaṁgraha, but having no attachment, that is, having no selfish desire for the fruit of the work done for Lokasaṁgraha. In fact, the basic teaching of Śri Kṛṣṇa that all actions should be performed without attachment to the fruit thereof, applies equally to Lokasaṁgraha. Tilak has drawn attention to this:

> Acts for Lokasaṁgraha must not be performed, entertaining any hope for fruit (phalāṣā); because if one entertains the hope for fruit, though it may be about Lokasaṁgraha, one cannot but suffer unhappiness, if that hope is frustrated. Therefore, a man should not entertain the proud or desireful thought that 'I shall bring about Lokasaṁgraha', and a man has to bring about Lokasaṁgraha merely as a duty.[36]

10.47. Gandhi also distinguished between desires of two kinds, of which the second one, namely the desire, 'to improve ourselves and to do good to others' is a part of true morality. Here are Gandhi's words:

> Desires are of two kinds. One is the pursuit of mere self-interest. To attempt to fulfil this kind of desire is immoral. the second kind of desire impels us constantly to improve ourselves and to do good to others. We should never become overweening with any amount of good that we may do. It is not for us to evaluate it, but rather should we have perpetual longing to become better and do more good. True morality consists in our efforts to realize such longing.[37]

10.48. In Raju's opinion, too, the Lokasaṁgraha-way of the Gītā involves 'not the killing of desires, but channelling them':

> Action is always prompted by desire, and desires are generated by instinctive urges. What then has man to do? Man should satisfy his desires according to the laws of the Cosmic Person. If desires are killed, there will be no action, and if there is no action, the world cannot be sustained. The Bhagavad-Gītā preaches not the killing of desires, but channelling them.
>
> Sustaining the world (Lokasaṁgraha) through the satisfaction of desires according to the laws of the Cosmic Person, which are not subjective but objective, is the ideal action. . . .[38]

TERMS WHICH IMPLICITLY REFER TO LOKASAṀGRAHA

10.49. Although the term 'Lokasaṁgraha' explicitly occurs only twice in the Gītā (III.20, 25), it does not mean that this important message is so narrowly confined and restricted to the Karma-yoga chpater alone. Another closely related term is 'sarva-bhūtahite ratāh' (persons who rejoice in doing good to all creatures) which occurs in Chapters V and XII. (V.25, XII.4) But these two terms taken together still do not exhaust the coverage of Lokasaṁgraha in the Gītā. There are several other terms that implicitly refer to Lokasaṁgraha, and they occur throughout the Gītā, and in conjunction with bhakti-yoga and

Jñāna-yoga as well. Three such terms or phrases need particular mention in this context:

(a) samaḥ sarveṣu bhūteṣu (even-minded towards all people) or sāmya (equality).
(b) ātmaupamya (equality of others with oneself)
(c) nirmamo nirahaṁkāraḥ (without any sense of mineness or egotism)

We shall indicate how each of these terms is associated with Lokasaṁgraha, and further that the concept of 'samatva', occurring in two forms, also provides a convenient, though implicit, way of distinguishing between śreyas and Lokasaṁgraha.

SAMATVA OR EVEN-MINDEDNESS

10.50. One form of even-mindedness, namely, that in success or failure of one's effort, has already been introduced by Śrī Kṛṣṇa in verse II.48, and it was mentioned as being synonymous with yoga. In a general way, this can be called "even-mindedness in all situations", and it can be viewed as an element of mental discipline, leading to śreyas or release from the binding effects of karma (IV.22). But Lokasaṁgraha also calls for an attitude of sympathy and compassion—say, a warm heart—the climax of which, according to Gītā, is "even-mindedness towards all people". The key Sanskrit word for even-mindedness in both these cases is the same—samatva—but the context in which it is used in any verse helps allocate it to one of the two categories.

10.51. As the most obvious example of highlighting separately the two categories of even-mindedness, we give below the translation of verses VI.8 and VI.9. In the former, samatva towards situations is again called yoga, but in the latter, samatva towards people is called "excellent":

> The yogi whose soul is satisfied with wisdom and knowledge, who is unchanging and master of his senses, to whom a clod, a stone and piece of gold are the same, is said to be firm in yoga." (VI.8)

> He who is equal-minded among friends, companions and foes, among those who are neutral and impartial, among those who are hateful and related, among saints and sinners, he excels. (VI.9)

10.52. The samatva-attitude towards a clod, a stone and a piece of gold which occurs in verse VI.8 is repeated in verse XIV.24 which forms part of the description of one who has risen above the three guṇas. In fact, the Gītā account of the characteristics of those who have attained perfection by different means is broadly similar. Radhakrishnan comments on the yogī who has samatva of the first category: "He is unperturbed by things and happenings of the world and is therefore said to be equal-minded to the events of this changing world."[39] And about the second category of samatva, he writes (in another place): "This view makes us look upon our fellow beings with kindliness and compassion. The wise see the one God in all beings and develop the quality of equal-mindedness which is characteristic of the Divine."[40] Verse V.19 says: God is the same in all, and this is repeated in verse IX.29 also.

10.53. Chidbhavananda also compares the two categories of samatva and while admiring both, stresses the supreme importance of the latter for the conflict-ridden humanity (or Lokasaṁgraha, as we would prefer to call it):

> Inert things are all viewed with an equal eye by the yogī. . . . The achievement of the Yogī is that he is the conqueror of the senses. . . .
>
> He stands supreme who has equal regard for people of varying status. His supremely benevolent attitude is the greatest gift made by him to the conflict-ridden humanity.[41]

SAMATVA TYPE I PROXY FOR ŚREYAS—AND TYPE II PROXY FOR LOKASAṀGRAHA

10.54. A convenient, though implicit, way of distinguishing between śreyas and Lokasaṁgraha, in the Gītā, is to refer to the former by 'samatva of the first category', and to the latter by 'samatva of the second category'. Furthermore, samatva of the first category is also denoted as being the same as 'liberation from the pairs of opposites (dvandvas). (XV.5, V.3). Similarly, samatva of the second category is also denoted as being the same as 'equality towards friend and foe'. (XII. 18, XIV.25)

10.55. Persons attaining perfection, according to the Gītā, achieve both śreyas and Lokasaṁgraha, and are, therefore described as possessing even-mindedness of both the categories. For example, among the characteristics of a bhakta given in verses XII.13 to XII.20, references to samatva of both the types occur side by side:

> He is alike to foe and friend, also to good and evil repute; . . . he is alike in cold and heat, pleasure and pain, . . . and is free from attachment. (XII. 18)
>
> He has no ill will to any being, . . . is friendly and compassionate, free from mineness and egotism, even-minded in pain and pleasure, . . . and patient. (XII. 13)

10.56. Similarly, holy ṛṣiṣ attaining brahmanirvāṇaṁ are not only pure but they also do good to all: "The holy men whose sins are destroyed, whose doubts and dualities are cut asunder, whose minds are disciplined, and who rejoice in doing good to all creatures, attain to the beatitude of God". (V.25)

Radhakrishnan comments on this verse as follows:

> The two sides of religion, the personal and the social, are emphasized by the Gītā. Personally, we should discover the Divine in us and let it penetrate the human; socially, society must be subdued to the image of the Divine. The individual should grow in his freedom and uniqueness and he should recognize the dignity of every man, even the most insignificant. Man has not only to ascend to the world of spirit but also to descend to the world of creatures.[42]

10.57. It is by no means necessary that even-mindedness of both the categories, associated with perfection, must occur in the same verse; these are often mentioned separately, so as to be appropriate to their respective contexts. For example, samatva of type one is associated with jñāna in verse XIII.9:

"... a constant equal-mindedness to all desirable and undesirable happenings..." (is a symptom of knowledge). (XIII.9). The fact that samatva of the second category also goes hand in hand with jñāna is convincingly brought out in verses V.18 and V.19:

> Men of knowledge see with an equal eye, a learned and humble Brāhmin, a cow, an elephant or even a dog or an outcaste. (V.18)
>
> Even here on earth the created world is overcome by those whose mind is thus established in equality (sāmya). God is flawless and the same in all. Therefore these persons are established in God. (V.19)

This with further details in verse V.23, is also referred to as jīvan-muktāvasthā (being liberated while still alive).

10.58. Verses XVIII.49 to XVIII.66 summarize the attainment of perfection in such a way that ultimately the distinction between karma-yoga, bhakti-yoga and jñāna-yoga disappears, and the Lokasaṁgraha-related characteristic of one who has become perfect is indicated in verse XVIII.54 by the phrase "samah sarveṣu bhūteṣu": "Having become one with Brahman, and being tranquil in spirit, he neither grieves nor desires. Regarding all beings as alike, he attains supreme devotion to Me". (XVIII.54)

10.59. In the description of the perfect person, given in verses XVIII.54-56, Sri Krishna Prem (a Gītā-commentator) finds a parallel with the Bodhisattva ideal of Mahāyāna Buddhism—of 'one who treads the Path not for his own salvation alone but for the salvation of all'. Here is an extract from Sri Krishna Prem's commentary:

> ... Serene in his true nature, he now, if he has come along the path of Love, attains to that supreme devotion which has no care for any conceivable personal gain, not even for the

greatly coveted goal of Liberation. Caring not for the intense bliss of personal liberation, the bliss of sheer self-loss in the absolutely blissful Brāhmik Being from which there is no return, he seeks only to serve Sri Krishna, the Purushottama, in whatever sphere his service is required.[43]

10.60. Aurobindo has also compared the Gītā-description of perfection with the Mahāyāna Buddhist ideal as well as with that of the Taoist thinkers. In Aurobindo's opinion, the Purushottama doctine of the Gītā leads to the most profound spiritual experience:

> The Gītā adds a phrase of immense import that alters everything, ātmani atho mayi. The demand is to see all things in the self and then in Me—the Ishwara, to renounce all action into the Self, Spirit, Brahman and thence into the supreme Person, the Purushottama. There is here a still greater and profounder complex of spiritual experience, a larger transmutation of the significance of human life, a more mystic and heart-felt sweep of the return of the stream to the ocean, the restoration of personal works and the cosmic action to the Eternal Worker. . .[44]

10.61. Although the term "sāmya" (occurring in V.19) conveys an idea similar to samatva of the second category, Vinoba thinks it can denote samatva of both the categories, and furthermore, it can be a preparation for reaching parama sāmya which (in Muṇḍakopaniṣad) stands for supreme identity, that is, Brahman. Vinoba explains why he prefers to call the Gītā "Sāmyayoga":

> I have named the Gītā Sāmayoga which is both the art and the philosophy of equality, equanimity and identity. . . . Parama Sāmya does not include the economic or the social equalities alone. They are, of course, desirable. But there is another kind of sāmya, namely equanimity or balance of mind, which is also implied in it. But this too is not adequate. The state that transcends all these sāmyas is the Supreme Identity, Parama Sāmya.[45]

10.62. Vinoba claims that spiritual gnosis and compassion for human beings are the two cardinal principles of Hinduism. He argues that to unite with God is to become like God, and he continues: "To become like Him amounts to being able to look upon all creatures with an equal eye or to meet all situations with equanimity."[46]

Although Vinoba refers to samatva of both the categories, he stresses the importance of Lokasaṁgraha-related attitude of equality (and practical action programmes based thereon).

EQUALITY OF OTHERS WITH ONESELF

10.63. The term 'ātmaupamya' meaning equality of others with oneself occurs in verse VI.32 which says: "He, O Arjuna, who sees with equality everything, in the image of his own self, whether in pleasure or in pain, he is considered a perfect yogi." (VI.32)

In Śaṅkara's words, "he sees that whatever is pleasant to himself is pleasant to all creatures, and that whatever is painful to himself is painful to all beings."[47] Even as he desires good to himself, he desires good to all.

10.64. The concept of ātmaupamya ultimately comes from the Upaniṣads, for example, Īśa Upaniṣad verse 6 says:

> The wise man who realises all beings as not distinct from his own self, and his own self as the self of all beings, does not, by virtue of that perception, hate any one. (Īśa verse 6)

Ranganathananda comments on the attitude and behaviour of such a person:

> Narrow-mindedness, secretiveness, and hatred spring always from a sense of separateness. The sense of separateness gives rise to all kinds of selfish desires; the desire to hide one's thoughts and possessions from others, the desire to exploit or overcome somebody else, and so on. But when this sense of separateness vanishes, such calculations also vanish, leaving in their place a feeling of universal friendship and benevolence towards other beings. . . .

All morality, all ethics and spirituality tell us that we are one, basically one. Jesus says. Love the neighbour as thyself. The Upaniṣads add: For you are your neighbour.[48]

10.65. From the above it is clear that a jñānin's metaphysical knowledge provides for him a firm foundation for ātmaupamya. The Gītā verse VI.29 says: "He whose self is harmonized by yoga seeth the Self abiding in all beings, and all beings in the Self, everywhere he sees the same."

Radhakrishnan says that "on the ethical plane, this means that (for a seeker of jñāna) there should grow a detachment from the world, and when jñāna is attained, a return to the world through love, suffering and sacrifice for it."[49]

10.66. Verses VI.30 and VI.31 state that a bhakta also experiences the profound unity of all beings from the devotional point of view:

> He who sees Me everywhere and sees all in Me, I am not lost to him nor is he lost to Me. (VI.30)
>
> The yogin who established in oneness, worships Me abiding in all beings lives in Me, howsoever he may be active. (VI.31)

Obviously, a bhakta's being active refers to the practical application of ātmaupamya in performing acts for universal welfare. The famous phrase "vasudhaiva kutuṁbakaṁ" meaning that "the whole world is just like one family" conveys the same idea.

GIVING UP MINE-NESS AND EGOTISM

10.67. A search for words or phrases which implicitly denote working for Lokasaṁgraha can be made by looking at the descriptions of persons who have attained perfection through Karma-yoga, bhakti-yoga and jñāna-yoga. In addition to the terms already mentioned, another phrase indicative of Lokasaṁgraha which has thus been identified by Vinoba is "nirmamo nirahaṁkāraḥ" literally meaning "giving up mine-ness and egotism". Vinoba's argument (specifically given with reference to verse II.71 which forms part of the description of a sthitaprajña) runs like this:

Nirmamo means that a sthitaprajña karmayogin has no selfish desires. Nirahaṁkāraḥ means that he has dedicated all his actions to Īśvara and does not regard himself as the doer. But still he puts in his best effort in whatever he does. What can he do other than Lokasaṁgraha? In fact, he lives only in order to benefit humanity."[50]

10.68. The same phrase "nirmamo nirahaṁkāraḥ" occurs also in verse XII.13 which describes a bhakta. Considering next the description of a jñānī who is worthy of becoming one with Brahman, verse XVIII.53 says that he is (among other things) nirmamaḥ and he casts away ahaṁkāraṁ. Therefore Vinoba's argument linking "nirmamo nirahaṁkāraḥ" with Lokasaṁgraha is fully justified.

Chapter Eleven

Multiplicity of Ways of Participation in Lokasaṁgraha

11.1. After introducing, in Chapter Ten, the main theoretical elements of what constitutes the social ideal, Lokasaṁgraha, the question now needs to be considered as to how that ideal can be actually put into practice. In this context, it may not be out of place to recall Nehru's observation that the high degree of perfection implied by some of the ancient Indian ideals could not possibly have much influence on practice.[1] While this remark might be generally true of some of the lofty ideals of ancient Hinduism and early Buddhism, it can be stated, following Bishop, Upadhyaya, Tilak, Gandhi, and others, that the approach of the Gītā, being relatively more flexible, encourages everyone's participation in the battle of life—and, therefore, also in Lokasaṁgraha—through the observance of the principles of svadharma according to one's capacity.

ENCOURAGEMENT BY GĪTĀ TOWARDS EVERYONE'S PARTICIPATION AND PURIFICATION

11.2. Bishop views the Gītā as a book which not only offers practical directions for people to follow in the battle of life but also has a big appeal, providing encouragement towards everyone's participation and purification:

> In life we are constantly engaged in a struggle both within and without between the forces of good and evil. . . . The Gītā gives us guidance or a set of beliefs to help us in that battle. . . . It is a source of inspiration. . . . The message of the Gītā is that the tendency of the universe is toward consolidation through purification. That consolidation consists of the harmony

of man with man and with nature on the Māyā level and the union of man with Brahman on the absolute level. That union is accomplished through participation on the part of both man and God, man becoming purified in the process. The Gītā, as a synthesis of Indian thought, describes different ways of joining with Brahman. It does not declare one to be better than the other, for each leads the sojourner to his true destination, God.[2]

11.3. Upadhyaya has put together in one place as many as eight Gītā-verses (or parts or sets thereof), to document his statement that 'the general tone of the Gītā is one of encouragement. . . . in carrying on one's worldly duties with a purity of purpose as far as possible.'[3] Of course, Upadhyaya's study is basically a comparison between early Buddhism and the Gītā, and the message of encouragement contained in the Gītā-verses applies mostly to svadharma-activities, which Śrī Kṛṣṇa wants to be performed in accordance with the teachings of the Gītā. However, works for Lokasaṁgraha are not envisaged to be in opposition to svadharma; rather the concept of svadharma is to be so adjusted as to include such of the Lokasaṁgraha - activities as are not beyond the capacity (pauruṣam, Gītā XVIII.25) of the person concerned. This issue will be discussed at some length in Chapter Twelve. The point to be recognized now is that the Gītā-verses of encouragement, picked up and put together by Upadhyaya, apply to the Gītā-teachings in general, and therefore include Lokasaṁgraha-activities also.

11.4. After providing the necessary clarification as above, Upadhyaya's long paragraph, containing eight Gītā-quotations 'of encouragement', as he calls them, is reproduced below:

> In the second chapter itself where Kṛṣṇa starts his exhortation to Arjuna, he declares: 'In this path, no effort is ever lost, no opposite result is ever produced. Even a little of this discipline saves one from great fear.' (II.40) Arjuna is repeatedly encouraged and cheered: 'Grieve not, O Arjuna, you are born with divine endowments'. (XVI.5) 'Casting aside all vacillating states of the mind come to me alone for shelter, I shall release you from all sins, do not grieve'. (XVIII.66) 'Know

it for certain, O Arjuna, that my devotee never perishes'. (IX.31) 'Even if one is of most vile conduct, if he worships me with unwavering devotion. . . . he soon becomes a righteous man and attains eternal peace'. (IX.30-1) 'One should not abandon one's natural duty, even though it is defective', . . . for 'man attains perfection devoted each to one's own duty'. (XVIII.48, 45) Though the Gītā also admits that 'there is nothing pure like wisdom in this world', yet it shows no urgency to attain it: 'He who acquires perfection in disinterested action, attains it (wisdom) of himself in course of time'. (IV.39, 38) When Arjuna, referring to the highly difficult process of yoga, asks Kṛṣṇa about the fate of those who, though endowed with faith, fail to follow the yoga to perfection, and being careless fall from it, Kṛṣṇa at once encourages him by saying: 'There is no destruction (setback) for him, O Arjuna, either here or elsewhere. One who has done good can never, O Arjuna, tread the path of woe'. Then it is pointed out how after having spent a happy life in heaven for long, he is born in the family of those who are pure and prosperous, or in the family of glorious yogins themselves and ultimately 'perfecting himself through many lives, he reaches the supreme goal'. (VI.33, 34, 37, 40-4)[4]

11.5. Tilak's statements about the participation of everyone in the society, in Lokasaṁgraha-activities, are even more explicit than those of Upadhyaya. However, before taking them up, it should be mentioned that two of the Gītā-verses, quoted by Rammohun Roy in his arguments against suttee-advocates, occur amongst the eight put together by Upadhyaya and therefore included as part of Upadhyaya's statement in the preceding paragraph. More specifically, Rammohun Roy used verses II.40 and VI.41 to convince his opponents that their doubts about the ability of widows to derive real benefit from *niṣkāma* karma were unfounded. Verse II.40 was translated by Rammohun Roy to be an assurance that 'the performance of even a small portion of a work without desire brings safety'.[5] Similarly, verse VI.41 was used by Roy to affirm that 'those who perform righteous actions without desire are assured of a continuous, upward spiritual mobility, for in their case, a heavenly stay is followed by a birth in the home of the pure, to enable them to complete their yoga till they attain final beatitude'.[6]

11.6. Tilak interpreted the Gītā in such a way as to assert, firstly, that its main message is Lokasaṁgraha-centred Karmayoga, and secondly, that, everyone, small or big, should, by performing svadharma in accordance with the teachings of the Gītā, contribute to one or the other aspect of Lokasaṁgraha. Summaries of these two conclusions drawn by Tilak in his *Gītā-Rahasya* are reproduced below:

> The Gītā religion proclaims to everybody, though nominally to Arjuna: 'perform lifelong your several worldly duties according to your respective positions in life, desirelessly, for the universal good (lokasaṁgraha) . . .[7]
>
> Every human being. . . acquires by birth, the high or low qualification of maintaining and uplifting society according to his or her own powers, and proportionately with whatever intellectual capacity, authoritative capacity, financial capacity, or physical capacity is either naturally possessed by him, or can be acquired by him having regard to his status in life. Just as extremely small wheels are necessary along with large wheels in order that any machine should work properly, so also is it necessary that the authority of common-place persons should be exercised properly and fully in the same way as the authority of superior persons like Vyāsa and others, in order that the immense and ponderous activity or mechanism of the Cosmos should continue to work in a properly regulated manner. . . . If the potters do not manufacture pots or weavers do not weave cloth, the maintenance of society (lokasaṁgraha) cannot be satisfactorily carried out, even if the king protects the society properly. . . ."[8]

11.7. Another important observation made by Tilak, to obtain maximum possible participation in Lokasaṁgraha-centred Karmayoga activities, is that, although purity of mind (of which unselfishness is a crucial element) is necessary to follow the teaching of the Gītā, one need not wait to achieve complete purity before engaging in action. According to Tilak's interpretation of verses II.40, VI.25, and others, participation in svadharma and efforts to achieve purity of mind, could go hand-in-hand:

Although the essential basis of proper conduct (sadācaraṇa) is the equable Reason (samatva buddhi), I must repeat here that, one cannot from that fact draw the inference that the man who performs Action, must wait for performing action until his Reason has reached that stage. It is the highest ideal of everybody to make his mind like that of a Sthitaprajña. But it is stated already in the commencement of the Gītā, that because this is the highest ideal, one need not wait for performing Action until that ideal has been reached; that one should in the meantime perform all Actions with as much unselfishness as possible, so that thereby the Reason will become purer and purer, and the highest state of perfection will ultimately be reached; and that one must not waste time by insisting on not performing any Action until the perfect state of the Reason has been reached.[9]

11.8. Upadhyaya also agrees with the above-mentioned interpretation of Tilak, namely the practice of *niṣkāma* karma from the very beginning without first realising the infallible stage of perfection. Upadhyaya further says that this teaching of the Gītā is "in contradistinction to early Buddhism which prescribes it (disinterested action) only after the attainment of perfection".[10] According to Upadhayaya's interpretation of Gītā-verses II.40, IV.38, VI.3, and others, perfection is gradually realised in the course of practising disinterested action—such action serving as the means of serenity. Here is a short extract from the detailed explanation given by Upadhyaya—which also contains an explicit reference to 'serving humanity' (Lokasaṁgraha):

> Thus, the Gītā speaks of two stages of disinterested action: the one which is performed by the aspiring saint (ārurukṣa) with a view to reaching perfection, and the other which is performed by the perfect or accomplished saint (siddha or yogārūḍha) with a view to serving humanity with perfect equanimity.[11]

11.9. Although Gandhi, like Tilak, also wanted mass-scale participation in the Lokasaṁgraha-activities, he (Gandhi) prescribed certain minimum standards for all such participants. The most obvious condition to be observed by all Satyāgrahīs (the ideal for whom was the Sthitaprajña of the Gītā), was that they could not cause physical injury to the opponent. Although Ahiṁsā (non-violence) ideally meant no injury by thought, word, and deed, it was obviously too much to expect that millions of ordinary people would come up to that lofty standard. Nevertheless, when cases of physical violence against the British officials or their supporters were brought to the attention of Gandhi, he suspended the movement itself.

11.10. Standards of self-discipline and purity, which Gandhi prescribed for the Āśrama-residents, were broadly patterned so as to come as close as possible to the Sthitaprajña-ideal. However, for ordinary participants in the Satyāgraha movements, certain feasible standards were indicated from time to time. For example, a list of 'seven qualifications', which Gandhi considered 'essential for every Satyāgrahī in India', reads as follows:

1. He must have a living faith in God, for He is his only Rock.
2. He must believe in truth and non-violence as his creed and therefore have faith in the inherent goodness of human nature which he expects to evoke by his truth and love expressed through his suffering.
3. He must be leading a chaste life and be ready and willing for the sake of his cause to give up his life and his possessions.
4. He must be a habitual Khādī-wearer and spinner. This is essential for India.
5. He must be a teetotaller and be free from the use of other intoxicants in order that his reason may be always unclouded and his mind constant.
6. He must carry out with a willing heart all the rules of discipline as may be laid from time to time.
7. He should carry out the jail rules unless they are specially devised to hurt his self-respect.

The above qualifications are not to be regarded as exhaustive. They are illustrative only.[12]

11.11. So much about the views of Gītā-scholars and activists on the issue of obtaining the maximum possible participation of people in Lokasaṁgraha-activities, and also on the related issue of having standards of 'purification' so as to ensure the observance of the Gītā-teachings. In the light of this, it is necessary to explore further, firstly, how the criteria of 'purification' applicable to Lokasaṁgraha-activities differ from those applicable to śreyas-oriented yoga. Secondly, there is an obvious need to list out all possible ways of participation in Lokasaṁgraha, with a view to accommodating persons placed in the various situations in life and following their respective svadharma. These two explorations, therefore, occupy the rest of this chapter.

VIRTUES THAT PURIFY—FOR ŚREYAS AND FOR LOKASAṀGRAHA

11.12. Paragraph 9.34 quoting Gītā-verses II.64-65, presents a chain of virtues, which starts from mental discipline—and proceeding through non-attachment, freedom from aversion, normal worldly activity, sense control, and serenity of mind-takes one up to Śreyas. This chain can be viewed as a linkage between 'dharma' and 'śreyas'.

11.13. Gītā-interpreters like Vivekananda, Tilak, Aurobindo, Gandhi and others have identified, in their own way, the main elements of the linkage between 'dharma' and 'lokasaṁgraha'. For example, Vivekananda emphasized, in this context, the importance of 'unselfishness', 'fearlessness' and 'spirit of dedicated service to the needy'. Tilak and Aurobindo, fully recognizing the supreme value of these three virtues, added thereto two more, namely 'respect for the values which have held the society together' and 'willingness to sacrifice for a just cause'—the latter assuming particular significance in the light of their confrontation with the British Empire. Gandhi did not deny the importance of the virtues identified by his predecessors, but added 'truth' and 'non-violence' to the list—almost placing non-violence on the top.

11.14. As a firm believer in the Gītā, Gandhi attached great importance to the chain of virtues, which from an analytic point of view, has been specified (in para 11.12) as leading to śreyas. However, Gandhi viewed these virtues, as well as those specified in para 11.13, as an integral part of 'dharma', the principal goal of which, for 'life on earth', as Iyer summarized Gandhi's thoughts, was Lokasaṁgraha (even mokṣa or śreyas being secondary thereto):

> Gandhi regards dharma as the highest human value, an end in itself, to which even mokṣa is secondary during life on earth. Dharma, in his view, has no meaning apart from Lokasaṁgraha, the welfare of the whole world.[13]

11.15. The subtle distinction between virtues that lead to śreyas and those that lead to Lokasaṁgraha has attracted the attention of scholars. A slightly different, though related, type of classification has been attempted by Hiriyanna, who utilized a list of nine virtues (dharmasādhanaṁ) given in Yājñavalkya Smṛti to illustrate the practical difference between "self-regarding" and "other-regarding" virtues:

> There are nine virtues which, according to Yājñavalkya, should be cultivated by all, namely, ahiṁsā, satya, honesty, cleanliness, sense-control, dānaṁ (charity), damaḥ (self-discipline), dayā (compassion), and forbearance. Some of these like ahiṁsā, dānaṃ, and dayā, have a reference to the good of others, while some others like satya, cleanliness, and damaḥ serve to develop one's own character and will. It should not, however, be thought that this division into self-regarding and other-regarding virtues is a hard and fast one; for, as an individual has no life of his own independent of society, the former has a bearing on the latter, as surely as the latter has on the former.[14]

11.16. Three of the above-mentioned virtues—damaḥ, dayā and dānaṁ—are the subject of a beautiful story occurring in the Bṛhadāraṇyaka Upaniṣad, which helps to clarify the difference between self-regarding and other-regarding virtues.

> Three kinds of Prajāpati's sons—gods, men, and demons—lived with their father as students. After finishing their studies,

the gods said to Prajāpati, 'Please teach us'. He told them the syllable 'Da' and asked, 'Have you understood?' The gods said, 'We have'. You say to us: discipline yourselves.' Prajāpati said, 'Yes, you have understood.'

"Then men said to him, 'Please teach us.' Prajāpati told them the same syllable 'Da' and asked, 'Have you understood?' Men said, 'We have. You say to us: be charitable.' Prajāpati said, 'Yes, you have understood.'

Then demons said to Prajāpati, 'Please teach us.' He told them the same syllable 'Da' and asked, 'Have you understood?' Demons said, 'We have. You say to us: have compassion.' Prajāpati said, 'Yes, you have understood'.[15]

11.17. Of the three virtues highlighted by Bṛhadāraṇyaka Upaniṣad, the first one, damaḥ or self-discipline, is self-regarding, while the other two—dayā and dānaṁ—are other-regarding. Ranganathananda has similarly derived a combination of both types of virtues from Īśā Upaniṣad, although the terms used there are dharma and amrita: "Dharma (outward-directed action) gives abhyudaya (social welfare), while amrita (inward-directed action) ensures niḥśreyas (spiritual freedom)"[16]

11.18. In verse XII.20 of the Gītā, the two terms: dharma and amrita, occur, and Ranganathananda interprets them as conveying a similar meaning:

> Śrī Kṛṣṇa's message is both dharma and amrita, capable of ensuring collective social welfare and the realization by the individual of his immortal divine nature, as defined by Himself in the Gītā.[17]

Ranganathananda continues to talk about both aspects, and how they have been harmonized by Vivekananda through his famous Sanskrit phrase describing the new goal of his brother-disciples:

> This is also the description that Swami Vivekananda gives of the scope of the mission of his master, Sri Ramakrishna: Ātmano mokṣārthaṁ jagaddhitāya ca"
>
> i.e. For the spiritual freedom of oneself and the general welfare of the world.[18]

11.19. A comprehensive list of twenty-six virtues (including damaḥ, dayā and dānaṁ) is given in the Gītā (verses XVI.1-3) while describing daivī sampat or divine endowments:

> Fearlessness, purity of mind, wise apportionment of knowledge and concentration, dānaṁ, damaḥ, yajña, study of scriptures, tapas, uprightness. (XVI.1)
>
> Ahiṁsā, satya, freedom from anger, spirit of renunciation, śānti, aversion to fault-finding, dayā to living beings, freedom from covetousness, gentleness, modesty, absence of fickleness. (XVI.2)
>
> Vigour, forgiveness, fortitude, purity, freedom from malice, and freedom from excessive pride—these, O Arjuna, are the endowments of him who is born with the divine nature. (XVI.3)

11.20. Obviously, the above list includes both self-regarding and other-regarding virtues. Subsequently, in Chapter eighteenth, while presenting a summary of the teaching, Śrī Kṛṣṇa has picked up three virtuous acts, namely, tapas, yajña, and dānaṁ, which everyone should perform, without attachment or desire for the fruits thereof:

> Acts of tapas, yajña, and dānaṁ are not to be relinquished but should be performed; for these are purifiers of the wise. (XVIII.5)
>
> But even these acts ought to be performed, without attachment or desire for fruits. This, O Arjuna, is my decided and final view. (XVIII.6)

11.21. Vinoba and Balkoba find in Bṛhadāraṇyaka Upaniṣad a passage which mention tapas, yajña, and dānaṁ (among others) as a means to know Brahman, and which also characterises Brahman as lokānāṁ asaṁbhedaḥ". This has been translated by these two scholars as "one who protects the worlds from falling apart".[19] In their opinion, this is similar to Lokasaṁgraha of the Gītā. A translation of the relevant passage from Bṛhadāraṇyaka Upaniṣad follows:

> That infinite Brahman is the lord of all, the ruler of beings,

> the protector of beings. It is like a bridge which protects the worlds from falling apart. It is the Brahman whom the Brāhmins wish to know by the study of the Vedas, and also by means of tapas, yajña, and dānaṁ, performed without attachment. (*Bṛhadāraṇyaka Upaniṣad* 4.4.22)

11.22. There is a close parallel (and partial identity) between "damaḥ, dayā, dānaṁ" on the one hand, and "tapas, yajña, dānaṁ" on the other. In fact, the Gītā verses XVII.14 to 16 have listed a number of virtues which are included in tapas, and one of these is ātmavinigrahaḥ or self-discipline, which is the same as damaḥ. So tapas can be viewed as a wider virtue than damaḥ. Similarly, yajña in the extended form formulated by the Gītā, is more comprehensive than dayā, and it has the additional advantage, of having within it the Gītā-inspired elements of selflessness, desirelessness and non-egotism. Tilak has summarized the extended meaning of yajña in the Gītā:

> The most important element in a yajña is the giving up of the idea of mineness (mamatva) with reference to the object thrown into the sacrificial fire, by uttering the words "na mama" (i.e. this is not mine) at the time of throwing. . . . In short, one may say that doing a particular karma, in which there is no selfish purpose, with a pure frame of mind, is a yajña in itself.[20]

11.23. In view of the above we can say that, although dharma stands for a large number of virtuous acts, the Gītā has presented a minimum of three, fundamentally important, practical action-programmes, which can be denoted by tapas, yajña, and dānaṁ. The primary role of tapas for attaining śreyas has already been referred to in para 9.36. The other two, namely, yajña and dānaṁ, are particularly relevant to Lokasaṁgraha. We shall indicate in Chapter Twelve what role these two concepts have played in Lokasaṁgrahā-oriented activities in India in recent years.

11.24. In addition to yajña and dānaṁ, the Gītā mentions, in two verses (V.25 and XII.4), the phrase 'sarvabhūtahite ratāḥ.', which means 'persons who rejoice in doing good to all creatures'.

Virtues like 'having no ill will or enmity to any creature, being friendly and kind to all' have also been stressed (e.g. in verses XI.55 and XII.13) Above all, the virtue of 'samatva' or even-mindedness to all creatures' is given in several verses as an important characteristic feature of those who have attained perfection. Since this particular virtue (samatva) has tremendous terminological significance, it has been discussed in detail in paragraphs 10.50 to 10.62.

11.25. Another reference to Hindu scriptures which specifically relates dharma and Lokasaṁgraha has been identified by Desai.[21] He says that the Bhāgavata Purāṇa has listed seven dharma-sādhanaṁ as applicable to all varṇās:

> ahiṁsā satyamasteyamakāmakrodhalobhatā
> bhūtapriyahitehā ca dharmoyaṁ sarvavārṇikaḥ.
> (11.17.21)

that is, "the basic dharmas common to all the varṇas are: ahiṁsā, satya, honesty, unselfishness, freedom from wrath, freedom from greed, and desire to do good to mankind."

11.26. Mishra has depicted the self-regarding and other-regarding virtues as 'vertical and horizontal development' respectively, of human character. Virtues like self-discipline and cleanliness which serve to develop one's character and will and to raise one's status in the spiritual field, represent vertical growth in a figurative sense. Other virtues like compassion and friendliness which strengthen one's bond to fellow human beings and extend one's sympathy to all creatures, represent horizontal development. These are the virtues which promote Lokasaṁgraha.[22]

11.27. The two categories of virtues can also be viewed as broadly corresponding to the two commandments which Jesus Christ highlighted in answering the question of the scribe:

> And one of the scribes. . .asked him 'Which commandment is the first of all? Jesus answered, 'The first is, . . . you shall love the Lord your God with all your heart, and with all your soul, and with all your mind, and with all your strength.' The

second is this, 'You shall love your neighbour as yourself'. There is no other commandment greater than these.[23]

11.28. In Western moral philosophy, some writers like Pierre Nicole make a distinction between self-love and charity, which represent broadly what we have called self-regarding and other-regarding virtues. Nicole says that, although self-love (which relates everything to itself) and charity (which relates everything to God) are very different from each other, yet they end up being similar in their effects:

> If charity extends its kindness to those from whom it has nothing to expect, and indeed to its very enemies because it looks only to their advantage and not to its own interest, self-love acts likewise, knowing that the more its kindnesses appear disinterested and free of all self-seeking, the more they will attract the affection of the world, since they afford everyone the hope of receiving similar kindnesses.[24]

11.29. Turning the attention from virtues to vices, it might be useful, though difficult, to attempt a classification of vices, corresponding to what Hiriyanna did for virtues, namely, self-harming vices and other-harming vices. Perhaps an illustrative classification could begin by designating ignorance and attachment as self-harming vices, and violence and egotism as other-harming vices. More specifically, it is pertinent to ask which of the vices can be identified as the most serious obstacle in the path to śreyas and Lokasaṁgraha—and particularly the latter. Followers of jñānamārga would regard ignorance as the root cause of all misery and bondage, that is, the main obstacle in the path of śreyas. Another approach would emphasize attachment, which has already been mentioned as the starting point of the chain of unhappiness.

11.30. Considering, next, the matter from the point of view of Lokasaṁgraha, the Gītā warns against mamatva or the feeling of mineness, which is intimately linked with attachment. Mamatva leads to selfish desires or kāma. But vices, put together in a sequence in such a way as if they constitute a parallel chain starting from ahaṁkāra or egotism, are also mentioned in verse

XVI.18: "Given over to egotism, force, insolence, and also to lust and anger, these malicious people despise Me dwelling in the bodies of themselves and others."

This chain of vices starting from ahaṁkāra and leading to hatred between different members of a society can be considered as most damaging to Lokasaṁgraha because while summarizing the main teaching of the Gītā. Śrī Kṛṣṇa repeats it in verse XVIII.53 and asks Arjuna to cast this chain aside and attain to the state of 'samaḥ sarveṣu bhūteṣu' (even-mindedness towards all people)

MULTIPLICITY OF ASPECTS OF PARTICIPATION IN LOKASAṀGRAHA

11.31. Chapter Ten gives a theoretical account of the teaching on Lokasaṁgraha contained in the Gītā-verses III.20-26—presented verse-by-verse, but in a slightly different order so as to fit into the sequence of ideas contained in that chapter. A deeper analysis of these verses taken together, supplemented by other socially oriented verses of the Gītā, can provide a new perspective on the meaning and purpose of karma. In order that every member of the society, engaged in one's svadharma, can participate in one aspect or the other of Lokasaṁgraha, it is important that all possible aspects of Lokasaṁgraha-activities, relevant to present-day conditions, be listed. Modern scholars and activists using different arguments have already identified several such aspects which, taken together, and expanded to incorporate the views of the author of this study, indicate what 'karma for Lokasaṁgraha' could stand for. Accordingly, ten aspects of participation in 'lokasaṁgraha' are presented below:

(i) Productive aspect
(ii) Protective aspect
(iii) Stability aspect
(iv) Service aspect
(v) Self-help aspect
(vi) Responsibility aspect
(vii) *Niṣkāma* aspect
(viii) Ethical aspect

(ix) Cohesive aspect
(x) Educative aspect

We shall present these aspects one by one.

PRODUCTIVE ASPECT

11.32. Subramaniam is one of those who have tried to analyse and interpret the Karma-yoga verses of the Gītā in the light of the modern economic theory of work. Nowadays productive employment of able-bodied persons is a key factor in the welfare of families as well as the society. So an important question is whether the term 'karma' in the Gītā can be interpreted as productive work. Subramaniam writes:

> Of the three meanings of karma in the text, only one pertains to work in modern parlance. . . .
>
> In the first place, karma is interpreted as rituals of all sorts, as for example in Chapter III where Krishna describes an injunction from Prajāpati to the humans to perform rituals and the devās to grant boons in return. . . .
>
> It is used in a second ultra comprehensive sense in the seme chapter to include every physical and physiologial movement. . . . In this sense karma includes productive work only by including every movement, useful or useless. . . .
>
> In a third sense karma is closer to productive work, when Krishna declares in the same (third) chapter that even he, the Lord, wanting nothing, does work incessantly to keep the world going and that it behooves the great to set an example to the rest of the world.[25]

11.33. In old days, productive and socially useful work was largely agricultural, although some non-agricultural work was also important, for example, handicraft, trade and other services. The importance of producing enough food for the society is still a priority, but industries producing items of basic need, and services like trade, education and health have also obtained greater recognition. One of the threats to world preservation, highlighted by Arapura and others, comes from the the vast increase in population outstripping the production of food. Therefore, Subramaniam's emphasis on productivity as an important element of karma for Lokasaṁgraha is fully justified. And it also fits in with the Gītā's characterization of yoga as 'karmasu kauśalam' (II.50) which has been translated by Subramaniam as 'efficiency in action'.

11.34. Indira Rothermund also feels that the modern summarizing of the Gītā as karmayogaśāstra (rather than mokṣaśāstra, as done by the traditionalists) has opened up possibilities for arousing the villagers to give up their passivity and to engage themselves in productive effort: "The Indian farmers could be persuaded to put in greater effort to improve their lot by pointing out to them, for example, that Lord Krishna in the Gītā had emphasized this type of activity."[26]

11.35. Productive activities, for bringing about 'rural uplift', have also been included in the work-programme of the Ramakrishna Mission. One of the main activities is known as 'Pallimangal'—or Integrated Rural Development—the coverage of which varies from area to area but is often quite wide, including, for example, pisciculture, cottage industries, aid to farmers and small business, training in know-how as also adult education and mobile medical service.[27]

11.36. Gandhi attached so much importance to utilizing the productive capability of villagers, in Khadi and village industries, that he termed the spinning wheel as 'yajña'—to emphasize that everyone should participate in it, as a symbol sharing the burden of poverty, which traditionally fell heavily on the neglected, landless villagers, including the so-called untouchables.

PROTECTIVE ASPECT

11.37. The protective and world-preservative aspect of karma for Lokasaṁgraha is highlighted by Śrī Kṛṣṇa when he says that, if he were to cease such work, the lokas as well as the people would be destroyed. For identifying the appropriate human work for Lokasaṁgraha, the nature of threats of mankind, animals, birds, plants and sea-life needs to be diagnosed.

According to environmental experts, many areas of the world are losing much of their wildlife because of indiscriminate tree-felling, chemical pollution, depletion of underground water, a high birth rate, and natural disasters. The forest area as a percentage of total land area is falling rapidly below the optimum level (say twenty-five per cent) needed to maintain the ecological balance. The forest area is falling because of excessive felling of trees for fuel and for construction of houses for rapidly growing populations. Problems are further aggravated by excessive consumerism which results in a rapid depletion of natural resources. Above all, low lying land areas may go under water due to the green house effect that might cause global warming and raise the sea level.

11.38. The environmental hazards and the nuclear threat call for world-wide action by policy-makers, scientists, industrialists and others, but ultimately everything depends on the right mental attitudes. The Lokasaṁgraha concept of the Gītā, if properly understood, can make people aware of their responsibility, and can provide the ethical rationale for curbing unnecessary consumption and reducing pollution and waste. The problems are so vast that a coordinated effort from all angles is needed before it is too late. In this context, Klostermaier's remarks about the provision of Hindu dharmaśāstras for protecting environment are worth quoting:

> The Manusmriti, as well as other dharmaśāstras, are quite up to date as regards protection of the environment. They punish by loss of caste the injuring of living plants, cutting down green trees for firewood, mining and all mechanical engineering that does damage to the environment, etc.[28]

11.39. How Gandhi's example inspired the hill-people of north India to apply non-violent methods to protect their forests, has been briefly described in para 6.98. This famous ecological movement became known throughout the world as 'Chipko'—which means hugging the trees. When all efforts for preventing the cutting of trees had failed, ordinary men and women 'hugged' the trees and flung their bodies before the axes—which proved effective.

11.40. A brief mention should also be made of Gandhi's suggestion that the traditional way of performing a yajña—involving burning of wood—needs to be discontinued. Gandhi attached much value to the Gītā-approach of modifying the meaning of yajña, and himself carried such modification still further so as to make it increasingly relevant to present socio-economic conditions and to serve the cause of Lokasaṁgraha. His comment on the yajña-related verses of the Gītā (reference paras 6.106-7) included the following:

> I cannot understand the idea that one can perform a yajña by lighting a few sticks. . . There were big forests in those (Vedic) days, and it may have been regarded as everyone's duty to help in clearing these forests, for it was a social necessity. . . . In burning wood in this age, we misuse the capital of our forefathers, or we show ourselves witless pedants by understanding the thing in a literal sense.[29]

STABILITY ASPECT

11.41. Radhakrishnan has given a detailed commentary on verse III.26 which advises a man of knowledge working for Lokasaṁgraha to encourage others also to act, but warns against using pressure or force to secure immediate abandonment of traditional practices. The Gītā does not believe in creating unstable conditions, in an attempt to bring about changes and improvements too rapidly. Radhakrishnan has highlighted the stability aspect:

> Traditional symbols are vital to those who believe in them. They become intolerable only if they are imposed on those who cannot accept them. . . . It is true that every one should reach the highest level but this can be attained generally by slow steps and not by sudden jumps. . . . Whatever we would like to do for others, we should do with love and reverence.[30]

11.42. Verse III.24 warns against creating disorder in society, against causing confusion. An avatāra establishes righteousness and justice. Stability does not mean inflexibility or perpetuation of injustice. Altekar, who has made a detailed study of whether Hinduism is a static structure or a dynamic force, writes:

> Our ancient rishis never expected that the rules that they had laid down would be regarded as binding for ever by their descendants. They themselves have pointed out the necessity of making periodical changes in them.[31]
>
> It was an evil day when the non-official change-sanctioning authority, the Dasavara Parisad of the Smriti was replaced by a government department presided over by the Minister of Religion. For, when Hindu rule came to an end by the thirteenth century, this department also disappeared, and during the last 600 years Hinduism has remained more or less static. With no authoritative and intelligent agency to guide him, the average Hindu believes that religious beliefs, philosophical theories and social practices, current in the twelfth century, are of hoary antiquity. It is his conviction that they are all sanctioned by the scriptures (which he does not understand), and that to depart from them is unpardonable sin.[32]

11.43. Maintaining social stability in the Indian context involves striking a balance between religious tradition and modernization. Bellah considers four possible responses,[33] of which the two extreme ones are: giving up the traditional religion in favour of the colonial powers' religion, or making no change in the tradition. Obviously, the Indian approach based on the Gītā is neither of these extremes. The two intermediate responses are: neo-traditionalism (keeping change to a minimum), and reformism (striking a balance between tradition and modernity). Although some of the leaders of modern India can be called neo-traditionalists, the main stream is represented by reformists. Thomas believes that such a balanced response has contributed to social stability in the midst of so many changes:

> By turning to a religious text, Gandhi and others were not shunting their responsibility to face the present. On the other hand, they tapped the possibilities of this religious text to make changes meaningful in the final analysis. One of the

conditions for modernization, according to David E. Apter, is a social system that can constantly innovate without falling apart, including innovation of beliefs about the acceptability of change. Through their commentaries on the Gītā, Tilak, Gandhi, et al, prepared the Indian society for change and even asserted that the Gītā calls for change.[34]

11.44. An individual-related variant of the problem of instability which has become serious in modern times can be expressed in terms of psychological disbalance. In the chain of unhappiness mentioned in the Gītā, a crucial factor is unrealistic desires for personal benefits, which, when not matched by acquisitions, lead to frustration. In old days, family support and sympathy was a good healing factor, but excessive individualism, on the one hand, and traditional restrictions, on the other, offer little comfort for disturbed minds. Klostermaier notices a parallel between Thomas McCarthy's description of such problems in the modern age and the chain of unhappiness given in the Gītā :

> Without referring to the Gītā , a modern writer describes the symptoms of the manifestation of crisis—and he clearly means our own time—in terms that could be taken straight from the Gītā as "loss of meaning, withdrawal of legitimation, confusion of orientations, anomie, destabilization of collective identities, alienation, psychopathologies, breakdowns in tradition, withdrawal of motivation."[35]

11.45. Although Klostermaier does sound a note of warning that "it is not so easy to establish the universal applicability of the ethics of the Gītā",[36] the fact that modern scholars find in the Gītā a vivid reflection of modern problems, is significant by itself. And even if "universal" solutions are not easy to find, limited progress in solving some of the problems in selected areas can possibly be made.

11.46. In order that social stability is understood in a comprehensive sense, Śrī Kṛṣṇa explains (in Chapter X) that things of beauty and splendour (that enrich the society culturally) constitute special revelations of the Divine. The use of the phrase "satyaṁ śivaṁ sundaraṁ" for identifying truth, goodness and beauty as attributes of perfection should help remind us not to forget the role of art and culture in social development and stability. Joan Price's description of a perfect being—or a gnostic being, in the terminology of Aurobindo—includes the following: "Acting as a free force with respect for truth, the gnostic being would live in peace; music, arts and crafts would be expressions of beauty and truth, the life and body would know the joy of purity and self-mastery. . . ."[37]

SERVICE ASPECT

11.47. Commenting on verse III.20 Radhakrishnan writes:

> Lokasaṁgraha stands for the unity of the world, the interconnectedness of society. If the world is not to sink into a condition of physical misery and moral degradation, if the common life is to be decent and dignified, religious ethics must control social action. . . . In an age of hope and energy we emphasize active service in the world. . . .[38]

Another Gītā commentator, Sarma also says that service to society is the main component of Lokasaṁgraha, and furthermore that "unsympathetic critics of Hinduism have often ignored the existence of the concept of Lokasaṁgraha, and said that social service forms no integral part of our religion."[39]

11.48. Upadhyaya thinks that the message of selfless service to the world draws its inspiration from three sections of the Gītā, namely (i) Lokasaṁgraha, (ii) divine origin of the world, and (iii) wheel of yajña or sacrifice:

> God himself is cited as an ideal who without any interest of his own is engaged in the work of maintaining the world-order. . . .
>
> As the origin of the world is traced to God, it becomes the duty of man to live in the world and promote its welfare. . .
>
> The wheel of the world, according to the Gītā, goes on by means of sacrifice or renunciation, and one who does not discharge his selfless service to the world lives only in vain.[40]

Reference has already been made to the Gītā phrase "sarvabhūtahite ratāḥ" (V.25 and XII.4) which means "persons who rejoice in doing good to all creatures", and this includes the rendering of selfless service to the needy.

11.49. Romain Rolland has described how Vivekananda emphasized the "social service" component of the Ramakrishna Mission's programme of work, and how the Gītā's teachings of "social unity and harmony" and "renouncing the fruits of action" were stressed by Vivekananda in his final message to the disciples, asking them to "serve others":

> One of the lay disciples pointed out the difficulty of establishing social unity and harmony in India. Vivekananda replied, "Your duty is to serve the poor and the distressed, without distinction of caste and creed. What business have you to consider the fruits of your action? . . . Let the reading of the Vedānta and the practising of meditation and the like be left to be done in the next life! Let this body go in the service of others—and then I shall know you have not come to me in vain![41]

11.50. Rolland also mentions Gandhi who took up another kind of service: "Another has taken up the holy struggle to give back to the untouchables their rights and their dignity—M.K. Gandhi".[42]

And it is well known how Gandhi drew inspiration from the Gītā and devoted his whole life to the service of the disadvantaged people.

11.51. Madeleine Biardeau made a special study of social service groups in India with a view to identifying their sources of inspiration. She observes:

> The term sevā, service, is one that recurs quite frequently in the names of many political or social reform groups . . . .
>
> Undoubtedly the influence of Vivekananda who had been so impressed in his travels to the West by charitable institutions, and of his Ramakrishna Mission as well, lent great credence to the idea of selfless service. It is nevertheless more than

likely that all of this took place within pre-existing ideological frames of references, and that the Bhagavad-Gītā was its greatest source of inspiration.[43]

SELF-HELP ASPECT

11.52. Although in the interest of those who are in a position to serve others, Vivekananda advised them to do their utmost, but with humility, still from the viewpoint of the receivers of such service, and also in general, he stressed the importance of self-help and self-confidence. He called 'self-help' as the 'greatest lesson' given by the Gītā-verse VI.5, which says, 'Thou thyself art thy only friend, thou thyself thy only enemy'. Vivekananda added: "It is a tremendous error to feel helpless. Do not seek help from anyone. We are our own help. If we cannot help ourselves, there is none to help us."[44]

11.53. 'Self-confidence' was given so much importance by Vivekananda that, in Practical Vedānta, it plays the same role as 'faith in God'. The essence of practical Vedānta was viewed by him to be a 'man-making' religion, and his main requirement for achieving success in his plans was 'men who believe in themselves'.

11.54. The main idea behind Gandhi's Khādī-programme also was that the poor villagers, instead of feeling helpless and asking for charity, should stand on their own feet, as much as possible. Furthermore, he derived the 'bread-labour law' from the yajña-related verses of the Gītā—suggesting that all must work and earn their bread by the sweat of their brow. He hoped that, in this way, distinctions between rich and poor, high and low, touchable and untouchable, could be minimised, and violent social conflicts could be avoided.

RESPONSIBILITY ASPECT

11.55. While clarifying the ideal of Lokasaṁgraha to Arjuna, Śrī Kṛṣṇa explained in verse II.24, 'If I do not act, the world would be ruined'. Dandekar discerns therein a strong emphasis on 'social obligations'. Any person following Śrī Kṛṣṇa's example will need to ask himself or herself: what will be the impact of my action or inaction on the society? Vivekananda illustrated this by pointing out the 'responsibility' of mothers to ensure that, by leading a 'pure life', they would give birth to healthy babies. "So long as you live in society", said Vivekananda, "it is your responsibility to prevent the very birth of evil".[45]

11.56. Vivekananda also wanted the richer sections of the society to recognize that they are at least partly responsible for the misery of the masses. He outlined the purposes of rendering service:

> . . . .to struggle unto life and death to bring bout a new state of things—sympathy for the poor and bread to their hungry mouths, enlightenment to the people at large, and struggle unto death to make men of them who have been brought to the level of beasts by the tyranny of your forefathers.[46]

NIṢKĀMA ASPECT

11.57. The most appropriate meaning of 'niṣkāma' in the context of Lokasaṁgraha is 'to have no selfish desire'. Tilak has clarified that the Gītā does not envisage the giving up of all desires—only desires for selfish gains are to be given up. In fact, in verse III.25, Śrī Kṛṣṇa asks Arjuna to 'act without any attachment, but with the desire for Lokasaṁgraha'. A fine distinction is made here between having the desire for Lokasaṁgraha, but having no attachment, that is, having no selfish desire for the fruit of the work done for Lokasaṁgraha. It is a sort of reminder that the basic teaching of the Gītā that all actions should be performed without attachment to the fruit thereof, applies equally to Lokasaṁgraha. In Tilak's words: ". . .a man should not entertain the proud or desireful thought that ' I shall bring about Lokasaṁgraha' . . . a man has to bring about Lokasaṁgraha merely as a duty".[47]

ETHICAL ASPECT

11.58. Karma for Lokasaṁgraha has to be such as may 'wean people from the tendency to take to the path of wrong', using

Śaṁkara's definition. Vinoba also stresses the need to keep the people on the right path. For this, the action itself has to be morally right. When verse III.21 speaks of setting an example, the ethical aspect of karma is implicit in it. Tilak says that the word śreṣṭha used in this verse is comparable to the ideal-setting person who should be followed, according to the Taittirīya Upaniṣad, if one is in doubt as to how to act in any particular contingency of life.[48] Kaveeshwar argues that sometimes, "giving up the desire for selfish gains" might not be enough to guarantee that the action itself is morally right, and that therefore the right-wrong consideration of an action should not be relegated to a secondary stage.[49] Another argument in support of the ethical content of karma is that an avatāra (God's incarnation) works for re-establishing righteousness, by supporting the good and by punishing the evil.

11.59. Fighting against evil and injustice is thus a part of karma for Lokasaṁgraha, and the possibility of doing this by peaceful means (as attempted by Gandhi) reinforces the ethical principle. Panikkar has explained how the ideals of Lokasaṁgraha and unselfishness, elaborated by Tilak, were supplemented by the Ahiṁsā doctrine of Gandhi—and how this resulted in an exemplification of the image of a Sthitaprajña in the personality of 'Gandhi, the ideal Satyāgrahī':

> To Gandhiji, it was not sufficient that the ideal should be Lokasaṁgraha or the welfare of all. It was even more important that the means should be ethically right. . . . Gandhiji's special contribution to the integral teachings of the Gītā is not selfless action for the welfare of the world but the emphasis on the means. There was a suggestion in Tilak's Gītā-Rahasya that the Karmayogin's action, as it was dedicated to God, was above moral laws so long as the object was clearly understood to be the common weal. It is this unexpresssed doctrine of Tilak that Gandhiji sought to set right by his commentary on the Gītā and the practical interpretation he gave to it through his own life.[50]

11.60. Under present-day conditions, the ethical aspect of works supposedly done for Lokasaṁgraha has assumed great significance. Even terrorists killing their opponents or innocent civilians often claim that they have no selfish interests to serve. By supplementing the criterion of selflessness with that of non-violence, the possibility of discouraging terrorism, by characterizing it as anti-Lokasaṁgraha, needs to be explored.

COHESIVE ASPECT

11.61. Karma for Lokasaṁgraha has to fulfil the basic purpose of keeping people together, not by force but voluntarily. As a prerequisite for this, grievances of one group of people against another have to be looked into, and resolved in such a manner as not to disrupt social unity and harmony. Reducing gross inequalities in the distribution of wealth by peaceful means would form a part of this. A legal approach can have only a limited role in achieving this. A non-official mechanism for resolving disputes peacefully also needs to be considered. These are big issues for which easy solutions do not exist. But tendencies to foment hatred and rivalry have to be discouraged. The Gītā has warned against getting entangled in a chain of hatred rooted in ahaṁkāra (Reference para 11.30).

11.62. The cohesive aspect of Lokasaṁgraha lends support to activities which create feelings of mutual cooperation and togetherness among the various members of the society, including inter-religious tolerance and fellow-feeling. One good example of this was the daily prayer-meeting of Gandhi where verses from different scriptures were recited and devotional hymns were sung. Furthermore, in Chinmayananda's opinion, the cultivation of a cooperative spirit is an important element of what the Gītā has indicated as 'yajña', and therefore, sharing of joys and sorrows through socially beneficial 'yajñas' would make the society more cohesive: ". . . . all causes for the sorrows in social life would be, no doubt, removed, if the good and socially-conscious members of a community were to feel satisfied in enjoying the 'remnants' of their co-operative work performed in the true Yajña-spirit".[51]

EDUCATIVE ASPECT

11.63. Since karma for Lokasaṁgraha is absolutely voluntary, the only possible way to give it the form of a mass movement is by creating favourable public opinion. Basic questions like: 'why should the good of the society receive a higher priority than the good of the individual?' need to be raised and answered by scholars and activists. Only through such awareness and knowledge can common people appreciate why Vivekananda said that, the philosopher, the worker, and the devotee all meet at one point, that one point being unselfishness. Furthermore, some of the underlying concepts like the preservation of a clean environment can be conveyed even to children in an appropriate manner. All such actions are included in the general term "educative", which constitutes an important aspect of karma for Lokasaṁgraha.

CHAPTER TWELVE

Two Stages of Lokasaṁgraha—Duty-Bound and Spontaneous

12.1. If we summarize (as is often done) the main teaching of the Gītā as *niṣkāma* karma or anāsakti or samatva, we are putting more stress on the mental attitude with which we discharge our duties rather than on determining what our duties are. Sarma raises a question connected with this limitation which applies only when the technique of Karma-yoga—but not its content or direction—is taken into account:

> But karmayoga is only the method of our work. It lays down only the manner in which we should discharge our duties. But what are our duties, what constitutes their content and substance?[1]

12.2. The content of duties is indicated in the Gītā in a variety of ways, taking into account both explicit and implicit teachings. However, the following two ways of describing duty are probably the most important:

(a) svadharma
(b) yajña, dānaṁ, tapas—often spoken of as a trio.

In this chapter we examine how svadharma, on the one hand, and yajña, dānaṁ and tapas, on the other, give an idea of the content of duty, and also how, in each case, the individual goal—śreyas—and the social goal—Lokasaṁgraha—can be achieved. Our main interest behind all this is to explore how either of these specifications of duty has (or can have) Lokasaṁgraha as an integral component. However, we need not always remain tied up to the idea that Lokasaṁgraha has to be accomplished only from a sense of duty or obligation, because ultimately Lokasaṁgraha has to be a spontaneous or natural activity. That possibility—representing, in a way, the second stage of Lokasaṁgraha —will also be considered towards the end of this chapter.

SVADHARMA AS DUTY

12.3. According to the traditional interpretation, svadharma denotes duty allocated to any particular individual by virtue of his or her belonging to one of the four varṇas—Brahmin, Kṣatriya, Vaiśya, Śūdra—into which the Indian society was divided in ancient times. In course of time, the four varṇas degenerated into the caste system, which became associated with narrow attitudes of loyality to small subgroups rather than to the society as a whole. Also, for lower castes, conditions of poverty and occupational immobility practically constituted a vicious circle, to escape from which usually meant breaking the tradition. Taking into account the drawbacks of the present-day caste system, many critics of the Gītā rebel against the very concept of svadharma.

12.4. Gītā-commentators have tried to soften the criticism launched by 'anti-caste' scholars. A plea that is commonly made is that the svadharma approach should not be judged in the light of the evils of the present-day caste system. If we accept the validity of this plea, attention needs to be focused on what the Gītā says about the varṇa system and the role of svadharma therein.

12.5. Verse IV.13 of the Gītā states that guṇa (i.e. quality or aptitude) and karma (i.e. work or function) constitute the basis of the varṇa system. Radhakrishnan comments:

> The emphasis is on guṇa (aptitude) and karma (function) and not jāti (birth). The varṇa or the order to which we belong is independent of sex, birth or breeding. A class determined by temperament and vocation is not a caste determined by birth and heredity. . . . The present morbid condition of India broken into castes and subcastes is opposed

to the unity taught by the Gītā, which stands for an organic as against an atomistic conception of society. . . .[2]

12.6. Verses XVIII.41-47 speak of the duties of each varṇa, determined in each case by svabhāva (i.e. nature), and efficacy of svakarma or svadharma (again determined by svabhāva). In these seven verses, the word 'svabhāva' occurs six times. However, in the closing verse of this section, namely, verse XVIII.48, the expression used is 'sahajaṁ karma'—the literal translation of 'sahajaṁ' being 'born with'. This single word 'sahajaṁ' has been picked up by the critics to denounce the svadharma doctrine. In order to facilitate a clear understanding of the pros and cons of the svadharma-debate, a translation of the verse XVIII.48 is given below—except that the Sanskrit expression 'sahajaṁ karma' is retained as it is: "One should not give up sahajaṁ karma, O Arjuna, even if it may be defective, for all enterprises are clouded by defects as fire by smoke". (XVIII.48)

12.7. Many critics of the Gītā in modern times like Pillai take the view that, since the term 'svadharma' essentially represents the duty of each varṇa, which was an early form of the caste system, the work ethics of the Gītā is too compartmentalized and narrow. For example, Pillai says:

> Even in a philosophical text like the Gītā, the Varṇa-system based on birth has acquired undue importance. . . . The Gītā simply accepted the age-old blind and cruel system of caste and gave it divine authority. . . . The mystic author of the Gītā, Vyāsa, put words into the mouth of Kṛṣṇa to establish the superiority of the Brahmins, and to allocate to the śūdras obligatory service work like that of a slave. Looking to the modern needs, we must reject the Gītā's teaching on varṇadharma. Such rejection is justified since Kṛṣṇa did not impose anything on Arjuna and only told him to do as he chooses after having reflected fully on the teachings.[3]

12.8. Attempts by the Gītā-commentators to answer the abovementioned criticism broadly fall into six groups. First, there are commentators like Gandhi and Vinoba who feel that svadharma linked with varṇa need not represent a weak point for the Gītā, even if varṇa was determined by birth. The Gītā according to Gandhi says: "Among the saints of revered memory, Senā was a barber, Sajanā was a butcher, Gorā a potter, Raidās a cobbler, Chokhamālā an untouchable, Tukārām a kumbi, and so on. None disclaimed his hereditary function but worked his salvation through a detached prayerful performance of it."[4] Similarly, Vinoba argues that when a man gives up his ancestral trade and takes up a new job, so many years are wasted in learning the new job.[5]

12.9. Secondly, there are commentators like Radhakrishnan who argue that varṇa in the Gītā depended not on birth but on qualities and functions, and furthermore that, since svabhāva (nature) has been specified six times as the basis of svadharma or svakarma, the word 'sahajaṁ', occurring only once and in the same context, should be translated as 'suited to one's nature'. In the opinion of Radhakrishnan, therefore, the concept of svadharma linked with such non-hereditary varṇa was designed 'for human evolution':

> The fourfold order is designed for human evolution. There is nothing absolute about the caste system which has changed its character in the process of history. Today it cannot be regarded as anything more than an insistence on a variety of ways in which the social purpose can be carried out. Functional groupings will never be out of date. . . .[6]

12.10. Thirdly, Chinmayananda links the word 'sahajaṁ' with a technical term 'vāsanās', which he defines as "the compelling deep urges in us, gathered in our past fields of action—that now determine our present emotional profile".[7] He explains this further in simpler language:

> That which determines one man's personality as distinctly different from another's, it is very well known, is the texture of the thoughts entertained by him. This texture of his thoughts is, again, in its turn, determined by the pattern of thinking (vāsanās), which his mind has gained from its own past. These pre-determined 'channels-of-thinking' created by one's own earlier ways of thinking are called the vāsanās.[8]

12.11. After explaining the term 'vāsanās', Chinmayananda interprets 'sahajaṁ karma' as 'the work ordained by the existing vāsanās', and his long commentary on verse XVIII.48 includes the following statement:

> The word 'sahajaṁ' means 'born with'. There is an ocean of difference between the meanings of the phrases 'born with' and 'born into'. Krishna is saying that one should not renounce actions which are ordered by the evil vasanas born with the individual. But the Lord has not said that one should pursue the evil action one is born into. . . . The vāsanās one is born with are to be lived through, without ego and desire; while the vāsanā-creating atmosphere into which one is born should not be allowed to contaminate one's personality. Krishna is very careful in indicating that a spiritual seeker must constantly strive hard to stand apart from the shackling effects of the environments. According to the Gītā, man is the master of circumstances. To the extent he comes to assert this mastery, to that extent he is evolved.[9]

12.12. Fourthly, there are scholars like Sarma who give to svadharma an individualistic interpretation. He argues

> If by svadharma the Gītā merely meant that the descendants of washermen should do nothing but wash clothes for all time and that the descendants of shoe-makers should do nothing but make shoes for all time, it would not be a scripture with a universal message. So by giving a narrow interpretation to the expression svadharma, we are doing great injustice to the Gītā and trying to hide its light under a bushel. In a remarkable verse (XVIII.47) the Gita connects svadharma with svabhāva, that is, one's duties with one's nature. . . . It is one of the remarkable features of the Gītā that it strikes an extraordinarily modern note in its clear and unmistakable recognition of the influence of natural dispositions on the individuality of man. . . . In no scheme of spiritual discipline can the natural dispositions of the individual be ignored. The Gītā repeats this statement in a hundred different ways.[10]

12.13. Fifthly, Aurobindo's detailed analysis, besides giving 'svabhāva' (which occurs six times) a bigger role than 'sahajaṁ' (which occurs only once), interprets 'svabhāva' not only as 'phenomenal nature' but also as 'Spiritual Nature' or the Divine Shakti. Brief extracts relating to both these aspects of Aurobindo's thoughts are reproduced below:

> The word 'sahaja' means that which is born with us, whatever is natural, inborn, innate; its equivalent in all other passages is 'svabhāvaja', The work or function of a man is determined by his qualities, karma is determined by guṇa; it is the work born of his svabhāva, and regulated by his svabhāva. This emphasis on an inner quality and spirit which finds expression in work, function and action is the whole sense of the Gītā's idea of karma. . . .[11]
>
> In the end, to arrive at the divinest figure and most dynamic soul-power of the fourfold activity is a wide doorway to a swiftest and largest reality of the most high spiritual perfection. This we can do if we turn the action of the svadharma into a worship of the inner Godhead, the universal Spirit, the transcendent Purushottama and, eventually, surrender the whole action into his hands. . . . The Spirit takes up the individual into the universal Svabhāva. . . . To live in the highest spiritual nature with the individual and natural being delivered from shortcoming and ignorance and made a conscious instrument for the works of the Divine Shakti is the perfection of which humanity is capable. . . .[12]

12.14. Sixthly, there are scholars and activists like Kalelkar and Tilak who argue that the Karma-yoga teaching can be dissociated from varṇa because the varṇa system has nothing to do with the central message of the Gītā. Kalelkar writes:

> The arrangement of society according to varṇas is not a necessary corollary of the Vedic philosophy of the Gītā. The development of social virtues mentioned in the sixteenth chapter does not need the four varṇas at all.[13]

On the basis of similar arguments, expressed even more forcefully, Tilak summarizes his view on the universality of svadharma-based Karma-yoga and its linkage with Lokasaṁgraha:

> The Gītā says that whether the society is a Hindu society or a non-Hindu society, whether it is an ancient society or a modern society, whether it is an Eastern society or a Western society, if the arrangement of four varṇas applies to that society then according to that arrangement, and if it does not apply then according to any other arrangement of society which may be applicable to it, that duty which has falled on one's shoulders or which, being possible, may have been taken up by one as a duty, of one's own choice, becomes a moral duty; and giving up these moral duties, and on the spur of the moment, taking up that which is proper for some one else, on some pretext or other, is wrong from the point of view of morality, as also from the point of view of public good.[14]

SVADHARMA AND LOKASAṀGRAHA

12.15. Tilak's justification of svadharma (with or without its linkage with varṇa), as presented in the preceding paragraph, rests on the contribution that svadharma can make to preservation of morality and to the advancement of "public good" (i.e. Lokasaṁgraha). A similar argument is given by Upadhyaya (although he is critical of the varṇa system) and he supports svadharma with a story from the Mahābhārata in which a meat-seller (vyādha) doing svadharma "for the good of others" is capable of teaching a Brāhmin who practices tapas "for his own good":

> Despite its advocacy of hereditary professions, the Gītā makes no mention of the intrinsic superiority or inferiority of any profession. It rather emphasizes that man attains perfection devoted each to his own duty. It is further said that all actions are associated with (more or less) defects as fire by smoke. This idea is conveyed more explicitly in the Mahābhārata in the course of the dialogue between the Brāhmin and the meat-seller (Vanaparva 206-215) wherein the latter, who discharges his duty devotedly for the good of others is not only defended

but is considered superior to the Brāhmin practising penance for his own selfish purpose.[15]

12.16. The above-mentioned views of scholars and activists represent possibilities of interpreting svadharma in ways appropriate to the present age, and particularly of combining svadharma and Lokasaṁgraha. On the general question as to whether svadharma would automatically include some obviously visible aspect of Lokasaṁgraha, Radhakrishnan says that it may or may not, depending on one's nature and circumstances:

> All forms of perfection do not lie in the same direction. Each one aims at something beyond himself, at self-transcendence, whether he strives after personal perfection, or lives for art, or works for one's fellows.[16]

12.17. However, Vinoba interprets svadharma from an idealist viewpoint and says that service of neighbours would naturally become a visible part of one's duty as one grows in full awareness of one's role in the community:

> Svadharma comes naturally, no one need go in search of it. The service of the parents to whom I was born, the service of the neighbours amongst whom I find myself, these duties come to me naturally. Then my other obligations are matters of everyday experience. I feel hungry, I feel thirsty. So to give food to the hungry and drink to the thirsty becomes my duty, my nature.[17]

12.18. From the above it is clear that a linkage between svadharma and the "service aspect" of Lokasaṁgraha (which might be significant enough to be visible) depends on how svadharma is interpreted. But even with a non-idealistic interpretation of svadharma, a linkage with the "stability aspect" of Lokasaṁgraha is possible, because each member of a society, carrying on one's limited duties to the best of one's ability or pauruṣaṁ (XVIII.25), can help maintain the social order, while fulfilling one's own legitimate goals.

12.19. From the functional and occupational viewpoint, svadharma denotes the means of earning one's livelihood, it being understood that the means are lawful or in accordance with the dharma of the society. The Gītā uses the term 'śarīrayātrā' (III.8), which literally means 'keeping the body moving'. The important contribution that svadharma makes to the self-help aspect of Lokasaṁgraha is thus obvious. Furthermore, svadharma carried on in conformity with the Gītā-technique of unselfishness implies that social interests are watched as much as one's circumstances permit. Radhakrishnan summarizes how the performance of svadharma according to the varṇa-rules envisaged in the Gītā can "contribute to the general good", although much of it might not be obviously visible (cf. para 12.16):

> The varṇa rules recognize that different men contribute to the general good in different ways, by supplying directly urgent wants of which all are conscious and by being in their lives and work witnesses to truth and beauty. Society is a functional organization and all functions which are essential for the health of society are to be regarded as socially equal. Individuals of varying capacities are bound together in a living organic social system. Democracy is not an attempt at uniformity which is impossible but at an integrated variety. All men are not equal in their capacities but all men are equally necessary for society, and their contributions from their different stations are of equal value.[18]

12.20. Tilak uses the analogy of small wheels in a machine to draw attention to the important role of ordinary svadharma-observers in bringing about Lokasaṁgraha:

> Just as extremely small wheels are necessary along with large wheels in order that any machine should work properly, so also is it necessary that the authority of common-place persons should be exercised properly and fully in the same way as the authority of superior persons like Vyasa and others, in order that the immense and ponderous activity or mechanism of the Cosmos should continue to work in a properly regulated manner. Because, if potters do not manufacture pots or weavers do not weave cloth, the maintenance of society—

Lokasaṁgraha—cannot be satisfacotrily carried out, even if the king protects the society properly. . . .[19]

SVADHARMA FORTIFIED WITH LOKASAṀGRAHA ENSURES ŚREYAS

12.21. The Gītā assures the attainment of perfection through the performance of one's duties—svakarma or svadharma—when this is done as a worship of the Supreme:

> Devoted each to his own duty man attains perfection. How one, devoted to one's own duty, attains perfection, that do thou hear. (XVIII.45)
>
> He from whom all beings arise and by whom all this is pervaded—by worshipping Him through the performance of his own duty does man attain perfection. (XVIII.46)

12.22. Another term used in the Gītā to convey the idea of 'worshipping the Divine through svadharma' is 'karma-samarpaṇaṁ', which literally means 'dedicating one's actions to God'. In order that actions are fit enough to be dedicated to God, they have to be pure, unselfish and conducive to the good of the society. In short, svadharma fortified with Lokasaṁgraha leads to śreyas. This is the message which Lokasaṁgraha-activists, drawing support from the Gītā, have been trying to convey in many different ways. For example, Tilak put it in the following words:-

> The Gītā-religion proclaims to everybody, though nominally to Arjuna: perform lifelong your several worldly duties according to your respective positions in life—svadharma—for the universal good—Lokasaṁgraha—with a self-identifying vision, and enthusiastically, and thereby perpetually worship the deity in the shape of the Paramātman . . . because therein lies your happiness in this world and in the next. . . .[20]

12.23. Tilak firmly believed that in times of social crisis, one's choice of svadharma could not be determined by varṇa-rules. He cited the example of the Brahmin Madhavrāo Peshva who was praised by Rama Shastribuva for taking up the duties of a solider instead of religious duties when Maratha affairs were in a crisis.[21] Faced with an oppressive foreign rule, Tilak declared his own svadharma to be to obtain swaraj—political independence—and he appealed to all followers of the Gītā to do likewise.

12.24. Gandhi too, in spite of his pointing out instances of low-caste people attaining perfection through their svadharma (reference para 12.8), believed in identifying duty not only according to one's svabhāva but also in the light of the changing social needs. For himself, he chose as his svadharma, 'the service of my country and humanity', but he viewed it as 'the road to salvation':

> For me the road to salvation lies through incessant toil in the service of my country and humanity. I want to identify myself with every thing that lives. I want to live at peace with both friend and foe. So my patriotism is for me a stage on my journey to the land of eternal freedom and peace.[22]

12.25. It could be considered a happy coincidence that Arjuna's svadharma (of fighting a battle against the evil forces for re-establishing the rule of the legitimate king) went hand-in-hand with a highly visible Lokasaṁgraha-activity. The Kauravas as the perpetrators of so many crimes needed to be removed from power in the interest of universal welfare. Śrī Kṛṣṇa as an avatāra was bound to ensure that the sins committed by the Kauravas should lead to their destruction. And since the killing of the evil-doers also happened to be the svadharma of Arjuna, the overlap between svadharma and Lokasaṁgraha was in this particular case perfect, and this also ensured Arjuna's śreyas.

12.26. Śrī Kṛṣṇa's teaching to Arjuna represents a combination of the traditional concept of svadharma, and the new Gītā technique of performing it with samatva. These two elements together mean that Arjuna should not have any desire for selfish gain, and also that he should maintain even-mindedness, irrespective of achieving success or failure. This is the way Arjuna is to act. But Śrī Kṛṣṇa also gives him an opportunity to have an advance vision of the divine plan for the destruction of the evil-doers:

Even without thy action, all the warriors standing arrayed in the opposing armies shall cease to be. (XI.32)

Therefore arise thou and gain glory. Conquering thy foes, enjoy a prosperous kingdom. By Me alone are they slain already. Be thou merely an instrument in the divine plan, O Arjuna. (XI.33)

Slay Droṇa, Bhīṣma, Jayadratha, Karṇa and other great warriors as well, who are already doomed by Me. Be not afraid. Fight, thou shalt conquer the enemies in battle. (XI.34)

12.27. The divine vision makes Arjuna realize that Śrī Kṛṣṇa is śāśvatadharmagoptā (undying guardian of dharma). (XI.18) He sees not only the destructive aspect of the divine power but also the spiritual presence and the law governing the universe. Arjuna's vision includes the feeling of delight which noble souls have on seeing God, and the fleeing away of the wicked ones out of fear, at the same time. (XI.36) This enables Arjuna to see his role as participating in the incorporation of the thrilling vision into his whole life.

12.28. Uderlying the above-mentioned analysis of how Arjuna was assured of his śreyas, is a modern interpretation of the Gītā wherein the Lokasaṁgraha-centred karma-yoga (involving the performance of svadharma) is a 'direct means' to perfection. Perhaps it should be mentioned that, according to the jñāna-yoga-oriented commentary of Śaṁkara, the role of svadharma was only citta-śuddhi or purification of the mind, because the ultimate goal was attainable only through the realisation of the identity of Ātman and Brahman. Without going into the philosophical details, we may point out that Tilak's *Gītā-Rahasya* opened the way for wide acceptance and practical application of the svadharma-doctrine, in the context of socio-political activities in India.

HOW LOKASAṀGRAHA AS WELL AS ŚREYAS ADVERSELY AFFECTED BY PARADHARMA

12.29. Verses III.35 and XVIII.47 contain the teaching that one should stick to one's svadharma (even if there are shortcomings in it), and avoid paradharma (someone else's duty, even if it looks more attractive):

> Better one's own duty, bereft of merit, than another's well-performed; better is death in the discharge of one's duty; another's duty is fraught with danger. (III.35)
>
> Better one's own duty, bereft of merit, than another's well-performed; doing duty which accords with one's nature, one incurs no sin. (XVIII.47)

12.30. Perhaps the most effective Lokasaṁgraha-oriented use of the svadharma-paradharma dichotomy was made by Gandhi, in support of the freedom struggle, when he declared that "svadharma applied to one's immediate environment means Swadeshi".[23] As is well known, the term 'Swadeshi' denoted an appeal by the Indian National Congress to all the people to patronize goods made in the country (like the hand-spun and hand-made cloth Khādī), in preference to goods imported from England because of the anti-India policy of the foreign rulers. Although scholars like Betai feel that this involved a stretching of the meaning of the word 'svadharma',[24] Lokasaṁgraha-activists see therein an extension of what the Gītā itself has done to words like 'yajña', 'sannyāsa', etc. The type of appeal which Gandhi made for Swadeshi, by linking it with svadharma, can be illustrated with the help of the following quotation:

> The Gītā says: 'It is best to die performing one's own duty or svadharma; paradharma or another's duty is fraught with danger'. Interpreted in terms of one's physical environment, this gives us the law of Swadeshi. What the Gītā says with regard to svadharma equally applies to Swadeshi, for Swadeshi is svadharma applied to one's immediate environment. . . .[25]
>
> A votary of Swadeshi will carefully study his environment, and try to help his neighbours wherever possible, by giving preference to local manufactures, even if they are of an inferior grade or dearer in price than things manufactured elsewhere. He will try to remedy their defects, but will not, because of their defects, give them up in favour of foreign manufactures. . .[26]
>
> A true votary of Swadeshi will never harbour ill-will towards the foreigner; he will not be actuated by antagonism towards

> anybody on earth. Swadeshism is not a cult of hatred. It is a doctrine of selfless service, that has its roots in the purest Ahiṁsā, i.e. Love. . . .[27]

12.31. As to the adverse effect of paradharma on śreyas, reference can be made to Vivekananda's views. Vivekananda interpreted 'svadharma' as 'one's own path', and he believed that the validity of following one's own path to growth was linked with the doctrine of evolution itself. In the course of his speech on the Gītā in California in 1900, Vivekananda said:

> In modern times we all know that every child brings with him all the past, not only of humanity, but of the plant life. . . . Everyone has his path mapped and sketched and planned out for him. . . . It is the universal chain of cause and effect, you receiving one link, one part, I another. . . . and that part is our own nature. . . . Now Śrī Kṛṣṇa says, 'Better die in your own path than attempt the path of another'. This is my path, and I am down here. And you are way up there, and I am always tempted to give up my path, thinking I will go there and be with you. And if I go up, I am neither there nor here. We must not lose sight of this doctrine. It is all a matter of growth. Wait and grow, and you attain everything; otherwise there will be great spiritual danger. Here is the fundamental secret of teaching religion. . . . Better die in your own path rather than giving it up and taking hold of another. . . .[28]

12.32. A possible combination of svadharma and Lokasaṁgraha, which also ensures śreyas, would be one practical way of reconciling individual and social goals. From the viewpoint of critics, the concept of svadharma needs to the dissociated from the compartmentalized varṇa system. Luckily, the Lokasaṁgraha concept operates in the wider framework of the society as a whole. Perhaps this fact could be utilized to supplement the efforts made by Tilak and others to soften the criticism launched by "anti-varṇa" and "anti-caste" scholars against the acceptability of the very notion of svadharma.

YAJÑA, DĀNAṀ, TAPAS—AS DUTY

12.33. We have already mentioned in paragraphs 11.16-23 that the Gītā (as well as the Bṛhadāraṇyaka Upaniṣad) attaches great importance to yajña, dānaṁ and tapas. Our present purpose is to see whether, in the Gītā, they have a role in identifying the content of one's duty. For this purpose, the most important statement is that of Śrī Kṛṣṇa in verses XVIII.5-6 (which he calls 'his firm and final view') that acts of yajña, dānaṁ and tapas are not to be relinquished, but should be performed, (along with other purifying acts, and like them) without attachment or desire for fruits. Although these two verses have been quoted in para 11.20, they are repeated below, for ready reference in the present context:

> Acts of yajña (sacrifice), dānaṁ (charity), and tapas (austerity) are not to be relinquished but should be performed; for these are purifiers of the wise. (XVIII.5)
>
> But even these acts ought to be performed, without attachment or desire for fruits. This, O Arjuna, is my firm and final view. (XVIII.6).

12.34. Besides the explicit teaching of verses XVIII.5-6, which relates to all three acts (of yajña, dānaṁ and tapas), there are several implicit statements emphasizing, separately, the importance of yajña and tapas. For example, the second part of verse IV.31 says: "This world is not for him who offers no yajña, how then any other world, O Arjuna?"

Similarly, the first part of verse XVIII.67 says: "Never speak the Gītā to one who does not do tapas" (among other things).

Furthermore, in the well-known verse IX.27, in which Śrī Kṛṣṇa asks Arjuna to dedicate all acts to Him, three of the acts specifically mentioned for dedication are: yajña, dānaṁ, tapas. A translation of the verse IX.27 is given below for ready reference: "Whatever thou doest, whatever thou eatest, whatever thou sacrificest (yajña), whatever thou givest away (dānaṁ), whatever austerities thou dost practise (tapas)—do that, O Arjuna, as an offering to Me". (IX.27)

We shall now discuss each element of this trio separately.

YAJÑA—NEW MEANINGS IN THE GĪTĀ

12.35. Yajña is a Vedic term and it denoted a particular type of ceremonial act in those days. The Gītā used the same term but modified its meaning and content. For example, the Gītā introduced the subject of yajña in verse III.9 by first mentioning the Mimaṁsā doctrine (reference para 9.44) of the advisability of performing yajña, and then adding its own doctrine of acting without attachment: "Except for work done as and for yajña, this world is in bondage to work. Therefore, O Arjuna, do thy work as a yajña, becoming free from all attachment." (III.9)

12.36. Radhakrishnan sees in this modified version of yajña an implicit reference to the "service of creation", which in our terminology is an important aspect of Lokasaṁgraha:

> All work is to be done in a spirit of sacrifice, for the sake of the Divine. Admitting the Mimaṁsā demand that we should perform action for the purpose of sacrifices, the Gītā asks us to do such action without entertaining any hope of reward. In such cases the inevitable action has no binding power. Sacrifice itself is interpreted in a larger sense. We have to sacrifice the lower mind to the higher. The religious duty to the Vedic gods here becomes service of creation in the name of the Supreme.[29]

12.37. The idea of sharing "food" with "others" is conveyed in the second part of the verse III.13 by condemning those who prepare food "only for themselves": "Those wicked people who prepare food only for themselves—verily they eat sin."

And the second part of the verse III.11 says that, through such acts of mutual care, one can attain śreyas:

> "Fostering each other you shall attain to the supreme śreyas" This statement is particularly significant because it tells Arjuna (who wanted to know how to attain śreyas) that one way of attaining śreyas is to perform acts for Lokasaṁgraha. It may be added that both the verses (quoted partly) fall within the yajña-related section of the Gītā.

12.38. In addition to the above-mentioned, simple variety of mutual dependence between "oneself" and "others", the Gītā presents, in verses III.14 to 16, a larger chain of interdependence involving yajña, performance of other acts, food production, human beings, all creation, nature, and God. It can be called "a wheel of yajña or karma" because yajña as well as karma constitutes an important link in this chain, and the wheel conveys the idea of continuity and preservation of the creation because God Himself is intimately connected therewith. Śrī Kṛṣṇa's instruction to human beings to help keep the wheel of yajña or karma moving on and on is contained in verse III.16: "He who does not, in this world, help to turn the wheel thus set in motion, is evil in his nature, sensual in his delight, and he, O Arjuna, lives in vain." (III.16)

12.39. Both Radhakrishnan and Upadhyaya see in these "wheel-related" verses a modified concept of yajña which includes within it the service aspect of Lokasaṁgraha. To quote Radhakrishnan first:

> In these verses the Vedic conception of sacrifice as an interchange between gods and men is set in the larger context of the interdependence of beings in the cosmos. The deed done in the sacrificial spirit are pleasing to God. God is the enjoyer of all sacrifices. Sacrifice is the Supreme. It is also the law of life. The individual and the cosmos depend on each other. There is a constant interchange between human life and world life. He who works for himself lives in vain.[30]

12.40. Upadhyaya also considers the "wheel-related" verses as establishing a close link between yajña and Lokasaṁgraha. What we have called the wheel of yajña or karma is designated by Upadhyaya as the "wheel of the world", which is kept in motion by yajña or *niṣkāma* karma. Upadhyaya's interpretation of the underlying message is similar to Radhakrishnan's, namely, to work for Lokasaṁgraha:

> As the origin of the world is traced to God, and God himself is engaged in the work of maintaining the world-order, it becomes the duty of man to live in the world and promote its welfare. The wheel of the world, according to the Gītā, goes on by means of sacrifice or renunciation, and one who does not discharge his selfless service to the world lives only in vain.[31]

12.41. Radhakrishnan interprets the yajña of the Gītā as "service of creation", and Upadhyaya qualifies such service as "selfless" so as not to forget the basic teaching of the Gītā. Śrī Kṛṣṇa draws specific attention to this requirement in verses XVII.11 to 13, by classifying yajña as sāttvika, rājasa or tamas. This shows that merely doing acts of service is not enough unless this is accompanied with the right attitude. A sāttvika yajña is done with śraddhā or faith that the cause for which one is dedicating one's energy and resources is just, and furthermore, the doer expects no selfish return or reward. If there is any expectation of reward, or if the yajña is performed for display, to earn prestige or name, then the yajña becomes rājas. Finally, if the doer of yajña lacks śraddhā or faith or sympathy for the intended beneficiaries, the yajña becomes tamas. Radhakrishnan says that performers of sāttvika yajña are like Socrates or Gandhi who are prepared to do the right, in the interest of the society, even at the cost of their life:

> The yajña of the Gita is not the same as the ceremonial sacrifice of the Veda. It is sacrificial action in general by which man dedicates his wealth and deeds to the service of the One Life in all. People with such a sacrificial spirit will accept even death gladly, though unjustly meted out to them, so that world may grow through their sacrifice.[32]

12.42. In verse IV.24, the process of realizing the Supreme through one's acts, by dedicating them to God, is symbolically presented as a yajña (and Radhakrishnan calls it a spiritual interpretation of yajña):[33]

> For him (who does work without attachment, as a sacrifice) the act of offering is God, the oblation is God, by God is it offered into the fire of God. Therefore God is that which is to be attained by him who realizes God in his works. (IV.24)

12.43. In verses IV.25 to 32, Śrī Kṛṣṇa indicates that the yogic performance of breath control (prāṇāyāma) and related practices prescribed in the Pātañjala-yoga, or even the performance of religious austerities (tapas) could be considered a yajña if the words agni (fire), havi (sacrificial offering), etc. are taken in their symbolic meanings. One such symbolic yajña consists in controlling the senses, that is, allowing them to perform their respective functions within proper limits. Later on, in verse X.25 Śrī Kṛṣṇa identifies japa or recitation of God's name as the highest yajña.

12.44. The above-mentioned idea of the Gītā to extend the meaning of yajña so as to include self-restraint, tapas, japa, and other means of getting merged into God has its parallel in Manusmṛti (2.27 and others) where five principal yajñas are prescribed for householders:

(i) Brahma-yajña or a study of Vedas
(ii) Deva-yajña or prayer to deities
(iii) Pitri-yajña or offerings dedicated to ancestors
(iv) Manuṣya-yajña or hospitality to human beings
(v) Bhūta-yajña or offering of food to other creatures.

The last two of the five yajñas, if interpreted in practical rather than ritualistic terms, can help strengthen linkages between yajña and Lokasaṁgraha.

YAJÑA—MORE MEANINGS GIVEN BY LOKASAṀGRAHA-ACTIVISTS

12.45. Lokasaṁgraha-activists were much inspired by the approach of the Gītā, which had retained the Vedic term, yajña, but modified its meaning drastically by introducing the concept of abandonment of selfish desires. Fresh studies into the whole subject were conducted by Tilak, Aurobindo, Gandhi, Vinoba and others. It was recalled how a clear distinction was made in the Vedās, Brāhmaṇas and Upaniṣads, between the Karmakāṇḍa and Jñānakāṇḍa, or the path of work and the path of knowledge. The Vedic Yajña was undoubtedly the most important element of Karmakāṇḍa. The famous Puruṣa Sūkta of Ṛgveda (X.90) attributed the creation of the universe itself to Yajña. Every desired object could be achieved if the specified Yajña was performed correctly. Every yajña had four components: dravya or sacrificial matter; tyāga or the relinquishing of the object sacrificed; a devatā or deity to be addressed as the recipient, and a mantra or the Vedic hymn to be chanted. The sacrificial fire was supposed to be the mouth of the gods. The sacrificial material like sesamum, rice, etc. was put into the fire, with a mantra saying that I offer it to such and such deity and it is not mine "idaṁ na mama". It was believed that the deity gets the offering through the medium of the fire, and gives to the person performing the sacrifice the desired object. Yajña thus helped the householders in obtaining children, grandchildren, cows, horses or other wealth in this life and a happy state after death.

12.46. At the time of the Upaniṣads, the emphasis shifted from Karmakāṇḍa to Jñānakāṇḍa, and the faith of the people in Vedic Yajña was shaken. The Upaniṣads taught that the maximum benefit a traditional yajña could give was to take a person to heaven which was only a temporary place of pleasures, and that a genuine release from the bondage of karma was possible only through knowledge. Keeping in mind the popularity of the term Yajña, symbolic meanings began to be attached thereto; for example, Chandogya Upaniṣad (3.16.1) considers the whole duration of a man's life as a Yajña and makes out (3.17.4) that the true payment for the priests is in the practice of the virtues of austerity, charity, uprightness, non-violence and truthfulness. Chandogya Upaniṣad also says (3.17.6) that a priest of the sun, Ghora Angirasa explained these ideas about Yajña to Kṛṣṇa, the son of Devakī. But the growing emphasis on the knowledge of Brahman as the only way to obtain release also strengthened renunciatory attitudes, for example, Bṛhadāraṇyaka Upaniṣad says (4.4.22) that the scients of yore did not have any desire for children, and after renouncing all objects of pleasure they used to roam about the world begging for alms.

12.47. The Gītā harmonized Karmakāṇḍa and Jñānkāṇḍa by emphasizing, on the one hand, that Yajña should not be performed for the fulfilment of selfish desires, and, on the other hand, that Jñāna should not lead people to a way of escapism from their duties. The doctrine of the Mimaṁsā school that "one should perform action for the purpose of the Yajña as it has not a binding effect", was amended and amplified by the Gītā as: "even the action to be performed for the purposes of the Yajña should be performed without entertaining the hope of fruit." With this modification, the prayers to the deities can only be for the benefit of the society, and not for personal benefit. But even to this position an objection can be raised by a Jñānamārgī by asking whether it is not better for obtaining release by escaping the bond of Karma altogether, implying that one should take to Sannyāsa and give up all Yajñas. The clear answer of the Gītā to this is that, once the concept of Yajña is modified so as to be oriented to the benefit of the society, then it includes the performance of svadharma or duties allocated to the various sub-groups of the society, and that Yajña in the form of svadharma, should not be given up. The modified meaning of Yajña as Svadharma is stressed in Jñāneśwarī which is a commentary on the Gītā written by Saint Jñāneśwara in Marathi language in the fourteenth century. Mahābhārata (San.237.12) and Manusmṛti (1.87) also accept the extended meaning of Yajña so as to include the performance of varṇa-duties.

12.48. Tilak believed that the re-awakening and freedom of India depends on the revival of her religion and the restoration of her ancient glory. These are interdependent, as he viewed history. He interpreted the Gītā to convey the message that through dedicated social and political action one can reach the supreme goal. He found ample justification for new interpretations of Vedic terms in the history of Hinduism:

> Considering the matter from the historical point of view, it can be seen that when the sacrifice of wealth of various kinds prescribed in the Śruti-texts for propitiating Indra, Varuṇa, and other deities fell into disuse, and the devices of attaining the state of the Parameśvara by Pātañjala yoga, Saṁnyāsa or metaphysical knowledge came more and more into vogue, the meaning of the word 'yajña' was widened, and it was made to symbolically include all the various devices of obtaining release. The principle at the root of this is the tendency to indicate subsequent religious methods by the same technical terms as had come to be formerly accepted in the religion.[34]

12.49. Tilak also draws attention to the fact that the word 'amṛtā' has been defined in the Manusmṛti (2.285) as meaning 'that which remains over after the performance of a yajña'. He argues that this principle applies equally to symbolic yajñas, and it is better to offer animal tendencies like desire, anger, egotism, etc. which are in everyone's body by way of sacrifice into the fire of mental control, than to offer commodities or animals into sacrificial fire. He summarizes his *Gītā-Rahasya*, by implying, among other things, that yajña and Lokasaṁgraha are practically the same:

> The Gita religion, which preaches that the whole of one's life should be turned into a yajña, contains the essence of the entire Vedic religion. . . . It proclaims to everybody, though nominally to Arjuna: Perform lifelong your several wordly duties according to your respective positions in life, desirelessly, for the universal good—Lokasaṁgraha. . . .[35]

12.50. Aurobindo used the concept of yajña to appeal to his countrymen about the need to make sacrifices in the struggle for freedom. Subsequently, in his "Essays on the Gita", he emphasized the symbolic meaning of yajña and linked it with Lokasaṁgraha:

> The fire of sacrifice, agni, is no material flame, but brahmāgni, the fire of the Brahman, or it is the Brahman-ward energy, inner Agni, priest of the sacrifice, into which the offering is poured; the fire is self-control or it is a purified sense-action or it is the vital energy in that discipline of the control of the vital being, . . . or it is the fire of self-knowledge. . . . For the man who has this knowledge and lives and acts in it, there can be no binding works, no personal and egoistically appropriated action. . . .[36]

12.51. Gandhi carried further the task of modifying the meaning of Yajña so as to make it increasingly relevant to present social conditions and to serve the cause of Lokasaṁgraha. This was a twofold process. On the one hand, it meant identifying new approaches and productive activities (like Khādī and village industries) which if undertaken in a spirit of Yajña could help the society. Secondly, Gandhi also suggested the abandonment of the traditional way of performing a Yajña, for examle, burning of wood. Although fire was the symbol of Yajña in Vedic times and is still so considered by religious organisations like Arya Samaj, the Gītā envisaged the possibility of using fire in a symbolic sense (IV.24). Gandhi tried to create public opinion in favour of subjecting every religious practice to the test of relevance in modern times. He gave the following comment on the yajña-related verses of the Gītā:

> I cannot understand the idea that one can perform yajña by lighting a few sticks. It does not do to say that doing so purifies the air. There are many other ways of purifying the air. Why should we at all pollute the air? But this is not the aim behind a yajña. When the Āryans first came to this country, they tried to civilize the non-Āryan races. Maybe the idea of yajña was originally conceived for the uplift of the latter. There were big forests in those days, and it may have been regarded as everyone's duty to help in clearing these forests, for it was a social necessity. And because the work was regarded as a duty, it came to be looked upon as a means of attaining mokṣa. Innumerable ceremonies were devised, all of which required the lighting of fire. In burning wood in this age, we misuse the capital of our forefathers, or we show ourselves witless pedants by understanding the thing in a literal sense.[37]

12.52. Gandhi is very emphatic that verses III.9 to III.16 which speak of the origin of Yajña and of the importance of continuing in motion the wheel of yajña, should be interpreted in such a way as to solve the most pressing problems of today's society. He raises the question: What is meant by saying that mankind was created along with Yajña?, and he suggests an answer: Just as we cannot escape the cycle of birth, old age and death, so also bodily labour is our lot in life from which there is no escape. In a country like India, extremely backward that it was, he saw not only laziness and a dislike for physical labour and lack of care to do one's own small jobs on one's own, he also saw that a sense of hatred for physical labour even for one's own needs existed in the society, and so he wanted that dignity of labour should be established. He also saw that for removing the grave sin of untouchability, the sense of dignity of labour and self-dependence as also keenness for service should be emphasized. He therefore took the view that labouring enough for one's food has been classed in the Gītā as a Yajña. He suggested similarly that the wheel of Yajña in verse III.16 should in today's conditions mean the spinning wheel. Whereas in old days cutting down trees and burning wood had become a yajña, at the present time spinning and other village industries have become a yajña. If water was scarce and we had to fetch it from a distance of two miles, fetching water would be a yajña.[38]

12.53. Vinoba carried further the Gandhian approach and argued that Chapter XVII of the Gītā, in which Yajña, Dānaṁ and Tapas are viewed as "triple duty", should be interpreted with reference to three levels of creation, namely, nature, society, and body. According to this interpretation, Yajña represents the effort made to replenish nature's loss, Dānaṁ is the help given through body, mind, material resources and other means to discharge the debt to society, and Tapas is self-discipline needed for removing the deficiencies and distortions in the body caused by normal wear and tear.[39] (Since Vinoba developed these ideas further in the context of his Bhoodāna (land-gift) movement, the chief elements thereof are described separately in paras 12.60-65 dealing with Dānaṁ).

12.54. Balkoba Bhave (Vinoba's younger brother) also interprets Yajña as consisting of those acts which can do good to the society. He specifically mentions the following:

(i) afforestation; tree-planting
(ii) better care of cows
(iii) not to burn wood and ghee as in a traditional yajña (since there is a shortage of these in the society these days)
(iv) village industries
(v) improvements in agriculture
(vi) better relations between the rich and the poor, and between urban and rural populations.[40]

12.55. The Gītā-portion of the T.V. serial "Mahābhārata"—produced by Doordarshan of India with the help of Chopra—also includes "afforestation" as one of the items of yajña and Lokasaṁgraha, thus representing a modern version of Śrī Kṛṣṇa's teaching.

DĀNAṀ—NOT ALWAYS SĀTTVIKA

12.56. The importance of dānaṁ (meaning charity, gift) as an expression of sympathy for the less fortunate and as a practical way of helping them, has been universally recognized. Its linkage with Lokasaṁgraha is thus obvious. Śaṁkara defines it as saṁvibhāgaḥ or equal division or sharing, and this interpretation can make dānaṁ acceptable even to those who prefer fundamental changes in distribution of resources rather than superficial acts of giving (which might encourage begging).

12.57. Before indicating the special contribution of the Gītā to provide checks on a possible misuse of dānaṁ, we may mention that the concept of dānaṁ (like that of yajña) can be traced to the Veda. Embree writes:

> The stress in the Vedic hymns on the offering of gifts tô the gods as an essential feature of religious experience was generalized to include the concept of the duty of liberality to all who were in need. The duty of giving dānaṁ, which is a prominent feature of all Indian religions, is clearly foreshadowed in the hymn X.117 of the Ṛg Veda.[41]

And a part of this hymn, as translated by Macdonell, is reproduced below:

> The wealthier man should give unto the needy,
> Considering the course of life hereafter;
> For riches are like chariot wheels revolving;
> Now to one man they come, now to another.
> The foolish man from food has no advantage;
> In truth I say: it is but his undoing;
> No friend he ever fosters, no companion;
> He eats alone, and he alone is guilty.[42]

12.58. Although the Gītā includes dānaṁ in the list of virtues that characterize divine nature (daivī saṁpat—XVI.1-3), it also sounds a note of caution by declaring that some types of dānaṁ could even be classified as undesirable. Verses XVIII.20-22 prescribe conditions which, if fulfilled, can help designate dānaṁ as sāttvika, rājas, or tamas, respectively. The most interesting case is that of tamas, and out of five conditions attached thereto, the most significant is "an unworthy recipient of dānaṁ". According to Chidbhavananda: "Persons unworthy of charity and gifts are they who are of questionable character, who are devoid of self-control, who do not engage themselves in the welfare of being, and who squander away money."[43]

In other words, one whose conduct is contrary to Lokasaṁgraha (among other things), is an unworthy recipient of dānaṁ. The full text of verse XVII.22 is: "And that gift which is made at a wrong place or time or to an unworthy person, without proper respect or with contempt, that is declared to be tamas." (XVII.22)

12.59. Three conditions make dānaṁ rājas, namely, giving involunatrily, hoping to receive personal benefit in return, expecting future gain. And dānaṁ which avoids the disqualifications of tamas as well as rajas, and is given to a "worthy person", is sāttvika, the full text pertaining to which is in verse XVII.20:

> That gift, which is made to one from whom no return is expected, with the feeling that it is one's duty to give, and which is given in proper place and time and to a worthy person, that gift is held to be sāttvika. (XVII.20)

Obviously, sāttvika danaṃ is an act for Lokasaṁgraha.

VINOBA'S USE OF DĀNAṀ FOR LOKASAṀGRAHA

12.60. Vinoba started the Bhoodan (land-gift) movement in the early fifties as a counter-point to the Communist activities in Telengana. The situation there acquired the characteristics of a class struggle when the tenants, under Communist leadership, siezed land from the landlords. Violent clashes took place between the peasants who tried to retain the land, and the police whose function according to the law of the country was to help return the land (by using force if necessary) to the landlords. Vinoba told the people that seizing land against the consent of the landlords as well as retaking land by force would only embitter relations between the peasants and the landlords and would cause widespread suffering. He also felt that there were many loopholes in the scheme of land reforms and redistribution attempted through legislative measures of the government. According to Vinoba, all three activities—forcible seizure, police protection, and compulsory re-distribution—involved the use of violence. Citing the Gītā and other scriptures, Vinoba made the plea that all land belongs to God and those who hold it in trusteeship should voluntarily part with one-sixth of what they have, to be re-distributed among the landless.

12.61. Although Vinoba uses a traditional word 'dānaṁ' (meaning charity, gift), his interpretation (drawing support from Śaṁkara) gives it a modern flavour. Śaṁkara defines dānaṁ as saṁvibhāgaḥ or equal division or sharing. (Reference para 12.56) Vinoba says that when he accepts land on behalf of the poor, he is not accepting it as charity from the rich. Rather he is offering a peaceful alternative to the rich to save themselves from a violent revolution. The rich should view dānaṁ as an act of expiation for the sins committed. According to Vinoba, it is by sinful covetousness that society developed the system of unlimited private ownership of land, and the means to mitigate the weight of this sin is to share it with the landless, in a spirit of voluntary sacrifice, like a yajña.[44]

12.62. Vinoba (and his brother Balkoba) present a four-way categorization of an individual's economic relationship with the society, namely:

(a) Theft
(b) Begging
(c) Earning one's livelihood (śarīrayātrā)
(d) Dānaṁ.

First, they define theft (in the light of the verse III.12 of the

Gītā) as a situation in which an individual takes from the society goods and services but gives nothing in return. The second category is begging when an individual takes more from the society than what he or she gives in return. The third category (śarīrayātrā) represents a state of equality of what one takes and what one gives. Fourthly, dānaṁ refers to a situation in which one is apparently giving more to society than what one is (currently) receiving in return, but Vinoba says, this should be viewed as discharging old debts:

> Dānaṁ, the rite of giving was instituted in order to discharge our debt to society. I have received from society boundless service, therefore I in my turn should serve society. 'Doing good' is serving someone from whom we have received no service, but in this case we have already received everything from society. The service that we render to free ourselves from this debt to society is dānaṁ, the help given through body, mind, substance and other means to discharge the debt to society in dānaṁ.[45]

12.63. Vinoba also links the concept of dānaṁ or equal distribution to samadṛṣṭi or equal vision, which is described in the Gītā-verse V.18 as a characteristic of a man of true knowledge. Vinoba argues that the ability to look upon all creatures with an equal eye would remain an incomplete virtue unless it is supplemented by the willingness to share one's wealth with those who are poor. In his preface to Gurubodha, selections from Śaṁkara, Vinoba presents his views about God, man and the world in the form of a couplet which may be translated as:

> Vinu (or Vinoba) has extracted the essence of the Vedas, the Vedānta, and Bhagavad Gītā, that Brahman is truly existent, the world is a vibrant manifestation, and that life consists in the pursuit of Truth.[46]

This is an obvious modification of the famous statement of Śaṁkara: "Brahman alone is truly existent, the world is an illusion, and the jīvātman is none other than Brahman itself."

Justifying his modification of Śaṁkara's couplet, Vinoba says:

> I do not think I have made any great departure from the

> general teaching of the Vedānta philosophy. On the contrary, my statement brings about a happy reconciliation between Vedānta and the age of science.[47]

Thomas comments: "By ascribing a relative reality to the world as opposed to total unreality, Bhāve is building a metaphysical basis for his ideology of serving the poor.[48]

12.64. The fact that land is the main productive resource in rural India imparts to Vinoba's movement a special importance from the viewpoint of creating a viable, just socio-economic system. Vinoba himself extended his concept of dānaṁ to include śrama-dān (voluntary labour for projects of public utility), buddhi-dān (dedicating one's intellectual capability, partly or wholly), sampatti-dān (sharing of one' wealth), etc. After several years of intense activity, the full momentum of Vinoba's movement could not be sustained. In Arapura's opinion, the real significance of the movement based on Dānaṁ lies not so much in measurable economic gains but rather in its attempt to build a spiritual and moral basis to the social life:

> The real aim of this movement is to put humanity through a spiritual discipline calculated to humanize it and to cure the basic ills that mar the spiritual image of man in the context of social existence.[49]

12.65. Vinoba's focus on the landless people (who are usually the poorest) helped give a practical shape to the sarvodaya ideology. Gandhi had pointed out the difference between sarvodaya and utilitarian approach by saying that the latter's aim, namely "the greatest good of the greatest number" was not so comprehensive as the Sarvodaya goal of "the uplift of all". By leaving out a minority as "unimportant", the utilitarians create class conflicts. More fundamentally, they violate the Vedanta doctrine of "equal vision" towards all. However, in practice, Vinoba pointed out, it is usually not feasible to serve the entire humanity, all at the same time, although sarvabhūtahitaṁ (the good of all) is the goal of the Gītā. He therefore suggested that, within the comprehensive ideology of Sarvodaya, particular attention should initially be given to Antyodaya (or uplift of the lowest). This is similar to what is called in modern terminology "a target-oriented approach", that is, an attempt to help directly the most needy, rather than hope that overall economic progress would ultimately trickle down to everyone. Antyodaya programmes are often adopted by developmental planners, although they are unable to go all the way with the Sarvodaya ideology (which does not encourage industrialization and the adoption of labour-saving technology).

TAPAS FOR ŚREYAS AND LOKASAṀGRAHA

12.66. As already mentioned in paras 11.15-23, tapas or austerity is primarily a self-regarding virtue and its linkage with Lokasaṁgraha is not so strong as that of yajña and dānaṁ. But some of the virtues which are included in the comprehensive definition of tapas in the Gītā are other-regarding. For example, in verses XVII.14 to 16, tapas of three types (of body, speech, mind) is described, and then in verses XVII.17-19), there is a description of sāttvika, rājas and tamas varieties of tapas (applicable to all three types of tapas). Without going into all these details, we need only refer to those virtues which are other-regarding.

12.67. Ahiṁsā or non-violence is mentioned as one of the elements of bodily tapas (in verse XVII.14). Similarly, tapas of speech (in verse XVII.15) includes the utterance of words which give no offence but are truthful, pleasant and beneficial. Besides these, the other virtues constituting tapas include self-discipline, purity of mind, and study of scriptures, which serve to develop one's own character and will. Radhakrishnan remarks that "for the Gītā, improvement in the individual nature is the way to social betterment."[50]

12.68. The importance of tapas as a basic virtue is stressed in the Vedas, and even more so in the Upaniṣads. For example, Muṇḍaka Upaniṣad (III.1.5) lists four basic virtues, namely, satya, tapas, jñāna, brahmacarya. Radhakrishnan also quotes the famous statement of Sāvitrī to Yama "santo bhūmiṁ tapasā dhārayanti", that is, good people maintain the world through their tapas.[51]

12.69. The Gītā sounds a note of caution against the tamas variety of tapas in verse XVII.19: "That tapas which is performed with a foolish obstinacy by means of self-torture or for causing injury to others is said to be tamas."

Chidbhavananda says that "occasionally, such performers of austerities stumble upon some psychic power which they utilize for hurting, wrecking or destroying others.[52]

12.70. In verses XVII.5 and 6 also, Śrī Kṛṣṇa warns against bodily torture inflicted through violent austerities:

> Those men, vain and conceited and impelled by the force of lust and passion, who perform violent austerities, which are not ordained by the scriptures,
>
> Being foolish (they) oppress the group of elements in their body and Me also dwelling in the body. Know these to be demoniac in their resolve. (XVII.5-6)

So the main message on tapas from the viewpoint of Lokasaṁgraha is: It would certainly be helpful if one is able to perform sāttvika tapas; but it is absolutely crucial to avoid tāmasika tapas.

12.71. Aurobindo viewed sāttvika tapas or tapasyā as "that which is done with a highest enlightened faith, as a duty deeply accepted or for some ethical or spiritual or other higher reason and with no desire for any external or narrowly personal fruit in the action."[53] Obviously, elements of both śreyas and Lokasaṁgraha are included in Aurobindo's concept of sāttvic tapas. He stressed his belief therein when he told Romain Rolland why he withdrew from 'mediocre politics' and how, in his opinion, a life of 'tapasyā' could contribute to the 'progress of humanity':

> India possesses in its past, a little rusty and out of use, the key to the progress of humanity. It is to this side that I am now turning my energies, rather than towards mediocre politics. Hence the reason for my withdrawal. I believe in the necessity for tapasyā (a life of meditation and concentration) in silence for education and self-knowledge and for the unloosing of spiritual energies. Our ancestors used these means under

different forms; for they are the best for becoming an efficient worker in the great hours of the world.[54]

12.72. Gandhi's concept of tapas was to prepare the Satyāgrahīs to undergo self-suffering, particularly in connection with the Civil Disobedience movement. According to Iyer's analysis, this represented a 'more difficult' type of Satyāgraha, because 'only a few' could be expected to practise 'tapas'. Here tapas was used to help an important Lokasaṁgraha-activity. Relevant portions of Iyer's statement, comparing two types of Satyāgraha—one of which particularly needed tapas on the part of participants—are given below:

> Non-co-operation was conceived in a much wider context as an instrument of social action....
>
> Civil disobedience is more difficult than non-co-operation because it presupposes the habit of willing obedience of laws without fear of their sanctions....
>
> Gandhi's emphasis was on Ahiṁsā in non-co-operation and on Tapas in civil disobedience, although both concepts contained elements of self-suffering and non-violence.
>
> Non-co-operation made fewer spiritual demands on its users.... Civil Disobedience called for a spirit of tapas or self-suffering, which in practice only a few were capable of exemplifying....[55]

HOW LOKASAṀGRAHA BECOMES SPONTANEOUS

12.73. The difference between duty-prompted acts for Lokasaṁgraha and the spontaneous ones—also called by us as the two stages of Lokasaṁgraha—is referred to in the Gītā-verse VI.3, a literal translation of which is given below: "Work is said to be the means of the sage who wishes to attain to yoga; when he has attained to yoga, serenity is said to be the means". (VI.3).

Radhakrishnan brings out the spontaneity-related meaning of this verse that is relevant to our present discussion:

> When we are aspirants for liberation, work done in the right spirit with inner renunciation helps us. When once we achieve

self-possession, we act, not for gaining any end but out of our anchorage in God-consciousness. . . . A yogin attains complete tranquillity by abandoning the fruit of action. He performs actions with a perfect equanimity. He overflows with a spontaneous vitality and works with a generosity which arises from his own inexhaustible strength.[56]

12.74. In short we can say that Lokasaṁgraha becomes a spontaneous activity for a person who has attained perfection. Such a person is also called 'Jīvanumukta'—i.e. liberated while still alive. The Gītā-verse V.19 is one of the verses which specifically says that the state of liberation is attainable here on earth: "Even here (on earth) the created world is overcome by those whose mind is established in equality. God is flawless and the same in all. Therefore are these persons established in God". (V.19)

12.75. Detailed descriptions of those who have achieved the state of perfection are given in the Gītā under several titles like Sthitaprajña, Bhakta, Jñānī, Brahmaniṣṭha, Yogī, and Triguṇātīta. These descriptions are broadly similar. All of them act spontaneously for Lokasaṁgraha because they are unselfish and pure, and they have equal vision for all. As to the methods by which one can achieve perfection, the Gītā describes Karmayoga, Bhaktiyoga, and Jñānayoga, and also indicates that the methods ultimately merge into one another.

12.76. Without going into the details of the various methods, we may say that, for a follower of the svadharma-doctrine, the easiest way to perfection has been indicated in verse XVIII.46 itself (reference para 12.21). A short title for this method is 'samarpaṇaṁ'—i.e. dedicating all actions to God. According to verse IX.27, the method of 'samarpaṇaṁ' is applicable also to those who perform yajña-dānaṁ-tapas as duty (reference para 12.34). Since this method is a harmonious combination of Karmayoga and Bhaktiyoga, further details pertaining thereto are given in Chapter Thirteen, where the role of Bhakti is discussed.

12.77. Another popular method involves a steady cultivation of sattva-guṇa which ultimately leads to a state of Triguṇātīta (Details in Chapter XIV of the Gītā). Acts vitiated with tamas and rajas guṇas are avoided, and sāttvika acts, too, are performed without any desires for selfish gains. This is similar to avoiding āsurī-elements and cultivating daivī-sampat. (Details in Chapter XVI of the Gītā.)

12.78. There is an important difference between Aurobindo and Tilak on the question as to whether Lokasaṁgraha-activities should be taken up only after achieving perfection or whether this could be done while still in the process of attaining perfection. According to Aurobindo, genuine Lokasaṁgraha was possible only after one has become a muktātmā—a liberated soul.[57] However, Tilak believed that one's purification could go hand-in-hand with participation in Lokasaṁgraha-activities.[58]

Chapter Thirteen

Bhakti, Jñāna and Puruṣārthas: Practically Incomplete Without Lokasaṁgraha

13.1. Most of the discussion in the preceding chapters was in the context of Karmayoga. However, it is well known that the Gītā attaches great importance to Bhakti-yoga and Jñāna-yoga also. Therefore, the first question raised in this chapter is: what is the role of Lokasaṁgraha in Bhakti-yoga? And similarly, the second question is: what is the role of Lokasaṁgraha in Jñāna-yoga?—

13.2. Hindu scriptures speak of four Puruṣārthas or goals of life or values, namely, Artha (wealth), Kāma (pleasure), Dharma, and Mokṣa. In this study which devotes special attention to Lokasaṁgraha, an obvious question is: what is the role of Lokasaṁgraha in the context of the Puruṣārthas? This is the third question that we raise in this chapter. Our attempt to answer this question naturally involves a look into possible linkages between Lokasaṁgraha, on the one hand, and each of the four Puruṣārthas, on the other. Finally, in continuation of the Lokasaṁgraha-related material that is presented for answering the three questions raised, we show that the harmonizing approach of the Gītā—which several scholars have applied to the means, i.e. karma, bhakti, and jñāna—applies equally to the goals, i.e. Lokasaṁgraha, śreyas, and preyas—the last two representing individual goals (meaning 'good' and 'pleasant' respectively).

BHAKTI IN THE GĪTĀ—THE ORIGINAL FORM OF BHĀGAVATA DHARMA

13.3. Upadhyaya, after making a detailed study of the possible sources of Bhakti or devotion in the Gītā, has traced it to what he calls the 'original' from of Bhāgavata Dharma.[1] The significance of the word 'original' is to distinguish it from later forms, which become associated with Bhāgavata Dharma, in course of time. This is further clarified in para 13.11.

13.4. Upadhyaya has made use of the Nārāyaṇīya section of the Mahābhārata (Śāntiparva 334-351) to supplement the relevant portion of the Gītā, in order to specify the following six main features of the original Bhāgavata Dharma:

(i) An active life was the foundation of this Dharma. Initially, this religion was followed by the warrior tribe known as Sātvatas. According to another reference in the Mahābhārata (Ādiparva 218.12), Vāsudeva himself belonged to this tribe. Illustrations of activism are provided, in the epic style, by means of wars fought by Kṣatriya kings to uphold just causes—like that of the Pāṇḍavas. The motive behind all such effort was supposed to be the preservation of Dharma, not personal gain.

(ii) A deep theistic sentiment of devotion to the highest deity—known as Hari, Nārāyaṇa, Vāsudeva, or Bhagavat—is the next most important feature of this religion. It is on account of this strong devotional element that the religion is known by the name of Nārāyaṇīya or Bhāgavata dharma. Furthermore, since it is devotion to a monotheistic conception of God, it is also called an Ekāntika dharma.

(iii) About the possibility of God revealing Himself to human beings, it is illustrated through the story of king Vasu Uparicara, that whole-hearted devotion is the only way to see God—provided that no animal is killed, even if yajñas like Ásvamedha (horse-sacrifice) are performed.

(iv) Not only that God does not reveal Himself to those who kill animals, He also punishes those who even give moral support to the practice of animal-killing. King Vasu Uparicara, acting as a mediator in a religious controversy between the gods (who favoured animal-killing) and the rishis (who opposed animal-sacrifice), gave moral support to the gods, and so had to suffer the curse of lying in a hole of the earth. The king was ultimately saved by virtue of his whole-hearted devotion to Nārāyaṇa.

(v) Austerities involving long periods of bodily torture are of no avail in obtaining a revelation of God. Prajāpati's sons—Ekata, Dvita and Trita—were not able to see God, although they practised austerities for four thousand years.

(vi) Along with an active life and devotion to God, knowledge contained in the teachings of the Araṇyakas and the Upaniṣads must be assimilated and reflected in life's conduct.[2]

13.5. The Bhakti-yoga of the Gītā, although recognizing the basic teachings of *Niṣkāma* karma, makes provision for those who initially pray to God for the fulfilment of worldly desires. In verses VII.16-18, Śrī Kṛṣṇa speaks of four kinds of Bhaktas, of whom two—seeking relief from distress, or seeking wealth—are still called noble, though not the best:

> The virtuous ones who worship Me are of four kinds, the man in distress, the seeker for knowledge, the seeker for wealth, and the man of wisdom, O Arjuna.
>
> Of these, the wise one, who is ever in constant union with the Divine, whose devotion is single-minded, is the best. For I am supremely dear to him and he is dear to Me.
>
> Noble indeed are all these, but the sage, I hold, is verily Myself. For, being perfectly harmonized, he resorts to Me alone as the highest goal. (VII.16-18)

13.6. Commenting on the above verses, Radhakrishnan says that by starting to turn towards God for material things, "slowly we feel that it is degrading to pray for luck in life. . ." and ultimately "we pray that we may know the Divine and be more and more like Him. . ."[3]

> Even if we pray for material things, turn prayer into a formal routine or use it as a mascot, we recognize the reality of the religious sense. . . . Through the exercise of prayer, we kindle a light in our consciousness which shows up our silly pride, our selfish greed, our fears and hopes. . . .While the first three types attempt to use God according to their ideas, the knowers belong to God to be used according to His will. Therefore they are the best of them all.[4]

13.7. The case of the jijñāsu or the seeker for knowledge (who is mentioned in verse VII.16 as one of the four types of Bhaktas) is, in a way, similar to an aspirant for perfection who is advised in verses II.59-61 to try to bring his senses under control, and if his own efforts in this direction do not succeed, then to seek the help of the Supreme. In fact, this is the first reference to the role of Bhakti in the Gītā, that is, as we proceed from Chapter One to Chapter Eighteen. Vinoba explains how a Satyāgrahī or any worker engaged in a just struggle can, in this way, invoke an infinite 'reserve' of 'divine strength':

> Our human powers, the powers that God has given us, find their last and supreme expression in faith and humility, culminating in these two virtues. The strength in us is the divine strength of Krishna, the strength of God. He bestows it upon us at the beginning, giving us a part and retaining a part as reserve. We mistake this God-given power for our own. It is not ours but God's. And the part that God holds in reserve for us belongs, conversely, to us and is ours. When we have fully utilized the share given to us at the start, expending it entirely, we win the right to ask for the remainder.[5]

13.8. Another way in which the Bhakti-yoga of the Gītā opens the door for all, is to declare that, even those who, being unable to understand the doctrine of monotheism, worship gods or manes or spirits, but with faith, are acceptable to the Supreme Godhead, although their methods of worship are not 'according to the true law'. Verses IX.23-25 contain this declaration:

> Even those who are devotees of other gods, worship them with faith, they also sacrifice to Me alone, O Arjuna, though not according to the true law.
>
> For I am the enjoyer and lord of all sacrifices. But these men do not know Me in My true nature and so they fall.
>
> Worshippers of the gods go to the gods, worshippers of the manes go to the manes, sacrificers of the spirits go to the spirits, and those who sacrifice to Me come to Me. (IX. 23-25).

13.9. How the open-door approach of the Gītā shows the way to spiritual advancement for persons in 'different stages of development', is explained by Radhakrishnan, in his comments on the above verses:

> The author of the Gītā welcomes light from every quarter of the heaven. It has a right to shine because it is light. . . . The shining gods, the spirits of the dead and the spirits in the psychic world all happen to be worshipped by men in different stages of development but they are all limited forms of the Supreme and cannot give the aspiring soul the peace that is beyond all understanding. The result of worship is assimilation to the form worshipped and these limited forms give limited results. No devotion fails of its highest reward. The lesser ones bring lesser rewards while devotion to the Supreme brings the supreme reward. All sincere religious devotion is a seeking after the Supreme Godhead.[6]

13.10. In order to avoid the risk that devotional practices of all sorts, if not subjected to a proper intellectual discipline, might lead to blind faith and superstitions, the Gītā, in verse X.10, connects Buddhi-yoga with Bhakti:

To those who are constantly devoted and worship Me with love, I grant buddhi-yoga by which they come unto Me." (X.10) This reference to Buddhi-yoga in conjunction with bhakti has been compared by Sarma to a similar reference to buddhi-yoga made in relation to karma (in verse II.49), and its practical implication, according to Sarma, is the avoidance of 'superstitious worship':

> Buddhi-yoga implies equanimity or evenness of mind, an attitude of detachment, freedom from error or delusion, and ability to rise above the mere letter of the books. In short, it is the preliminary discipline of the mind indispensable to every kind of spiritual life—whether it is karma-yoga, bhakti-yoga, dhyāna-yoga or jñāna-yoga. . . .
>
> The Gītā is aware that without a disciplined mind, karma-yoga would result only in rash action, bhakti-yoga in superstitious worship, and jñāna-yoga in vague abstractions. Though the Gītā is a theistic gospel, its object is not to bring to the

feet of God a rash or a sentimental or an anaemic soul, but a fully developed, well integrated, dynamic soul.[7]

13.11. Before moving on to the linkage between Bhakti and Lokasaṁgraha, it is necessary to clarify the significance of the expression 'original form of Bhāgavata Dharma', which was used in para 13.3 to characterize the Bhakti-yoga of the Gītā. Upadhyaya says that, whereas in the original form, the importance of Bhakti was tempered "on account of the combination and prominence of Niṣkāma Karma", in the later forms of the Bhāgavata Dharma, Bhakti by itself was emphasized more and more, and "the Bhāgavata Dharma came to be regarded as an exclusive cult of Bhakti or devotion".[8] One of the sources used by Upadhyaya to draw this conclusion is a statement of the Bhāgavata Purāṇa, about which Upadhyaya writes as follows:

> The Bhāgavata Purāṇa is clearly said to have been composed after the Gītā and the Mahābhārata. In the very beginning of this Purāṇa (I.4-5) it is stated that the purpose of its composition is to bring into full prominence the element of devotion which according to the author had not been given its rightful place in the Mahābhārata including the Gītā, where it was somewhat subordinated to Niṣkāma Karma.[9]

BHAKTI-YOGA AND LOKASAṀGRAHA

13.12. In order to study the role of Lokasaṁgraha in Bhakti-yoga, four aspects of this Yoga (including the way it has been used) are particularly important, namely,

(i) Samarpaṇaṁ of svadharma or svakarma
(ii) Virtues and conduct of a Bhakta
(iii) Samarpaṇaṁ of sarvadharmān (XVIII.66)
(iv) Use for bringing about social harmony

These will now be taken up one-by-one.

(i) *Samarpaṇaṁ of Svadharma or Svakarma*

13.13. Hiriyanna has sounded a note of caution for ordinary people that they need to avoid a sense of self-importance, arising out of actions done for Lokasaṁgraha:

> The process of abandoning selfish interest and purusing only the good of the society is not always conducive to one's spiritual growth. A conscious assumption by an individual, of the role of a social benefactor, is likely to result in a sense of self-importance which is ruinous to all spiritual growth. . . .[10]

13.14. In the Gītā itself, the practical problem raised by Hiriyanna is recognized, namely, that a person working for Lokasaṁgraha runs the risk of developing a sense of self-importance or ahaṁkāra or egotism. In order to stress this point, Śrī Kṛṣṇa mentions, immediately after the Lokasaṁgraha verses (III.20-26), that

'ahaṁkāravimūḍhātmā kartāhamiti manyate'

that is, he whose soul is bewildered by ahaṁkāra thinks "I am the doer". (III.27)

Although egotism presents a very serious obstacle on the journey to Lokasaṁgraha, a relatively convenient way to get over this problem is suggested in verse III.30, in the form of "dedicating all actions to God" or karma-samarpaṇaṁ: "Dedicating all thy works to me, with thy consciousness fixed in the Self, being free from desire and egotism, fight, delivered from thy fever." (III.30)

Perhaps it should be clarified that the expression 'fight' has been used in the Gītā (for example, in verse VIII.7 also—reference para 13.22) to convey the advice 'do thy duty or svadharma'.

13.15. The most well-known verse containing the teaching on dedication of all acts to God, is IX.27:

> Whatever thou doest, whatever thou eatest, whatever thou sacrificest, whatever thou givest away, whatever austerities thou dost practise, do that, O Arjuna, as an offering to me. (IX.27)

Since 'all acts' to be dedicated, specifically include yajña, dānaṁ, and tapas, this verse has already been referred to in para 12.34, in connection with the discussion on the trio—'yajña-dānaṁ-tapas'.

13.16. The act of dedication is a harmonious combination of karma-yoga and bhakti-yoga, and it has several important implications. For one thing, the person becomes free from ahaṁkāra which is the starting point for the chain of hatred (reference para 11.30). An attitude of samarpaṇaṁ makes it easier to give up the desire for selfish gains or mamatva. Another great advantage is that one would feel the urge to do only sāttvika or pure deeds, because how can impure deeds be dedicated to God? (Reference para 13.19)

13.17. Among those who tried to put into practice the method of dedication or karma-samarpaṇaṁ, names of Gandhi and Vinoba easily come to mind. Gandhi went so far as to say that "the renunciation of the fruit of action is impossible without devotion (bhakti)".[11] He continues:

> We learn from the ninth chapter that devotion means attachment (āsakti) to God. This is the royal road (rāja-mārga) to the cultivation of a selfless spirit. Therefore we are told at the very beginning that devotion is the sovereign yoga and is easy to practice. It is easy to practise if it takes hold of our heart, but hard going if it does not.[12]

13.18. Vinoba gives the simile of "seed-throwing" and "seed-sowing" to bring home the advantage of combining karma-yoga and bhakti-yoga:

> Karma-yoga says: 'Perform action; but renounce the fruit, do not desire it.'...
>
> What is bhakti-yoga? It means becoming one with the Lord through devotion....
>
> In Rāja-yoga, both karma and bhakti are combined in a beautiful manner. Rāja-yoga says, 'Do not give up the fruit, do not throw it away, but dedicate it to the Lord. What you throw away is wholly lost. The action dedicated to the Lord is like a seed sown. It fills our life with endless joy and holiness.[13]

13.19. Vinoba argues that, although only sāttvika actions are worthy of being offered to the Lord, a beginning of the process of dedication could be made with non-sāttvika acts as well, with prayers that traces of selfishness in human effort may be eliminated gradually in the process:

> The ninth chapter spoke of surrendering all actions to the Lord. In the seventeenth chapter, this idea is more fully dealt with. It is specially stressed here that the action which is surrendered to the Lord should be sāttvika, for only then will it be worthy of being offered to the Lord. . . .
>
> But a question arises: If dedication is only for the pure man, what is the sinner to do? He should also, wishing that his acts should become progressively purer, surrender all his actions to the Lord. Dedication is a mental attitude, and the mere utterance of words of dedication are neither necessary nor sufficient.[14]

13.20. The teaching about dedication of actions to God is conveyed in a different terminology in verse XI.33, namely, that one should have the feeling that one is doing God's work like an instrument or nimittamātraṁ: "Therefore arise thou and gain glory. Conquering thy foes, enjoy a prosperous kingdom. By me alone are the kauravas slain already. Be thou merely the instrument, O Arjuna." (XI.33)

This verse enunciates the doctrine of causality that wicked persons like the Kauravas die in the battle as a result of their own misdeeds because God follows the law of karma. Therefore, as Tilak interprets it, one who is fighting a just battle and kills unrighteous foes is only helping the cosmic process by becoming a nominal cause, and so such killing does not cause any bondage. In fact, work done with the feeling that one is doing God's work is considered by the Gītā as worship of the Supreme: "He from whom all beings arise and by whom all this is pervaded—by worshipping Him through the performance of his own duty does man attain perfection" (XVIII.46)

(ii) *Virtues and Conduct of a Bhakta*

13.21. Development of an attitude of karma-samarpaṇaṁ is not the only way in which the bhakti-input into karma-yoga helps

Lokasaṁgraha. Another great advantage is that bhakti-yoga gives a strong support to the cultivation and growth of what Hiriyanna calls "other-regarding" virtues like compassion. (reference para 11.15) Radhakrishnan lists "the particular qualities associated with bhakti" as humility, readiness to serve, compassion, love and devotion, mercy and tender love.[15]

13.22. Those who interpret Bhakti in a narrow sense, often consider its main feature to be "telling of beads and the like, but not getting involved with the worries of the world." However, Śrī Kṛṣṇa clearly indicates in the Gītā that a Bhakta carries out his (or her) normal duties in the world (VIII.7, VI.31), and moreover, his (or her) conduct is in conformity with the virtues that go hand-in-hand with Bhakti (as mentioned in the preceding para). Before we consider the practical implications of this statement, we give below a translation of verses VIII.7 and VI.31:

> Therefore, at all times remember Me and fight. When thy mind and understanding are set on Me, to Me alone shalt thou come without doubt. (VIII.7)
>
> The yogin who, established in oneness, worships Me abiding in all beings, lives in Me, howsoever he may be active. (VI.31)

13.23. As an important practical application of the teaching 'to worship God abiding in all beings' , Vivekananda coined the famous phrase "Daridra-Nārāyaṇa" which meant that the service of the poor was the service of God. To Śiva-worshippers he said, "Jīva is Śiva", and explained it further:

> He who sees Śiva in the poor, in the weak and in the diseased, really worships Śiva; and if he sees Śiva only in the image, his worship is but preliminary. He who has served and helped one poor man, seeing Śiva in him, without thinking of his caste, or creed, or race, or anything, with him Śiva is more pleased than with the man who sees Him only in temples.[16]

13.24. A description of how a Bhakta lives in the world is contained in verses XII.13-20. This is similar to other statements of the Gītā in respect of those who have attained perfection, for example, a Sthitaprajña or a Yogī. Without going into all the details, we notice that a Bhakta's relationship with the society is stressed in the very beginning of the description (i.e. in verse XII.13)—by specifying, among other things, that a Bhakta has no ill will towards any being, and is friendly and compassionate to all (XII.13). Tilak clarifies the social dimensions of Bhakti in the Gītā:

> If a man seeks unity with the Deity, he must necessarily seek unity with the interests of the world also, and work for it. If he does not, then the unity is not perfect, because there is union between two elements out of the three (man and Deity), and the third (the world) is left out. I have thus solved the question for myself and I hold that serving the world, and thus serving His will, is the surest way of salvation, and this way can be followed by remaining in the world and not going away from it.[17]

13.25. Those who follow the bhakti-mārga of the Gītā, oriented to social concerns as indicated above, can do a lot for bringing about a sense of harmony and unity in the society, because Śrī Kṛṣṇa recognizes no distinctions of race, sex, caste, or method of worship (IX.26-31). When Gandhi was confronted by orthodox Hindus and asked to quote scriptural authority supporting the abolition of untouchability, he referred to verse IX.32 of the Gītā which says: "Those who take refuge in Me, O Arjuna, though they are lowly born, women, Vaiśyas, as well as Śūdras, they also attain to the highest goal." (IX.32)

Radhakrishnan comments:

> The message of the Gītā is open to all wihout distinction of race, sex or caste. This verse is not to be regarded as supporting the social customs debarring women and Śūdras from Vedic study. It refers to the view prevalent at the time of the composition of Gītā. The Gītā does not sanction these social rules. The Gītā gets beyond racial distinctions in its emphasis on spiritual values. Its gospel of love is open to all men and women, persons of all castes as well as those outside caste. . . . The great teachers of bhakti have striven for equality and proclaimed that belivers in God, whatever their origin, are the best of the twice born.[18]

13.26. Bhakti-yoga offers several possibilities of organizing community-level programmes in which men and women of all age-groups and coming from different backgrounds, can join in a spirit of harmony and fellow-feeling. Verses X.9 and X.10 can be read as illustrating some of these possibilities:

> The thoughts of my bhaktas are fixed in Me, their lives are devoted to Me, they are contented and rejoicing in Me, enlightening one another and ever narrating my kathā to each other. (X.9)
>
> To these who are constantly devoted and worship Me with love, I grant buddhi-yoga by which they come unto me. (X.10)

The significance of linking 'buddhi-yoga' with bhakti has already been pointed out in para 13.10.

13.27. Narrating God's kathā (for example, Rāmāyaṇa and Gītā-based stories from Mahābhārata) in groups and pointing out what men, women and children can learn therefrom, and doing all this in a lively manner (avoiding boredom and orthodoxy)—such activities have been found to be conducive to bringing about social harmony and integration. In fact, the success achieved by the Indian T.V. serials on Rāmāyaṇa and Mahābhārata has been universally recognized to be beyond all expectations. Shorter programmes suited to the needs and interests of children of different age-groups can also be devised.

(iii) *Samarpaṇaṁ of Sarvadharmān*

13.28. The Gītā takes the path of karma-samarpaṇaṁ a step further when Śrī Kṛṣṇa closes the teaching with a message of complete surrender. Radhakrishnan believes that, for a Bhakta, the act of surrendering to God implies an acceptance of the duty 'to participate in God's work for the world':

> When the soul surrenders itself to God, He takes up our knowledge and our error and casts away all forms of insufficiency, and transforms all into His infinite light and, the purity of the universal good. Bhakti is not merely the flight

of the alone to the Alone, the soul's detachment from the world and attachment to God, but is active love for the Divine who enters into the world for redeeming it. . . . Participation in God's work for the world is the duty of all devotees.[19]

13.29. The closing verses of the teaching of the Gītā, namely, XVIII.54-66, present a harmonious combination of karma, bhakti, and jñāna. The doctrine of saṁpūrṇa-samarpaṇaṁ (or complete dedication to God) which is conveyed in verse XVIII.66, is sometimes called prapatti (or taking shelter in God). Before coming to that, we give below a translation of this verse, which many Bhaktas consider to be the 'carama śLoka' (i.e the key verse) of the Gītā: "Abandoning sarvadharmān, come to Me alone for shelter. Be not grieved, for I shall release thee from all evils. (XVIII.66)

13.30. Radhakrishnan analyses the fine distinction between bhakti and prapatti:

> The difference between bhakti and prapatti is symbolized by the ape way (markaṭakiśoranyāya) and the cat way (mārjārakiśoranyāya). The young ape clings fast to the mother and is saved, but a little effort on the part of the young is called for. The mother cat takes the young in her mouth; the young one does nothing to secure its safety. In bhakti the grace of God is earned to an extent; in prapatti it is freely bestowed. . . .[20]
>
> Man's effort is involved in the total surrender to the Supreme. It cannot be unintentional or effortless. The doctrine of grace is not to be interpreted as one special election, as such a conception conflicts with the general trend of the Gītā that the Supreme is the same to all beings.[21]

13.31. Verse XVIII.54 also summarizes supreme devotion to God as being synonymous to "regarding all beings as alike", which has been identified (in paras 10.54-62) as being closely linked with Lokasaṁgraha. In the purified vision of a jñāni bhakta, Vāsudeva Śrī Kṛṣṇa is all that is (VII.19). In popular language we have the well-known Indian dictum that "Mānava sevā is Mādhava sevā, that is, that service of man is service of God."

13.32. Aurobindo has written extensively about 'samarpaṇaṁ of sarvadharmān' or 'surrender without reservations', but the main idea to be stressed in our present context is that this, according to Aurobindo, leads to "universal good'—Lokasaṁgraha, as the following short extract from "Essays on the Gītā" shows:

> The Gītā indicates that the surrender must be without reservations; our Yoga, our life, our state of inner being must be determined freely by the living Infinite, not predetermined by our mind's insistence on this or that dharma or any dharma. . . . An omniscient consciousness will take up our knowledge and our ignorance, our truth and our error, cast away their forms of insufficiency, sarvadharmān parityajya, and transform all into its infinite light. An almighty Power will take up our virtue and sin, our right and wrong, our strength and our weakness, cast away their tangled figures, sarvadharmān parityajya, and transform all into its transcendent purity and universal good and infalliable force. . .[22]

(iv) *Use for Bringing About Social Harmony*

13.33. Bhakti-yoga of the Gītā has been used, along with other elements of the Indian tradition, in trying to bring about social harmony through religious tolerance. One of the main authoritative sources on which the Hindu attitude of religious tolerance is based is the verse IV.11 of the Gītā: "As men approach me, so do I accept them; men on all sides follow my path, O Arjuna." (IV.11)

Radhakrishnan comments:

> This verse brings out the wide catholicity of the Gītā religion. . . . The Hindu thinkers are conscious of the amazing variety of ways in which we may approach the Supreme, of the contingency of all forms. . . . The forms we worship are aids to help us to become conscious of our deepest selves. . . . Meditation on any favourite form may be adopted. . . . Name and form are used to reach the Formless. . . .
>
> Udayanācārya writes: Whom the Śaivas worship as Śiva, the Vedāntins as Brahman, the Buddhists as Buddha, the Naiyāyikās who specialize in canons of knowledge as the chief agent, the followers of the Jaina code as the ever free,

> the ritualists as the principle of law, may that Hari, the Lord of the three worlds, grant our prayers. If he had been writing in this age, he would have added: whom the Christians devoted to work as Christ and Mohammedans as Allah.[23]

13.34. The Hindu doctrine of Avatāra makes it relatively easy for Indians to take a comprehensive view and to visualise how the Supreme can appear in various forms and assume different names in order to save mankind and to ensure the rule of righteousness. Arnold Toynbee has characterized this as "India's gift to the world":

> The spiritual variety of human nature needs the variety of religious aid that the historic religions provide between them. This is a hard saying for adherents of the religions of the Judaic family (Judaism, Christianity, Islam), but is a truism for Hindus. The spirit of mutual goodwill, esteem and veritable love that is stringing among the adherents of all the religions, is the traditional spirit of the religions of the Indian family. This is India's gift to the world. No gift could be greater, and is more timely in the atomic age.[24]

12.35. Sri Ramakrishna discovered, in his own personal, religious experience, that all the deities of Hinduism as well as Buddha, Christ, Allah—were identical in the communion of the mystic. All experience was seen by him as part of a total unity. Subsequently, when Vivekananda spoke at the Parliament of Religions held in USA in 1893, he presented to the world an image of Hinduism—a religion tolerant of all faiths, profoundly spiritual, yet utterly simple in its creed:

> To the Hindu, then, the whole world of religions is only a travelling, a coming up, of different men and women, through various conditions and circumstances, to the same goal. Every religion is only an evolving a God out of the material man, and the same God is the inspirer of all of them. Why, then, are there so many contradictions? They are only apparent, says the Hindu. The contradictions come from the same truth adapting itself to the varying circumstances of different natures.[25]

13.36. Gandhi's prayer meetings included recitation of hymns from the scriptures of the various religions. The chanting of God's names was the most popular part, and he specifically added 'Allah' along with the Hindu names so as to make it acceptable to the Muslims. Gandhi describes how this practice of including non-Hindu names of God was started when he was still in South Africa:

> In Phoenix (South Africa) we had our daily prayers in the same way as in Sābarmati (India), and Musalmans as well as Christians attended them along with Hindus. . . .
>
> Joseph Royeppen's favourite hymn was Vaishnava Jana meaning: He is a Vaishnava (worshipper of Vishnu) who succours people in distress. He loved music, and once sang this hymn saying 'Christian' in place of Vaishnava. The others accepted his reading with alacrity, and I observed that this filled Joseph's heart with joy.[26]

13.37. Iyer sees a link between Gandhi's emphasis on satya and ahiṁsā, and the modern concepts of tolerance and civility. This can be called a "forward linkage". Iyer also mentions the corresponding "backward linkage", namely, that between satya and ahiṁsā, on the one hand, and mokṣa and tapas, on the other. In deriving satya and ahiṁsā from the traditionally religious notions of mokṣa and tapas, Gandhi gave spiritual values a social significance. Similarly, in linking tolerance and civility with his doctrine of satya and ahiṁsā, Gandhi highlighted the importance of religious tolerance and social harmony in the context of India's independence, unity and progress. Iyer summarizes the advantage of this approach:

> There is no doubt that by deflating satya and ahiṁsā to tolerance and civility something significant is lost, just as by inflating satya and ahiṁsā to mokṣa and tapas there is also an important change of meaning. The advantage of this procedure is merely to reveal the metaphysical roots as well as the immediate social relevance of Gandhi's concepts of satya and ahiṁsā.[27]

13.38. Those who try to create an atmosphere of religious tolerance in India on the basis of the teachings of the Gītā, use other sources also in support of their views, namely, the Buddhist Emperor Aśoka of the third century B.C., and the fifteenth century prophet of Hindu-Muslim unity, Kabir. Áśoka made it known that harmony is good, and that all faiths of men are to be respected. Some writers trace the influence of the Gītā on the liberal policies of Aśoka. Similarly, the following utterance of Kabir is truly in line with the spirit of the Gītā: The Hindu God lives in Banaras, the Muslim God at Mecca, but He who made the world lives not in a city made by hand. There is one Father of Hindu and Muslim, one God in all matter.

13.39. Closely linked with the issue of religious tolerance is the ideology of a secular state which the Indian nation has accepted. Although some scholars like Panikkar believe that the roots of the secular state have to be sought in the west,[28] Radhakrishnan thinks that secularism is only an extension of the Hindu attitude of tolerance and affirmation of the unity of all religions:

> Secularism here does not mean irreligion or atheism or even stress on material comforts. It proclaims that it lays stress on the universality of spiritual values which may be attained by a variety of ways.[29]

13.40. Thomas rightly observes that attempts to create an atmosphere of religious tolerance have so far achieved only a limited success in overcoming the immense religious conflicts rampant in India. In his opinion, this is part of a wider struggle to integrate Western and Indian ideologies, and further that such integration would be facilitated by emphasizing samatva and Lokasaṁgraha:

> The ideological struggle in India is basically a struggle to accommodate and integrate modern Western ideologies with the Indian ideologies. This means a radical re-examination as to the goal of ideology: from salvation through knowledge, gnosis, to salvation through a concept of equality, samatva, from the salvation of the individual self to the salvation of the community.[30]

JÑĀNA IN THE GĪTĀ—NOT DIVORCED FROM CONDUCT

13.41. Sāttvika knowledge is defined in verse XVIII.20 as "the knowledge by which the one Imperishable Being is seen in all existences, undivided in the divided." In Vedāntic language, this means the identity of Brahman and Ātman. Chāndogya Upaniṣad (Chapter VI) describes how Uddālaka Āruṇī conveyed this teaching to his son Śvetaketu by using the well-known words: tattvamasi (meaning, that thou art).

13.42. The process of acquisition of knowledge starts with jijñāsā or a genuine desire to know (or inquiry). Radhakrishnan highlights the role of jijñāsā:

> Ascent to higher levels of living, losing oneself to find the higher self can be achieved through jijñāsā or disinterested passion for knowledge. It lifts man out of his narrow limits and makes him forget his self in the contemplation of the universal principles of existence. Knowledge pursued for the sake of power or fame does not take us far. It must be sought for attaining truth.[31]

13.43. Although a study of scriptures could be one way of acquiring knowledge, the Hindu tradition assigns a crucial role to a guru or teacher who is himself a man of wisdom and who has to be approached properly by a seeker of knowledge. Verse IV.34 specifies the conditions to be fulfilled before knowledge can thus be acquired: "Learn the knowledge by humble reverence, by inquiry and by service. The men of wisdom who have seen the truth will instruct thee in knowledge." (IV.34)

It is further mentioned in the second part of the verse IV.38 that "he who acquires perfection in karma-yoga, attains knowledge, by himself, in course of time." And then in verse IV.39, the need for faith is also stressed: "He who has faith, who is absorbed in the pursuit of knowledge and who has subdued his senses, gains knowledge and then he attains quickly the supreme peace." (IV.39)

13.44. We mentioned in para 9.25 that followers of jñāna-yoga consider the starting point of the chain of misery to be ignorance (which is one step beyond desire or attachment, highlighted by karma-yoga). If ignorance is the root cause of bondage, then jñāna is viewed as the only means of liberation (śreyas) from the chain of avidyā-kāma-karma. However, according to Tilak, even after one has achieved the state of perfection through jñāna, there can be no escape from Lokasaṁgraha-activities. As Tilak put it, this type of "action must be done to keep the world going by the right path of evolution which the Creator has destined the world to follow".[32]

13.45. Strong support to Tilak's interpretation is provided by verses XIII.7-11, in which the concept of jñāna has been widened so as to include the practice of as many as twenty virtues (of which nearly one-third are 'other-regarding virtues'—reference para 11.15). At the head of the list of all these virtues is 'amānitvaṁ' meaning humility or freedom from vanity, and the same idea is conveyed through the popular saying: vidyā dadāti vinayaṁ (knowledge leads to humility). Tilak has stressed that, since vanity and egotism often become a serious handicap for those who want to utilize their knowledge for Lokasaṁgraha-activities, the need to get rid of these (i.e. vanity and egotism) is highlighted in these verses.[33] Other virtues which have to be reflected in the conduct of a jñānin towards other people, and which are similarly included in the above verses, are: non-violence, forgiveness, absence of deceit, absence of ahaṁkāra or egotism, non-attachment, evenness of mind in the occurrence of the pleasant or the unpleasant. And after listing these (and other self-regarding virtues like self-control and purity of body and mind) Śrī Kṛṣṇa says in the second part of the verse XIII.11: "(All these virtues) are declared to be (true) knowledge and all that is different therefrom is non-knowledge or ignorance."

Radhakrishnan comments: "It is clear from this list of qualities that jñāna or knowledge includes the practice of moral virtues. Mere theoretical learning will not do."[34]

13.46. We have mentioned in para 10.50 that the term 'samatva' meaning "evenness of mind" is used in the Gītā in two senses, namely, evenness towards all situations, and evenness towards all people. The term used in the verse XIII.9 may or may not specifically include the second type of evenness which is particularly relevant to Lokasaṁgraha. But one who has knowledge of the identity of ātman and brahman and who applies this knowledge to one's conduct automatically has evenness towards all people, as stated in verse VI.29: "He whose self is harmonized by yoga seeth the self abiding in all beings, and all beings in the self; everywhere (in the world) he sees the same."

Radhakrishnan interprets the conduct of such a jñānin as characterized by "love, suffering, and sacrifice" for the world ("on the ethical plane").[35]

JÑĀNA-YOGA AND LOKASAṀGRAHA

13.47. Those who follow jñāna-yoga are depicted in Chapter XII of the Gītā as "those who seek oneness with the Absolute, one and impersonal, and worshipping the Imperishable and the Unmanifested" (or doing nirguṇa upāsanā). Śrī Kṛṣṇa declares in verse XII.4 that such persons also come to Me because they are engaged in the welfare of all creatures:

> By restraining all the senses, being even-minded in all conditions, rejoicing in the welfare of all creatures, they come to Me indeed (just like the worshippers of God in His manifested form, who do saguṇa bhakti). (XII.4)

13.48. For the followers of Jñāna-yoga, that is, those who rely more on knowledge than on faith, the teaching about giving up of egotism is conveyed in the Gītā by utilizing a modified version of Kapila-sāṁkhya philosophy. The argument (presented briefly in verses III.27-29) runs as follows: Prakṛti and the Ātman are different from each other; Prakṛti (with its three guṇas—sattva, rajas, tamas) does everything; the Ātman is a witness, a non-doer; therefore only ignorant people (who identify themselves with the body and not with the Ātman) have the egotism that they are the doers of actions. An elaboration of these ideas is presented in verses XVIII.13-16 which list five factors which together cause all actions to be accomplished. These five factors are: the seat of action, the doer, the instruments of various sorts, the many kinds of efforts, and finally providence. Mentioning providence as the last of these causes but assigning to it a limited role in the accomplishment of any action is noteworthy. The Gītā recognizes human effort as the major cause, but one cannot be sure of success due to the (minor) role of the non-human factor which is popularly called chance, luck, fate or destiny.

13.49. In the case of those who prefer to use an intellectual approach outlined above, the act of dedication or karma-samarpaṇaṁ is expressed in the Gītā in terms of "Brahman" rather than "Śrī Kṛṣṇa or Īśvara": "He who works, having given up attachment, resigning his actions to Brahman, is not touched by sin, even as a lotus leaf (is untouched) by water." (V.10)

13.50. Hiriyanna, designating the two ways of samarpaṇaṁ—that is, of a Bhakta and a Jñānī—as "theistic" and "absolutistic", respectively, considers the ultimate result of both to be essentially similar:

> Really therefore the distinction between the two teachings is not much; only while the absolutistic teaching may suit the few whose minds are well cultivated, the theistic teaching has decidedly a stronger appeal to common people with their simple trust in a personal God.[36]

13.51. Perhaps the best illustration of uniting Jñāna-yoga and Lokasaṁgraha is provided by Vivekananda's formulation of the concept of Practical Vedānta, and its continued implementation through the Ramakrishna Mission. 'Practical Vedānta', according to Vivekananda, meant an harmonization of theoretical knowledge—Vedānta—and practical action—Karma-yoga:

> Raise once more that mighty banner of Vedānta for on no other ground can you have that wonderful love until you see that the same Lord is present everywhere. The nation is sinking, the curse of unnumbered millions is on our heads—the unnumbered millions to whom we have talked of Vedānta and whom we have hated with all our strength, to whom we have talked theoretically that we are all the same and all are one with the same Lord, without even an ounce of practice. . . .

throw away everything, even your own salvation, and go and help others. Ay, you are always talking bold words, but here is Practical Vedānta before you. The first part of this is that you should go to the sinking millions of India, and take them by hand, remembering the words of Lord Krishna. . . .[37]

13.52. Sarma observes that, prior to the time of the Gītā, jñāna often had a renunciatory connotation because it was "coupled with karma-sannyāsa or physical renunciation of karma".[38] By coupling jñāna with Lokasaṁgraha, the Gītā presented, according to Sarma, a more balanced and realistic view and helped integrate jñāna with dharma and hence with society:

> The Gītā supplied a much needed corrective to the overemphasis on jñāna and renunciation, which had led to mere quietism. It may be said that the whole Gītā is a long and sustained protest against the dangers of quietism.[39] . . . The unique feature of Jñāna, as taught in the Gītā, is that it is never divorced from service to society.[40] . . . Unsympathetic critics of Hinduism have often ignored the Lokasaṁgraha message of the Gītā and said that social service forms no integral part of our religion. They forget that the service to society is fundamental to the very concept of Hindu dharma as taught by the Gītā.[41]

PURUṢĀRTHAS—NONE OF THE FOUR NEGLECTED IN GĪTĀ

13.53. The concept of the four Puruṣārthas or goals of life or values is an important element of the Hindu tradition. Ranganathananda translates the word 'Puruṣārtha' as 'sought after by the human being', and says that "that all human urges, aspirations, and purposes are covered by the four comprehensive puruṣārthas. . . ."[42] There is no unanimity about the order in which the puruṣārthas should be mentioned—some put 'artha' in the beginning, some others put 'kāma', while some begin with 'dharma'. For our present purposes, we take the order 'artha-kāma-dharma-mokṣa'. Following Kathopaniṣad, the ultimate goal is also denoted by 'śreyas', and some verses of the Gītā (e.g. II.7 and III.2) use the word 'śreyas' in the same sense.

From this consideration, 'mokṣa' and 'śreyas' become synonyms.[43] Some scholars like Mishra (reference para 13.64) believe that 'śreyas' could denote both dharma and mokṣa, depending on the context. We have talked about 'śreyas' before (e.g. in Chapter Nine), but the puruṣārtha-centred discussion of this chapter, covering all the four goals (and not only the ultimate goal 'śreyas'), obviously has a wider scope.

13.54. Although the Gītā does not specifically mention all the four puruṣārthas together in any single verse, they are referred to either singly or in groups of two's or three's, and the importance of each of them is stressed in different contexts. Traditional commentators devoted most of the attention on dharma and mokṣa, and even in the twentieth century, dharma remained the most prominent goal. It seems to us that putting aside artha and kāma completely does not do justice to the comprehensive and practical approach of the Gītā to individual goal specification. Therefore, we shall first look into Śrī Kṛṣṇa's teaching on these two individual goals, i.e. artha and kāma, and particularly their linkage with the wider, social goal of Lokasaṁgraha. Discussion on dharma and mokṣa (or variants thereof) and their close relationship with Lokasaṁgraha will then follow.

13.55. Rather than covering artha and kāma as two vast goals (with no level-wise gradation of each), the Gītā has adopted a practical "Distributional approach", and mentioned separately the "basic needs" part of both of these as an important subcategory called śarīra yātrā (or the maintenance of body, both physically and psychologically). The idea is not to make three goals out of two, but emphasize that, in practical life, certain minimum levels of artha and kāma have to be achieved by each and every individual. In a way, this is comparable to the modern ideal of universal fulfilment of basic needs, denoted in terms of "crossing the poverty line" and of satisfying fundamental human rights. Therefore, we cover in our discussion śarīrayātrā as the basic goal, and then higher levels of artha and kāma as caution-demanding goals because otherwise they can lead one astray from dharma.

ŚARĪRA YĀTRĀ—THE BASIC NEED FOR ALL

13.56. The Karma-yoga approach of the Gītā envisages that every able-bodied person should perform karma or productive work as a means of livelihood. No such person should take recourse to begging. In his state of delusion Arjuna had suggested the possibility of running away from the battlefield and of maintaining himself by begging, but Śrī Kṛṣṇa did not show any sympathy with such an escapist approach. In terms of the modern theory of employment, the śarīrayātrā concept can be compared (as already mentioned) with the basic needs approach, according to which the satisfaction of minimum needs of each family (including food, clothing, shelter, health, education, recreation) should normally be achieved through the provision of freely chosen productive work for able-bodied members of the family. Such work would be called 'svadharma' in the language of the Gītā, and its performance in accordance with the teachings of the Gītā would also help the cause of Lokasaṁgraha.

13.57. Good health, physical as well as mental, would be an essential part of the basic goal of śarīrayātrā. Sāttvika food, according to the Gītā, (verse XVII.8) promotes vitality, strength, health, joy, and cheerfulness. The Gītā stresses the usefulness of moderation, in food as well as recreation. Within the limitations of the available resources, bhakti of Śrī Kṛṣṇa can be practised because it calls for faith and devotion, not money. In fact, bhakas need not worry about yogakṣema, that is, the availability of what is not already possessed, and the preservation of what is in possession: "Those who worship Me, meditating on Me alone, to them who ever persevere, I bring attainment of what they have not and security in what they have." (IX.22)

Of course, content with what they have, they need to be free from jealousy:

> He who is satisfied with whatever they get, who has passed beyond the dualities (of pleasure and pain), who is free from jealousy, who remains the same in success and failure, even when he acts, he is not bound. (IV.22)

This shows that "common people" earning their livelihood by proper means and leading a normal life can help the cause of Lokasaṁgraha if they participate in community-level activities in a spirit of harmony, and free from discontentment and jealousy.

ARTHA AND LOKASAṀGRAHA

13.58. Since a minimum, "basic needs" level of artha has already been included in śarīrayātrā, we have to ask: what is the Gītā's approach to artha over and above such a minimum level? The Gītā approves of prosperity if the wealth is earned by just means, and if there is no misuse nor attachment to wealth nor arrogance because of it. For example, Śri Kṛṣṇa tells Arjuna in verse XI.33: enjoy a prosperous kingdom. And in the closing verse of the Gītā, namely, XVIII.78, Sañjaya associates fortune with the presence, jointly, of Śrī Kṛṣṇa and Arjuna: "Wherever there is Kṛsṇa, the lord of yoga and Arjuna the archer, I think there will surely be fortune, victory, welfare and morality." (XVIII.78)

13.59. But the Gītā is equally emphatic about the conditions under which wealth is to be acquired. For example, acquisition of wealth by unjust means is characterized as demoniac in verse XVI.12, and limitless hankering after wealth is similarly condemned in verse XVI.13:

> Bound by hundreds of ties of desire, given over to lust and anger, they strive to amass hordes of wealth, by unjust means, for the gratification of their desires." (XVI.12)
>
> This today has been gained by me; this desire I shall attain; this is mine and this wealth also shall be mine in future. (XVI.13)

13.60. Similarly, because of arrogance of wealth, "the demoniac" "hypocritically" associate themselves with acts of Lokasaṁgraha, but only to derive personal gain:

> I am rich and well-born. Who is there like unto me? I shall sacrifice, I shall give, I shall rejoice: thus they say, deluded by ignorance. (XVI.15)

> Self-conceited, obstinate, filled with extreme arrogance of wealth, they perform yajñas which are so only in name, with ostentation and without propriety. (XVI.17)

13.61. The conditions which convert wealth into demoniac prosperity are ultimately the result of ignorance (ajñānaṁ), as mentioned in the above-quoted verse XVI.15, and also in several other verses. Therefore scholars like Tilak have summarized the above ideas by saying that the Gītā advocates a combination of aiśvaryaṁ (prosperity) and jñānaṁ (knowledge).[44] Alternatively, the evils associated with an indiscriminate pursuit of wealth can be avoided by bhakti, for example, in verses VII.16 to 18, seekers for wealth who are bhaktas are termed as noble. Only when wealth is thus sanctified (by bhakti or jñānaṁ), can genuine acts of Lokasaṁgraha be performed therewith, and that would mark its proper utilization, say in sāttvika dānaṁ (reference paras 12.56-59).

KĀMA AND LOKASAṀGRAHA

13.62. Kāma meaning pleasure represents psychological value. Hiriyanna argues:

> If kāma stands for pleasure, we may say that it is desired by all, for pleasure is always welcome to everyone. Indeed we cannot help desiring our own felicity. But not everything desired is necessarily desirable. A sick person may long for a certain kind of food, but it may not at all be advisable for him to partake of it from the standpoint of his physical wellbeing. That is, kāma, while it may be an object of desire, may not always be desirable; and, though appearing to be a true value of life, it may not really be so or may even prove to be a disvalue.[45]

13.63. The question is: how to draw the line between kāma as a true value and kāma as a disvalue. The Gītā brings in dharma, the moral value, to answer this question. That variety of kāma is a true value which is in accord with the requirements of dharma, but not any other. This conception of dharma as a regulative principle is stressed by Śrī Kṛṣṇa when he says in the second part of the verse VII.11: "In beings I am the kāma which is not contrary to dharma, O Arjuna."

13.64. Mishra includes both artha and kāma in the category of preyas (the pleasant), and considers dharma as śreyas (the good). He also finds a hierarchy in this scheme of values:

> Artha represents the fulfilment of the gross physical needs like food, shelter, etc. Physical or biological needs are certainly different from desires which are more mental or psychological and therefore subtler and more refined. In this sense kāma may be regarded as higher to artha in the value-hierarchy. Dharma is still higher, for artha and kāma can be sacrificed in favour of dharma.[46]

13.65. The most obvious use of dharma to discriminate between good and bad kāma is to avoid excesses, and not to let kāma be considered as the sole cause of the world or the sole object of life. According to the last part of verse XVI.8, the demoniac consider kāma as the sole cause or the sole object. Such a distorted view leads them to act against Lokasaṁgraha as explained in the verse XVI.9: "Holding fast to this view (stated in XVI.8), these lost souls of feeble understanding, commit cruel deeds, and rise up as the enemies of the world for its destruction."

13.66. The need to avoid excesses and to observe self-restraint is stressed in verse VI.17: "For the man who is temperate in food and recreation, who is restrained in his actions, whose sleep and waking are regulated, there ensues yoga which destroys all sorrrow."

If self-restraint is applied to kāma by householders, we would see (in developing countries like India) only a modest increase in population, whereas unrestrained kāma (under conditions of inadequate health and family planning facilities) has caused a population explosion which is threatening a basic goal like śarīrayātrā. Śrī Kṛṣṇa's statement in the verse X.28 that "I am the God of conjugal love" is to be understood in this light.

13.67. Persons who lead normal lives and who participate in worldly pleasures in moderation can benefit themselves as well as the society. Only a society in which such people have freedom of creative expression can produce artists, musicians, sculptors, dancers, and literary writers. Śrī Kṛṣṇa's support for art, culture, and things of beauty and splendour is implied by his statements listing his various manifestations in the world; for example, he says, in the last parts of verses X.37 and X.35, respectively: "Of the poets, I am the poet Uśanā" (X.37) and "Of the seasons, I am the flower-bearer spring." (X.35)

And in verse X.41, Śrī Kṛṣṇa makes a general statement about things of beauty and grace: "Whatsoever being there is, endowed with glory and grace and vigour, know that to have sprung from a fragment of my splendour." (X.41)

Radhakrishnan comments that:

> While all things are supported by God, things of beauty and splendour reveal Him more than others. Every deed of heroism, every life of sacrifice, every work of genius, is a revelation of the divine.[47]

Cultural advancement of a society has been identified in para 11.46 as a part of the stability aspect of Lokasaṁgraha, and contribution thereto by kāma (regulated by dharma) can be quite significant.

DHARMA AND LOKASAṀGRAHA

13.68. The role of dharma as a regulatory principle has been referred to in para 13.63, in conjunction with kāma. Ranganathananda stresses the 'uniting' and 'integrating' role of dharma, which is viewed by him as 'the principle for integrating human being with human being in society'.[48] Here is an extract from Ranganathananda's long statement on this subject:

> A mere accumulation of bricks does not constitute a building; there is the cement to unite brick with brick. Similarly, no accumulation of human beings can constitute a society. There is something that unites human being to human being; and that is what Vedānta calls dharma. It is a set of spiritual values, acting silently from within. . . .Dharma stresses the concept of mutuality and interdependence. There is no full freedom for the human being within the social context. . . .[49]

13.69. Possible linkages between svadharma and Lokasaṁgraha were discussed in paras 12.15-32. In that context, it was considered useful by several Gītā-scholars if svadharma could be dissociated from the traditional concept of varṇa. This can be done by viewing dharma in a wider sense—namely, Sādhāraṇadharma —which is not tied down to varṇa. Three elements of sādhāraṇadharma (i.e. dharma common to all), that occur in the Gītā in different contexts, are, in our opinion, inter-related namely:

(a) Daivī sampat or development of divine virtues
(b) Sattva guṇa or development of sāttvika virtues
(c) Participation in God's work (or mat-karma or My work).

Our purpose is to explore how the common core of these three concepts has a social dimension and is linked with Lokasaṁgraha.

13.70. To start with daivī samat, we have already mentioned (in para 11.19) the twenty-six virtues which according to verses XVI.1 to 3 constitute divine endowments. Of these, the following (being "Other-regarding virtues"—reference para 11.15) are particularly relevant to Lokasaṁgraha: "fearlessness, ahiṁsā, dayā to living beings, aversion to fault-finding, dānaṁ, freedom from covetousness, forgiveness, freedom from malice, freedom from excessive pride."

13.71. Next, the development of sāttvika virtues implies, according to the Gītā, pushing down (in the scale of priorities) tamas and rajas, but not their complete elimination, because the three guṇas taken together (in whatever proportions) constitute human nature. Verse XIV.10 states this fundamental proposition according to which no one can be completely "good" or completely "bad": "Sattva guṇa prevails, overpowering rajas and tamas, O Arjuna. Similarly, rajas prevails overpowering sattva and tamas, and even so tamas prevails overpowering sattva and rajas." (XIV.10)

Radhakrishnan explains this further:

> The three guṇas are present in all human beings, though in different degrees. No one is free from them and in each soul

> one or the other predominates. Men are said to be sāttvika, rajas or tamas according to the guṇa which prevails. . . .
>
> The sāttvika nature aims at light and knowledge; its activities are free, calm and selfless. . . .
>
> The rajas nature is restless, full of selfish desires connected with things outward, it cannot sit still. . . .
>
> The tamas nature is dull and inert, its mind is dark and confused and its whole life is one continuous submission to environment.[50]

13.72. The three-guṇa classification has been applied in the Gītā to karma as well as to its doer (along with other concepts like jñāna, buddhi, etc.). An interesting aspect of this is the following characterization of tāmas karma in verse XVIII.25:

> The action which is undertaken through ignorance, without regard to consequences or to loss and injury and without regard to one's human capacity, that is said to be tamas. (XVIII.25)

It is clear from this that, the Gītā teaching of giving up the fruit of action does not mean carelessness or neglect of what the consequences of one's action (particularly on others) are likely to be. As Radhakrishnan says: the effects of actions on others must always be considered; only selfish aims are to be renounced.[51] Lokasaṁgraha considerations are thus (implicitly) inherent in sāttvika karma. Of course, whatever one takes up as a part of one's duty, has to be feasible and consistent with one's capacity, because otherwise it becomes tamas (according to the above-quoted verse).

13.73. Similarly, to qualify as a sāttvika doer of action, one needs to avoid deceit, malice and violence, because these are included (in verses XVIII.27-28) among the characteristics of a tāmas or rājas doer. Other features of a sāttvika doer are mentioned in verse XVIII.26: "The doer who is free from attachment, who does not talk with egotism, who is full of resolution and zeal, and who is unmoved by success or failure, he is said to be a sāttvika doer." (XVIII.26)

13.74. Fortified with sattva guṇa and with daivī sampat, one is exhorted by Śrī Kṛṣṇa in verse XI.55 to do "My work" and "to be free from enmity to all creatures": "He who does My work, he who looks upon Me as his goal, he who worships Me, free from attachment, he who is free from enmity to all creatures, he goes to Me, O "Arjuna." (XI.55)

According to Śaṁkara, this verse is the substance of the whole teaching of the Gītā. To be free from enmity to all creatures is obviously an element of Lokasaṁgraha. But Śrī Kṛṣṇa's message to translate such "freedom from enmity" into practical action is conveyed by the words "do My work". Although some commentators read this as meaning "dedicate actions to Me", another possible interpretation is "participate in My work of Lokasaṁgraha" or "follow my example". Tilak writes:

> The Gītā asks us to work in imitation of the Lord, for the purpose of Lokasaṁgraha or the good of the society—the unification of humanity in universal sympathy. . . . the Gītā reconciles and harmonizes spiritual freedom with work in the world.[52]

13.75. Participation in God's work, after being equipped with daivī sampat and sattva guṇa, would imply giving a social dimension to divine endowments and sāttvika virtues. In other words, this would extend the meaning of Kurukṣetra to refer to a battle between the divine and the demoniac elements "in the society", as also between the sāttvika forces on the one hand, and tamas and rajas forces, on the other, (considering the society again as the battlefield). It was Gandhi who interpreted Kurukṣetra as "the heart of every person where a duel between dharma and adharma is perpetually going on."[53] This "inward-looking" interpretation can be extended "outward" so as to assume a social dimension. In Chapter XVI of the Gītā, the divine qualities include compassion towards all (XVI.2) while the demoniac elements try to destroy the world (XVI.9) Radhakrishnan's comments on the words "dharmakṣetra" and "kurukṣetra" also lend support to this society-oriented interpretation:

> The world is dharmakṣetra, the nursery of saints where the sacred flame of spirit is never permitted to go out. . . . Life

> is a battle, a warfare of dharma against the spirit of evil. ... By their mutual conflict, the development is advanced and the cosmic purpose furthered.... Kurukṣetra is also called tapahkṣetra, the field of penance, of discipline.[54]

Thus an extended interpretation of sādhāraṇadharma (which views dharma from a social angle—but not linked with varṇa) further strengthens its close relationship with Lokasaṁgraha. (Para 11.25 refers to a similar idea in the Bhāgavata Purāṇa).

MOKṢA AND LOKASAṀGRAHA

13.76. The ultimate goal of life, mokṣa or spiritual freedom or release, is referred to in the Gītā by using a variety of terms, for example, (as listed by Radhakrishnan):

> The end of perfection is called the highest (III.19), emancipation (III.31, IV.15), the eternal state (XVIII.56), the path from which there is no return (V.17), perfection (XII.10), the highest rest (IV.39), the entering into God (IV.9, 10, 24), contact with God (VI.28), rest in Brahman (II.72), transformation into divine existence (XIV.26), transmutation into Godhead (V.24)....[55]
>
> Any one who attains this transcendent condition is a yogin, a siddhapuruṣa, a realized soul, a jitātman, yuktacetas, a disciplined and harmonized being for whom the Eternal is ever present.[56]

13.77. Mishra warns against any narrow, negativistic interpretation of mokṣa:

> Mokṣa is not an other-worldly and after-death value, nor is it an individualistic a-social value. The negativistic interpretation of mokṣa found in some sections of the Indian tradition is not correct. The true picture of mokṣa which we find in the Vedas, Upaniṣads and the Gītā is a very positive one.... Self-realization is a process of gradual uncovering of the higher or the deeper self, proportionate to self-purification through the means of the cleansing of heart and universal love.[57]

13.78. There is ample evidence in the Gītā to support Mishra's view of mokṣa, namely perfection related to cleansing of heart and to universal love, and the possibility of this being achieved in this world. Śrī Kṛṣṇa describes in verse V.18 the state of even-mindedness towards all beings which sages have, and then confirms, in verses V.19 and V.23, the attainability of perfection while still alive:

> Even here (on earth) the saṁsāra (worldly sorrow) is overcome by those whose mind is established in equality. God is flawless and the same in all. Therefore are these persons established in God. (V.19)
>
> He who is able to resist the rush of desire and anger, even here before he gives up his body, he is a yogin, he is the happy man. (V.23)

13.79. We have already mentioned in paragraphs 10.54-67 that a sthitaprajña karmayogin or a bhakta or a jñānin—each of these performs acts for Lokasaṁgraha, irrespective of the fact that the state of perfection is achieved by them through different paths. Radhakrishnan says: "We do not proceed on the same lines but that which we seek is the same. We may climb the mountain by different paths but the view from the summit is identical for all."[58]

It may be added that, a triguṇātīta also (one who goes beyond the three guṇas) performs acts for Lokasaṁgraha, being "the same to friends and foes", as characterized in verse XIV.25.

13.80. There is, however, an important difference between the state of striving for mokṣa and the state after the attainment of mokṣa, in regard to "why" one carries on Lokasaṁgraha activities. In the former state (of striving), such acts are done because of a sense of duty, whereas in the latter state (of perfection), such acts become natural or spontaneous. (reference paras 12.73-78). Hiriyanna elaborates this change of perspective, both from the viewpoint of jñāna and bhakti:

> No doubt, he was doing unselfish work even before he became free; but that was, more or less, the result of conscious strife. Now (after perfection) it becomes quite spontaneous. This

is for a jñānin. For a bhakta also, the same will be the case, the only difference being that the enlightened person will help others, prompted by compassion rather than ātmaupamya (or because of atman being the same)."[59]

HOW GĪTĀ'S HARMONIZATION APPLIES TO GOALS

13.81. In paragraphs 9.48-53 we described how the karma-yoga of the Gītā presents an harmonization between the Vedic karma-kāṇḍa (or Pravṛtti) and the Upaniṣadic Jñāna-kāṇḍa (or Nivṛtti). Broadly speaking, such harmonization has three main elements:

(a) Redefining nivṛtti as renunciation of selfish desires but not of worldly duties
(b) Redefining pravṛtti as the performance of worldly duties without attachment to the fruits, that is, without expecting selfish gains
(c) Introducing bhakti to fill the gap because normal human beings would find it hard to give up the desire for fruits of their actions but may find it easier to dedicate the actions as well as the fruits to God.

In this process, the Gītā achieved harmonization not only between karma and jñāna, but also between karma, jñāna and bhakti. In either case, this can be called "harmonization of means" because karma, bhakti and jñāna are essentially means for achieving the ultimate goal of life for which various terms and illustrations have been given in the Gītā (Reference para 13.76).

13.82. The harmonization of karma, bhakti and jñāna has been studied in detail by many interpreters, based on verses XVIII.54-56, IX.13-14, II.60-61, and many others. For example, Aurobindo calls the harmonious synthesis of the three yogas "the triune way of knowledge, works and devotion."[60] Vinoba compares the harmonization of the three yogas to "Triveṇī", that is, the confluence of the three rivers, Gaṅgā, Yamunā and Sarasvatī.[61] Upadhyaya, after explaining and illustrating the various aspects of such harmonization, summarizes his findings in the following terms:

The Gītā tries its best to show that it is wrong to see any

> intrinsic superiority or inferiority in these paths which are meant for people of different temperament to start with, but ultimately they all converge in one and lead to the same goal. They are said to be mutually complementary and essentially the same. . . .[62]
>
> Although not explicitly stated, the Gītā shows indirectly its preference for karma, bhakti and jñāna in a descending order.[63] But this is done more on the ground of expediencey than on the basis of any intrinsic superiority. To show a preference for one or the other path on the ground of its being easier and more expedient is one thing, and to speak of one having greater intrinsic worth is quite a different thing. Indeed the compromising attitude of the Gītā is too strong to allow it to recognize a difference of value or even to accept the independence of the different paths.[64]

It may be added that Upadhyaya's statement about preference being shown on grounds of ease and expediency also applies to yoga in relation to sāṁkhya (V.1-7) and to saguṇa bhakti in relation to nirguṇa upāsanā (XII.1-7).

13.83. Rather than giving further details about the harmonization of means, we move to the subject of "harmonization of goals" in the Gītā. Although goals are extremely important, not much research has so far been conducted on the subject of their harmonization—in fact, very little in comparison to the harmonization of means. In our opinion, the approach of the Gītā is so comprehensive that two stages of harmonization of goals can be identified therein, namely:

Stage one:	Harmonizing śarīrayātrā, artha, kāma and dharma (that is, the individual goals of preyas and śreyas)—adopting Mishra's classification (para 13.64) according to which śreyas could stand for dharma as well as mokṣa
Stage two:	Harmonizing śreyas and Lokasaṁgraha (that is, individual and social goals)

13.84. The terms "preyas" and "śreyas" owe their popularity to the conversation between Yama and Nachiketa in Kathopaniṣad.

Some scholars interpret the Upaniṣadic text as presenting a choice between the two, and as asking one to strive for śreyas to the exclusion of preyas. Tilak's interpretation (as summarized by us in para 9.11) is different, namely, that the three blessings enabled Nachiketa to obtain both preyas and śreyas. The last mantra (II.iii.18) of Kathopaniṣad says that Nachiketa obtained both "yogavidhi" and "vidyā", the former leading to preyas and the latter leading to śreyas.

13.85. In the Gītā, fulfilment of preyas (that is, śarīra yātrā, artha, kāma) is approved, subject to certain conditions, for example, avoidance of extremes, observance of dharma, non-attachment, even-mindedness, having no selfish desires and no egotism. (Details are given in paras 13.56-67.) How to attain śreyas was the main question of Arjuna, and Śrī Kṛṣṇa told him in verses II.31-38 that performance of svadharma with even-mindedness would lead him śreyas. The overall message of the Gītā is that of harmonizing preyas and śreyas. (This is stage one of the harmonizing of goals). One of the similes given by Śrī Kṛṣṇa to convey this message is that of "the sea" which can absorb so many flows and yet retain its motionlessness: (verse II.70): "He unto whom all desires enter as waters into the sea, which, though ever being filled is ever motionless, attains to peace and not he who hugs his desires."

13.86. Stage two of the harmonization of goals is of particular interest to us, namely, harmonizing śreyas and Lokasaṁgraha. Both these goals are mentioned together in the verse III.20: "It was even by karma that Janaka and others attained to perfection (or śreyas). Thou shouldst do karma also, keeping an eye to Lokasaṁgraha." (III.20)

In the second part of the verse III.11, a linkage between Lokasaṁgraha and śreyas is brought out: "Fostering each other you shall attain to śreyas."

This is similar to the first principle of sarvodaya (uplift of all) enunciated by Gandhi: "The good of the individual is contained in the good of all."[65]

13.87. Vinoba harmonizes Lokasaṁgraha and śreyas by saying that service to society and personal salvation can be achieved simultaneously from the same action if performed in accordance with the teaching of the Gītā:

> The service that is being rendered to the world through my external actions can itself, viewed from within, be described as spiritual exercise. The service of creation and the development of the spirit do not demand two different courses of action; service and spiritual growth are not different things. For both, the effort made, and the action performed is the same.[66]

13.88. Radhakrishnan sees a similar harmonization in the concluding verse XVIII.78 of the Gītā, although the terms used there are 'yoga' and 'dhanuḥ':

> The tremendous facts of life divine are yoga, the realization of God through worship and entire submission to His will, and dhanuḥ or active participation in the furtherance of the cosmic plan. Spiritual vision and social service should go together. The double purpose of human life, personal perfection and social efficiency, is indicated here.[67]

13.89. Vivekananda conveys the same idea by the phrase "ātmano mokṣārthaṁ jagaddhitāya ca" which means that individual salvation and universal welfare can be achieved simultaneously by the followers of Sri Ramakrishna. (Reference para 11.18) Since the Gītā relates śreyas to "even-mindedness in success or failure", and Lokasaṁgraha to "equal vision towards all beings", the simultaneous achievement of śreyas and Lokasaṁgraha is confirmed by the inclusion of both types of samatva in the characteristics of those who have attained perfection through karma, bhakti or jñāna or a synthesis thereof (II.56-57, 71; V.18-20; XII.13, 18-19; XIV.24-26; XVIII.54-56).

13.90. We mentioned above (in para 13.81) that the Gītā harmonizes pravṛtti and nivṛtti by introducing bhakti to fill the gap. In fact, the harmonizing role of bhakti is noticed also in the case of śreyas and Lokasaṁgraha, because "attaining to God" is a synonym for śreyas, and verse XII.4 says: "Those who (worship the Unmanifested) and rejoice in the welfare of all creatures, they come to Me."

Other aspects of harmonization of śreyas and Lokasaṁgraha are referred to in paras 13.76-80.

CHAPTER FOURTEEN

Updated Lokasaṁgraha: A Potentially Dynamic Social Ideal

14.1. The second part of this study (consisting of Chapters Eight onwards) was intended to answer the question: Why was it possible for modern interpreters of the Gītā to have this particular scripture play an important social role, initially in the context of a specific (women's) problem, but ultimately spanning the vast socio-political field? An answer to this question, based on the life and/or work of activists and scholars, has been attempted in Chapters Eight to Thirteen. A summary of the main elements that constitute this answer is presented in this chapter.

14.2. In order to understand clearly the introduction of a social ideal—Lokasaṁgraha—in a religious text, the background situation needs to be properly appreciated. A basic point emerging from our study is that, Arjuna and Śrī Kṛṣṇa viewed the "crisis-situation" of the Kurukṣetra-battlefield from two different perspectives. Among the first words used by Śrī Kṛṣṇa in the Gītā, while addressing Arjuna, were the following: "Engulfed in a crisis (viṣame samupasthitaṁ) (II.2), give up faint-heartedness and stand up to fight".

But what was the real nature of this crisis ? Arjuna took a narrow view as if it was only a 'personal crisis' for himself—how to choose between duty and family-loyalty. But, more importantly, the unlawful unsurption of the entire kingdom by the Kauravas—who were durbuddhiḥ (I.23) or evil-minded, and ātatā-yinaḥ (I.36) or felons—was a social crisis'. Obviously, people's welfare (Lokasaṁgraha) could not be expected from the Kauravas.

14.3. It was because of Śrī Kṛṣṇa's appreciation of the real nature of the crisis that He imparted the Lokasaṁgraha-related teaching on His own initiative, after He had answered Arjuna's initial questions that reflected his (i.e. Arjuna's) narrow vision. To sharpen the focus, we have used the expressions "first stage" and "second stage" of the Gītā-teaching—the first stage notionally ending with the verse III.19, and the second stage beginning with III.20. A brief review of the details follows.

DISTINGUISHING FEATURES OF THE TWO STAGES OF TEACHING

14.4. Arjuna representing an ordinary human being is initially depicted as too much engrossed in narrow personal problems. He knew very well that all possible attempts had been made to avoid the war, including Śrī Kṛṣṇa's mediation efforts and Pāṇḍavas' willingness to accept only a small part of the kingdom, the whole of which legitimately belonged to them. Regarding the mentality and conduct of the Kauravas, too, Arjuna knew that they had an insatiable greed, an uncompromising attitude, and had committed so many crimes, thus prompting him to use the word 'ātatāyinaḥ' (meaning felons) for them (I.36). According to Hindu tradition, felons were punishable by death, no sin attaching to one who killed them. In spite of all this, the actual sight of kinsmen (svajanaṁ), elders, teacher, and friends on the battlefield and the imminence of the battle, suddenly raised a doubt in Arjuna's mind whether his duty to fight for a just cause should really have priority (in a moral sense) over his family ties. His questions to Śrī Kṛṣṇa, at such a critical juncture, had three main elements, namely, how not to incur sin (pāpaṁ), how to obtain release from śokaṁ (sorrow), and how to attain śreyas (the good of the individual, possibly extended to the family).

14.5. Since Arjuna's questions are framed within the confines of a narrow vision (he does not show any concern about the effect of his action or inaction on the society as a whole), the initial teaching of Śrī Kṛṣṇa also concentrates on the way to achieving individual goals. For example, Arjuna is told that the evil or virtue (pāpaṁ or puṇyaṁ) that we ascribe to any particular action does not lie in the action itself but depends on the frame of mind of the person who does it. Similarly, the root cause of grief and bondage is not karma but attachment. In fact, a chain of vices and misery starting from attachment is presented, in which kāma (or desire for selfish gains) also plays a crucial role (II.62-63) After narrating these fundamentals, Śrī Kṛṣṇa teaches the doctrine of *niṣkāma* karma or performance of svadharma without attachment to the fruits of one's action (II.47 and III.19).

14.6. The need to give up attachment and selfish desires can be viewed as a "negative" formulation of the teaching. On the "positive" side, Śrī Kṛṣṇa stresses the immense importance of samatva or even-mindedness in success or failure (II.38 and II.48) Also, corresponding to the above-mentioned chain of vices, the Gītā introduces a chain of virtues starting from mental discipline (or mental tapas) (II.64-65 and III.7) An enthusiastic implementation of the teaching imparted in stage one would enable one to attain both preyas and śreyas—meaning 'pleasant' and 'good', respectively, in the terminology of Kathopanisad. (One of these two terms—śreyas—occurs explicitly in the Gītā also, while the other term—preyas—is implicitly understood, although not occurring explicitly.)

14.7. The second stage of the teaching, dealing with Lokasaṁgraha (or the social goal), is introduced by Śrī Kṛṣṇa on His own initiative in verses III.20 to III.26. As compared to the first stage, the goal is obviously widened, from individual śreyas to social harmony and welfare, and further extending to world preservation, following Śrī Kṛṣṇa's own example given in the Gītā. Perhaps the most effective message conveyed to Arjuna was that he should take into account as to how his action or inaction would affect the society and the world, not merely his own self or his svajanaṁ or own people.

14.8. Side by side with the widening of goals and the placing of a new emphasis on social responsibility, the framework for sorting out questions of dharma is also modified, although the fundamental teaching of *niṣkāma* karma remains intact as a "method of work". Corresponding to the chain of misery starting from attachment (introduced in stage one), we now have a chain of hatred and ill-will in society, starting from egotism (ahaṁkāra) (XVI.18-19) Similarly, whereas mental discipline (or mental tapas) marks the beginning of a chain of virtues in stage one, virtues like compassion and friendliness towards all are highlighted in stage two (XI.55, XII.13, V. 25) Furthermore, although the term 'svadharma' can be used to denote the "content of duty", in a broad sense, in both the stages, the actual connotation and coverage of svadharma has to be much wider in stage two, as compared to stage one. This is further explained in paras 14.40-44.

14.9. A similar observation (but having a more interesting implication) can be made with the term 'samatva', which, when used in the context of śreyas, means "even-mindedness in all situations" (II.48, VI.8) Although the same term 'samatva' is used in the context of Lokasaṁgraha, its new meaning is "even-mindedness towards all people" (VI.9, V.18) The ability to achieve samatva of the second category is designated as practically behaving like God, who looks upon all creatures with an equal eye (V.19) That is why, Śrī Kṛṣṇa gives His own example and says: If I should cease to work for Lokasaṁgraha, all these worlds would fall in ruin and I would be the creator of disordered life and destroy these peoples (III.24). There is an obvious reference here to the 'social dimension' of dharma, whereas the initial confusion of Arjuna about his dharma (II.7) represented mainly the 'individual dimension'. The social dimension of dharma is again highlighted in the verse IV.8, when one of the purposes of God's incarnation, Avatāra, is declared to be the establishment of dharma.

TEN ASPECTS OF KARMA FOR UPDATED LOKASAṀGRAHA

14.10. The above-mentioned summarization of the main differences between the two stages of Śrī Kṛṣṇa's teaching can be viewed as an internal appeal for focusing attention on Lokasaṁgraha. However, as soon as the concept of social responsibility was brought home to leaders of social movements, details of the appropriate action programmes were thought of, so as to suit the prevailing circumstances. In other words, Lokasaṁgraha became a rallying point for obtaining mass support for social causes, and the internal appeal for Lokasaṁgraha was re-inforced by what happened in the external world. The life and work of socio-spiritual leaders and political activists contributed a lot to bring before the people and the thinkers the Gīta-message of Lokasaṁgraha—perhaps with more meanings attached thereto than those specifically mentioned in the Gītā. For example, Vivekananda made 'social service' an integral part of the work-programme of the Ramakrishna Mission. Tilak explained at length why Lokasaṁgraha-centred Karma-yoga was the main teaching of the Gītā, and when he acted accordingly to win the country's independence, leading to his imprisonment, he willingly went through the sufferings. Aurobindo elaborated this further and incorporated the Lokasaṁgraha-approach (with some modification) in his Integral Yoga also.

14.11. Gandhi, on the basis of his extensive experiments, made non-violence an essential prerequisite for Lokasaṁgraha. In other words, the concept of Lokasaṁgraha was 'updated' so as to suit the changing socio-political needs of the country. And it was because of such updating—and possibilities of further modifications in the future if the need arose—that the Lokasaṁgraha ideal attracted so much attention. Obviously, the potentially dynamic nature of this ideal motivated people to participate in Lokasaṁgraha-oriented work-programmes in all directions.

14.12. But what does 'karma for updated Lokasaṁgraha' stand for? As many as ten aspects of such karma have been identified in the present study, using the views of activists and scholars (and also of the author of this study):

(i) Productive aspect
(ii) Protective aspect
(iii) Stability aspect
(iv) Service aspect
(v) Self-help aspect
(vi) Responsibility aspect
(vii) Niṣkāma aspect
(viii) Ethical aspect

(ix) Cohesive aspect
(x) Educative aspect

Brief statements about the significance of each aspect follow.

14.13. In a poor country like India, Lokasaṁgraha would remain an empty dream if basic needs like food, nutrition, clothing, shelter, health and education, are not fulfilled. The best way of doing this would be to ensure that able-bodied persons of working age have productive and useful work in their hands. If the productivity aspect of karma is ignored, the society would be ruined. Of course it is true that man does not live by bread alone, but it is equally true, as Sri Ramakrishna said, that "religion is not for empty bellies."[1] Gandhi's Constructive Programme included productive activities like Khādī and village industries, which became a symbol of the Swadeshi spirit.

14.14. The Gītā's support for productive activities is by no means confined to the fulfilment of basic needs only. Artha or wealth is recognized as a legitimate goal provided it is achieved by just means—i.e. in accordance with dharma, and also if it is not accompanied with arrogance, misuse or waste. (XVI.12-17) Śrī Kṛṣṇa tells Arjuna in verse XI.33: enjoy a prosperous kingdom. And in the closing verse of the Gītā (XVIII.78), Sañjaya associates fortune as well as morality with the presence, jointly, of Śrī Kṛṣṇa and Arjuna. Using the terminology of Kathopaniṣad, we can say that the Gītā links 'preyas' with 'dharma'—preyas including both Artha and Kāma (pleasure), that is, two of the four Puruṣārthās (the other two Puruṣārthās being Dharma and Mokṣa) Just as the Gītā regulates Artha through Dharma, it regulates Kāma also through Dharma. (VII.11)

14.15. The protective and world-preservative aspect of karma for Lokasaṁgraha is highlighted by Śrī Kṛṣṇa when he says that, if he were to cease such work, the Lokas as well as the people would be destroyed (II.24) While the divine spirit and the natural phenomena have created the proper environment for life in all forms to be sustained—that is, mankind, animals, birds, plants, sea-life—man-made threats in the form of nuclear weapons, chemical pollution, population explosion, indiscriminate tree-felling, excessive consumerism, careless habits causing waste and environmental degradation, etc. are becoming more and more serious, as stressed by Arapura.[2] The problems are undoubtedly vast but a co-ordinated effort to tackle the threats from all angles must be made before it is too late. Klostermaier has rightly described the Gītā as "a book of crisis",[3] and the Lokasaṁgraha-related teaching can help us make some contribution towards meeting the critical situation facing the society and the world.

14.16. To appreciate the stability aspect of Lokasaṁgraha, it is necessary to see how the Gītā, as interpreted by modern commentators, tries to strike a balance between tradition and change. Stability does not mean inflexibility or perpetuation of injustice, but, equally, the Gītā does not believe in creating confusion and disorder in the society, in an attempt to bring about changes too rapidly. Using the terminology of Bellah, India's response to the challenge of modernity can be called "reformism" which has been defined by Bellah as " a movement that re-interprets a particular religious tradition to show not only that it is compatible with modernization but also that, when truly understood, the tradition vigorously demands at least important aspects of modernity."[4] For example, the modern concept of "efficiency" can be linked to the Gītā's characterization of yoga as "karmasu kauśalaṁ." Similarly, "rationality" can be linked to "buddhi-yoga." However, while attaching great importance to buddhi-yoga, the Gita also warns (III.26) against creating "buddhī-bheda" or confusion which can arise when traditional beliefs and practices are subjected to unsympathetic argumentation. As Radhakrishnan says:

> Traditional forms charged with historical associations are the vehicles of unspoken convictions, though they may not be well understood. . . . It is true that every one should reach the highest level but this can be attained generally by slow steps and not by sudden jumps.[5]

14.17. An individualistic variant of the problem of instability which has become serious in modern times can be expressed in terms of psychological disbalance. In the chain of unhappiness mentioned in the Gītā, a crucial factor is unrealistic desires for personal benefits, which, when not matched by acquisitions, lead to frustration. In old days, family support and sympathy was a good healing factor, but excessive individualism, on the one hand, and traditional restrictions, on the other, offer little comfort for disturbed minds. In the ultimate analysis, family instability and social instability are inter-linked.

14.18. In order that social stability is understood in a comprehensive sense, Śrī Kṛṣṇa explains that things of beauty and splendour (that enrich the society culturally) constitute special revelations of the Divine (X.41) The use of the phrase "satyaṁ śivaṁ sundaraṁ" for identifying truth, goodness and beauty as attributes of perfection, should help remind us not to forget the role of art and culture in social development and stability.

14.19. Rendering of selfless service to the needy is a very important aspect of Lokasaṁgraha, and the phrase "sarvabhūtahite ratāḥ" meaning "persons who rejoice in doing good to all creatures" occurs twice in the Gītā (V.25, XII.4) Upadhyaya thinks that the message of selfless service to the world draws its inspiration from three sections of the Gītā, namely, (i) Lokasaṁgraha, (ii) divine origin of the world, and (iii) wheel of yajña or sacrifice:

> God himself is cited as an ideal who without any interest of his own is engaged in the work of maintaining the world-order. . . .
>
> As the origin of the world is traced to God, it becomes the duty of man to live in the world and promote its welfare. . . .
>
> The wheel of the world, according to the Gītā, goes on by means of sacrifice or renunciation, and one who does not discharge his selfless service to the world lives only in vain.[6]

14.20. The ideal of selfless service is also strengthened by bhakti-yoga, and the age-old tradition of saints moving from place to place, preaching the gospel of love and human brotherhood, and providing a concrete demonstration thereof by their own deeds. Vivekananda also linked this ideal with his new interpretation of Vedānta, which he called 'practical Vedānta'. It was through his initiative, pursued against the escapist attitudes of the traditionalists, that the Ramakrishna Mission identified service to the needy as worship of the Divine. While describing how Vivekananda was able to give this new orientation to Hinduism in the last decade of the nineteenth century, Ursula King also mentions that he (Vivekananda) even extended the social service idea to the bodhisattva ideal of giving priority to the salvation of others before one's own: "The karma-yogī wants everyone to be saved before himself. His only salvation is to help others to salvation. . . This true worship leads to intense self-sacrifice."[7]

14.21. Although in the interest of those who are in a position to help others, Vivekananda advised them to do their utmost, but with humility, still from the viewpoint of the recipients of such service, and also in general, he stressed the importance of self-help and self-confidence. He called 'self-help' as the 'greatest lesson' given by the Gītā-verse VI.5. Similarly, the main idea behind Gandhi's Khādī-programme was that the poor villagers, instead of feeling helpless and asking for charity, should stand on their own feet.

14.22. While clarifying the ideal of Lokasaṁgraha to Arjuna, Śrī Kṛṣṇa explained in verse III.24, 'If I do not act, the world would be ruined'. Dandekar discerns therein a strong emphasis on 'social obligations'.[8] Any person following Śrī Kṛṣṇa's example will need to ask himself or herself: what will be the impact of my action or inaction on the society? Vivekananda illustrated this by pointing out the 'responsibility' of mothers to ensure that, by leading a 'pure life', they would give birth to healthy babies.[9]

14.23. The most appropriate meaning of 'niṣkāma' in the context of Lokasaṁgraha is 'to have no selfish desires'. Tilak has clarified that the Gītā does not envisage the giving up of all desires—only desires for selfish gains are to be given up.[10] It is a sort of a reminder that the basic teaching of the Gītā that all actions should be performed without attachment to the fruit thereof, applies equally to Lokasaṁgraha'. In Tilak's words: " . . . a man should not entertain the proud or desireful thought that 'I shall bring about Lokasaṁgraha' . . .a man has to bring about Lokasaṁgraha merely as a duty".[11]

14.24. Karma for Lokasaṁgraha has to be such as may 'wean people from the tendency to take to the path of wrong', using Śaṁkara's definition. Vinoba also stresses the need to keep the people on the right path. For this, action itself has to be morally right. When verse III.21 speaks of setting an example, the ethical aspect of karma is implicit in it. Kaveeshwar argues that sometimes, "giving up the desire for selfish gains" might not be enough to guarantee that the action itself is morally right, and that therefore the right-wrong consideration of an action should not be relegated to a secondary stage.[12] Another argument in support of the ethical content of karma is that an avatāra (God's incarnation) works for re-establishing righteousness, by supporting the good and by punishing the evil (IV.8) Fighting against evil and injustice is thus a part of karma for Lokasaṁgraha, and the possibility of doing this by peaceful means (as attempted by Gandhi) re-inforces the ethical principle.

14.25. Panikkar attaches great importance to the way Gandhi modified Tilak's approach to Lokasaṁgraha, namely, that whereas Tilak applied only the criterion of 'unselfishness', Gandhi added thereto the criterion of Ahiṁsā' or non-violence as well.[13] This has a great practical significance, because even the so-called 'terriorists' while killing innocent people, claim to be completely unselfish. Although they might satisfy Tilak's criterion, they cannot meet Gandhi's standards, and so cannot pass off as Lokasaṁgraha-activists.

14.26. Karma for Lokasaṁgraha has to fulfill the basic purpose of keeping people together, not by force but voluntarily. As a prerequisite for this, grievances of one group of people against another have to be looked into, and resolved in such a manner as not to disrupt social unity and harmony. Reducing gross inequalities in the distribution of wealth by peaceful means would form part of this. A legal approach can have only a limited role in achieving this. A non-official mechanism for resolving disputes peacefully also needs to be considered. These are big issues for which easy solutions do not exist. But tendencies to foment hatred and rivalry have to be discouraged. The Gītā has warned against getting entangled in a chain of hatred rooted in ahaṁkāra. (XVI.18-19)

14.27. Since karma for Lokasaṁgraha is absolutely voluntary, the only possible way to give it the form of a mass movement is by creating favourable public opinion. Furthermore, some of the underlying concepts like the preservation of a clean environment can be conveyed even to children in an appropriate manner. Both of these actions—which are only illustrative—are included in the general term "educative" which constitutes an important aspect of karma for Lokasaṁgrah.

TWO KURUKṢETRAS FOR EVERY INDIVIDUAL

14.28. Gandhi gave a symbolic interpretation to Kurukṣetra when he wrote that "under the guise of physical warfare, the Gītā describes the deal that perpetually goes on in the hearts of mankind."[14] This inward-looking interpretation (according to which every human heart is a Kurukṣetra) can be extended outward so as to assume a social dimension. According to such an extended, symbolic interpretation, Kurukṣetra could refer to a battle between the divine and demoniac elements in the society. Chapter XVI of the Gītā lends support to this society-centred meaning of Kurukṣetra (XVI.2, 9, etc.) When Tilak applied the Gītā to the socio- political struggle for swaraj, he stated that not only one's immediate field of activity but the whole of India is the dharmakṣetra of modern Indians.[15] Panikkar finds this extended interpretation of Kurukṣetra to be of great significance when he says: "Hindu Reformation. . . was indeed a significant fact, but it would have remained basically a religious movement but for the rediscovery of the Bhagavad-Gītā as the political and social gospel of Hindu India."[16] In relation to the two-stage exposition of Śrī Kṛṣṇa's teaching (referred to in paras 14.4-9), the Lokasaṁgraha component of the teaching goes hand-in-hand with the society-centred meaning of Kurukṣetra.

LINKS BETWEEN AN INDIVIDUAL AND OTHER MEMBERS OF SOCIETY

14.29. After telling Arjuna of the importance of having Lokasaṁgraha as an important goal of life, Śrī Kṛṣṇa also advises him about setting an example to others by his own conduct. (II.21) The underlying teaching here is that mere theoretical knowledge about what is good and what is real is not enough unless this knowledge is reflected in one's conduct. Furthermore, in order to bring about a unity of purpose and cooperative effort in society for a just cause, Śrī Kṛṣṇa asks the men of knowledge not to be content by their own actions, but also to encourage others to act as well (II.26). Obviously, the idea is not to push people around, against their will; nor is it to perpetuate their ignorance. The plea is in favour of a slow and steady effort to educate common people and to encourage them to follow voluntarily the example of the wise. Ultimately, each individual has to choose one's own path, as the Gītā teaches in verse VI.5 which says that: "Let a man lift himself by himself; let him not degrade himself, for the self alone is the friend of the self, and the self alone is the enemy of the self." In this way, without endangering individual rights, a suggestion is made to a man of knowledge to put in his efforts for Lokasaṁgraha, not only in regard to the material needs of the common people but also for their intellectual and spiritual advancement.

14.30. Cooperative effort for achieving the good of all is viewed in the Gītā as a Yajña—a Vedic term given new meanings, of which one mentioned in the first part of this sentence was extensively made use of for Lokasaṁgraha-activities.17 'Fostering each other, you shall attain the supreme śreyas' (III.11)—this path leading to śreyas, which originally envisages cooperation between human beings and gods, was interpreted by modern commentators as being applicable to all the members of the society. Similarly, the ancient practice of ' Dānaṁ' or charity was interpreted, following Saṁkara, as 'saṁvibhāgaḥ' or equal division or sharing. Vinoba applied this idea to obtain voluntary donation of land, and thus evolved an important Lokasaṁgraha-activity from a traditionally religious concept.[18] Finally, out of the famous trio—yajñā-dānaṁ-tapas—the ancient practice of tapas or austerity, became, in Gandhi's Satyāgraha an important source of strength for a social cause, because a new meaning—'willingness to suffer the consequences of Civil disobedience'—was associated with tapas.[19] In this way, a strong Lokasaṁgraha-orientation was given to each of the three elements which have traditionally had mainly religious connotations.

JÑĀNA INCOMPLETE WITHOUT LOKASAṀGRAHA

14.31. In pre-Tilak days, the Gītā-commentary of Śaṁkara, highlighting the crucial role of Jñāna, was largely viewed as representing the real meaning of this scripture. Sāttvika jñāna is defined in the Gītā (XVIII.20) as the knowledge by which the one Imperishable Being is seen in all existences, undivided in the divided. Followers of Śaṁkara believed that, after the acquisition of true knowledge, karma or social duties could be given up. However, new interpretations given by Vivekananda, Tilak, Aurobindo and others, stressed the importance of 'karma for Lokasaṁgraha', for all including those who have acquired knowledge.

14.32. Regarding the method of acquiring knowledge, Śrī Kṛṣṇa tells Arjuna, (among other things): Learn the knowledge by humble reverence, by inquiry and by service (IV.34) Humility is stressed not only for a seeker of knowledge, but also in describing the conduct of a jñānin. In fact, verses XII.7 to 11 widen the scope of jñāna so as to include the practice of as many as twenty virtues, headed by "amānitvaṁ" (or freedom from vanity), and including non-violence, forgiveness, absence of ahaṁkāra or egotism, and so on.

14.33. The importance of nirahaṁkāra or absence of egotism is stressed in the Gītā in many contexts, so much so that the phrase "nirmamo nirahaṁkāraḥ"—literally meaning "giving up mineness and egotism"—practically denotes the achievement of perfection—through karma, bhakti, or jñāna. According to Vinoba, this phrase also indicates one working for Lokasaṁgraha. As Vinoba explains:

> Nirmamo means he has no selfish desires. Nirahaṁkāraḥ means that he has dedicated all his actions to Īśvara and he does not regard himself as the doer. But still he puts in his best effort in whatever he does. What can he do other than Lokasaṁgraha? In fact, he lives only in order to benefit humanity.

14.34. The linkage between Jñāna and Lokasaṁgraha is stressed by saying that a man of knowledge is even-minded towards all people, friend and foe alike, and he also rejoices in doing good to all (sarvabhūtahite ratāḥ) (V.18-19, VI.9) Sarma observes that, prior to the time of the Gītā, jñāna often had a renunciatory connotation because it was coupled with karma-saṁnyāsa or physical renunciation of karma. By coupling jñāna with Lokasaṁgraha, the Gītā presented a more balanced and realistic view and helped integrate jñāna with dharma and hence with society:

> The Gītā supplied a much-needed corrective to the over-emphasis on jñāna and renunciation, which had led to mere quietism. It may be said that the whole Gītā is a long and sustained protest against the dangers of quietism. . . The unique feature of jñāna, as taught in the Gītā, is that it is never divorced from service to society.[21]

BHAKTI ORIENTED TO SERVICE OF SOCIETY

14.35. Those who interpret bhakti in a narrow sense, often consider its main feature to be "telling of beads and the like, but not getting involved with the worries of the world." However, Śrī Kṛṣṇa clearly indicates in the Gītā that a bhakta carries out his normal duties in the world (VIII.7, VI.31), has no ill will towards any being, and is friendly and compassionate to all (XII.13) Tilak clarifies the social dimensions of bhakti in the Gītā:

> If a man seeks unity with the Deity, he must necessarily seek unity with the interests of the world also, and work for it. If he does not, then the unity is not perfect, because there is union between two elements out of the three (man and Deity), and the third (the world) is left out.[22]

14.36. Those who follow the bhakti-mārga of the Gītā, oriented to social concerns as indicated above, can do a lot for bringing about a sense of harmony and unity in the society, because Śrī Kṛṣṇa recognizes no distinctions of race, sex, caste, or method of worship (IX.29—32) When Gandhi was confronted by orthodox Hindus and asked to quote scriptural authority supporting the abolition of untouchability, he referred to verse IX.32. Gandhi's prayer meetings included recitation of hymns from the scriptures of the various religions—including the Gītā and the Kurān. The chanting of God's names—called the highest Yajña in the Gītā (X.25)—was the most popular part, and Gandhi specifically added 'Allah' along with the Hindu names so as to make it acceptable to the Muslims. This was a practical step taken to try to bring about social harmony and unity through religious tolerance, the basis of which was the verse IV.11 of the Gītā: "As men approach Me, so do I accept them; men of all sides follow My path, O Arjuna". (IV.11)

14.37. Although shraddhā (faith) is the basis of bhakti, verse X.10 also connects buddhi-yoga with bhakti. Sarma sees in this an attempt to dissociate bhakti from superstition:

> Buddhi-yoga implies equanimity or evenness of mind, an attitude of detachment, freedom from error or delusion, and ability to rise above the mere letter of the books. In short, it is the preliminary discipline of the mind, . . . without which karma-yoga would result only in rash action, bhakti-yoga in superstitious worship, and jñāna-yoga in vague abstractions.[23]

14.38. Furthermore, verses XVIII.54 to 57 (which again refer to buddhi-yoga), characterize supreme devotion to God as being synonymous to "regarding all beings as alike" which, in the Gītā, is the commonest way of implicitly referring to Lokasaṁgraha. In popular language we have the well-known Indian dictum conveying the same idea, namely, that "Mānava sevā is Mādhava sevā, that is, that service of man is service of God."

14.39. One of the closing verses of the Gītā (XVIII.66), which many Bhaktas consider to be the 'carama śLoka' (i.e. the key verse), enunciates the doctrine of 'saṁpūrṇa-samarpaṇaṁ' or 'samarpaṇaṁ of sarvadharmān'. Aurobindo has written extensively about this, which he calls 'surrender to God without reservations'. The main conclusion of Aurobindo is that the "almighty Power will take up our virtue and sin, our right and wrong, our strength and our weakness, cast away their tangled figures, sarvadharmān parityajya, and transform all into its transcendent purity and universal good and infallible force. . . ."[24] Obviously, 'universal good' or Lokasaṁgraha is highlighted in Aurobindo's interpretation of 'saṁpūrṇa-samarpaṇaṁ'.

SVADHARMA, MAT-KARMA AND LOKASAṀGRAHA

14.40. It could be considered a coincidence that Arjuna's svadharma (of fighting a battle against the evil forces for re-establishing the rule of the ligitimate king) went hand-in-hand with Lokasaṁgraha (provided that svadharma was performed with samatva) But the concept of svadharma has to be considered in general, not confined to Arjuna. On the question as to whether svadharma would, in general, include the "service aspect" of Lokasaṁgraha, opinions differ. Radhakrishnan says that it may or may not, depending on one's nature—and, of course, circumstances.[25] However, Vinoba takes an idealist interpretation and says that service of neighbours would naturally become a part of one's duty as one grows in full awareness of one's role in the community.[26] In any case, a linkage between svadharma and the "stability aspect" of Lokasaṁgraha is always possible, because each member of a society, carrying on one's limited duties to the best of one's ability, can help maintain the social order, while fulfilling one's own legitimate goals.

14.41. The Gītā assures the attainment of perfection through the performance of one's duties as a worship of the Supreme (XVIII.45-46). Another term used in the Gītā for denoting the Bhakti-input in karma is: dedicating one's acts to God—or karma-samarpaṇaṁ. This is a relatively easy way to avoid feelings of self-importance which an ordinary human being, engaged in Lokasaṁgraha-activities, might normally have. This way of harmonizing karma-yoga and bhakti-yoga, highlighted in the Gītā-verse IX.27 (and several other verses), was often referred to by Gandhi and Vinoba.

14.42. In an important verse (XI.55), which, according to Śaṁkara, summarizes the Gītā-teaching, Śrī Kṛṣṇa asks Arjuna to do "Mat-karma" or "My work". Although many commentators interpret this as referring to karma-samarpaṇaṁ, perhaps an equally appropriate interpretation of "Mat-karma" would be "to do God's work". Examples of Janaka and Śrī Kṛṣṇa have been cited in the Gītā, to clarify the meaning of Lokasaṁgraha. Tilak's suggestion is in conformity with this: "The Gītā asks us to work in imitation of the Lord, for the purpose of Lokasaṁgraha or the good of the society—the unification of humanity in universal sympathy."[27]

14.43. Although Gandhi and Vinoba feel that svadharma interpreted as hereditary function does not imply a narrow, rigid approach, there are critics like Pillai who see in the varṇa-based svadharma an early form of the caste system, which (in Pillai's opinion) has brought ruin to India.[28] Radhakrishnan tries to soften such criticism by arguing that varṇa in the Gītā depended not on birth but on qualities and functions.[29] Sarma gives an individualistic interpretation by saying that svadharma is linked with svabhāva (that is, one's nature)[30] Tilak feels that the karma-yoga teaching of the Gītā can be dissociated from varṇa, and linked primarily with Lokasaṁgraha,—a concept operating in the wider framework of the society as a whole, without the varṇa-based compartments.[31]

14.44. Upadhyaya too (although he is critical of the varṇa system) believes that admiration traditionally shown for followers of svadharma was because of their contribution to Lokasaṁgraha:

> Despite its advocacy of hereditary professions, the Gita makes no mention of the intrinsic superiority or inferiority of any profession. It rather emphasizes that man attains perfection devoted each to his own duty. It is further said that all actions are associated with (more or less) defects as fire by smoke. This idea is conveyed more explicitly in the Mahābhārata in the course of the dialogue between the Brāhmin and the meat-seller, wherein the latter, who discharges his duty devotedly for the good of others is not only defended but is considered superior to the Brāhmin practising penance for his own selfish purpose.[32]

ŚREYAS AND LOKASAṀGRAHA

14.45. Mokṣa or śreyas, the ultimate goal of life, is depicted in the Gītā through descriptions of the characteristics of those who have achieved perfection either by karma-yoga, or bhakti or jñāna or, (as interpreted by Aurobindo) by a harmonious synthesis of all these. The fact that each of these siddhapuruṣas (perfect men) while still alive, acts for Lokasaṁgraha is conveyed by describing him (among other things) as "samaḥ sarveṣu bhūteṣu" (even-minded towards all people). Since the journey to śreyas thus passes through Lokasaṁgraha, these two goals are said to be 'harmonized'. As Gandhi put it:

> For me the road to salvation lies through incessant toil in the service of my country and humanity. I want to identify myself with every thing that lives. I want to live at peace with both friend and foe. So my patriotism is for me a stage on my journey to the land of eternal freedom and pece.[33]

14.46. Vivekananda coined the famous phrase "ātmano mokṣārthaṁ jagaddhitāya ca", meaning that followers of Śrī Ramakrishna should realize that the two goals—one's salvation and the good of the world—were being simultaneously achieved through the work-programme of Practical Vedānta. Some of his own colleagues protested against this approach, but Vivekananda's deep conviction won them over. In the terminology of the present study, an alternative version conveying the same meaning as Vivekananda's phrase could be "ātmanaḥ śreyorthaṁ Lokasaṁgrahāya ca".

14.47. There is, however, an important difference between the state of striving for mokṣa and the state after the attainment of mokṣa, in regard to "why" one carries on Lokasaṁgraha activities. In the former state (of striving), such acts are done because of a sense of duty, whereas in the latter state (of perfection), such acts become natural or spontaneous. Radhakrishnan interprets the Gītā-verse VI.3 to lend support to this.[34] Desai finds this spontaneity described also in a song of Kabīr which says:

> For me this state of samādhi (complete immersion in the

Absolute) has become natural. Whatever I do is sevā (service), whatever I hear is God's name, whatever I eat or drink is pūjā (God's worship)[35]

MULTIPLE INSTANCES OF HARMONIZATION

14.48. "Harmonization" is an important concept to understand the approach of the Gītā. We have, in this study, mentioned not only the harmonization of śreyas and Lokasaṁgraha, but also four other instances of harmonization, and it will be useful to list them together in one place, as we do below:

(i) Pravṛtti (karma-kāṇḍa or activism) and Nivṛtti (jñāna-kāṇḍa or quietism or renunciation) harmonized into karma-yoga

(ii) Karma-yoga and bhakti-yoga harmonized into karma-samarpaṇaṁ (dedicating actions along with fruits to God)

(iii) Karma, bhakti and Jñāna harmonized into the final teaching of the Gita, namely "brahmavidyāyāṁ yogaśāstra". In popular language this is compared to Triveṇī (confluence of three rivers, Gaṅgā, Yamunā, Saraswatī, at Prayāga)

(iv) Harmonization of preyas and śreyas (the pleasant and the good)—the word 'śreyas' being used to denote 'dharma' as well as mokṣa, as suggested by Mishra.

(v) Harmonization of śreyas and Lokasaṁgraha (the good of the individual and the good of the society)

An application of the harmonizing approach of the Gītā to the goals—preyas, śreyas, and Lokasaṁgraha—can be viewed as a special feature of our study, because the general tendency so far has been to look into the details of how only the means—karma, bhakti, and jñāna—have been harmonized.

14.49. A practical lesson, that was expected to contribute to smooth relations in a complex society like that of India, and which Lokasaṁgraha-activists wanted people to learn from the harmonizing approach of the Gītā was: "Do not have a narrow, exclusive vision." Śrī Kṛṣṇa calls them unwise who are "nānyadastīti vādinaḥ", that is, "who say that there is nothing other than this". (II.42) Similarly, one of the characteristic features of tamas buddhi is "Kṛtsnavadekasmin", that is, "to consider only one view as if it were the whole". (XVIII.22) Only by means of such an open-minded approach did the Gītā succeed in bringing together so many divergent views, and in evolving out of them an harmonized way to attain both śreyas and Lokasaṁgraha. As Radhakrishnan puts it:

> The different elements which, at the period of the composition of the Gītā, were competing with each other within the Hindu system, are brought together and integrated into a comprehensive synthesis, free and large, subtle and profound. The teacher refines and reconciles the different currents of thought, the Vedic cult of sacrifice, the Upaniṣad teaching of the transcendent Brahman, the Bhāgavata theism and tender piety, the Sāṁkhya dualism and the Yoga meditation. He draws all these elements of Hindu life and thought into an organic unity. He adopts the method, not of denial but of penetration and shows how these different lines of thought converge towards the same end. . .[36]
>
> The Gītā gives us not only a philosophical interpretation, brahmavidyā, but also a practical programme, yogaśāstra. Our world is not a spectacle to contemplate; it is a field of battle. Only for the Gītā improvement in the individual nature is the way to social betterment.[37]

SUMMING UP

14.50. Finally, the answer to the question posed in para 14.1 can, in the interest of clarity, be summed up very briefly: the Lokasaṁgraha-ideal of the Gītā, elaborated, modified and updated to suit the changing socio-political needs, proved to be such a strong source of inspiration for millions of Indians that they voluntarily participated in a revolutionary process that brought about all-round change and development to a significant extent. The Lokasaṁgraha-teaching of the Gītā had cited the examples of Janaka and Śrī Kṛṣṇa. Ursula King has rightly observed that additional, new examples (like that of Gandhi) "are a sign of the creativity of Hinduism and of its religious activity, sensitive to the needs of modern men".[38] It is because of possibilities of further 'updating and modifactions if necessary' that Lokasaṁgraha emerged as 'a potentially dynamic social ideal' carrying a strong appeal.

Notes

PART ONE

CHAPTER ONE

1. Robert N. Bellah, "Epilogue", in Religion and Progress in Modern Asia, ed. by him. Free Press, New York, 1965, p. 215.
2. Suttee (or sati) was a Hindu custom according to which a widow burnt herself to death with the body of her dead husband. Rammohun Roy worked for suttee-abolition.
3. Brahmo Samaj was a religious organization set up by Rammohun Roy as a part of his effort to bring about religious reform.
4. Ainslie T. Embree (ed.), The Hindu Tradition, Random House, New York, 1972, p. 279.
5. E.J. Sharpe, The Universal Gita; Western Images of the Bhagavad Gita, A Bicentenary Survey. La Salle: Open Court, 1985, p. 14.
6. The Age of Consent Bill, 1891 was intended to put legal restrictions on child marriages.
7. Ainslie T. Embree (ed.), The Hindu Tradition, op. cit., p. 299.
8. Romain Rolland, The Life of Ramakrishna. Advaita Ashrama, Calcuta, eighth edition, 1970, p. 142.
9. Ainslie T. Embree (ed.), The Hindu Tradition, op. cit., p. 301.
10. Romain Rolland, The Life of Ramakrishna, op. cit., p. 151.
11. Ibid., pp. 151-2.
12. Ainslie T. Embree (ed.), The Hindu Tradition, op. cit., p. 301.
13. Romanin Rolland, The Life of Ramakrishna, op. cit. p. 85.
14. Romain Rolland, The Life of Vivekananda and the Universal Gospel. Advaita Ashrama, Calcutta, seventh impression, 1970, p. 285.
15. Quoted by D.V. Tahmankar, Lokamanya Tilak, Father of Indian Unrest and Maker of Modern India, John Murray, London, 1956, p.62.
16. K.M. Panikkar, The Foundations of New India. Allen and Unwin, London, 1963, p. 36.
17. Ursula King, "Who is the Ideal Karmayogin ? The Meaning of a Hindu Religious Symbol". In Religion, vol. X, Spring 1980, p. 43.
18. Ibid., p. 44.
19. K.M. Panikkar, The Foundations of New India, op. cit., p. 44.

CHAPTER TWO

1. Brahmo Samaj, Leaders of the Brahmo Samaj. Natesan and Co., Madras,

1926, p. 6.
2. Ibid., p.9.
3. D.S. Sarma, The Renaissance of Hinduism. Banaras Hindu University, 1944, p. 74.
4. Brahmo Samaj, Leaders of the Brahmo Samaj, op. cit., p.11.
5. Ibid., p. 63.
6. Quoted by Arvind Sharma (with A. Ray, A. Hejib and K. Young). Sati—Historical and Phenomenological Essays, Motilal Banarsidass, Delhi, 1988, p. 27.
7. Ibid., p. 29.
8. Benoy Bhushan Roy, Socio-economic Impact of Sati in Bengal and the Role of Raja Rammohun Roy. Naya Prokash, Calcutta, 1987, pp. 26-7.
10. P.V. Kane, History of Dharmashastra. Poona, 1941, vol. II, part I, pp. 635-6.
11. Quoted by Benoy Bhushan Roy, Socio-economic Impact of Sati, op. cit., p. 78.
12. Ibid., p. 78.
13. Ibid., pp. 78-9.
14. Ibid., p. 92.
15. Ibid., p. 92.
16. Max Muller has pointed out that an unscrupulous priest in Medieval times purposely distorted the meaning of the Rig-Veda verse by changing agre to agne. Agre means "sitting in front"; Agne means "O Fire !". See Arvind Sharma, Sati—Historical and Phenomenological Essays, op. cit., pp. 63-4.
17. Arvind Sharma, Sati, op. cit., p. 64.
18. K. Nag and D. Burman (eds.), The English Works of Raja Rammohun Roy. Sadharan Brahmo Samaj, Calcutta, 1945, p. 91.
19. Ibid., p. 92.
20. Ibid., p. 93.
21. Ibid., p. 94.
22. Ibid., p. 93.
23. Ibid., p. 105.
24. Ibid., pp. 105-6.
25. Arvind Sharma (with A. Ray, A. Hejib and K. Young) Sati, op. cit., pp. 75-81.
26. Ibid., p. 94.
27. Ibid., p. 83.
28. K. Nag and D. Burman (eds.), The English Works of Raja Rammohun Roy, op. cit., p. 120.
29. Ibid., p. 96.
30. Ibid., p. 96.
31. Ibid., p. 97.
32. Ibid., p. 111.
33. Ibid., p. 112.
34. Ibid., p. 111.
35. Ibid., p. 134.
36. Ibid., p. 111.

37. Ibid., pp. 112-3.
38. Ibid., p. 113.
39. Ibid., p. 134.
40. Ibid., p. 114.
41. Ibid., p. 116.
42. Ibid., pp. 125-6.
43. Ibid., p. 117.
44. Ibid., p. 115.
45. Ibid., p. 117.
46. Arvind Sharma (with A. Ray, A. Hejib and K. Young), Sati, op. cit., p.44.
47. Ibid., p. 44.
48. Ibid., p. 45.
49. Benoy Bhushan Roy, Socio-economic Impact of Sati, op.cit., p. 117.
50. K. Nag and D. Burman (eds.), The English Works of Raja Rammohun Roy, op. cit., p. 134.
51. Benoy Bhushan Roy, Socio-economic Impact of Sati, op. cit., pp. 108-9.
52. Brahmo Samaj, Leaders of the Brahmo Samaj, op. cit., p. 54.
53. Robert N. Bellah, Religion and Progress in Modern Asia, op. cit., p. 215.
54. Ainslie T. Embree (ed.), The Hindu Tradition, op. cit., p. 279.
55. Arvind Sharma, "The Gita, Suttee and Rammohun Roy", in Indian Economic and Social History Review, vol.XX, No.3 (1983), pp. 341-7.
56. Arvind Sharma, (with A. Ray, A. Hejib and K. Young), Sati, op. cit., p. 72.
57. E. J. Sharpe, The Universal Gita, op. cit., p. 14.
58. The Lokasamgraha-verses of the Gita are III.20-6.
59. M.N.Jha, Modern Indian Political Thought: Rammohun Roy to Present Day. Meenakshi Prakashan, Meerut, 1975, p. 14,.

CHAPTER THREE

1. Romain Rolland, The Life of Ramakrishna, op. cit., p. 222.
2. Ibid., p. 223-4.
3. Ibid., p. 226.
4. Ibid, p. 228.
5. Swami Nikhilananda, Vivekananda: A Biography. Advaita Ashrama, Mayavati, third edition, 1975, p. 16.
6. Romain Rolland, The Life of Ramakrishna, op. cit., pp. 228-9.
7. R.C. Majumdar, Swami Vivekananda: A Historical Review. General Printers, Calcutta, 1965, p. 13.
8. Romian Rolland, The Life of Ramakrishna, op. cit., pp. 84-5.
9. Ibid., p. 85.
10. Ibid., p. 230.
11. Ibid., p. 231.
12. Ibid., p. 234.
13. R.C. Majumdar, Swami Vivekananda: A Historical Review, op. cit., pp. 18-9.

14. Ibid., pp. 19-20.
15. Indira Patel, Vivekananda's Approach to Social Work. Sri Ramakrishna Math, Madras, 1987, p.1.
16. R.C. Majumdar, Swami Vivekananda: A Historical Review, op. cit., pp. 20-1.
17. Romain Rolland, The Life of Ramakrishna, op.cit., pp. 258-9.
18. R.C. Majumdar, Swami Vivekananda: A Historical Review, op. cit., p. 12.
19. D.S. Sarma, The Renaissance of Hinduism, op.cit., p. 265.
20. Romain Rolland, The Life of Vivekananda and the Universal Gospel, op. cit., p. 21.
21. Swami Vivekananda, Complete Works. (eight volumes). Advaita Ashrama, Calcutta, fourteenth edition, 1972, vol.V, p. 441.
22. R.C. Majumdar, Swami Vivekananda: A Historical Review, op. cit., p. 121.
23. Ibid., p. 132.
24. Ibid., p. 132.
25. Ibid., p. 115.
26. Swami Vivekananda, Complete Works, op. cit., vol. III, pp. 220-2.
27. Ibid., vol. IV, p. 405.
28. Seminar on Swami Vivekananda's Teaching. Sri Ramakrishna Vidyalaya, Coimbatore, 1964, p. 109.
29. Swami Vivekananda, Complete Works, op. cit., vol. V, p. 10.
30. Seminar on Swami Vivekananda's Teaching, op. cit., p. 98.
31. Swami Vivekananda, Complete Works, op. cit., vol.III, p. 301.
32. R.C. Majumdar, Swami Vivekananda: A Historical Review, op. cit., p. 132.
33. Swami Vivekananda, Complete Works, op. cit., vol. VI, pp. 450-2.
34. Ibid., vol. III, pp. 213-27.
35. Ibid., vol. VII, p. 163 and vol.III, p. 141.
36. Ibid., vol. III, pp. 142-3.
37. Ibid., vol. III, pp. 430-3.
38. Sri Krishna Prem, The Yoga of the Bhagavad Gita. Penguin Books, Baltimore, 1958, p. 217.
39. Swami Vivekananda, Complete Works, op. cit., vol. VII, p. 163.
40. Ibid., vol. III, p. 143.
41. Ibid., vol. III, p. 142.
42. Swami Vivekananda, Karmayoga, Advaita Ashrama, Calcutta, seventeenth impression, 1984, p. 91.
43. Ibid., p. 83.
44. Swami Vivekananda, Complete Works, op. cit., vol. III, p.133.
45. Ibid., vol. III, p. 432.
46. Ibid., vol. II, p. 140.
47. Ibid., vol. I, p. 478.
48. Ibid., vol. III, pp. 223-4.
49. Romain Rolland, The Life of Vivekananda and the Universal Gospel, op. cit., p. 286.
50. Ibid., p. 10.
51. Ibid., p. 285.
52. Swami Vivekananda, Karmayoga, op. cit., p. 72.
53. Swami Nikhilananda, Vivekananda: A Biography. op. cit., p. 236.

54. R.C. Majumdar, Swami Vivekananda: A Historical Review, op. cit., pp. 69-70.
55. Ibid., p. 71.
56. Swami Nikhilananda, Vivekananda: A Biography, op. cit., p. 244.
57. Ibid., p. 246.
58. Ibid., pp. 246-7.
59. Romain Rolland, The Life of Vivekananda and the Universal Gospel, op. cit., p. 166.
60. Ibid., pp. 324-5.
61. R.C. Majumdar, Swami Vivekananda: A Historical Review, op. cit., p. 111.
62. Life of Swami Vivekananda by his Eastern and Western Disciples. Advaita Ashrama, Calcutta, fifth edition, 1981, vol. II, p. 328.
63. R.C. Majumdar, Swami Vivekananda: A Historical Review, op. cit., p. 72.
64. Indira Patel, Vivekananda's Approach to Social Work, op. cit., p. 92.
65. Swami Vivekananda, Complete Works, op. cit., vol. VI, p. 504. This famous Sanskrit phrase was coined by Vivekananda to summarize the Karmayoga-based socio-spiritual approach to India's problems.
66. Ibid., vol. VI, pp. 504-5.
67. Ibid., vol. VIII, p. 89.
68. Ibid., vol. VI, pp. 511-2.
69. R.C. Majumdar, Swami Vivekananda: A Historical Review, op. cit., p. 41.
70. The "Karmayoga" publication proved to be the most popular written work of Vivekananda.
71. Swami Vivekananda, Complete Works, op. cit., vol. I, pp. 86-90.
72. Ibid., vol. I, p. 457.
73. Ibid., vol. I, p. 457.
74. Ibid., vol. I, p. 457.
75. Ibid., vol. I, p. 457.
76. Ibid., vol. I, p. 459-61.
77. Ibid., vol. I, p. 459-60.
78. Ibid., vol. I, p. 467-8.
79. Ibid., vol. I, p. 468.

CHAPTER FOUR

1. Stanley A. Wolpert, Tilak and Gokhale: Revolution and Reform in the Making of Modern India. University of California Press, 1962, p. 2.
2. D.V. Tahmankar, Lokamanya Tilak, op. cit., p. 11.
3. Ibid., p. 205.
4. Ibid., p. 24.
5. Ibid., p. 27.
6. T.V. Parvate, Bal Gangadhar Tilak. Navajivan, Ahmedabad, 1958, p. 23.
7. Stanley A. Wolpert, Tilak and Gokhale, op. cit., p. 29.
8. D.V. Tahmankar, Lokamanya Tilak, op. cit., p. 62.
9. Stanley A. Wolpert, Tilak and Gokhale, op. cit., p. 81.
10. Ainslie T. Embree (ed.) The Hindu Tradition, op. cit., p. 310.

11. D.S.Sarma, The Renaissance of Hinduism, op. cit., p.145.
12. Stanley A. Wolpert, Tilak and Gokhale, op. cit., p. 15.
13. D.V. Tahmankar, Lokamanya Tilak, op. cit., p. 253.
14. D.S. Sarma, The Renaissance of Hinduism, op. cit., p. 143.
15. K.M. Panikkar, The Foundations of New India, op. cit., p. 36.
16. T.V. Parvate, Bal Gangadhar Tilak, op. cit., p. 475.
17. Ibid., p. 477.
18. D.V. Tahmankar, Lokamanya Tilak, op. cit., pp. 49-50.
19. Ibid., p. 50.
20. Ibid., p. 50.
21. Stanley A. Wolpert, Tilak and Gokhale, op. cit., p. 302.
22. Arvind Sharma (with A. Ray, A. Hejib and K. Young), Sati, op. cit., pp. 43-8.
23. Ibid., p. 48.
24. Ibid., p. 46.
25. T.V. Parvate, Bal Gangadhar Tilak, op. cit., pp. 42-3.
26. D.P. Karmarkar, Bal Gangadhar Tilak: A Study. Popular Book Depot, Bombay, 1956, pp. 107-8.
27. Ibid., p. 111.
28. Stanley A. Wolpert, Tilak and Gokhale, op. cit., p. 101.
29. D.V. Tahmankar, Lokamanya Tilak, op. cit., Prelude.
30. Stanley A. Wolpert, Tilak and Gokhale, op. cit., pp. 96 and 259.
31. D. P. Karmarkar, Bal Gangadhar Tilak: A Study, op. cit., pp. 133-4.
32. Stanley A. Wolpert, Tilak and Gokhale, op. cit., p. 170.
33. Ibid., p. 169.
34. Ibid., p. 191.
35. D.S. Sarma, The Renaissance of Hinduism, op. cit., pp. 143-4.
36. Stanley A. Wolpert, Tilak and Gokhale, op. cit., p. 220.
37. Ibid., p. 221.
38. T.V. Parvate, Bal Gangadhar Tilak, op. cit., p. 213.
39. D.V. Tahmankar, Lokamanya Tilak, op. cit., p. 196.
40. B.G. Tilak, Writings and Speeches. Ganesan, Madras, 1922, pp. 259-61.
41. B.G. Tilak, Gita Rahasya. Tilak Brothers, Poona, sixth edition, 1986, pp. 90-1.
42. P.M. Thomas, Twentieth Century Indian Interpretations of Bhagavad Gita: Tilak, Gandhi and Aurobindo,. Indian Society for Promoting Christian Knowledge, Delhi, 1987, p.188.
43. K.M.Panikkar,The Foundations of New India, op. cit., p. 43.
44. B.G. Tilak, Gita Rahasya, op. cit., pp. 460-1.
45. K.M. Panikkar, The Foundations of New India, op. cit., p. 42.
46. B.G. Tilak, Gita Rahasya, op. cit., p. 151.
47. Ibid., p. 697.
48. K.M. Panikkar, The Foundations of New Delhi, op. cit., pp. 39-40.
49. D. Mackenzie Brown, "The Philosophy of Bal Gangadhar Tilak: Karma vs. Jnana in the Gita Rahasya", in The Journal of Asian Studies, vol. XVII, No.2, (Feb. 1958), p. 202.
50. B.G. Tilak, Gita Rahasya, op. cit., p. 404.
51. Ibid., p. 469.

52. D.V. Tahmankar, Lokamanya Tilak, op. cit., p. 217.
53. Stanley A. Wolpert, Tilak and Gokhale, op. cit., pp. xii and 305-6.
54. Quoted by D.S. Sarma, The Renaissance of Hinduism, op. cit., pp. 144-5.
55. Stanley A. Wolpert, Tilak and Gokhale, op. cit., p. 260.
56. D.V. Tahmankar, Lokamanya Tilak, op. cit., p. 231.
57. R.C. Majumdar, History of the Freedom Movement in India. Mukhopadhyay, Calcutta 1963, vol. II, p. 369.
58. T.V. Parvate, Bal Gangadhar Tilak, op. cit., p. 314.
59. D.V. Tahmankar, Lokamanya Tilak, op. cit., p. 230.
60. Ibid., p. 242.
61. Ibid., p. 253.
62. Ibid., p. 253.
63. Stanley A. Wolpert, Tilak and Gokhale, op. cit., p. 291.
64. Ibid., p. 291.
65. Ibid., p. 292.
66. T.V. Parvate, Bal Gangadhar Tilak, op. cit., pp. 529-30.
67. Ibid., p. 530.
68. B.G. Tilak, Gita Rahasya, op. cit., p. 713.
69. K. Damodaran, Indian Thought: A Critical Survey. Asia Publishing House, Bombay, 1967, p. 394.
70. P.M. Thomas, Twentieth Century Indian Interpretations of Bhagavad-Gita, op. cit., p. 73.
71. B.G. Tilak, Writings and Speeches, op. cit., pp. 259-60.
72. B.G. Tilak, Gita Rahasya, op. cit., p. 147.
73. Ibid., p. 148.
74. Ibid., p. 466.
75. Ibid., p. 554.
76. Ibid., p. ix.

CHAPTER FIVE

1. Karan Singh, Prophet of Indian Nationalism. George Allen and Unwin, London, 1963, p. 155.
2. R.C. Majumdar, History of the Freedom Movement in India, op. cit., vol. I, p. 461.
3. Ibid., pp. 243 and 330.
4. Ibid., p. 333.
5. Ibid., p. 333.
6. Ibid., p. 423.
7. Karan Singh, Prophet of Indian Nationalism, op. cit., p. 42.
8. D.S.Sarma, The Renaissance of Hinduism, op. cit., pp. 308-9.
9. Sri Aurobindo Birth Centenary Library (30 volumes), vol. 22, p.121.
10. Karan Singh, Prophet of Indian Nationalism, op. cit., p. 138.
11. Ibid., p. 136.
12. Ibid., p. 143.

13. T.V. Parvate, Bal Gangadhar Tilak, op. cit., pp. 529-30.
14. Ibid., p. 530.
15. Karan Singh, Prophet of Indian Nationalism, op. cit., pp. 143-4.
16. D.S. Sarma, The Renaissance of Hinduism, op. cit., p. 340.
17. Joan Price, An Introduction to Sri Aurobindo's Philsophy. Pondicherry, second edition, 1982, p. 14.
18. Ibid., pp. 18-9.
19. Karan Singh, Prophet of Indian Nationalism, op. cit., pp. 155-6.
20. R.C. Majumdar, History of the Freedom Movement in India, op. cit., vol. II, pp. 92 and 186-7.
21. Ibid., p. 24.
22. Ibid., pp. 23-4.
23. Ibid., pp. 166-7.
24. Ibid., p. 24.
25. D.S. Sarma, The Renaissance of Hinduism, op. cit., p. 310.
26. R.C. Majumdar, Swami Vivekananda: A Historical Review, op. cit., p. 115.
27. Ibid., p. 120.
28. R.C. Majumdar, History of the Freedom Movement in India, op. cit., vol. I, p. 447.
29. Sri Aurobindo, On Nationalism. (First Series). Pondicherry, 1965, p. 73.
30. Ursula King, "Who is the Ideal Karmayogin?", op. cit., p. 50.
31. Ibid., p. 51.
32. R.C. Majumdar, History of the Freedom Movement in India, op. cit., vol. II, pp. 141-3.
33. Ibid., pp. 140-1.
34. Ibid., pp. 203-4.
35. Ibid., p. 191, and Sri Aurobindo, On Nationalism, op. cit., p. 63.
36. R.C. Majumdar, History of the Freedom Movement in India, op. cit., vol. II, p. 180.
37. Ibid., p. 176.
38. Ibid., p. 180.
39. Ibid., p. 186.
40. Ibid., p. 187.
41. Ibid., p. 178.
42. Sri Aurobindo, The Doctrine of Passive Resistance. Pondicherry, 1952, pp. 80-1.
43. Ibid., pp. 77-8.
44. Ibid., p. 29.
45. Ibid., p. 81.
46. Ibid., p. 29.
47. Karan Singh, Prophet of Indian Nationalism, op. cit., pp. 58-9.
48. Ibid., pp. 143.
49. Ibid., p. 145.
50. Sri Aurobindo, Essarys on the Gita (Second Series). Arya Publishing House, Calcutta, 1949, pp. 222-7.
51. Ibid., p. 224-5.
52. Ibid., p. 4-9.
53. Joan Price, An Introduction to Sri Aurobindo's Philosophy, op. cit., pp.

26-7.

54. Sri Aurobindo, Essays on the Gita (Second Series), op. cit., p. 407.
55. Sri Aurobindo, Essays on the Gita (First Series). Arya Publishing House, Calcutta, 1949, p. 45.
56. Ibid., p. 134.
57. Ibid., p. 30.
58. P.M. Thomas, Twentieth Century Indian Interpretations of Bhagavad Gita, op. cit., p. 108.
59. Sri Aurobindo, Essays on the Gita (First Series), op. cit., p. 126.
60. Ibid., p. 162-5.
61. Ibid., p. 171-2.
62. Ibid., p. 173.
63. Sri Aurobindo, Essays on the Gita (Second Series), op. cit., pp. 179-80.
64. Ibid., p. 180.
65. Ibid., p. 408.
66. R.S. Betai, Gita and Gandhiji. Gujarat Vidyapith, Ahmedabad, 1970, pp. 70-2.
67. Ibid., p. 65.
68. S. Radhakrishnan and C.A. Moore (eds.), A Sourcebook in Indian Philosophy. Princeton Univ. Press, 1957, p. 577.
69. Joan Price, An Introduction to Sri Aurobindo's Philosophy, op. cit., p. 29.
70. Karan Singh, Prophet of Indian Nationalism, op. cit., p. 67.
71. B.K. Lal, Contemporary Indian Philsophy. Motilal Banarsidas, Delhi, 1987, p. 200.
72. Ibid., p. 202-3.
73. Ibid., p. 201.
74. Ibid., p. 203.
75. Ibid., p. 219-20.
76. Ibid., p. 219.
77. Karan Singh, Prophet of Indian Nationalism, op. cit., p. 68.
78. Ibid., p. 68.
79. B.K.Lal, Contemporary Indian Philosophy, op. cit., p. 209.
80. Ainslie T. Embree (ed.), The Hindu Tradition, op. cit., pp. 334-5.
81. Joan Price, An Introduction to Sri Aurobindo's Philosophy, op. cit., pp. 125 and 134.
82. Robert McDermott (ed.), The Essential Aurobindo. Schocken Books, New York, 1973, p. 240.
83. V. Madhusudan Reddy, Seven Studies in Sri Aurobindo. Institute of Human Study, Hyderabad, 1989, pp. 68 and 32.
84. B.K. Lal, Contemporary Indian Philosophy, op. cit., p. 222.
85. Sri Aurobindo, Essays on the Gita (First Series), op. cit., p. 172.
86. Ibid., p. 168.
87. R.S. Betai, Gita and Gandhiji, op. cit., p. 69.
88. Sri Aurobindo, Essays on the Gita (Second Series), op. cit., pp. 224-5.
89. Ibid., pp. 4-9.
90. K.M. Panikkar, The Foundations of New India, op. cit., p. 45.
91. R.C. Majumdar, History of the Freedom Movemnt in India, op. cit., vol.

II, pp. 140-1.
92. Ursula King, "Who is the Ideal Karmayogin?", op. cit., p. 50.
93. Karan Singh, Prophet of Indian Nationalism, op. cit., pp. 143-4.
94. D.S. Sarma, The Renaissance of Hinduism, op. cit., p. 338.
95. S. Radhakrishnan and C.A. Moore (eds.), A Sourcebook in Indian Philosophy, op. cit., p. 577.
96. B.K. Lal,Contemporary Indian Philosophy, op. cit., pp. 219-20.
97. V. Madhusudan Reddy, Seven Studies in Sri Aurobindo, op. cit., p. 32.

CHAPTER SIX

1. M.K.Gandhi, The Story of My Experiments with Truth. Beacon Press, Boston, 1957, p.4.
2. Ibid., p. 7.
3. Ibid., p. 33.
4. D.S. Sarma, The Renaissance of Hinduism, op. cit., p. 408.
5. M.K. Gandhi, The Story of My Experiments with Truth, op. cit., pp. 63-6.
6. Ibid., pp. 70-2.
7. Ibid., p. 67.
8. Jawaharlal Nehru, The Discovery of India. Oxford Univ. Press, New Delhi, 1983 (third impression), p. 358.
9. Mahadev Desai, The Gospel of Selfless Action or The Gita according to Gandhi. Navajivan, Ahmedabad, 1977, pp. 125-7.
10. K. M. Panikkar, The Foundations of New India, op. cit., p. 44.
11. M.M. Verma, Gandhi's Technique of Mass Mobilization. R.K. Gupta, New Delhi, 1990, p. 124.
12. Ibid., p. 124.
13. R.S. Betai, Gita and Gandhiji, op. cit., p. 154.
14. Ibid., p. 155.
15. Ibid., p. 156.
16. D.S. Sarma, The Renaissance of Hinduism, op. cit., p. 440.
17. Ibid., pp. 440-1.
18. Ibid., pp. 436-7.
19. Ibid., p. 449.
20. Raghavan Iyer, The Moral and Political Thought of Mahatma Gandhi. Oxford Univ. Press, New York, 1978, p. 326.
21. V.P. Verma, The Political Philosophy of Mahatma Gandhi and Sarvodaya. Laxmi Narain, Agra, 1959, p. 59.
22. D.S. Sarma, The Renaissance of Hinduism, op. cit., p. 477.
23. Ibid., p. 477.
24. Ibid., p. 480.
25. Ibid., p. 480.
26. Raghavan Iyer, The Moral and Political Thought of Mahatma Gandhi, op. cit., p. 282.
27. D.S. Sarma, The Renaissance of Hinduism, op. cit., p. 502.

28. Jawaharlal Nehru, The Discovery of India, op. cit., p. 361.
29. Shriman Narayan (ed.), The Selected Works of Mahatma Gandhi. (Six volumes). Navajivan, Ahmedabad, 1968, vol.IV, pp. 344-6.
30. Jawaharlal Nehru, The Discovery of India, op. cit., pp. 361-2.
31. Raghavan Iyer, The Moral and Political Thought of Mahatma Gandhi, op. cit., pp. 275-83.
32. Ibid., p. 275.
33. D.S. Sarma, The Renaissance of Hinduism, op. cit., p. 532.
34. Ibid., p. 533.
35. Ibid., p. 533.
36. V. P. Verma, The Political Philosophy of Mahatama Gandhi and Sarvodaya, op. cit., p. 160.
37. Ibid., p. 161.
38. Jawaharlal Nehru, The Discovery of India, op. cit., p. 360.
39. Ibid., p. 361.
40. M.M. Verma, Gandhi's Technique of Mass Mobilization, op.cit., pp. 205-7.
41. Ibid., p. 207.
42. Harijan, 7th April, 1946, quoted by V.P. Verma, The Political Philosophy of Mahatma Gandhi and Sarvodaya, op. cit., p. 31.
43. Quoted by V.P. Verma, The Political Philosophy of Mahatma Gandhi and Sarvodaya, op. cit., p. 72.
44. Shriman Narayan (ed.), The Selected Works of Mahatma Gandhi, op. cit., vol. IV, p. 39.
45. V.P. Verma, The Political Philosophy of Mahatma Gandhi and Sarvodaya, op. cit., p. 83.
46. Ibid., p. 89.
47. Young India, 20th Sept. 1928, quoted by R.S. Betai, Gita and Gandhiji, op. cit., p. 249.
48. R.S. Betai, Gita and Gandhiji, op. cit, p. 150.
49. Raghavan Iyer, The Moral and Political Thought of Mahatma Gandhi, op. cit., p. 194.
50. D.S. Sarma, The Renaissance of Hinduism, op. cit., p. 488.
51. Ibid., p. 489.
52. Ibid., p. 532.
53. Ibid., p. 532-3.
54. M.M. Verma, Gandhi's Technique of Mass Mobilization, op. cit., pp. 125-6.
55. D.S. Sarma, The Renaissance of Hinduism, op. cit., p. 546.
56. R.S. Betai, Gita and Gandhiji, op. cit., p. 196.
57. M.M. Verma, Gandhi's Technique of Mass Mobilization, op. cit., p. 207.
58. Ibid., p. 207.
59. Ibid., p. 207.
60. R.S. Betai, Gita and Gandhiji, op. cit., pp. 3 and 155.
61. D.S. Sarma, The Renaissance of Hinduism, op. cit., p. 406.
62. Ursula King, "Who is the Ideal Karmayogin?", op. cit., p. 52.
63. Jawaharlal Nehru, The Discovery of India, op. cit., p. 29.
64. Mahadev Desai, The Gospel of Selfless Action or The Gita according to

Gandhi, op. cit., p. 132.
65. R.S. Betai, Gita and Gandhiji, op. cit., p. 237.
66. Ibid., p. 235.
67. Raghavan Iyer, The Moral and Political Thought of Mahatma Gandhi, op. cit., p. 51.
68. Ibid., p. 52.
69. R.S. Betai, Gita and Gandhiji, op. cit., p. 242.
70. Ibid., p. 243.
71. Ursula King, "Who is the Ideal Karmayogin?", op. cit., p. 52.
72. Ibid., p. 55.
73. P.M. Thomas, Twentieth Century Indian Interpretations of Bhagavad Gita, op. cit., p. 193.
74. Sissela Bok, "Toward a Practical Ethic of Non-violence". In Speaking of Truth, Diana Eck and Devaki Jain (eds.), New Society Publishers, 1987, p. 256.
75. Devaki Jain, "Gandhian Contributions towards a Feminist Ethic". In Speaking of Truth, Diana Eck and Devaki Jain (eds.) op. cit., pp. 290-1.
76. Radha Bhatt, "Lakshmi Ashram: A Gandhian Perspective in the Himalayan Foothills". In Speaking of Truth, Diana Eck and Devaki Jain (eds.), op. cit., p. 185.
77. M.K. Gandhi, Satyagraha in South Africa. Navajivan, 1950, p. 206.
78. Quoted by Raghavan Iyer, The Moral and Political Thought of Mahatma Gandhi, op. cit., pp. 311-2.
79. Ibid., p. 316-7.
80. Ibid., p. 316.
81. Ibid., p. 318.
82. Ibid., p. 319.
83. D.S. Sarma, The Renaissance of Hinduism, op. cit., p. 436.
84. R.S. Betai, Gita and Gandhiji, op. cit., p. 56.
85. Raghavan Iyer, The Moral and Political Thought of Mahatma Gandhi, op. cit., p. 194.
86. K.M. Panikkar, The Foundations of New India, op.cit., p. 44.
87. Ibid., p. 43-4.
88. T.V. Parvate, Bal Gangadhar Tilak, op. cit., p. 530.
89. M.K.Gandhi, The Bhagavad Gita. Orient Paperbacks, New Delhi, pp. 79-80.
90. D.S. Sarma, The Renaissance of Hinduism, op. cit., p. 406.

CHAPTER SEVEN

1. K. Nag and D. Burman (eds.), The English Works of Raja Rammohun Roy, op. cit., p. 105.
2. Ibid., p. 134.
3. Ibid., p. 97.
4. Swami Vivekananda, Complete Works, op. cit., vol. VI, p. 504.
5. Ibid., vol.VI, pp. 450-2.

6. Swami Vivekananda, Karmayoga, op. cit., pp. 130-1.
7. Madeleine Biardeau, Hinduism: The Anthology of a Civilization. Oxford Univer. Press, Delhi, 1989, pp. 164-5.
8. K.M. Panikkar, The Foundations of New India, op. cit., pp. 39-40.
9. V. Subramaniam, "Karmayoga and the Rise of the Indian Middle Class", in The Journal of Arts and Ideas, Nos. 14-5, pp. 137-9.
10. B. G. Tilak, Gita Rahasya, op. cit., p. 713.
11. P. M. Thomas, Twentieth Century Indian Interpretations of Bhagavad Gita, op. cit., p. 188.
12. K. Damodaran, Indian Thought: A Critical Survey, op. cit., p. 394.
13. P.M. Thomas, Twentieth Century Indian Interpretations of Bhagavad Gita, op. cit., p. 73.
14. Stanley A. Wolpert, Tilak and Gokhale, op. cit., p. 191.
15. B.G. Tilak, Gita Rahasya, op. cit., p. 554.
16. D. Mackenzie Browm "The Philosophy of Bal Gangadhar Tilak", op. cit., p. 202.
17. R.C. Majumdar, History of the Freedom Movement in India, op. cit., vol. II, pp. 203-4.
18. Karan Singh, The Prophet of Indian Nationalism, op. cit., p. 138.
19. Ursula King, "Who is the Ideal Karmayogin?",op. cit., p. 50.
20. V. Subramaniam, "Karmayoga and the Rise of the Indian Middle Class", op. cit., p. 139.
21. Karan Singh, The Prophet of Indian Nationalism, op. cit., p. 143.
22. Ibid., pp. 143-4.
23. T.V. Parvate, Bal Gangadhar Tilak, op. cit., pp. 529-30.
24. Ibid., p. 530.
25. D.S. Sarma, The Renaissance of Hinduism, op. cit., p. 340.
26. K.M. Panikkar, The Foundations of New India, op. cit., p. 45.
27. S. Radhakrishnan and C.A. Moore (eds.), A Sourcebook in Indian Philosophy, op. cit., p. 577.
28. V. Madhusudan Reddy, Seven Studies in Sri Aurobindo, op. cit., p. 32.
29. P.M. Thomas, Twentieth Century Indian Interpretations of Bhagavad Gita, op. cit., p. 182.
30. Stanley A. Wolpert, Tilak and Gokhale, op. cit., p.291.
31. Ibid., p. 291.
32. R.S. Betai, Gita and Gandhiji, op. cit., p. 56.
33. K.M. Panikkar, The Foundations of New India, op. cit., p. 44.
34. M.K. Gandhi, The Bhagavad Gita, Orient Paperbacks, op. cit., pp. 79-80.
35. Ibid., p. 86.
36. Ursula King, "Who is the Ideal Karmayogin?", op. cit., p. 52.

PART TWO

CHAPTER EIGHT

1. Donald H. Bishop (ed.), Indian Thought: An Introduction. John Wiley

and Sons, New York, 1975, p. 42.
2. Gita verses VII.11, XVI.12 and others.
3. D.S. Sarma, "The Path of Yoga in the Gita". In the Cultural Heritage of India, Vol. III, H. Bhattacharyya, ed. The Ramakrishna Mission Institute of Culture, Calcutta, 1983, p. 422.
4. Ibid., p. 422.
5. Balkoba Bhave, Gītā Tattva Bodh (in Hindi), Sarva Seva Sangh Prakashan, Varanasi, 1981, p. 130.
6. B.G. Tilak, Gita Rahasya, op. cit., pp. 490-1.
7. K. M. Panikkar, The Foundations of New India, op. cit., pp. 39-40.
8. D.M. Brown, "The Philosophy of Bal Gangadhar Tilak", op. cit., p. 200.
9. V. Subramaniam, "Karmayoga and the Rise of the Indian Middle Class", op. cit., pp. 137-9.
10. K.M. Panikkar, The Foundations of New India, op. cit., p. 44.
11. P.M. Thomas, Twentieth Century Indian Interpretations of Bhagavad-Gita, op. cit., p. 23.
12. B.G. Tilak, Gita Rahasya, op. cit., p. 944.
13. Sri Aurobindo, Essays on the Gita, 1950 New York edition, p. 156.
14. Ibid., p. 156.
15. K. Klostermaier, A Survey of Hinduism. State University of New York Press. Albany, New York, 1989, p. 105.
16. Ibid., pp. 105-6.
17. M. Hiriyanna, "Philosophy of Values". In the Cultural Heritage of India, Vol. III, H. Bhattacharyya, ed., op. cit., pp. 647-648.
18. Donald H. Bishop (ed.) Indian Thought, op. cit., p. 42.

CHAPTER NINE

1. Chidbhavananda, The Bhagavad Gita. Sri Ramakrishna Tapovanam, Tirupparaitturai, 1975, pp. 105-106.
2. S. Radhakrishnan, The Bhagavad Gita. Harper and Row, New York, 1973, p. 68.
3. Vinoba, Talks on the Gita, Sarva Seva Sangh Prakashan, Varanasi, 1978, p. 4.
4. Ranganathananda, The Message of the Upanisads. Bharatiya Vidya Bhavan, Bombay, 1971, p. 292.
5. B. G. Tilak, Gita Rahasya, op. cit., pp. 159-160.
6. S. Radhakrishnan, The Bhagavad Gita, op. cit., p. 105.
7. D.S. Sarma, "The Path of Yoga in the Gita", op. cit., pp. 406-411.
8. K. N. Upadhyaya, Early Buddhism and the Bhagavad Gita, op. cit., pp. 364-5.
9. Ibid., p. 441.
10. B.G. Tilak, Gita Rahasya, op. cit., p. 148.
11. Mahadev Desai, The Gospel of Selfless Action or The Gita according to Gandhi. Navajivan, Ahmedabad, 1977, p. 131.
12. Ibid., p. 131.

13. K.N. Upadhyaya, Early Buddhism and the Bhagavad Gita, op. cit., p. 441.
14. Ibid., p. 427.
15. Vinoba, The Steadfast Wisdom, Sarva Seva Sangh Prakashan, Varanasi, 1985, p. 27.
16. Ibid., pp . 22-23.
17. Ibid., p. 39.
18. Ibid., p. 32.
19. Chidbhavananda, The Bhagavad Gita, op. cit., p. 823.
20. Ibid., p. 197.
21. B. G. Tilak, Gita Rahasya, op. cit., p. 904.
22. S. Radhakrishnan, The Bhagavad Gita, op. cit., p. 121.
23. B.G. Tilak, Gita Rahasya, op. cit., pp. 466-483.
24. Ibid., pp. 404 and 469.
25. Ibid., p. 770.
26. K.N. Upadhyaya, Early Buddhism and the Bhagavad Gita, op. cit., pp. 456-7.
27. Ibid., p. 479.
28. Aurobindo, Essays on the Gita. Sri Aurobindo Ashram, Pondicherry, 1980, p. 108.

CHAPTER TEN

1. Swami Vivekananda, Complete Works, op. cit., vol. I, p. 468.
2. B.G. Tilak, Gita Rahasya, op. cit., pp. 456-7.
3. Ibid., p. 457.
4. Ibid., p. 451.
5. Mahadev Desai, The Gospel of Selfless Action or The Gita according to Gandhi, op. cit., p. 176.
6. M.K. Gandhi, The Bhagavad Gita. Orient Paperbacks, New Delhi, pp. 94-5.
7. Sri Aurobindo, Essays on the Gita, 1950 New York edition, p. 122.
8. Ibid., p. 123.
9. S. Radhakrishnan, The Bhagavad-Gita, op.cit., p. 139.
10. Ibid., p. 69.
11. Vinoba, The Steadfast Wisdom, op. cit., pp. 20-23.
12. R. N. Dandekar, "The Bhagavad-Gita". In Wm. Theodore de Bary (ed.), Sources of Indian Tradition. Motilal Banarsidass, Delhi, pp. 280-1.
13. P.T. Raju, The Philosophical Traditions of India. George Allen and Unwin, London, 1971, pp. 215-6.
14. J.G. Arapura, Personal Discussion at McMaster University, Aug. 1990.
15. M. Rangacharya, The Philosophy of Hindu Conduct: Lectures on the Bhagavad-Gita. Educational Publishing Co., Madras, 1957, vol.I, p. 207.
16. Mahadev Desai, The Gospel of Selfless Action, op. cit., p. 183.
17. Vinoba, Talks on the Gita, op. cit., pp. 28-32.
18. Swami Vivekananda, Complete Works, op.cit., vol.I, p. 457.
19, Ibid., p. 457.

20. Ibid., p. 457.
21. Ibid., p. 457.
22. Ursula King, "Who is the Ideal Karmayogin?", op. cit., p. 51.
23. Swami Chidbhavananda, The Bhagavad-Gita, op. cit., p. 244.
24. Shriman Narayan (ed.), The Selected Works of Mahatma Gandhi, op. cit., vol. VI, pp. 158-164.
25. B.G. Tilak, Gita Rahasya, op. cit., pp. 460-1.
26. K. Mishra, "Indian Value System and Social Development". Paper presented at the Annual Conference of the Association of Asian Studies at Laval University, Quebec, 1989, p.1.
27. S. Radhakrishnan, The Bhagavad-Gita, op. cit., p. 140.
28. Shriman Narayan(ed.), Selected Works of Mahatma Gandhi, op. cit., vol.VI, pp. 167-71.
29. Swami Vivekananda, Complete Works, op. cit., vol. I, pp. 58-9.
30. B.G. Tilak, Gita Rahasya, op. cit., pp. 531-2.
31. Sri Aurobindo, Essays on the Gita, op. cit., pp. 200-1.
32. Raghavan Iyer, The Moral and Political Thought of Mahatma Gandhi, op. cit., p. 326.
33. Swami Nikhilananda, Vivekananda, op. cit., p. 236.
34. Quoted by V.P. Verma, Political Philosophy of Mahatma Gandhi, op.cit., p. 72.
35. B.G. Tilak, Gita Rahasya, op. cit., pp. 147-8.
36. Ibid., p. 466.
37. Shriman Narayan (ed.), Selected Works of Mahatma Gandhi, op. cit., vol. IV, p.9.
38. P.T. Raju, Philosophical Traditions of India, op. cit., p. 216.
39. S. Radhakrishnan, The Bhagavad-Gita, op. cit., p. 192.
40. Ibid., p. 182.
41. Chidbhavananda, The Bhagavad-Gita, op. cit., pp. 366-7.
42. S. Radhakrishnan, The Bhagavad-Gita, op. cit., p. 184.
43. Sri Krishna Prem, The Yoga of the Bhagavad-Gita. Penguin Books, Baltimore, 1958, p. 184.
44. Sri Aurobindo, Essays on the Gita, op. cit., 1950 New York edition, p. 488.
45. Vasant Nargolkar, The Creed of Saint Vinoba. Bharatiya Vidya Bhavan, Bombay, 1963, pp. 58-9.
46. Ibid., p. 57.
47. S. Radhakrishnan, The Bhagavad-Gita, op. cit., p. 205.
48. Swami Ranganathananda, The Message of the Upanisads, op. cit., p. 109.
49. S. Radhakrishnan, The Bhagavad-gita, op. cit., p. 204.
50. Vinoba, The Steadfast Wisdom, op. cit., p. 114.

CHAPTER ELEVEN

1. Jawaharlal Nehru, The Discovery of India, op. cit., pp. 93-6.
2. Donald H. Bishop (ed.), Indian Thought, op.cit., pp. 62-79.
3. K.N. Upadhayaya, Early Buddhism, and the Bhagavad-Gita, op. cit., p. 466.

4. Ibid., pp. 464-6.
5. K. Nag and D. Burman (eds.), The English Works of Raja Rammohun Roy, op. cit., p. 115.
6. Ibid., p. 114.
7. B.G. Tilak, Gita Rahasya, op. cit., p. 713.
8. Ibid., p. 464-5.
9. Ibid., p. 534.
10. K.N. Upadhyaya, Early Buddhism and the Bhagavad-Gita, op. cit., p. 462.
11. Ibid., p. 462.
12. Shriman Narayan (ed.), Selected Works of Mahatma Gandhi, op. cit.., vol. VI, pp. 189-90.
13. Raghavan Iyer, Moral and Political Thought of Mahatma Gandhi, op. cit., p. 67.
14. M. Hiriyanna, "Philosophy of Values". In The Cultural Heritage of India, op. cit., vol. III, pp. 647-8.
15. Brhadaranyaka Upanisad, 5.2.1-3.
16. Swami Ranganathananda, The Message of the Upanisads, op. cit., p. 150.
17. Ibid., p. 152.
18. Ibid., p. 152.
19. Balkoba Bhave, Gita Tattva Bodh, op. cit., p. 130.
20. B.G. Tilak, Gita Rahasya, op. cit., p. 407.
21. Mahadev Desai, The Gospel of Selfless Action, op. cit., p. 103.
22. K. Mishra, "Indian Value System and Social Development", op. cit., and Personal Discussion in Canada, Aug. 1990.
23. The New Testament, Mark 12.
24. J.B. Schneewind, Moral Philosophy from Montaigne to Kant: An Anthology. (Mimeo). Johns Hopkins Univ., Baltimore, 1989, p. 689.
25. V. Subramaniam, "Karmayoga and the Rise of the Indian Middle Class", op. cit., pp. 133-42.
26. Indira Rothermund, "Discussion", in Tradition and Modernity in India, ed. by A. B. Shah and C.R. M. Rao, Manaktalas, Bombay, 1965, p. 125.
27. Indira Patel, Vivekananda's Approach to Social Work, op. cit., p. 91.
28. K. Klostermaier, A Survey of Hinduism. op. cit., p. 459.
29. M.K. Gandhi, The Bhagavad-Gita. Orient Paperbacks, op. cit., pp. 79-80.
30. S. Radhakrishnan, The Bhagavad-Gita, op. cit., p. 142.
31. A.S. Altekar, "Hinduism: A Static Structure or a Dynamic Force", in Nehru Abhinandan Granth, Calcutta, 1949, p. 421.
32. Ibid., p. 421.
33. Robert N. Bellah, Religion and Progress in Modern Asia, op. cit., p. 215.
34. P.M. Thomas, Twentieth Century Indian Interpretations of Bhagavad-Gita, op. cit., p. 186.
35. K. Klostermaier, A Survey of Hinduism, op. cit., p. 105.
36. Ibid., p. 106.
37. Joan Price, An Introduction to Sri Aurobindo's Philosophy, op. cit., p. 134.
38. S. Radhakrishnan, The Bhagavad-Gita, op. cit., p. 139.
39. D.S. Sarma, "The Path of Yoga in the Gita", op. cit., p. 422.
40. K.N. Upadhyaya, Early Buddhism and the Bhagavad-Gita, op. cit., p. 488.

41. Romain Rolland, The Life of Vivekananda and the Universal Gospel, op. cit., p. 166.
42. Ibid., p. 167.
43. Madeleine Biardeau, Hinduism: The Anthology of a Civilization, Oxford University Press, Delhi, 1989, pp. 164-5.
44. Swami Vivekananda, Complete Works, op. cit., vol.I, p. 478.
45. Swami Vivekananda, Our Women, Advaita Ashrama, Caltutta, 1990, p. 43.
46. Quoted by Swami Ranganathananda, The Message of Kanyakumari. Vivekananda Kendra, Madras, 1981. p.9.
47. B.G. Tilak, Gita Rahasya, op. cit., p.466.
48. Ibid., pp. 927-8.
49. G.W. Kaveeshwar, The Ethics of the Gita. Motilal Banarsidass, Delhi, 1971, p. 245.
50. K.M. Panikkar, The Foundations of New India, op. cit., p. 44.
51. Swami Chinmayananda, The Holy Geeta. Central Chinmaya Mission Trust, Bombay, p. 173.

CHAPTER TWELVE

1. D.S. Sarma, "The Path of Yoga in the Gita". In The Cultural History of India, op. cit., vol. III, p. 406.
2. S. Radhakrishnan, The Bhagavad-Gita, op. cit., pp. 160-1.
3. Kuttipuzha Krishna Pillai, Selected Essays. National Book Stall, Kottayam, 1969, pp. 343-5. (Summary of ideas translated from Malayalam to English by P.M. Thomas).
4. Mahadev Desai, The Gospel of Selfless Action, op. cit., p. 104.
5. Vinoba, Talks on the Gita, op. cit., pp. 168-9.
6. S. Radhakrishnan, The Bhagavad-Gita, op. cit., p. 161.
7. Swami Chinmayananda, The Holy Geeta, op. cit., p. 203.
8. Ibid., pp. 202-3.
9. Ibid., pp. 1067-8.
10. D.S. Sarma, "The Path of Yoga in the Gita", op. cit., pp.407-8.
11. Sri Aurobindo, Essays on the Gita, op. cit.., 1950 New York edition, p. 458.
12. Ibid., pp. 461-7.
13. Kakasaheb Kalelkar, The Geeta or Jeevan Yoga. Bharatiya Vidya Bhavan, Bombay, 1967, p. 23.
14. B.G. Tilak , Gita Rahasya, op. cit., p. 697.
15. K.N. Upadhyaya, Early Buddhism and the Bhagavad-Gita, op. cit., p. 508.
16. S. Radhakrishnan, The Bhagavad-Gita, op. cit., p.368.
17. Vinoba, Talks on the Gita, op. cit., p. 168.
18. S. Radhakrishnan, The Bhagavad-Gita, op. cit., pp. 366-7.
19. B.G. Tilak, Gita Rahasya, op. cit., pp. 464-5.
20. Ibid., p. 713.
21. D.M. Brown, "The Philosophy of Bal Gangadhar Tilak", op. cit., p. 201.

22. V.P. Varma, Political Philosophy of Mahatma Gandhi, op. cit., p. 72.
23. Shriman Narayan (ed.) , Selected Works of Mahatma Gandhi, op. cit., vol. IV, p. 257.
24. R.S. Betai, Gita and Gandhiji, op. cit., p. 253.
25. Shriman Narayan (ed.), Selected Works of Mahatma Gandhi, op. cit., vol. IV, p. 257.
26. Ibid., p. 260.
27. Ibid., p. 260.
28. Swami Vivekananda, Complete Works, op. cit., vol. I, pp. 472-3.
29. S. Radhakrishnan, The Bhagavad-Gita, op. cit., p. 135.
30. Ibid., p. 137
31. K.N. Upadhyaya, Early Buddhism and the Bhagavad-Gita, op. cit., p. 488.
32. S. Radhakrishnan, The Bhagavad-Gita, op. cit., p. 346.
33. Ibid., p. 165.
34. B. G. Tilak, Gita Rahasya, op. cit., p. 958.
35. Ibid., p. 713.
36. Sri Aurobindo, Essays on the Gita, op. cit., pp. 112-3.
37. M.K. Gandhi, The Bhagavad Gita, op. cit., pp. 79-80.
38. Ibid., p. 86.
39. Vinoba, Talks on the Gita, op. cit., pp. 202-3.
40. Balkoba Bhave, Gita Tattva Bodh, op. cit., pp. 107-8.
41. Ainslee T. Embree (ed.), The Hindu Tradition, op. cit., pp. 33-4.
42. S. Radhakrishnan and Charles A. Moore (eds.), A Sourcebook in Indian Philosophy. Princeton University Press, New Jersey, 1973, pp. 29-30.
43. Swami Chidbhavananda, The Bhagavad-Gita, op. cit., p. 829.
44. S. K. Ramachandra Rao, The Idea of Sarvodaya, Bangalore, 1951, p. 50.
45. Vinoba, Talks on the Gita, op. cit., p. 203.
46. Quoted by Vasant Nargolkar, The Creed of Saint Vinoba, op. cit., p. 62.
47. Ibid., p. 62.
48. P.M. Thomas, Twentieth Century Indian Interpretations of Bhagavad-Gita, op. cit., p. 164.
49. J.G. Arapura, "Sociological Alienation and Gandhian Philosophy". Panchshila, vol. I, No.4 (1956), p. 24.
50. S. Radhakrishnan, The Bhagavad-Gita, op. cit., p. 96.
51. Ibid., p. 346.
52. Swami Chidbhavananda, The Bhagavad-Gita, op. cit., p. 827.
53. Sri Aurobindo, Essays on the Gita, op. cit., 1950 New York edition, pp. 435-6.
54. D.S. Sarma, The Renaissance of Hinduism, op. cit., p. 340.
55. Raghavan Iyer, The Moral and Political Thought of Mahatma Gandhi, op. cit., pp. 275-83.
56. S. Radhakrishnan, The Bhagavad-Gita, op. cit., p. 188.
57. R.S. Betai, Gita and Gandhiji, op. cit., pp. 64-72.
58. B.G. Tilak, Gita Rahasya, op. cit., p. 534.

CHAPTER THIRTEEN

1. K.N. Upadhyaya, Early Buddhism and the Bhagavad-Gita, op. cit., pp. 134-46.
2. Ibid., p. 140-4.
3. S. Radhakrishnan, The Bhagavad-Gita, op. cit., p. 220.
4. Ibid., p. 220.
5. Vinoba, The Streadfast Wisdom, op. cit., pp. 39-40.
6. S. Radhakrishnan, The Bhagavad-Gita op. cit., p. 248.
7. D.S. Sarma, "The Path of Yoga in the Gita", op. cit., pp. 403-4.
8. K.N. Upadhyaya, Early Buddhism and the Bhagavad-Gita, op. cit., p. 140.
9. Ibid., p. 138.
10. M. Hiriyanna, The Essentials of Indian Philosophy. Macmillan, New York, 1949, pp. 54-6.
11. Shriman Narayan (ed.), Selected Woks of Mahatma Gandhi, op. cit., vol. IV, p. 303.
12. Ibid., p. 302.
13. Vinoba, Talks on the Gita, op. cit., pp. 94-104.
14. Ibid., pp. 212-5.
15. S. Radhakrishnan, The Bhagavad-Gita, op. cit., p. 61.
16. Swami Vivekananda, Complete Works, op. cit., vol. III, p. 142.
17. B.G. Tilak, Writings and Speeches. Ganeshan, Madras, 1922, p. 263.
18. S. Radhakrishnan, The Bhagavad-Gita, op. cit., pp. 252-3.
19. Ibid., pp. 62-5.
20. Ibid., p. 62.
21. Ibid., p. 64.
22. Sri Aurobindo, Essays on the Gita, op. cit., 1950 New York edition, pp. 498-9.
23. S. Radhakrishnan, The Bhagavad-Gita, op. cit., pp. 158-9.
24. Quoted by Ramacharita Manasa Jnanayajna Samiti, Brochure for Morari Bapu's Katha, Baltimore, 1990, cover page.
25. Ainslie T. Embree (ed.), The Hindu Tradition, op. cit., p. 321.
26. Shriman Narayan (ed.), Selected Works of Mahatma Gandhi, op. cit., vol. IV, p. 242.
27. Raghavan Iyer, The Moral and Political Thought of Mahatma Gandhi, op. cit., p. 245.
28. Cf. K.M. Panikkar, The State and the Citizen. Asia Publishing House, Bombay, 1956, p. 28.
29. S. Radhakrishnan, "Foreword", in S. Abid Hussain, The National Culture of India, Jaico Publishing House, Bombay, 1956, p.8.
30. P.M. Thomas, Twentieth Century Indian Interpretations of Bhagavad-Gita, op. cit., p. 180.
31. S. Radhakrishnan, The Bhagavad-Gita, op. cit., p. 55.
32. B.G. Tilak, Writings and Speecdhes, op. cit., pp. 259-60.
33. B. G. Tilak, Gita Rahasya, op. cit., p. 1112.
34. S. Radhakrishnan, The Bhagavad-Gita, op. cit., p. 305.
35. Ibid., p. 204.
36. M. Hiriyanna, The Essentials of Indian Philosophy, op. cit., p. 56.

37. Swami Vivekananda, Complete Works, op. cit., vol. III, pp. 430-3.
38. D.S. Sarma, "The Path of Yoga in the Gita', op. cit., p. 403.
39. Ibid., p. 403.
40. Ibid., p. 422.
41. Ibid., pp. 422-3.
42. Swami Ranganathananda, Science of Human Uniqueness: Vikram Sarabhai Memorial Lecture, Ahmedabad, 1991, pp. 54-5.
43. Donald H. Bishop, Indian Thought, op. cit., p. 42.
44. B.G. Tilak, Gita Rahasya, op. cit., p. 161.
45. M. Hiriyanna, "Philosophy of Values", op. cit., p. 648.
46. K. Mishra, "Indian Value System and Social Development", op. cit., p. 3.
47. S. Radhakrishnan, The Bhagavad-Gita, op. cit., p. 268.
48. Swami Ranganathananda, Science of Human Uniqueness, op. cit., p. 55.
49. Ibid., p. 55
50. S. Radhakrishnan, The Bhagavad-Gita, op. cit., p.319.
51. Ibid., p. 360.
52. B.G. Tilak, Gita Rahasya, op. cit., pp. 696-7.
53. Mahadev Desai, The Gospel of Selfless Action, op. cit., pp. 127-8.
54. S. Radhakrishnan, The Bhagavad-Gita, op. cit., pp. 79-80.
55. S. Radhakrishnan, The Bhagavad-Gita, op. cit., p. 75.
56. Ibid., p. 76.
57. K. Mishra, "Indian Value System and Social Development," op. cit., pp.2-3.
58. S. Radhakrishnan, The Bhagavad Gita, op. cit., p. 75.
59. M. Hiriyanna, "Philosophy of Values", op. cit., p. 653.
60. Aurobindo, Essays on the Gita, op. cit., p. 34.
61. Vinoba, The Steadfast Wisdom, op. cit., p.9.
62. K.N. Upadhyaya, Early Buddhism and the Bhagavad-Gita, op. cit., p. 475.
63. Ibid., p. 482.
64. Ibid., p. 475.
65. Shriman Narayan (ed.), The Selected Works of Mahatma Gandhi, Vol. IV, op. cit., p. 39.
66. Vinoba, Talks on the Gita, op. cit., p. 205.
67. S. Radhakrishnan, The Bhagavad Gita, op. cit., p. 383.

CHAPTER FOURTEEN

1. Romain Rolland, The Life of Vivekananda and the Universal Gospel, op. cit., p. 286.
2. J.G. Arapura, Personal Discussion at McMaster University, Aug. 1990.
3. K. Klostermaier, A Survey of Hinduism, op. cit., p. 105.
4. Robert N. Bellah, "Epilogue", in Religion and Progress in Modern Asia, op. cit., p. 215.
5. S. Radhakrishnan, The Bhagavad Gita, op. cit., p. 142.
6. K.N. Upadhyaya, Early Buddhism and the Bhagavad-Gita, op. cit., p. 488.
7. Ursula King, "Who is the Ideal Karmayogin? The Meaning of a Hindu

Religious Symbol," op. cit., p. 45.
8. R.N. Dandekar, "The Bhagavad-Gita", in Wm. Theodore de Bary (ed.), Sources of Indian Tradition, op. cit., pp. 280-1.
9. Swami Vivekananda, Our Women, op. cit., p. 43.
10. B.G. Tilak, Gita Rahasya, op. cit., pp. 147-8.
11. Ibid., p. 466.
12. G.W. Kaveeshwar, The Ethics of the Gita, op. cit., p. 245.
13. K. M. Panikkar, The Foundations of New India, op. cit., p. 44.
14. Mahadev Desai, The Gospel of Selfless Action or The Gita according to Gandhi, op. cit., p. 127.
15. P.M. Thomas, Twentieth Century Indian Interpretations of Bhagavad-Gita, op. cit., p. 188.
16. K.M. Panikkar, The Foundations of New India, Allen and Unwin, London, 1963, p. 36.
17. Paras 12. 45-55.
18. Paras 12. 60-5.
19. Para 12.72.
20. Vinoba, The Steadfast Wisdom, op. cit., p. 114.
21. D.S. Sarma, "The Path of Yoga in the Gita". In The Cultural Heritage of India, Vol. III, H. Bhattacharyya, ed., op. cit., p. 403.
22. B.G. Tilak, Writings and Speeches, op. cit., p. 263.
23. D.S. Sarma, "The Path of Yoga in the Gita", op. cit., p. 404.
24. Sri Aurobindo, Essays on the Gita, op. cit., 1950 edition, pp. 498-9.
25. S. Radhakrishnan, The Bhagavad-Gita, op. cit., p. 368.
26. Vinoba, Talks on the Gita, op. cit., p. 168.
27. B.G. Tilak, Gita Rahasya, op. cit., pp. 696-7.
28. Kuttipuzha Krishna Pillai, Selected Essays, op. cit., pp. 343-5.
29. S. Radhakrishnan, The Bhagavad-Gita, op. cit., pp. 160-1.
30. D.S. Sarma, "The Path of Yoga in the Gita", op. cit., pp. 407-8.
31. B.G. Tilak, Gita Rahasya, op. cit., p. 697.
32. K.N. Upadhyaya, Early Buddhism and the Bhagavad Gita, op. cit., p. 508.
33. Quoted by V.P. Verma, Political Philosophy of Mahatma Gandhi, op. cit., p. 72.
34. S. Radhakrishnan, The Bhagavad-Gita, op. cit., p. 188.
35. Madhadev Desai, The Gospel of Selfless Action or The Gita according to Gandhi, op. cit., p. 70.
36. S. Radhakrishnan, The Bhagavad Gita, op.cit., pp. 13-14.
37. Ibid., p. 96.
38. Ursula King, "Who is the Ideal Karmayogin? ", op. cit., pp. 52-5.

Index

References are to paragraph numbers, not to pages